Voices of pedagogical development - Expanding, enhancing and exploring higher education language learning

Edited by Juha Jalkanen,
Elina Jokinen and Peppi Taalas

Published by Research-publishing.net, not-for-profit association
Dublin, Ireland; Voillans, France, info@research-publishing.net

© 2015 by Research-publishing.net (collective work)
Each author retains their own copyright

Voices of pedagogical development - Expanding, enhancing and exploring higher education language learning
Edited by Juha Jalkanen, Elina Jokinen, & Peppi Taalas

Rights: All articles in this collection are published under the Attribution-NonCommercial -NoDerivatives 4.0 International (CC BY-NC-ND 4.0) licence. Under this licence, the contents are freely available online (as PDF files) for anybody to read, download, copy, and redistribute provided that the author(s), editorial team, and publisher are properly cited. Commercial use and derivative works are, however, not permitted.

Disclaimer: Research-publishing.net does not take any responsibility for the content of the pages written by the authors of this book. The authors have recognised that the work described was not published before, or that it is not under consideration for publication elsewhere. While the information in this book are believed to be true and accurate on the date of its going to press, neither the editorial team, nor the publisher can accept any legal responsibility for any errors or omissions that may be made. The publisher makes no warranty, expressed or implied, with respect to the material contained herein. While Research-publishing.net is committed to publishing works of integrity, the words are the authors' alone.

Trademark notice: Product or corporate names may be trademarks or registered trademarks, and are used only for identification and explanation without intent to infringe.

Copyrighted material: Every effort has been made by the editorial team to trace copyright holders and to obtain their permission for the use of copyrighted material in this book. In the event of errors or omissions, please notify the publisher of any corrections that will need to be incorporated in future editions of this book.

Typeset by Research-publishing.net
Cover design by © Antti Myöhänen

ISBN13: 978-1-908416-25-4 (Paperback - Print on demand, black and white)
Print on demand technology is a high-quality, innovative and ecological printing method, with which the book is never 'out of stock' or 'out of print'.

ISBN13: 978-1-908416-26-1 (Ebook, PDF, colour)
ISBN13: 978-1-908416-27-8 (Ebook, EPUB, colour)

Legal deposit, Ireland: The National Library of Ireland, The Library of Trinity College, The Library of the University of Limerick, The Library of Dublin City University, The Library of NUI Cork, The Library of NUI Maynooth, The Library of University College Dublin, The Library of NUI Galway.

Legal deposit, United Kingdom: The British Library.
British Library Cataloguing-in-Publication Data.
A cataloguing record for this book is available from the British Library.

Legal deposit, France: Bibliothèque Nationale de France - Dépôt légal: septembre 2015.

Table of contents

v   Notes on contributors

1   Voices of pedagogical development: an introduction
Juha Jalkanen, Elina Jokinen and Peppi Taalas

Section 1. Expanding perspectives

13   Teaching process writing in an online environment
Fergal Carolan and Anna Kyppö

31   Teaching networking: an interpersonal communication competence perspective
Lotta Kokkonen and Merja Almonkari

57   Virtual Slovak: insight into learning Slovak in an e-learning environment
Anna Kyppö

85   Developing a conceptual framework: the case of MAGICC
Teija Natri and Anne Räsänen

Section 2. Enhancing practices

105   Feedback on individual academic presentations: exploring Finnish university students' experiences and preferences
Adrienn Károly

131   Sharing and promoting disciplinary competences for university teaching in English: voices from the University of Jyväskylä language centre's TACE programme
Kirsi Westerholm and Anne Räsänen

159   Enabling the full participation of university students with disabilities: seeking best practices for a barrier-free language centre
Margaret Trotta Tuomi and Camilla Jauhojärvi-Koskelo

Table of contents

171   Doing what we teach: promoting digital literacies for professional development through personal learning environments and participation
Ilona Laakkonen

197   Learner agency within the design of an EAP course
Riina Seppälä

Section 3. Exploring perceptions

225   Learning paths on elementary university courses in Finnish as a second language
Johanna Eloranta and Juha Jalkanen

241   From canon to chaos management: blogging as a learning tool in a modern Finnish literature course
Elina Jokinen and Heidi Vaarala

279   Grammar is the heart of language: grammar and its role in language learning among Finnish university students
Pekka Saaristo

319   Use your languages! From monolingual to multilingual interaction in a language class
Anna Kyppö, Teija Natri, Margarita Pietarinen and Pekka Saaristo

337   Students' choice of language and initial motivation for studying Japanese at the University of Jyväskylä Language Centre
Pauliina Takala

359   Name Index

Notes on contributors

Editors

Juha Jalkanen, MA, is a lecturer and a pedagogical developer at the Language Centre. His research focuses on pedagogical development and language and literacy practices in technology-rich environments. His interest in pedagogical development lies in understanding the complexities of expertise, learning and technology in multilingual and multicultural contexts of higher education.

Elina Jokinen, PhD, is a lecturer at the Language Centre. She has a special interest in writing as an academic profession and the creative process for art and research. She also has extensive work experience in the world of literature and publishing houses. Her current work involves developing pedagogy for writing in an academic context and coaching and mentoring writers struggling with their first academic essays as well as those more experienced writers who publish their research results for wider audiences and through different media.

Peppi Taalas, PhD, adjunct professor, is the director of the Language Centre. Her current research interests are educational and organisational change processes on both policy and practical levels, including change in learning and teaching cultures, staff development and teacher roles, and attitudes in technology-enhanced language learning settings. She has been involved in many national and international research and development projects on the knowledge society, teaching innovation and the future of education. She is currently vice-president of Eurocall.

Contributors

Merja Almonkari, PhD, is a senior lecturer at the Language Centre. She has expertise in the study of political communication, communication skills and emotions as well as in the pedagogical development of speech communication courses for academic purposes. She has published articles and edited books on

Notes on contributors

political communication, academic speech communication, communication apprehension and social anxiety.

Fergal Carolan, MA, is currently a lecturer of English at the Language Centre. He primarily teaches academic reading, academic communication skills and academic writing at both the basic and intermediate levels. His interest in pedagogical development lies in understanding the uses and limitations of ICT, such as online learning platforms, in the academic writing process.

Johanna Eloranta, MA, is a lecturer at the Language Centre. Her research focuses on internationalisation and integration, especially in the contexts of higher education and second language learning. Her interest in pedagogical development lies in learning and teaching Finnish as a second language in an academic setting. She is also involved in national and international collaboration related to second language pedagogy.

Camilla Jauhojärvi-Koskelo, MA, is a lecturer in Swedish at the Language Centre. Her research focuses on motivation and attitudes towards studying Swedish among university students. She has also been involved in developing a barrier-free Language Centre.

Adrienn Károly, PhD, is a lecturer at the Language Centre. She has 15 years of teaching experience in higher education (in Hungary and Finland). Currently, she teaches English for Academic/Specific Purposes and research communication courses at all levels. Her main research interests lie in the intersection of foreign language learning and teaching, translation studies, language policy, multilingualism, intercultural communication and education. Her current research focuses on improving instructional (particularly feedback) practices in higher education.

Lotta Kokkonen, PhD, is a lecturer at the Language Centre. Her research focuses on interpersonal communication relationships and social networks. Her interest in pedagogical development lies in understanding the communication challenges and opportunities that global, multicultural and multilingual working life presents to future professionals. She is also involved in university-level development projects aimed at enhancing students' internationalisation competences.

Anna Kyppö, PhD, is a lecturer of Slovak and English at the Language Centre. Her research focus is on the development of new language learning and teaching environments and on the impact of technology on learning the less commonly taught languages (LCTL). In addition to the development of Slovak studies in the context of Finnish higher education, she is involved in a development project aimed at the integration of students' multilingual and multicultural academic communication competence.

Ilona Laakkonen, MA, is a coordinator at the Division for Strategic Planning, University of Jyväskylä. She works with the development of learner-centred environments and university pedagogy. Her research is focused on personalised learning in digital environments and on the development of digital literacies for professional learning and communication.

Teija Natri, LicPhil, is a senior lecturer of French at the Language Centre. Her specific interest in pedagogical development lies in multilingual competences in higher education language learning as well as in assessment and evaluation practices. She has been involved in two EU Lifelong Learning programmes: Raising awareness and enhancing intercultural communicative competences for students and lifelong learners, 2009–2011 (CefCULT) and Modularising Multilingual and Multicultural Academic Communication Competence, 2012–2014 (MAGICC).

Margarita Pietarinen, MA, is a lecturer of Russian at the Language Centre. Her interest in pedagogical development lies in multilingual competences in higher education as well as in language testing.

Anne Räsänen, LicPhil, worked at the Language Centre as a lecturer of English until her retirement at the end of 2014. Her main responsibilities included teaching research evaluation and research writing at master's and postgraduate levels and participating in numerous internal, national and international development projects in the fields of ESP, EAP and multilingualism as well as in integrated content and language instruction. She was also responsible for setting up the University of Jyväskylä's TACE programme in intercultural and interdisciplinary pedagogy. Her main research interests and publications are also in these fields.

Pekka Saaristo, MA, is a senior lecturer in Swedish, teaching Swedish mainly for students in the social sciences, philosophy, and sport and health sciences. His research interests include themes within the sociology of language and sociolinguistics, such as language ideologies, attitudes, identities, nationalism, language choices, geosemiotics/linguistic landscapes, and grammatical variation in spoken Swedish. His pedagogical interests are focused on the ideas and theories behind different forms of second language learning and teaching.

Riina Seppälä, MA, is a lecturer of English at Aalto University Language Centre. She is also a postgraduate student of applied linguistics at the Centre for Applied Language Studies, University of Jyväskylä and has previously worked as a lecturer of English at the University of Jyväskylä Language Centre (2004–2013). Her research focuses on learner agency on EAP courses. Her interest in pedagogical development lies in exploring the concept of learner agency and supporting it through learning designs on higher education English courses.

Pauliina Takala, MA, is a lecturer in Japanese language and culture at the Language Centre. Her research focuses on language choice and motivation. Her interest in pedagogical development lies in understanding learning and teaching LCTLs, students' language choices and persistence in studying, and creating technology-enhanced learning environments.

Margaret Tuomi, PhD, is a lecturer of English at the Language Centre. She is an educational sociologist specialising in the development of diversity-positive learning environments in classrooms, teacher training and teachers' professional development. Her research has focused on the creation of just and proactive school environments that provide children with tools such as consultation to prevent problems and resolve those that arise. She has conducted numerous teacher training seminars in Finland, Lebanon and the Balkans.

Heidi Vaarala, PhD, is on leave from her lecturer position at the Language Centre and currently works as a senior researcher at the Centre for Applied Language Studies at the University of Jyväskylä. She has taught Finnish as a second language at the University of Jyväskylä in Finland and other European countries. Her research interests include language education policies, social media as a tool in language learning and reading in a second language as well as understanding and interpreting literature in a second language context.

Kirsi Westerholm, MA, is a lecturer at the Language Centre. Her teaching focuses on academic writing and academic literacies in English medium master's programmes. Her area of research is university pedagogical training for staff lecturing in a foreign language. She is also involved in EU projects dealing with the challenges and quality of multilingual and multicultural learning spaces in higher education across Europe.

A very warm thank you to our reviewers

Anna-Leena Aira, PhD, Research Center for Sport and Health Sciences, Helsinki, Finland

Riikka Alanen, Professor, Department of Teacher Education, University of Jyväskylä, Finland

Mari Aro, PhD, Department of Languages, University of Jyväskylä, Finland

Hannele Dufva, Professor, Department of Languages, University of Jyväskylä, Finland

Päivi Häkkinen, Professor, Institute for Educational Research, University of Jyväskylä, Finland

Notes on contributors

Jyrki Kalliokoski, Professor, Department of Finnish, Finno-Ugrian and Scandinavian Studies, University of Helsinki, Finland

Leena Kuure, University Lecturer, Adjunct Professor, English Philology, University of Oulu, Finland

Josephine Moate, University researcher, Department of Teacher Education, University of Jyväskylä, Finland

Paula Pietilä, Disability Coordinator, Educational Development and Counselling Services, University of Turku, Finland

Terttu Rajala, Lecturer, Foreign Languages and Translation Studies, University of Eastern Finland

Sari Sulkunen, Professor, Institute for Educational Research, University of Jyväskylä, Finland

Mirja Tarnanen, Professor, Department of Teacher Education, University of Jyväskylä, Finland

Jaana Toomar, Lecturer, Department of Languages, University of Jyväskylä, Finland

Kaisa Tukia, Lecturer, vice-rector, Tiirismaa School, Finland

Translation and proofreading

Sirpa Vehviläinen, Language Services at the Language Centre, University of Jyväskylä, Finland

Matthew Wuethrich, Language Services at the Language Centre, University of Jyväskylä, Finland

1 Voices of pedagogical development: an introduction

Juha Jalkanen[1], Elina Jokinen[2] and Peppi Taalas[3]

1. Introduction

This volume is a collection of articles that demonstrate the longstanding tradition of pedagogical development work at the University of Jyväskylä Language Centre. The teacher-researchers who present their work in these articles share their ideas and development results while advancing their thinking by writing about the work they are doing. The chapters thus represent a spectrum of voices and perspectives and show different stages of pedagogical thinking and perception.

The Language Centre system in Finland dates back to the mid-1970s when a system of language teaching units was established in many Finnish universities. Some years later, these units were then set up as autonomous institutes whose responsibility was, and still is, to offer language and communication courses to all university students. All university degrees in Finland include compulsory language credits in a student's L1 (written and/or spoken academic communication), in the second national language (Swedish or Finnish depending on the language of the degree) plus in at least one foreign language. Many students also take optional courses in various languages and communication studies.

---

1. Language Centre, University of Jyväskylä, Finland; juha.jalkanen@jyu.fi

2. Language Centre, University of Jyväskylä, Finland; elina.k.jokinen@jyu.fi

3. Language Centre, University of Jyväskylä, Finland; peppi.taalas@jyu.fi

How to cite this chapter: Jalkanen, J., Jokinen, E., & Taalas, P. (2015). Voices of pedagogical development: an introduction. In J. Jalkanen, E. Jokinen, & P. Taalas (Eds), *Voices of pedagogical development - Expanding, enhancing and exploring higher education language learning* (pp. 1-10). Dublin: Research-publishing.net. doi: 10.14705/rpnet.2015.000284

Chapter 1

In 2015, the University of Jyväskylä Language Centre is a mid-size autonomous institution with about 90 employees. The Centre offers courses in 14 languages to about 12,000 students. Moreover, it is a multilingual, multicultural and multidisciplinary expert organisation that supports the internationalisation of the university.

The operations of the Centre can be divided into three dimensions: academic language teaching, support for teaching and research, and pedagogic and strategic development (Table 1). Internationalisation is the principle underpinning all three of the dimensions. It incorporates the internationalisation of the students and staff as well as structures for supporting the university's international staff (e.g. through Finnish language courses that support learning a language at work).

Table 1. The operations of the Language Centre

Language Centre		
Languages, communication, and internationalisation		
Academic language teaching	Support for teaching and research	Pedagogic and strategic development
• Degree students (BA, MA) • International students	• PhD students • Staff training	• Research and development projects and initiatives
Internationalisation (including translation and proofreading services)		

To be successful in these demanding and extensive operations, the Centre has to set clear goals for its operations. In the continuing discussions among the staff, the following goals have been identified to support the Centre in its role:

- embed aspects of future working life skills, including digital literacies and a sense of global citizenship;

- promote active participation in disciplinary discourses and support the development of academic literacies;

- offer modern approaches to learning in pedagogy and content;

- ensure good working conditions for the staff.

Achieving these goals requires dynamic pedagogical development that is grounded in theory as well as concerned with ways of working and development at the Centre. Embedded in the goals is the idea that the future is not predetermined nor is it something that just happens. Instead, we, as practitioners, make it happen. We become, in essence, designers of the future.

2. New directions for educating the academic experts of the future

The drivers for change in higher education language teaching come in many forms. For our work, the following perspectives are not just relevant but essential: societal, organisational, pedagogical and individual.

The societal and organisational perspectives deal with the expectations laid out in policy documents as well as the changing demands of society. These expectations and demands are related to the uncertainty and unpredictability of the contemporary world. The labour market, for instance, is in a state of flux: a growing number of jobs are knowledge-intensive and require the capacity to operate in different languages and to use a range of technologies in order to navigate the expanding sea of information. In addition, legislation on university degrees increasingly emphasises language and communication competence while at the same time cutting down on the time for students to comply with their subject-study requirements.

The pedagogical perspective, in turn, deals with objectives and ideals such as multilingual interaction and the development of academic expertise. However, in practice, multilingual interaction is often reduced to English only, and language and communication studies are isolated from the subject studies. Thus, language and communication competence is not always understood as an element of academic expertise. In this respect, there is a need to shift the focus from teaching to learning and from teaching students to educating future academic professionals.

Finally, the individual perspective takes into account the personal goals and challenges of both teachers and students. One of the key challenges is that of epistemic practices: information overload and the fast pace of working increases the demands on literacy skills and knowledge work. Students need to cope with academic texts in foreign languages from the very beginning of their studies – often without much systematic support. Moreover, students are expected to work in flexible ways that require a self-directed approach. The complexity increases even further when one considers how students' backgrounds differ in terms of education, nationality, goals and learning cultures. Moreover, teachers need to stay up to date on the changing content of various disciplines while not being experts in any of them.

3. A culture of teaching development and research

To be able to deal with these changing conditions, a research-based approach to work has been a central feature of the working culture at the Language Centre. Since 1994, the whole staff has been engaged in systematic action research. This research has been one of the key tools for quality management, continuous development and proactive measures. Over the years, the focus areas and the approaches have varied, but the 20-year period of action research came to a natural conclusion with the final cycle in 2012–2014. A need had been identified for a more dynamic way of working as well as for a more sustainable impact of the development findings and outcomes. This ending, however, was the beginning of a new developmental mechanism to initiate a large-scale transformation of the compulsory language and communication courses.

In an attempt to emphasise the importance of pedagogical development, 2014 was declared to be the Year of Teaching. During the year different ongoing development initiatives were brought to a close and their implications and results were discussed in staff meetings and pedagogical sessions. This was also when all of the more than 500 courses in the Language Centre curriculum were re-evaluated for accuracy in outcomes and assessment, as well as to see whether they still had a valid role in the curriculum.

4. Voices of pedagogical development: an overview

4.1. Expanding perspectives

The book is structured in three parts. In part one, the four chapters aim at **expanding perspectives** on the multilayered and multivoiced reality of pedagogical development in higher education. The chapters are situated within different theoretical and empirical domains, but also echo the multiple voices of practitioners at the Centre.

In Chapter 2, **Carolan** and **Kyppö** focus on how process writing is taught in a particular online environment. In the context of an academic writing course in English, they describe the potential and pitfalls of the process approach. They offer both student and teacher perspectives on the writing process.

In Chapter 3, **Kokkonen** and **Almonkari** address the role of interpersonal communication competence in modern working life and higher education from a pedagogical perspective. They give a comprehensive overview of the research in the area and argue that interpersonal communication competence is at the core of being an expert in contemporary networked society. They seek to expand the scope of the current discussion in a pedagogical direction.

In Chapter 4, **Kyppö** examines how a less commonly taught language, Slovak, is handled in an online teaching environment. She provides an extensive theoretical background – from sociocontructivism and agency to motivation and language learning awareness – for the design of an online course. These concepts are then used as the basis for an investigation of student learning within the course.

In Chapter 5, **Natri** and **Räsänen** describe the process of developing a conceptual framework for multilingual and multicultural academic and professional communication competence. They present MAGICC, a Europe-wide project in which language practitioners worked together to expand the current assessment practices and the Common European Framework of Reference (CEFR).

4.2. Enhancing practices

Part two consists of five chapters that look into **enhancing practices** by engaging teachers, students and other cooperating partners in reflection and development. New practices are co-designed with students and other partners and it is important to ensure that their voices are heard at all stages of the process. This way it is also possible to ensure that the development reflects current needs and demands.

In Chapter 6, **Károly** explores the notion of assessment for learning from the perspective of feedback practices. She reports the results of a survey that aimed to reveal students' previous experiences of feedback as well as their views and preferences regarding feedback. The results emphasise the importance of aligning feedback practices in terms of why and how.

In Chapter 7, **Westerholm** and **Räsänen** report the participant voices of a staff development programme in intercultural university pedagogy. They portray the challenges posed by increasing internationalisation for teaching and describe how the programme aims at responding to these challenges.

In Chapter 8, **Tuomi** and **Jauhojärvi-Koskelo** focus on enabling full participation of university students with disabilities. As a backdrop for the development work, they describe the results of a survey targeted at the language centre staff that aimed at finding out what kind of knowledge and resources teachers needed regarding barrier-free education. Based on the results, the working group for barrier-free language centre designed, among other things, a website to provide useful resources for both teachers and students.

In Chapter 9, **Laakkonen** examines the role of digital literacy as part of pedagogical design. The main concept is the Personal Learning Environment (PLE), which is operationalised in a language course where students are allowed and encouraged to use digital tools that both feel natural and best support their learning.

In Chapter 10, **Seppälä** focuses on learner agency and investigates how it is enabled and expressed on a higher education language course. The chapter contributes to the discussion of how to develop learner agency and empower university students to meet the demands of today's society and working life.

4.3. Exploring perceptions

Finally, the five chapters in part three aim at **exploring perceptions** of language, language learning, and literature. The chapters tackle three central questions of language teaching: what we teach, how we teach it and why we teach it.

In Chapter 11, **Eloranta** and **Jalkanen** examine the perceptions of language and language learning in university students' descriptions of learning Finnish as a second language. In the middle of growing pressures for internationalisation, there is an immense need to understand when, where and for which purposes learners need Finnish. This chapter takes a step in that direction by examining the learning paths of three international students who studied Finnish on a one-term elementary course.

In Chapter 12, **Jokinen** and **Vaarala** explore how literature and language are perceived and re-conceptualised as a social practice on a modern Finnish literature course targeted at students studying Finnish in universities across Europe. The teaching experiment reported in the chapter illuminates how blogging can broaden learners' conceptions of literature and strengthen their language proficiency.

In Chapter 13, **Saaristo** analyses students' views on grammar and its role in formal language learning. He reports the results of a questionnaire which aimed, among other things, to provide a pedagogical basis and a point of departure for the use of grammar in teaching and to help bridge the potential gap between the teacher's and students' understandings.

In Chapter 14, **Kyppö**, **Natri**, **Pietarinen** and **Saaristo** and introduce a pilot course that aims at the enhancement of students' skills in multilingual and multicultural communication. The course design provides a space for exploring, enhancing and expanding one's conception of language competence in multilingual and multicultural settings.

In Chapter 15, **Takala** investigates why students decide to study Japanese and anchors her exploration in the theory of motivation. The results of her survey illuminate the motivational aspects behind students' language choices. This final chapter of the book contributes to the notion that students' reasons for studying different languages vary greatly and the pedagogical challenge is to combine the diverse personal goals with the course design.

5. A multiplicity of voices forms the basis for promoting expertise

The need to re-conceptualise language learning in higher education is clearer than ever: language learning must be seen as the development of a strategic capacity to work with other experts in multilingual, multicultural, multidisciplinary and multimodal contexts that are characterised by change and uncertainty.

In our larger development framework, we recognise the fact that many of the characteristics of the future academic professional belong to language and communication education. These characteristics include the notions of expertise, agency and co-configuration. Expertise is, in our view, always relational (see Edwards 2010) and deals with the ability to communicate and share one's expertise with others and for different purposes through various media and in a range of contexts. In this light, expertise is seen as distributed across networks, negotiated with others around tasks, a resource for joint action, and mediated through languages, cultures, and technologies. Such a view places interaction and languages at the core of expertise.

Agency, in turn, is "understood as the breaking away from a given frame of action and the taking of initiatives to transform it" (Engeström 2005, cited in Virkkunen 2006: 43). Such a break is required of both students and teachers if pedagogical change is to happen. Co-configuration can be considered as one form of modern work (cf. Victor & Boynton 1998) and in which interaction is one of the central features. All this means that there is a growing need for both teachers and students to build an understanding of how expertise is constructed, manifested, negotiated, contested and re-constructed through languaging and across multiple spaces and timescales.

In this collection of articles we have only touched upon some of these elements. With these voices, visions and ideas, we have looked to convey an array of perspectives on teaching practice and thought. By doing so, we present diverse approaches and endeavours that may, on the surface, appear to be different but which on a deeper level share the same purpose; to better understand the context we work in and to use that increased understanding to make a difference and move us a few steps towards new practices and worlds of thinking. It is these worlds we want to open and offer for our students to further explore, expand and enhance.

We truly hope you will find our work thought-provoking, useful and enjoyable.

References

Edwards, A. 2010. *Being an expert professional practitioner: the relational turn in expertise*. Dordrecht: Springer.

Engeström, Y. 2005. Development, movement and agency: breaking away into mycorrhizae activities. *Paper presented at the International Symposium 'Artefacts and Collectives: Situated Action and Activity Theory' (ARTCO), Lyon.* Retrieved from http://lchc.ucsd.edu/mca/Mail/xmcamail.2008_12.dir/att-0247/Yrjo.dev.pdf

Victor, B. & Boynton, A. C. 1998. *Invented here: Maximizing your organization's internal growth and profitability.* Boston: Harvard Business School Press.

Virkkunen, J. 2006. Dilemmas in building shared transformative agency. *Activités, 3* (1), 44–66.

Section 1.
Expanding perspectives

2 Teaching process writing in an online environment

Fergal Carolan[1] and Anna Kyppö[2]

Abstract

This reflective practice paper offers some insights into teaching an interdisciplinary academic writing course aimed at promoting process writing. The study reflects on students' acquisition of writing skills and the teacher's support practices in a digital writing environment. It presents writers' experiences related to various stages of process writing, their growing awareness of becoming good writers but also the constant struggle with common writing problems. Preconceived attitudes towards the process of writing provide further obstacles for students to overcome in an interdisciplinary and intercultural learning environment. A writer often overcomes the barriers to effective writing by acquiring strategies for independent, self-directed learning. Course experiences may help teachers develop efficient writing courses for the new language learning environments and thus to promote students' academic writing competence.

Keywords: process writing, self-directed learning, language learning environments, common writing problems.

1. Background

This case study offers some insights into teaching an interdisciplinary academic writing course aimed at promoting process writing. In addition to the description

---

1. Language Centre, University of Jyväskylä, Finland; fergal.carolan@jyu.fi

2. Language Centre, University of Jyväskylä, Finland; anna.kyppo@jyu.fi

How to cite this chapter: Carolan, F., & Kyppö, A. (2015). Teaching process writing in an online environment. In J. Jalkanen, E. Jokinen, & P. Taalas (Eds), *Voices of pedagogical development - Expanding, enhancing and exploring higher education language learning* (pp. 13-30). Dublin: Research-publishing.net. doi:10.14705/rpnet.2015.000285

of the course content and the learning space, the study reflects on students' acquisition of writing skills and the teacher's support practices in an online learning environment.

The English intermediate academic writing course is an elective, blended course (4 ECTS credits) offered by the University of Jyväskylä Language Centre in the autumn and spring terms. For over one decade, the course has been an essential part of the learner pathway for language and communication skills for study purposes across the university. The history of the course dates to 2003, when the web-based learning platform Optima was adopted and the English academic writing course became one of the first pilot projects aimed at the efficient use of digital environments for language teaching and learning. Due to the immense popularity of the course – the roots of which were undoubtedly in the growing need for tailored writing courses aimed at the development of academic writing – the course was offered for two levels: basic and intermediate. At the same time, the course became one of the Language Centre's action research projects aimed at the enhancement of independent, autonomous learning.

2. Writing process or process writing?

As one of the main goals of the academic writing course is to develop the students' skills in the process of writing and the nature of the writing course is process-like, this section attempts to clarify the concepts of the *writing process* and *process writing*.

In this context, the *writing process* involves teaching the students how to write in a variety of genres and how to incorporate academic writing conventions into their texts. The course has a number of special focuses: explicitness (i.e. signalling and signposting the ideas in the text), responsibility, providing supporting arguments for claims, properly acknowledging the sources of the ideas presented in the text, and the shift from informal to formal language. The objective is to make the students fully aware of the danger of plagiarism and to provide them with the tools to avoid it.

Raimes and Miller-Cochran (2014) perceive the *process of writing* as focusing on content, fluency, personal voice and revision. Because writing always implies a process, instead of the term *process writing* she suggests the term *the process approach to teaching writing*. A process approach can be used with any content (e.g. academic, personal, literature). Seow (2002), however, considers process writing to be more than a writing process approach to teaching writing. He proposes the writing process to be an activity that broadly comprises the stages of planning, drafting (writing), revising (redrafting) and editing. Process writing, on the other hand, is seen as "a program of instruction which provides students with a series of planned learning experiences to help them to understand the nature of writing at every point" (Seow 2002: 316). In addition, process writing incorporates three other highly important skills: responding (sharing), evaluating and post-writing, which comprises re-reading the text for the logical structures and cohesion, eliminating the redundant text and proofreading for spelling, grammar and vocabulary.

Even though this course follows the basic steps of the writing process, it also maintains its process-like nature. The course is built on the spiral method of learning (Veladat & Mohammadi 2011), according to which after acquiring the basic knowledge, students expand on their skill level through 'learning by doing', and they construct the new knowledge. In the context of this academic writing course, students acquire the basic knowledge and become familiar with various genres of academic writing. After producing shorter texts, they proceed towards longer, more sophisticated ones. Revisiting the basic concepts of academic writing and building on the previously acquired knowledge results in an increase in both their learning awareness and in their confidence of themselves as writers.

As they explore the phenomena of academic writing, they progress from the topic sentence to the paragraph, from the paragraph to the essay and so on. They expand their writing skill level with each learning session. The class proceeds through the writing stages as a group, with postwriting consisting of teacher and peer feedback. Multiple forms of feedback generally results in a new draft. To support the idea of the above mentioned learner portfolio, learners are expected to save everything they create (e.g. drafts) or obtain (e.g. peer and teacher feedback) in order to be able to reflect on the overall process of writing.

3. Course content and demography

This section provides basic demographics and the information about the content, modes and expected outcomes of the course.

The main focus of the course is on the development of independent writing skills and the enhancement of self-directed learning. After the completion of the course, students are expected to have developed their academic writing skills, especially the skills of process writing, and enhanced their skills of independent, self-directed learning. They are also expected to have developed their skills in giving and receiving peer feedback on writing and reflecting on their own writing and learning process.

The course participation is open to all university students – Finnish and international degree and short-time (exchange) students – who wish to develop their writing skills. In addition, postgraduate students may participate in the course. Course participants are expected to have the proficiency level B2–C1 (CEFR 2009) in English. In addition to 10–14 contact lessons, the students are expected to participate in the online interaction related to the writing assignments and respond to continuous teacher and peer feedback to the extent of approximately 20 hours. They are assessed according to their participation and completion of the writing assignments.

4. Learning space and learner portfolio

This section introduces the web-based learning platform Optima and the course workspace from the viewpoint of the optimality and efficiency of the learning environment.

Optima is an adaptable web-based learning platform that supports independent, self-directed learning. It enables the sharing of various types of resources, such as documents, websites and audiovisual materials. It also offers various interactive functions, such as chatting, a diary, a collaborative writing platform and commenting and feedback functions. Malone (2012), in his articles on second-language acquisition, presents a social interactionist view, which emphasises the importance of an optimal learning environment. Such a learning environment provides the language learners with multiple opportunities to use the target language and may serve as a uniting factor (i.e. a student works alone but is still with the others). It therefore facilitates the acquisition of a common learning experience. The Optima learning platform fulfils this definition an optimal learning environment.

The course workspace is composed of several folders, which include all the course materials and activities. The main *writer's folder* contains the course plan and resources (e.g. writing-related websites, teacher materials and course assignments). Course participants have their own folders for mapping their learning outcomes through the peer and teacher feedback they give and receive and by reflecting on their writing process.

The course learning materials contained in the main folder and subfolders follow the basic steps of the writing process: planning, prewriting, brainstorming and outlining, drafting, revising and editing. The nature and technological properties of the Optima platform offer the learners the possibility to build a learner portfolio. Learner folders partially follow the structure of a personal learning portfolio (Morrison 2013), which involves a personal profile. A profile consists of various elements, including a student's introduction, course expectations, learning/writing needs, a record of the course (e.g. assignments, reflections, peer and teacher feedback), and the student's personal space for complementary writing or storing of learning- and writing-related resources (e.g. websites, media materials, blogs).

According to Barrett (2005), a traditional learner portfolio includes collecting, selecting, reflecting, projecting and celebrating. In the context of this course, collecting and selecting are related to the completion of writing assignments and other writing-related materials. The focus of reflecting is on one's own writing process, and projecting is related to the learner's self- and peer-evaluation, collaborative writing and group brainstorming. Celebrating refers to the final evaluation of one's achievements as well as the final assessment of the course.

5. Course design and content

This section offers insight into the course design and explains the content of the *writer's folder*, which, in its structure, reflects and supports the writing process.

The main folder consists of the following named subfolders: (1) first writing assignments, (2) academic writing, (3) critical reading and writing, (4) paragraph and essay, (5) research reporting, (6) summarising and paraphrasing, (7) referencing and incorporating sources, and (8) revising. In addition, the folder offers links to various writing-related websites and online tools, such as the Purdue University Online Writing Lab (OWL 2013), the UVIC Writer's Guide (1995) and Using English for Academic Purposes, Andy Gillett's (2014) online guide for students in higher education. There are also web materials related to the specific problems of academic writing (e.g. writing and grammar, punctuation in academic writing). In addition to information on writing-supportive skills, such as summarising, paraphrasing and the instructions on citing and incorporating sources into one's text (e.g. the IEE Citation Style Guide and Using English for Academic Purposes), the writer's folder provides guidelines on how to give peer feedback, what to focus on when reading texts written by others, and how to respond to the feedback received. This section continues with a description of how the course introduces students to academic writing as a genre and to the initial stages of the writing process.

The first of the subfolders, *first writing assignments*, is also the most important. It offers the initial writing assignments, one of which helps students and the teacher get to know each other and establish the course goals. Almost all of them want to learn 'how to write', 'how to produce academic texts', 'to write essays in English' and so on. The first written assignment is called 'Am I a writer?', and it is aimed at the enhancement of creative thinking and exploring multiple uses of an image in writing. Its purpose is to develop strategies for fluency, speed and the free flow of ideas. Students are asked to look at their computer and write about it for 15 minutes. They do not need to worry about spelling, grammar or style. The only rule is that they may not stop writing. After 15 minutes they read their texts in class. The results are often surprising. The texts are usually long and fluent, the language is rich in idiomatic expressions and mostly correct. The purpose of this rapid-writing task is to encourage the students to write and at the same time, to reveal their real writing abilities. The assignment is generally welcomed by the students, because it is both encouraging and fun.

The focus of the academic writing subfolder is on the basic features of academic writing. It also offers sample texts that reveal the variety of academic genres. The structure of academic texts is best demonstrated by scholarly articles related to the students' fields of study, because these generally follow a standard pattern: an introduction providing background information on the subject (general statements on the topic, specific details about a sub-area, review of relevant literature and other research in the field, and a research niche), the problem (i.e. a thesis statement), procedures and methods (description of the methods used in the research, data collection and analysis), results (reporting on the results), discussion (assessment of the results) and references (the cited literature). After getting familiar with the structure of academic texts, the basic steps of process writing are introduced: planning/brainstorming, prewriting, drafting (writing), revising, followed by editing and rewriting.

6. The writing process, from paragraph to finished essay

This section provides a step-by-step description of the writing process. The whole process is first demonstrated on the paragraph level. The main focus is on the structure of the paragraph and the topic sentence. The focus of paragraph writing is on exploring, in a concise manner the stated topic, evaluating the evidence, expounding on the idea, and creating an argument that concerns the idea/topic. Once this outcome is reached, the barrier to writing an essay is overcome.

After practicing different types of paragraphs – descriptive (static and process description), problem/solution, argumentative and persuasive – students begin to prepare an expository five-paragraph essay on a topic of their choice. The essay consists of an introductory paragraph, three supporting body paragraphs and a conclusion. Special focus is on the development of a thesis statement. The thesis statement is an assertion about the topic and it points to the purpose and direction of the paper, and thus it is important that the writers write one that is clear and concise. The major focus is on logical transitions between the paragraphs as well as on the evidential support of the arguments presented in the body (i.e. the main part of the text).

Students practise writing a problem-solving and argumentative expository essays before getting started with the essay related to their field of study. The prewriting stages are completed in pairs or small groups, and the writing itself is implemented individually, but students often benefit from the online area for collaborative writing. After completing the essay, feedback is given in pairs or small groups. Students are expected to reflect on the received feedback and implement the changes recommended by their peers. If the feedback is unclear or a writer does not understand a peer's comments, she may ask for clarification. When reviewing a colleague's essay, reviewing instructions are to be followed. These are targeted at the overall structure of the text (the introduction, body and conclusion), linguistic aspects (grammar and vocabulary), textual organisation (criteria of development, continuity, balance and completeness) and cohesion (use of linking words and phrases). Referring to sources and the relevancy of the topic is also taken into consideration. Rewritten texts (drafts) are reviewed by peers and the teacher. Generally two to three drafts are produced. Nevertheless, not all the students are capable of giving and receiving constructive feedback. For example, some students consider the peer feedback to be less professional than the teacher's feedback:

> "Peer evaluation is not always good in my opinion. A classmate can give you small pieces of advice but it is very difficult to find one who really knows what to tell you in order to make your essay/paper better. For instance, I am not able to do it".

> "The best part of the course was the teacher's constant feedback…"

For assigned topics, the online collaborative writing area may be used for brainstorming and writing. Students enjoy writing together, as they often claim. One of the benefits of the collaborative writing area is its accessibility. Writers do not have to give access to their readers, because comments are visible immediately upon entering the area. When students write together, ideas flow more rapidly and students may get the inspiration they seek from the previously written text. However, one of the disadvantages is that the area cannot be used simultaneously by more than one writer. So even though the final text is the product of the whole group, the text is written in the one-by-one method. One solution is simultaneous writing, everybody writing on the same topic, at the same time. However, the texts must be imported into the writing area and cohesively linked together. In the context of this study, the writing area has been used for text editing in small groups. Each group produced its own draft, which was then edited by other groups. Because all the texts may be displayed in the area, it is easy to compare them and search for some distinctive features of academic texts (e.g. the use of academic vocabulary, linking words, punctuation).

After the practice writing come the writing and revising stages. In these, students start to write an essay related to their field of study. One of the most difficult tasks is the choice of the topic. The topic is related to the student's field of study and its extent is six to seven standard pages including the references. The MA thesis writers and postgraduate students may write a research paper. The instructions for writing a research paper are available in the writer's folder and are usually specified by the teacher. As can be seen in the comments below, students value the possibility to write about their own studies and research topics:

> "I enjoyed the fact that it was possible to cover the topics related to your own field of study in the assignments. If it had not have been possible to write the texts about the issues from my own field of study, I would have felt considerably less motivated to write".

> "In my opinion, it was a good idea to write the final paper on my own research, because that has a purpose, it is not 'just' writing…"

Identifying the topic is often connected with the development of the thesis statement. Writing a focused statement is one of the greatest challenges for students. It should indicate the purpose, scope and direction of the paper while also previewing the sub-theses to follow and identifying the relationships between the pieces of evidence used to support of the writer's arguments. To break the barrier and let the ideas flow, the students may spontaneously tell their peers (or the teacher) what they want to write about. Asking some questions about the topic often helps the writer to organise ideas and create a solid statement. Brainstorming is implemented in small groups. To make the best of the peers' contribution, students create a mind map or poster for generating the ideas. They ask their colleagues for the feedback in the form of comments or questions on the statement related to the topic. If necessary, this process is repeated until a sufficient number of ideas is generated. Interestingly, the best ideas are not always generated during the brainstorming period.

The most productive step of the writing process is writing the first draft. This is the most time-consuming stage, but it is also the most rewarding. The first draft is generally followed by the second and sometimes even the third draft. Even though writing usually takes place offline (i.e. outside of class), students are often in the Optima learning environment either writing or retrieving information or just hanging out. In addition to regular face-to-face tutorials and online sessions, course participants spend time together outside of the class, which underlines the social aspect of the learning process.

One of the most fruitful stages of the writing process is revising and editing. Revising (i.e. making the text sound better) includes organising the text, replacing informal non-academic terms with more formal academic ones, adding details, clarifying explanations and focusing on cohesion. Editing (i.e. making the text look better) means correcting spelling and punctuation as well as finalising the text layout. In this stage of the writing process, students talk about their texts with their peers and the teacher, which results not only in the improvement of the structure, but also in the clarification of the ideas presented in the paper and refinement of the writers' arguments and contrary evidence. This stage usually makes the students think about what they are doing and what they are writing about and thus promotes their skills of critical literacy:

> "I believe I have made a progress as a writer. In the beginning of the course, writing in English demanded more effort and thinking. Writing now is more effortless and it comes fluently".

> "I learned how to pay more attention to my writing. Maybe I earlier just wrote without thinking…"

This writing and thinking often resulted in rewriting. The aphorism on writing that 'writing is rewriting' is close to the reality. Or, as H. Shaw, the author of *Errors in English and Ways to Correct Them* (as quoted in Shope 2002: para. 1), says, "There is no such thing as good writing. There is only good rewriting".

7. Student reflections

Finally, at the end of the course, students are required to reflect on their writing progress and evaluate the course. Students' reflections relate most often to the process of process writing, writing topics, becoming academic writers, self-confidence in writing, course atmosphere, feedback (teacher and peer feedback) and the Optima learning environment. Some findings based on the students' excerpts from course reflections and course feedback forms are presented below.

The process of writing was perceived as long, demanding and requiring patience and concentration, but all of the students considered the course to be useful for their future studies and working life:

> "Now, as I look at the list of assignments in my folder, I realise that the course has been quite a long one, but that is what process writing takes. I feel I have improved as a writer. I did manage quite well before, but I have done most of my writing in Finnish. Getting more accurate in academic English writing has been the main learning experience for me in this course and these skills will be useful in the future".

> "I have never written as much as I have on this course…"

They all valued the continuous teacher feedback and the pleasant atmosphere on the course. They believed that they made clear progress in academic writing and were optimistic about their writing in the future. Some praised the abundance of learning resources in Optima, but others would have preferred a more traditional learning environment:

> "I think that Optima environment is adequate for the purpose of this course and it supported the learning process quite well. It was also nice to be able to exchange feedback and to be able to see the texts of other students".

> "Optima works well, but there are too many folders and subfolders, which makes it exhausting to look for information. The common writing area was also hard to control or finish…"

The excerpts of students' reflections reveal that they take genuine pleasure in writing, despite the difficulties related mostly to searching for the appropriate academic vocabulary, struggling with structures and the impact of language interference:

> "Sometimes I enjoyed writing, sometimes writing was difficult. I had no

ideas or no clear structure. After writing for a while it went better but the beginning was always very difficult for me. My biggest problem is the translation from German into English. I translate directly. I should think more about the structure and not translate…"

"I enjoyed writing. I learned new things, like the correct essay structure. But it was difficult…"

Being able to write about one's own field of study in English was also a source of pleasure:

"Writing was somewhat boring because the paper did not allow the use of all kinds of expressions (e.g. rhetorical or humorous utterances). However, I enjoyed the feeling of being able to write about my field in foreign language. It was like exploring a new environment".

"Writing is a kind of therapy for me. I always feel good when I am writing. The best thing is when I realise that I can express my ideas in a foreign language. And I wrote the essay about my major subject…"

For some students, writing an essay was their first encounter with academic writing:

"I have become a better writer. I know I should have enough information about the topic and I have to learn more vocabulary. I made progress because this essay was the first academic essay that I wrote and I used academic language for the first time".

"I have learned important things about academic writing, for example, academic expressions and how to improve the paragraphs. I believe that information will be useful in the future".

"I think my writing skills have improved. I know now that I should avoid long sentences. The essay was a good exercise for practicing academic writing. In addition, the course provided me with lots of background information about writing an academic essay".

As mentioned earlier, one of students' frequent writing problems is a lack of self-confidence. The course not only contributed to the development of students' academic writing skills, but it also helped them to acquire self-confidence:

> "I have learned how to use the academic language. Besides, I learned how to write an essay in a focused way. The intermediate academic writing course helped me to improve my writing skills to become more self-confident in writing".

> "My vocabulary and writing skills have absolutely developed. Thanks to the feedback, I learned about my writing problems related to grammar and structure".

> "I learned about the structure of an essay. My academic skills got developed. This course helped me with academic writing. Moreover, I got rid of my worries about writing an essay".

8. Teacher reflections

This section opens a discussion about the so-called successful and less successful writers. Some of the barriers to successful writing are listed, as are some tips on how to overcome these barriers. Some of the students' ideas related to the impact of writing on their personal development are also introduced. Academic intermediate writing poses several challenges to the teacher, the greatest of which are the differences in learners' language proficiency and culture-related approaches to self-directed learning. Personal engagement, readiness to learn, motivation and above all, the urge to develop the learners' academic writing skills are often present. Nevertheless, it is up to the teacher to design a cooperative learning environment that motivates the students and facilitates their learning efforts.

Course participants are expected to have the proficiency level B2–C1 (CEFR 2009) in English. They are expected to be able to produce various types of written texts and to demonstrate their capability to use the language in a variety of contexts:

> "Users at this level…should be able to produce written texts of various types, showing the ability to develop an argument as well as describe or recount events. This level of ability allows the user a certain degree of independence when called upon to use the language in a variety of contexts" (CEFR 2009[3]).

However, only a few students can perform to that level. The Finnish students often lack confidence in their own skills and the international students generally lack the writing experience. In addition, they are not familiar with the strategies of independent, self-directed learning. The digital learning platform itself poses a challenge:

> "In the beginning I was confused because at my home university we don't have this kind of online work space. It was interesting though that after I got used to it (in a couple of weeks…maybe three), I realised how useful it is. We didn't have to print or write anything, because everything we needed to know was already there".

Furthermore, students can often feel overwhelmed when first surveying the course contents in Optima. When the course begins, students can see the full range of work that lies ahead of them. All of the course material, plus the wide range of assignments, are initially visible. Though this gives students a realistic impression of the time they will put into the course, some may find daunting the sight of all the course material at once. To counter this feeling, it is vital to reassure students of their abilities as writers from the first in-class meeting.

Confidence building is a key component, and many students experience a so-called eureka moment at some point. Students that lack the confidence to apply

---

3. Cited in Teaching Standards in Chile: B2 (Alte Level Three); retrieved from http://www.sccinternational.org/?p=82.

their writing skills effectively overcome this barrier when they perceive that they have been given a system with which to write. Once these students discover their own personal writing process, they overcome their lack of confidence and develop as writers.

9. Implications for the future

The overall positive reaction of students to the digital learning platform is encouraging for its use in the future. As the classroom, and indeed the world, continue to become more technologically rich environments, it is only prudent that this course continues to develop along with modern technology. One perceived limitation of the course is the fact that it is currently taught in a computer lab. Computer labs, in some cases, can be at a premium. If, for example, the instructor is reliant on booking a computer lab for the course, it can limit the timetabling options for the course. While laptops and other devices are now in widespread use, students have been reluctant to bring their own devices to the classroom. As stated previously, many of the course participants are students on exchange. These students cite the poor condition of their devices and short battery life as the main reasons for their reluctance to use them in class. Perhaps in the future the use of tablet devices or similar technologies will become even more common and widespread, which might serve to negate this issue.

While considering the future of the course it is also important to reflect on how technology can detract from the writing process. Writing on a computer with a keyboard has a somewhat different dynamic to writing by hand with a pen or pencil. Excessive use of technology is likely to speed up the entire writing process, which is not necessarily a positive outcome. When they write by hand, students tend to take more time to consider what exactly they will include in each sentence. The extra time that a student spends writing by hand can be valuable in improving the content and quality of students' texts. For this reason, older writing methods should not be discarded while developing this course for the future.

Similarly, the ease with which source material can be accessed online poses problems. If a student has to go to a library or archive to find source material, it takes much more time than if they access the same materials through online resources. That extra time spent travelling to the library and physically locating the source material can be crucial in a student's thought process. By physically locating source material for their work, the student has time to consider why they are getting that particular piece of information, how it is relevant to their topic and in what way they will incorporate it into their piece of text. It is vital that these elements of the thought process are not lost as the use of technology increases. This course will continue to develop in ways that preserve these crucial aspects of the writing process.

Optima has proved to be a functional interactive learning environment and an excellent platform for process writing. Its greatest benefit is its functionality, organising learning resources and making them easily accessible. The current version of Optima offers a wide variety of multimedia tools that can be incorporated seamlessly into the writing process. Simard (1997) has highlighted the changes multimedia environments bring to the writing process. In these environments, the writing process becomes the sum of various interactive processes that utilise a range of skills for a specific purpose. Even though the explicit purpose of our course has been the production of written academic texts, the course hopefully offers something deeper, namely, the intellectual excitement and pleasure of new learning experiences.

References

Barrett, H. C. 2005. *Researching digital portfolios and learner engagement*. White Paper. Retrieved from http://www.taskstream.com/reflect/whitepaper.pdf

CEFR (Common European Framework of Reference for Languages). 2009. *Learning, teaching, assessment. A Guide for Users*. Strasbourg: Language Policy Division.

Gillett, A. 2014. *Using english for academic purposes. A guide for students in higher education*. Retrieved from http://www.uefap.com/

Malone, D. 2012. Theories and research of second language acquisition. *Reading for day 2, Topic SLA Theories*. Bangkok: MLE WS.

Morrison, D. 2013. *How to create a personal learning portfolio: students and professionals. online learning insights*. Retrieved from http://onlinelearninginsights.wordpress.com/2013/01/30/why-students-need-personal-learning-portfolios-more-than-we-do/

OWL Purdue University Online Writing Lab. 2013. Retrieved from https://owl.english.purdue.edu/owl/resource/980/02/

Raimes, A. & Miller-Cochran, S. K. 2014. *Keys for writers*. Boston: Wadsworth Cengage Learning.

Seow, A. 2002. The writing process and process writing. In J. C. Richards & W. A. Renandya (eds.), *Methodology in language teaching. An Anthology of Current Practice*. Cambridge: Cambridge University Press, 315–320. doi:10.1017/CBO9780511667190.044

Shope, B. 2002. True writing is rewriting. *Holly Lisle's Vision. A resource for writers*. Retrieved from http://fmwriters.com/Visionback/Issue9/true.htm

Simard, J. 1997. The Writing process in a multimedia environment. *The Technology Source*. Retrieved from http://technologysource.org/article/writing_process_in_a_multimedia_environment/

UVIC. 1995. *Writer's Guide*. Retrieved from http://web.uvic.ca/wguide/Pages/MasterToc.html

Veladat, F. & Mohammadi, F. 2011. Spiral learning teaching method: Stair stepped to promote learning. *Procedia - Social and Behavioral Sciences, 29*, 1115–1122. doi:10.1016/j.sbspro.2011.11.345

3 Teaching networking: an interpersonal communication competence perspective

Lotta Kokkonen[1] and Merja Almonkari[2]

Abstract

Modern working life calls for competences that enable people to be creative, innovative and effective. Studies looking at contemporary enterprises and organisations such as businesses and schools have shown that many of the qualifications that graduating students would need, including informal learning (see Gielen, Hoeve & Nieuwenhuis 2003), innovativeness (e.g. Moolenaar & Sleegers 2010; Obstfeld 2005) and creativity (e.g. Burt 2004; Perry-Smith & Shalley 2003), are associated with interpersonal relationships and social networks. According to a report on the national career survey (EK 2011a), effective networking is dependent on social skills such as the ability to establish contacts in multicultural environments, the ability to discuss with others, understanding the perspectives of others and listening skills. For speech communication teachers and researchers, those skills listed above are communication skills, and more precisely, interpersonal communication skills. In this article, social networks are perceived from a perspective of interpersonal communication and networking is viewed as interpersonal communication competence. To date, the talents, characteristics and skills which people need when networking have not been consistently described from the perspective of interpersonal communication competence. Because it is possible to enhance this competence, we argue that networking is something that students could, and should, learn at the higher education level.

Keyword: networking, interpersonal communication competence, teaching communication, higher education.

1. Language Centre, University of Jyväskylä, Finland; lotta.o.kokkonen@jyu.fi

2. Language Centre, University of Jyväskylä, Finland; merja.almonkari@jyu.fi

How to cite this chapter: Kokkonen, L., & Almonkari, M. (2015). Teaching networking: an interpersonal communication competence perspective. In J. Jalkanen, E. Jokinen, & P. Taalas (Eds), *Voices of pedagogical development - Expanding, enhancing and exploring higher education language learning* (pp. 31-56). Dublin: Research-publishing.net. doi:10.14705/rpnet.2015.000286

Chapter 3

1. Introduction

Puhakka, Rautopuro and Tuominen (2010) discuss employability among Finnish university graduates. They found that the most needed skills and forms of knowledge for graduates entering today's job market are interpersonal skills and academic skills. Interpersonal skills included negotiation skills, teamwork and social skills, organisation and coordination skills, and communication skills in Finnish (see also EK 2011b). Since the Bologna process, which defines employability as "the ability to gain initial employment, maintain employment, and to be able to move around within the labour market"[3], universities have become more aware that they have to ensure graduates obtain the skills and knowledge that make them employable (Puhakka et al. 2010).

Changes in modern working life have created new kinds of needs for communication competence. Employees will have to deal with globalisation, internationalisation, and the rapid development of technology. The development of organisation models that rely heavily on computer-mediated communication involving people from different parts of the world dealing with increasingly abstract elements represent just a few of the aspects that have enhanced the need for communication competence at work. It is anticipated that the significance of one's communication competence is going to be even greater in the future working life (Aalto, Ahokas & Kuosa 2008; "FinnSight 2015" 2006; Huotari, Hurme & Valkonen 2005; Linturi 2007).

One of the communication requirements of modern working life includes the ability to create and maintain interpersonal relationships. For example, multinational cooperation and teamwork as well as the development of creative and innovative projects call for interpersonal relationships and social networks consisting of those relationships. Expertise is no longer something that an individual can create and enhance alone, but rather it is an ability to create a team and a community in which each individual's personal areas of expertise complement the knowledge and skills of others. Indeed, the Confederation of

---

3. Retrieved from http://www.ehea.info/article-details.aspx?ArticleId=16

Finnish Industries (EK 2011a)[4] has concluded in their report that networking is one of the key skills and qualifications required in the future job market.

In this article, social networks are seen as being constructed by and maintained within the interpersonal relationships that people have. Taking into consideration what is being said about the future working life, we address the question of whether interpersonal competence should be taught as part of communication and language courses at the university level, and raise the question of whether interpersonal competence is indeed already being taught on university-level communication and language courses and how this instruction could be developed further to benefit graduating students who are preparing themselves for future employment.

In many studies and reports on the current and possible future requirements for employees, the communication competence needed in working life is emphasised (Gaboury 1999; Himanen 2004; Kostiainen 2003; Lang, Cruse, McVey & McMasters 1999; Morreale, Osborn & Pearson 2000; Pyöriä 2006). It seems that communication competence is one of the key factors influencing wellbeing at work and the success of both individuals and organisations alike. Regardless of the vast amount of research that supports the claim that communication training is important, there is not much research specifying the types of communication skills that might be most appropriately incorporated in the curricula of particular fields. For example, Darling and Dannels (2003: 3-4) studied communication skills needed in engineering and they point out that, not much is known "about what kinds of communication tasks practicing engineers face (e.g. team presentations, one-on-one meetings with employees, formal PowerPoint presentations), the typical audiences for whom those speaking tasks occur (e.g. clients, employees, public forums, the government), and the perceived consequences of these speaking tasks for workplace success". Since 2003, there have been some attempts to look at work-related interpersonal communication skills and the communication competences needed in work-related interpersonal relationships. The question of whether this knowledge and

---

4. Oivallus Final Report is also to be found in English at http://ek.multiedition.fi/oivallus/fi/liitetiedostot/arkisto/Oivallus-Final-Report.pdf

information has reached the higher education communication training offered on university language centre courses will be addressed in this article.

This article first provides a brief overview of social networks and the interpersonal communication perspective on them. It then goes on to look at what kind of interpersonal skills and competences are related to networking, and what we know about learning these things. Finally, we examine the possibilities and challenges of teaching networking and interpersonal communication competence in a higher educational setting and some directions for future research are proposed.

2. Social networks as the focus and goal of learning

Social networks are everywhere. The ubiquity of networks in contemporary political and economic life, networking and interactivity seem to be a part of our everyday life. Network thinking is so broadly applied that authors such as Castells (1996, 2000) have started to talk about 'the network society'. Networks as a metaphor and model of individual and collective life seem to dominate contemporary Western thinking (Barry 2001; Riles 2000). Network theory and theories of networks have enabled researchers to analyse not only the chains within social networks, but also to find explanations to various phenomena in human social life (Frankham 2006; Gould 2003; Riles 2000; Trevillion 2000).

Indeed, network theory and related theories have become extremely popular in various fields and "The network approach spans a broad range of disciplines, including sociology, social psychology, mathematics, political science, communication, anthropology, economics, and epidemiology" (Katz, Lazer, Arrow & Contractor 2004: 311; see also Newman, Barabási & Watts 2006). As Borgatti and Halgin (2011) point out, the term social network is applied to almost everything from a trade associations to listservs and social media websites, while the number of studies on social networks has increased dramatically in recent decades.

Overall, social networks can be seen as method, metaphor and form (see Knox, Savage & Harvey 2006) and social network analysis is seen as a method or a perspective that is applied to great number of areas. Trevillion (2000: 514) points out that "[w]hereas network analysis is one among many specific methodologies available to social scientists including social work research, the social network approach is much broader and is best seen as an orientation to the social world which attempts to understand it in terms of sets, patterns and linkages".

Generally, social networks are said to consist of a set of actors and relations between these actors. In the human sciences, actors, also called nodes, can be individuals, groups, organisations or societies depending on the approach and perspective (see Katz et al. 2004). The relations, also called ties or edges, between the actors can be information flows, economic exchange and ties that provide social support to the actors in question. These social networks can also be defined simply as "interconnected individuals who are linked by patterned communication flows" (Rogers & Kincaid 1981: 82).

If one considers the myriad approaches, theoretical considerations and methodologies, it is understandable that there is no single formal statement of the network perspective, nor is there a single network theory that could be applied everywhere. In this article we see that social networks, also called interpersonal networks, communication networks and personal communities, are constructed by the interpersonal relationships that a person has. We use the term social network, but wish to stress that within these networks of interpersonal relationships communication is not only seen as a flow between the actors. Instead, interpersonal relationships are initiated and maintained through communication. Communication is therefore a fundamental and inseparable element within these relationships and social networks.

We use the term interpersonal relationships when referring to the relations between individuals. When defining an interpersonal relationship, we rely on what Wilmot (1996) has said about the nature of these relationships. He points out that partners need to be aware of the other and of the relationship for it to exist (see also Neuliep 1996). Furthermore, interpersonal relationships are seen as a process in which meanings are constantly negotiated in relation to shared history, the present and the anticipated future. What we mean by this is that interpersonal relationships are being initiated and maintained through communication and their qualities and meanings are negotiated in interaction between partners and over a period of time (Littlejohn 2002; Sigman 1998). Consequently, networking is seen as developing and maintaining interpersonal relationships.

3. The benefits of networking and why we should teach it

Numerous studies on social networks make clear the reasons why social networks are such a relevant phenomenon and why higher education graduates should know about them. Furthermore, they make a case for why graduates should have the skills to develop and maintain social networks.

Within the human sciences, it seems to be a common belief that networking is beneficial and recommended to individuals, organisations and companies alike. For example, in management research social networks are being discussed in relation with creativity (Burt 2004; Perry-Smith & Shalley 2003), informal learning (Gielen et al. 2003), innovation (Obstfeld 2005), and job performance (Sparrowe, Liden, Wayne & Kraimer 2001), among many others (see also Borgatti & Halgin 2011).

Benefits and positive outcomes related to social networks include social support (see Mitchell & Trickett 1980) and the health outcomes related to social networks have been discussed widely (see Albrecht & Goldsmith 2003). Furthermore, the importance of social networks can also be linked to adaptation to a life change (Mitchell & Trickett 1980), as well as to integration and belonging to a new cultural environment. These studies show that social networks and individuals' interpersonal relationships can be seen as the glue that ties a person to a group, a community, a physical environment or even a society (see Kokkonen 2010).

Communication studies looking at social networks have often dealt with questions such as what groups of people there are in an individual's networks (e.g. relatives, friends, acquaintances), what kinds of relationships there are within the networks (weak or close relationships), and what kinds of resources these networks, or different relationships within networks, provide to a person (Wellman 2007). Studies have often focused on the size or density of the network (Mitchell & Trickett 1980) and modern technology has further multiplied the possibilities to research these aspects. Since their introduction, social network sites such as Facebook have attracted millions of users, many of whom have integrated these sites into their daily practices. Contemporary technology enables researchers to look at the thousands, even millions of connections and relationships people have (Boyd & Ellison 2007). Consequently, many recent studies on social networks and network sites are nowadays published in channels such as the *Journal of Computer-Mediated Communication*.

Another network characteristic commonly studied in the field of communication is the degree of connections, that is, the average number of relationships that each member has with other members of the network. Furthermore, social networks have also been studied by looking at the intensity, durability, multidimensionality, directness and reciprocity of those linkages. Relationship dispersion, frequency and homogeneity are among the other characteristics of social networks that have been studied (Mitchell & Trickett 1980).

The benefits of social networks seem to be well addressed and, indeed, the question of why people create, maintain, dissolve and reconstitute network ties has been explained by multiple schools of thought or groups of theories (for analyses of existing theories, see Monge & Contractor 2003). Discussing networking and networks in general with students is beneficial not only in terms of their enhanced networking competence. The benefits might be even more extensive and, as Alatarvas (2013) has stated, understanding social networks and network processes in general would benefit people when developing social technologies in the future. Furthermore, Alatarvas (2013) suggests a deeper understanding of networks and network processes will support the understanding of different invasive phenomena, from gossip to infectious diseases. As all of these studies suggest, an understanding of social networks is, on numerous levels, highly relevant for modern working life.

4. Networking and interpersonal communication competence

A number of studies have examined networking as a skill or set of skills or as a competence. In contemporary research, terms such as networking competence or simply networking are frequently used (see Ritter & Gemünden 2003). Network competence has been described as the ability of an individual or the relationship of individuals or as an ability of organisations (e.g. Mittilä 2006; Thornton, Henneberg & Naudé 2013).

Little is said, however, about network competence from an individual or interpersonal perspective. Leskinen (2011) is among the few who have adopted an individual's point of view when researching entrepreneurial networking process. Her case study included an entrepreneurial networking project involving 25 firms operating in the service market, and the results revealed that the key elements in the entrepreneurial networking process are dialogue, trust and commitment. The practices and routines that are based on good and respectful dialogue encouraged partners in innovative discussions, creativeness and cooperation as well as in developing new services. Entrepreneurs received support and encouragement from other entrepreneurs in their network, and their relationships and cooperation in networks generated new business possibilities and channels. Networking also helped them cope with the various challenges entrepreneurs face.

In addition to Leskinen's (2011) study, Purhonen (2008, 2012) has explored networking from a communication and interpersonal communication perspective. She looked at the interpersonal communication competence from the perspective of small and medium-sized enterprises in the contexts of networking and business collaboration (Purhonen 2008). In her results, Purhonen (2008: n. p.) lists "information sharing, the management of diversity, adaptation and adjustment, integrative negotiation, and the creation and management of relationships" as focal areas of interpersonal communication competence in the networking and collaboration of SME during an internationalisation process. In the context of collaboration and networking, the key criteria for competent information sharing are mutuality, reciprocity and openness (Purhonen 2008). Based on the given criteria and considering that the broader networks of the involved parties are also closely connected, it seems to be useful for the cooperating parties to be aware of the larger social networks of their partners. This enables them to determine the sources, such as knowledge and skills that could be available for them too. "For SME owners, managers and employees it is thus important to recognize what kind of information and other resources exist within their interpersonal networks, and how these resources could help their collaborating group or partners", Purhonen (2008: n. p.) concludes.

While discussing the creation and management of relationships, Purhonen (2008) refers to lists of communication skills or behaviours that could be considered broadly as relational communication skills. Also other researchers have discussed this issue and they have listed skills such as showing concern for others, reasoning with others, expressing trust, elaborating, directness and mutual concessions, and providing face support (Hardy, Phillips & Lawrence 2003; Hargie & Tourish 1997; Purhonen 2008) as relational skills.

Since networking is, in this article, seen as developing and maintaining interpersonal relationships, and because there are so few studies analysing it from this perspective, we will briefly look into what has been said about interpersonal communication competence in contemporary working life in general.

5. Interpersonal communication competence for working life

In communication research on interpersonal communication, the foundation of competence often relies on ideas from Spitzberg and Cupach (1984). Communication competence in general can be defined "as an impression of appropriateness and effectiveness, which is functionally related to individual motivation, knowledge, skills, and contextual facilitators and constraints" (Spitzberg 2013: 126). Along the same lines, Purhonen and Valkonen (2013: n. p.) have defined interpersonal communication competence by using Valkonen's definition from 2003 as "knowledge about effective and appropriate interpersonal communication, motivation to engage in social interaction, meta-cognitive communication skills, as well as the interpersonal communication skills needed to act in a way that the interactants perceive to be both effective and appropriate" (Valkonen 2003: 26).

Interpersonal communication competence is understood as "construction of cognitive, affective and behavioural dimensions. The cognitive dimension refers to knowledge and metacognitive skills [...] such as knowledge of the communication partner of conversing and the topic", communication processes, strategies and context (Purhonen 2008: n. p.). Metacognitive skills include planning, perceiving, evaluating, controlling and analysing communication (Spitzberg 2000, 2003; Valkonen 2003).

Furthermore, interpersonal communication competence can be seen as an influence or impression formed by interaction partners about each other's communication behaviour. The impression can be formed by an observer about a participant's behaviour (Lakey & Canary 2002; Spitzberg 2000). Spitzberg (2013) has also discussed interpersonal communication competence as evaluations attributed and formed on the basis of how effective and appropriate communication behaviour is perceived to be, rather than considering it to be a certain set of skills, abilities or tactics.

Context also affects interpersonal communication competence, because interaction always takes place in a certain culture, time, relationship, situation and function. This context influences as well as gets incorporated into both actions and judgments of actions. Communication skills, for example, are evaluated differently in different contexts. The participants' and observers' perception of the context determines the expectations for interpersonal communication competence (Spitzberg 2000, 2013). It is therefore relevant to also look at the interpersonal communication competence needed in different professions and professional contexts.

Recent research has focused on the communication competence requirements for a range of professions (see Frymier & Houser 2000 on teachers, Darling & Dannels 2003 on engineers, Rouhiainen-Neuenhäuserer 2009 on managers, Ala-Kortesmaa & Välikoski 2008 on judges, and Laajalahti 2014 on researchers). Studies have also been interested in the educational methodologies and contexts used for teaching interpersonal competence in, for example, a healthcare context (Koponen 2012), among pharmacists (Hyvärinen 2011) and among accountants (Gray 2010).

As an example, Laajalahti's (2014) study focused on researchers' experiences and understanding of the need for interpersonal competence and learning interpersonal competence at work. In the study, researchers reported having work-related interpersonal relationships with at least 16 different groups of people. These included relationships with other researchers, students, professors and other academic professionals, participants in their studies, possible clients, officials and media representatives, among many others. According to these researchers, communication competence affected their personal career development, publications, funding and other resources, and job opportunities. Belonging to the academic community was also reported to be dependent on respondents' interpersonal communication competence. In addition, the research work itself was influenced by the communication competence of the researcher. For example, publicising the work, its societal relevance, the applicability of the results as well as their reliability and validity were all dependent on the researcher's interpersonal communication competence (Laajalahti 2014).

In Frymier and Houser's (2000) study of communication skills within teacher-student interpersonal relationships, they applied an interpersonal competence tool developed by Burleson and Samter (1990) for measuring interpersonal relationships. The tool, adapted to measure specific communication skills in a given context, included eight elements:

> "conversational skill (the ability to initiate, maintain, and terminate enjoyable casual conversations), referential skill (the ability to convey information clearly and unambiguously), ego supportive skill (the ability to make another feel good about himself or herself), comforting skill (the ability to make others feel better when depressed, sad, or upset), conflict management (the ability to reach mutually satisfying solutions in conflicts), persuasive skill (the ability to get people to modify their thoughts and behaviours), narrative skill (the ability to entertain through jokes, gossip, stories, etc), and regulation (the ability to help someone who has violated a norm to fix the mistake effectively)" (Frymier & Houser 2000: 208).

In their study, Frymier and Houser (2000) found that these methods for measuring communication skills within friendships are also applicable in teacher–student relationships. Whether the model is applicable to professional relationships such as those between managers and employees or collegial relationships between co-workers is still a question mark and requires more empirical research.

In summary, the skills mentioned earlier in the various networking contexts include information sharing, integrative negotiation, respectful dialogue, as well as "showing concern for others, reasoning with others, expressions of trust, using elaboration, directness and mutual concessions and providing support for others" (Purhonen 2008: n. p.). All of these skills are basic interpersonal communication skills. Similar sets of skills are highlighted in many other contexts as well (see Hargie & Dickson 2004; Spitzberg 2013).

All the examples mentioned above provide relevant information about interpersonal communication competence in working life. Yet, as Laajalahti (2007: 335) concludes in her article about the development of interpersonal communication competence at work, there have been many attempts to "define the interpersonal communication competence needed in current working life or in specific professions, but many of these [result in fragmented] lists of requirements" (see also Kostiainen 2003). Instead of listing all the different possible forms of interpersonal communication competence and skills, this section has introduced its key aspects. In the following section we discuss if it is possible to teach any of interpersonal competence in a higher educational context.

6. Teaching networking: interpersonal competence as a target for teaching and learning

Despite many studies, there still exists a widely held belief about networking and interpersonal communication skills that they are like personality traits: inborn and not possible to learn. In this section of our article we discuss the possibilities and challenges of teaching networking and interpersonal communication competence in a higher educational setting. The discussion is based on the assumption that, like any communication skill, interpersonal communication competence can also be taught, enhanced and learned in formal educational settings.

The idea of interpersonal communication competence being something that one can learn and something that can be taught is widely accepted. The learning process contains many stages, for example observation, emulation, self-control and self-regulation. Skilled behaviour improves with practice and feedback (for more on skilled interpersonal communication, see Hargie & Dickson 2004). As Laajalahti (2007: 341) mentioned "communication scholars disagree about how much interpersonal communication competence can change over time, the general idea that it can develop and be developed is widely accepted" (see also Greene 2003; Hargie & Dickson 2004).

In this article we are interested in the training provided to students entering working life. We know that the majority of significant learning experiences seem to take place in informal learning (Merriam & Clark 1993). Furthermore, we know that interpersonal communication competence is often acquired through informal learning (Segrin & Givertz 2003). However, like Puhakka, Rautopuro and Tuominen (2010: 45) point out "employers want graduates who are well prepared for the world of work". Thus, we argue that enhancing students' interpersonal communication competence prior to entering working life would give them certain advantages in the job market.

Development of language and communication skills in infancy and childhood have drawn more attention within the field of communications and further research is needed in order to develop theoretical and empirical methods for exploring the development of interpersonal communication competence at work (Laajalahti 2007). Comprehensive reviews of communication training, let alone of interpersonal communication training, in higher educational institutions is difficult to find.

However, studies conducted in specific areas such as healthcare and education do exist. For example communication skills training in healthcare teaching in pre-registration nurse education were reviewed in the United Kingdom in the early 2000s (Chant et al. 2002; see also Hargie, Boohan, McCoy & Murphy 2010). The results show that methods used in communication skills training included experiential methods, use of standardised patients, videos, lectures, groupwork and drama workshops, role-play, group discussion, readings, and audiovisual methods. Skills identified as being facilitated and evaluated in communication skills training in the UK nurse training programmes include empathy, anti-stereotyping practices, self-awareness, interviewing skills and critical thinking (Chant et al. 2002).

In Finland, Hyvärinen (2011) studied interpersonal communication competence in the field of pharmacy. Her results show that professional communication competence is connected to students' knowledge of their own field and to students' knowledge of interpersonal communication. Practical training in real work situations, constructive feedback, the role of mentors and communication between mentors and students were central in learning interpersonal communication competence (Hyvärinen 2011).

Another example from the Finnish context is a study by Koponen (2012) in which she compared Finnish medical students' perceptions of the suitability of three experiential methods in learning interpersonal communication competence. The students' self-reported learning outcomes included becoming aware of interpersonal communication competence, knowledge of professional communication and patient-centeredness. The students' own attitudes to learning communication skills became more positive (Koponen 2012).

In speech communication, interpersonal communication competence consists of more than skills; it also addresses motivational and ethical considerations. This is not to say that interaction skills do not have an important role in interpersonal competence. On the contrary, Spitzberg (2013: 131) suggests that

> "to be competent, an interactant needs have the motivation to create a competent impression, and avoid being debilitated by anxiety. Further, an interactant needs to have the knowledge relevant to the context, topics, activity procedures, norms, and the like. Having motivation and knowledge, however, may not be sufficient if the person cannot demonstrate the actual interaction skills required to implement their goals and understandings".

As a consequence, the focus of teaching and learning interpersonal communication has shifted from situation-specific behaviour and skills to broader dimensions. In particular, the importance of knowledge has increased. Teaching knowledge of communication processes is relevant, for example, in planning interaction (Isotalus 2006, Isotalus & Mäki 2009).

Communication teaching methods are often diverse, and formal learning of interpersonal communication competence, provided in the Finnish context by trained teachers of speech communication, is usually based on activities within a structured learning setting (see Gerlander, Hyvärinen, Almonkari & Isotalus 2009; Kaipomäki 2011; Koponen 2012). Furthermore, at Finnish university language centres, there are a number of courses in different languages that discuss and talk about various communication competences. What is unclear, however, is the extent to which this content is being acknowledged as explicit course content and communicated to the students. As pointed out by Pullin

(2010), the communication skills required in the workplace are far more varied than giving formal presentation. Studies have shown that for newly employed graduates informal discussions that enable team work and building and maintaining relationships, are the most frequent and important type of communication (Carnevale, Gainer & Meltzer 1990; Crossling & Ward 2002; Zorn & Violanti 1996).

In order to develop a more coherent foundation for teaching networking competence on university language courses, we first ought to determine exactly what is already being taught in relation to the subject as well as regarding interpersonal skills, knowledge and motivation. Only then will we be able to address the question of how communication and language courses at the university level answer to the needs for networking skills that are such a prominent feature of today's job market.

7. Challenges and suggestions for future research

One of the main aims of this paper was to discuss networking as a competence that is possible to acquire. The context is higher education and the focus is on language centre courses that deal with communication skills. We have discussed as an example the situation within Finnish higher education from the viewpoint of the Language Centre of the University of Jyvaskyla, where communication courses are taught not only in foreign languages, but also in Finnish.

We know that networking is considered to be one of the fundamental competences of the future job market (see EK 2011a; Puhakka et al. 2010). We have discussed social networks as being constructed by the interpersonal communication relationships that a person has. Thus, networking requires interpersonal competence that enables a person to develop and maintain his or her interpersonal relationships effectively and appropriately. A part of interpersonal competence is the understanding of the contextual nature of the phenomenon (see Spitzberg 2013).

While studying the networks of first-year college students, McEwan and Guerrero (2012) found that there is a difference between close and casual friendship networks, and that the maintenance behaviour differed accordingly. This makes us wonder whether there are different skills required for maintaining different kinds of networks such as those consisting of close friends vs. casual friends or those of work colleagues vs. free time acquaintances. In order to enhance university student networking skills that would also be applicable in the ever changing job market in the future, we would also need to know if one needs a different set of skills when networking in different contexts, such as at work and in leisure time, or in a healthcare context versus a business context.

Furthermore, even though Purhonen (2008) looked at networking and cooperation within an intercultural context, there remains a need to investigate different cultural perspectives on networking. For example, members of different cultural groups have knowledge of the meanings of different relationships. When a relationship is being defined as a friendship, a romantic relationship or a professional relationship is dependent on the cultural context. Culture, in a broad sense, can affect the expectations of how one should behave in different kinds of relationships, for example, how different interpersonal relationships are manifested and played out (Fitch & Sanders 1994; Gudykunst & Ting-Toomey 1996; Sigman 1998).

What language centres can offer is teaching aimed at language and culture competence as well as interpersonal communication competence. But what is still missing is the knowledge of the particular elements and skills related to interpersonal communication competence in various fields.

In relation to the cultural aspects of social networks, there is also a need for more information on the negative phenomena related to social networks (see Cho, Lee, Stefanone & Gay 2005). For example, the so-called old-boy networks (*hyvä veli –verkostot*) in Finland, meaning closely tied, closed networks of businessmen who operate with compromised ethics dealing favours to one another, sometimes leading to corruption, is an example of the ethically dubious phenomena related to social networks that are not consistently discussed or studied from the interpersonal communication perspective. Yet Finland is said to be one of the least corrupt countries in the world (Transparency International 2015). In contexts such as these, a deeper overall understanding of the cultural and interpersonal elements of social networks would be welcome.

What is clearly missing is empirical research that examines the development of students' networking competences. In addition to studies trying to determine or explain the factors influencing an individual's learning of networking competences, more qualitative research that offers in-depth information about interpersonal relationships and networking is still needed. For example, Purhonen (2008: n. p.) states the following:

> "The literature emphasises the significance of network relationships, but deeper analysis of their creation, management and development is still required. No work has either been done to examine what kinds of social or communicative competencies are needed in the contexts of networking".

In his discussion of interpersonal competence in the healthcare education context, Spitzberg (2013: 132) has also pointed out that models of communication competence "could be translated into some curricular and assessment content". However, like Spitzberg (2013: 132) points out, referring to his own model, "any curricular or assessment translations of this model will require subsequent research to establish the skills that most consistently predict preferred impressions of competence and outcomes".

8. Conclusion

Social networks are widely studied phenomena. Different perspectives and theories are being developed, applied and discussed by scholars in many fields and with diverse backgrounds. Communication network theories and groups of theories have provided extensive understanding of the reasons why individuals create, maintain, dissolve and recreate social networks. The advantages and benefits networks provide to individuals and organisations alike have been reported in various studies. The focus of this article is from an educational and pedagogical perspective of trying to understand how to enhance an individual's opportunities and abilities to engage in today's global world and ever changing working life.

Adapting network competence as a more explicit part of language centre courses should benefit both students and teachers. In order to do so, one should however have a comprehensive understanding of the processes and nature of networks as social phenomena. Furthermore, the understanding of interpersonal relationships, their development and maintenance would enable teachers and students to grasp the communication, and more specifically, the interpersonal approach to networking.

At the University of Jyväskylä, there is currently an ongoing development of cooperation between different departments and the Language Centre aiming at deeper integration of communication and language studies with subject studies. This integration should also be seen as a possibility to create understanding of the cultural expectations different fields have for networking. In this approach, a deeper understanding of the cultural and contextual expectations and norms of networking in different fields would be available for the students.

There is still a lack, however, of more focused and multidisciplinary research on the possibilities for teaching interpersonal communication networking competence more coherently at higher education units such as language centres. Furthermore, because interpersonal communication competence is, as we see it, the core phenomenon of networking in general, what is needed are empirical studies on the effectiveness of the formal teaching of such competence.

This article provided a brief overview of the concept of social networks from an interpersonal communication perspective. We are ready to hypothesise that networking competences are already being taught on language centre courses. One of the main ideas of this article is to stimulate discussion among language and communication teachers, and to make each of us think about how much interpersonal communication competence we actually teach. We are hoping for a broader understanding and awareness of what is being taught and what should be taught to enhance students' networking competence.

References

Aalto, H.-K. Ahokas, I. & Kuosa, T. 2008. *Yleissivistys ja osaaminen työelämässä 2030 – menestyksen eväät tulevaisuudessa. Hankkeen loppuraportti. Tutu-julkaisuja 1/2008.* Turku: Tulevaisuuden tutkimuskeskus ja Turun kauppakorkeakoulu.

Ala-Kortesmaa, S. & Välikoski, T.-R. 2008. Käräjätuomareiden ja syyttäjien käsitykset kuuntelemisesta. In P. Isotalus, M. Gerlander, M. Jäkälä & T Kokko (eds.), *Prologi: puheviestinnän vuosikirja 2008.* Prologos, Jyväskylä, 28-50.

Alatarvas, R. 2013. *Ihmisten vuorovaikutusverkostojen fysiikkaa* [Fysics of human communication networks]. Retrieved from http://www.aka.fi/fi/tietysti/tekniikka/nyt-pinnalla1/ihmisten-vuorovaikutusverkostojen-fysiikkaa/

Albrecht, T. L. & Goldsmith, D. J. 2003. Social support, social networks, and health. In T. L. Thompson, A. M. Dorcey, K. I. Miller & R. Parrott (eds.), *Handbook of health communication.* Mahwah, New Jersey: Lawrence Erlbaum Associates, 263–284.

Barry, A. 2001. *Political machines: governing a technological society.* London and New York: Athlone Press.

Borgatti, S. P. & Halgin, D. S. 2011. On network theory. *Organization Science, 22* (5), 1268–1181. doi:10.1287/orsc.1100.0641

Boyd, D. M. & Ellison, N. B. 2007. Social network sites: definition, history and scholarship. *Journal of Computer Mediated Communication, 13* (1), 210–230. doi:10.1111/j.1083-6101.2007.00393.x

Burleson, B. R. & Samter, W. 1990. Effects of cognitive complexity on the perceived importance of communication skills in friends. *Communication Research, 17* (2), 165–182. doi:10.1177/009365090017002002

Burt, R. S. 2004. Structural holes and good ideas. *American Journal of Sociology, 110* (2), 349–399. doi:10.1086/421787

Carnevale, A., Gainer, L. J. & Meltzer, A. S. 1990. *Workplace basics: the essential skills employers want.* San Francisco, CA: Jossey-Bass.

Castells, M. 1996. The net and the self: working notes for a critical theory of the informational society. *Critique of Anthropology, 16* (1), 9–38. doi:10.1177/0308275X9601600103

Castells, M. 2000. *The information age. Vol. 1, the rise of the network society*. Oxford and Malden, MA: Blackwell.

Chant, S., Jenkinson, T., Randle, J., Russel, G. & Webb, C. 2002. Communication skills training in healthcare: a review of the literature. *Nurse Education Today*, 22 (3), 189–202. doi:10.1054/nedt.2001.0690

Cho, H., Lee, J.-S., Stefanone, M. A. & Gay, G. 2005. Development of computer-supported collaborative social networks in a distributed learning community. *Behaviour & Information Technology*, 24 (6), 435–447. doi:10.1080/01449290500044049

Crossling, G. & Ward, I. 2002. Oral communication: the workplace needs and uses of business graduate employees. *English for Specific Purposes*, 21 (1), 41–57. doi:10.1016/S0889-4906(00)00031-4

Darling, A. L. & Dannels, D. P. 2003. Practicing engineers talk about the importance of talk: a report on the role of oral communication in the workplace. *Communication Education*, 52 (1), 1–16. doi:10.1080/03634520302457

EK 2011a. *Oivallusraportti* [Report of the national career survey]. Retrieved from http://ek.fi/mita-teemme/innovaatiot-ja-osaaminen/osaaminen-ja-koulutuspolitiikka/oivallus/

EK 2011b. *Osaava henkilöstö – menestyvät yritykset. EK:n koulutus- ja työvoimapoliittiset linjaukset vuoteen 2015*. Retrieved from http://ek.fi/wp-content/uploads/Osaava_henkilosto_menestyvat_yritykset.pdf

FinnSight 2015 [foresight project]. 2006. T*ieteen, teknologian ja yhteiskunnan näkymät* [The outlook for science, technology, and society]. Helsinki: The Academy of Finland and Tekes.

Fitch, K. L. & Sanders, R. E. 1994. Culture, communication, and preferences for directness in expression of directives. *Communication Theory*, 4 (3), 219–245. doi:10.1111/j.1468-2885.1994.tb00091.x

Frankham, J. 2006. Network utopias and alternative entanglements for educational research and practice. *Journal of Education Policy*, 21 (6), 661-677. doi:10.1080/02680930600969191

Frymier, A. B. & Houser, M. L. 2000. The teacher-student relationship as an interpersonal relationship.*Communication Education, 49*(3),207–219.doi:10.1080/03634520009379209

Gaboury, J. 1999. 30 ways to be a better IE. *IIE Solutions, 31* (1), 28–35.

Gerlander, M., Hyvärinen, M-L., Almonkari, M. & Isotalus, P. 2009. Mitä ja miten puheviestinnän opintojaksoilla opetetaan? In M. Almonkari & P. Isotalus (eds.), *Akateeminen puheviestintä. Kuinka opettaa puheviestintää yliopisto-opiskelijoille?* Helsinki: Finn Lectura, 8–24.

Gielen, P. A., Hoeve, A. & Nieuwenhuis, L. F. M. 2003. Learning entrepreneurs: learning and innovation in small companies. *European Educational Research Journal*, 2 (1), 90–106. doi:10.2304/eerj.2003.2.1.13

Gould, R. V. 2003. Uses of network tools in comparative historical research. In J. Mahoney & D. Rueschemeyer (eds.), *Comparative historical analysis in the social sciences*. Cambridge: Cambridge University Press, 241–269. doi:10.1017/cbo9780511803963.008

Gray, F. E. 2010. Specific oral communication skills desired in new accountancy graduates. Business *Communication Quarterly*, 73 (1), 40–67. doi:10.1177/1080569909356350

Greene, J. O. 2003. Models of adult communication skill acquisition: practice and the course of performance improvement. In J. O. Greene & B. R. Burleson (eds.), *Handbook of communication and social interaction skills*. Mahwah: Lawrence Erlbaum, 51–91.

Gudykunst, W. B. & Ting-Toomey, S. 1996. Communication in personal relationships across cultures. An introduction. In W.B. Gudykunst, S. Ting-Toomey & T. Nishida (eds.), *Communication in personal relationships across cultures*. Thousand Oaks, CA: Sage, 3–16.

Hardy, C., Phillips, N. G. & Lawrence, T. B. 2003. Resources, knowledge and influence: the organizational effects in intraorganizational collaboration. *Journal of Management Studies*, 40 (2), 321–347. doi:10.1111/1467-6486.00342

Hargie, O., Boohan, M., McCoy, M. & Murphy, P. 2010. Current trends in communication skills training in UK schools of medicine. *Medical Teacher*, 32 (5), 385–391. doi:10.3109/01421590903394603

Hargie, O. & Dickson, D. 2004. *Skilled interpersonal communication: research, theory and practice* (4th ed.). London: Routledge.

Hargie, C. T. C & Tourish, D. 1997. Relational communication. In O. Hargie (ed.), *The Handbook of communication skills* (2nd ed.). London: Routledge, 358–382.

Himanen, P. 2004. (toim.) *Globaali tietoyhteiskunta. Kehityssuuntia Piilaaksosta Singaporeen*. Helsinki: Tekes, Teknologiakatsaus 155/2004.

Huotari, M.-L., Hurme, P. & Valkonen, T. 2005. *Viestinnästä tietoon: tiedon luominen työyhteisössä*. Helsinki, WSOY.

Hyvärinen, M-L. 2011. *Alakohtainen vuorovaikutus farmasiassa*. Acta Universitatis Tamperensis 1604. Tampere: Tampereen yliopisto.

Isotalus, P. 2006. Virkaanastujaisesitelmä: Puheviestintä tietona. In T-R. Välikoski, E. Kostiainen, E. Kyllönen & L. Mikkola (eds.), *Prologi. Puheviestinnän vuosikirja 2006*. Jyväskylä: Prologos ry.

Isotalus, P. & Mäki, E. 2009. Tiedon rooli puheviestinnän opetuksessa? In M. Almonkari & P. Isotalus (eds.), *Akateeminen puheviestintä. Kuinka opettaa puheviestintää yliopisto-opiskelijoille?* Helsinki: Finn Lectura.

Kaipomäki, E. 2011. *Suomalaisten yliopistojen kieli- ja viestintäopintoihin kuuluvan puheviestinnän opetuksen nykytila ja haasteet.* Retrieved from http://urn.fi/urn:nbn:fi:uta-1-22019

Katz, N., Lazer, D., Arrow, H. & Contractor, N. 2004. Network theory and small groups. *Small Group Research, 35* (3), 307–332. doi:10.1177/1046496404264941

Knox, H., Savage, M. & Harvey, P. 2006. Social networks and the study of relations: networks as method, metaphor and form. *Economy and Society, 35* (1), 113–140. doi:10.1080/03085140500465899

Kokkonen, L. 2010. *Pakolaisten vuorovaikutussuhteet: Keski-Suomeen muuttaneiden pakolaisten kokemuksia vuorovaikutussuhteistaan ja kiinnittymisestään uuteen sosiaaliseen ympäristöön* [Interpersonal relationships of refugees in Central Finland]. Jyvaskyla Studeis in Humanities, 143. University of Jyvaskyla.

Koponen, J. 2012. *Kokemukselliset oppimismenetelmät lääketieteen opiskelijoiden vuorovaikutuskoulutuksessa* [Professionally-oriented communication education in the field of medicine]. Acta Universitatis Tamperensis 1734. Tampere: Tampereen yliopisto.

Kostiainen, E. 2003. *Viestintä ammattiosaamisen ulottuvuutena* [Communication as a dimension of vocational competence]. Jyväskylä studies in humanities 1. University of Jyvaskyla.

Laajalahti, A. 2007. The development of interpersonal communication competence at work. In N. Carpentier, P. Pruulmann-Vengerfeldt, K. Nordenstreng, M. Hartmann, P. Vihalemm, B. Cammaerts & H. Nieminen (eds.), *Media technologies and democracy in an enlarged Europe: the intellectual work of the 2007 European media and communication doctoral summer school.* The researching and teaching communication series (3). Tartu: Tartu University Press, 335–345.

Laajalahti, A. 2014. Vuorovaikutusosaaminen ja sen kehittyminen tutkijoiden työssä [Interpersonal communication competence and its development in the work of researchers]. *Jyväskylä studies in Humanities, 225.* Jyväskylä: Jyväskylä University Press.

Lakey, S. G. & Canary, D. J. 2002. Actor goal achievement and sensitivity to partner as critical factors in understanding interpersonal communication competence and conflict strategies. *Communication Monographs, 69* (3), 217–235. doi:10.1080/03637750216542

Lang, J. D., Cruse, S., McVey, F. D. & McMasters, J. 1999. Industry expectations of new engineers: A survey to assist curriculum designers. *Journal of Engineering Education, 88* (1), 43–51. doi:10.1002/j.2168-9830.1999.tb00410.x

Leskinen, R. 2011. *A longitudinal case study of an entrepreneurial networking process.* Helsinki: Aalto University. Retrieved from http://epub.lib.aalto.fi/pdf/diss/Aalto_DD_2011_032.pdf

Linturi, H. 2007. *Matkalla sivistysyhteiskuntaan.* Opetusministeriön sivistysbarometri 1997-2017. Väliraportti 2007. Metodix & Internetix.

Littlejohn, S. W. 2002. *Theories of human communication* (7th ed.). Belmont: Wadsworth.

McEwan, B. & Guerrero, L. K. 2012. Maintenance behavior and relationship quality as predictors of perceived availability of resources in newly formed college friendship networks. *Communication Studies, 63* (4), 421–440. doi:10.1080/10510974.2011.639433

Merriam, S. B. & Clark, C. 1993. Learning from life experience. What makes it significant? *International Journal of Lifelong Education, 12* (2), 129–138. doi:10.1080/0260137930120205

Mitchell, R. E. & Trickett, E. J. 1980. Task force report: Social networks as mediators of social support. An analysis of the effect and determinants of social networks. *Community Mental Health Journal, 16* (1), 27–44. doi:10.1007/BF00780665

Mittilä, T. 2006. *Verkosto-osaaminen – liiketoimintaosaamisen uusi mantra.* Retrieved from http://www.edu.fi/perusopetus/historia_yhteiskuntaoppi/liiketoimintaosaaminen

Monge, P. R. & Contractor, N. 2003. *Theories of communication networks.* New York: Oxford University Press.

Moolenaar, N. M. & Sleegers, P. J. C. 2010. Social networks, trust, and innovation. How social relationships support trust and innovative climates in Dutch schools. In A. Daly (ed.), *Social Network Theory and Educational Change.* Cambridge, MA: Harvard University Press, 97–114.

Morreale, S. P., Osbon, M. M. & Pearson, J. D. 2000. Why communication is important: a rationale for the centrality of the study of communication. *Journal of the Association for Communication Administration, 29*, 1–25.

Neuliep, J. W. 1996. Human communication theory. Applications & case studies. Boston: Allyn and Bacon.

Obstfeld, D. 2005. Social networks, the tertius iungens orientation, and involvement in innovation. *Admin. Sci. Quart, 50* (1), 100–130.

Perry-Smith, J. E. & Shalley, C. E. 2003. The social side of creativity: a static and dynamic social network perspective. *Academy of Management Review, 28* (1), 89–106.

Puhakka, A., Rautopuro, J. & Tuominen, V. 2010. Employability and Finnish university graduates. *European Educational Research Journal, 9* (1), 45–55. doi:10.2304/eerj.2010.9.1.45

Pullin, P. 2010. Small talk, rapport, and international communicative competence: lessons to learn from BELF. *International Journal of Business Communication, 47* (4), 455–476. doi:10.1177/0021943610377307

Purhonen, P. 2008. SME internationalization as a challenge to interpersonal communication competence: an analysis of interpersonal communication competence in networking and collaboration. *Journal of Intercultural Communication, 18.* Retrieved from http://www.immi.se/intercultural/nr18/purhonen.htm

Purhonen, P. 2012. *Interpersonal communication competence and collaborative interaction in SME internationalization.* Jyväskylä studies in humanities 178. Jyväskylä: University of Jyväskylä.

Purhonen, P. & Valkonen, T. 2013. Measuring interpersonal communication competence in SME internationalization. *Journal of Intercultural Communication, 33.* Retrieved from http://immi.se/intercultural

Pyöriä, P. 2006. *Understanding work in the age of information.* Finland in Focus. Tampere: Tampere University Press.

Riles, A. 2000. *The network inside out.* Ann Arbor: University of Michigan Press.

Ritter, T. & Gemünden, H. G. 2003. Network competence: its impact on innovation success and its antecedents. *Journal of Business research, 56* (9), 745–755. doi:10.1016/S0148-2963(01)00259-4

Rogers, E. M. & Kincaid, D. L. 1981. *Communication networks: toward a new paradigm for research.* New York: Free Press.

Rouhiainen-Neuenhäuserer, M. 2009. *Johtajan vuorovaikutusosaaminen ja sen kehittyminen : johtamisen viestintähaasteet tietoperustaisessa organisaatiossa* [The interpersonal communication competence of leaders and its development: leadership communication challenges in a knowledge-based organization]. Jyväskylä studies in humanities 128. Jyväskylän University.

Segrin, C. & Givertz, M. 2003. Methods of social skills training and development. In J. O. Greene & B. R. Burleson (eds.), *Handbook of communication and social interaction skills.* Mahwah: Lawrence Erlbaum, 135–176

Sigman, S. J. 1998. Relationships and communication: A social communication and strongly consequential view. In R. L. Conville & L. E. Rogers (eds.), *The meaning of "relationship" in interpersonal communication*. Westport, Connecticut: Praeger, 41–82.

Sparrowe, R. T., Liden, R. C., Wayne, S. J. & Kraimer, M. L. 2001. Social networks and the performance of individuals and groups. *Academy of Management Journal, 44* (2), 316–325. doi:10.2307/3069458

Spitzberg, B. H. 2000. What is good communication? *Journal of the Association for Communication Administration, 29,* 103–119.

Spitzberg, B. H. 2003. Methods of skill assessment. In J. O. Greene & B. R. Burleson (eds.), *Handbook of communication and social interaction skills*. Mahwah, NJ: Lawrence Erlbaum, 93–134.

Spitzberg, B. H. 2013. (Re)Introducing communication competence to the health professions. *Journal of Public Health Research, 2* (23), 126–135. doi:10.4081/jphr.2013.e23

Spitzberg, B. H. & Cupach, W. R. 1984. *Interpersonal communication competence*. Beverly Hills, CA: Sage.

Thornton, S. C, Henneberg, S. C. & Naudé, P. 2013. Understanding types of organizational networking behaviors in the UK manufacturing sector. *Industrial Marketing Management, 42* (7), 1154-1166. doi:10.1016/j.indmarman.2013.06.005

Transparency International 2015. Retrieved from https://www.transparency.org/cpi2014/results

Trevillion, S. 2000. Social work, social networks and network knowledge. *British Journal of Social Work, 30* (4), 505–517. doi:10.1093/bjsw/30.4.505

Valkonen, T. 2003. *Puheviestinnän arviointi. Näkökulmia lukiolaisten esiintymis- ja ryhmätaitoihin* [Assessing speech communication skills. perspectives on presentation and group communication skills among upper secondary school students]. University of Jyväskylä. Jyväskylä Studies in Humanities 7.

Wellman, B. 2007. Editorial. The network is personal: introduction to a special issue of *Social Networks. Social Networks, 29* (3), 349–356. doi:10.1016/j.socnet.2007.01.006

Wilmot, W. W. 1996. The relational perspective. In K. M. Galvin & P. J. Cooper (eds.), *Making connections. Readings in relational communication* (4th ed). Los Angeles, CA: Roxbury, 16-24.

Zorn, T. E. & Violanti, M. T. 1996. Communication abilities and individual achievement in organizations. *Management Communication Quarterly, 10* (2), 139–167. doi:10.1177/0893318996010002001

4 Virtual Slovak: insight into learning Slovak in an e-learning environment

Anna Kyppö[1]

Abstract

This paper offers insight into learning Slovak in an e-learning environment. The need to reach distance-learners of Slovak led to the implementation of a web-based course on Slovak language and culture in 2008–2010. The pedagogical basis of the course, called Virtual Slovak, is the socioconstructivist approach to teaching and learning, in which the focus is on the development of learners' communicative competence. This teaching experiment led to a study in which the focus was on learners' beliefs and experiences regarding learning Slovak in an e-learning environment. The results showed that this particular learning environment had a positive impact on the development of learners' agency. This impact was demonstrated by an evident increase in motivation and language learning awareness as well as in a conscious approach to learning. At the centre of this investigation is the evaluation of the e-learning environment, especially its appropriateness at the beginners' level for the acquisition of a less commonly taught language, as well as of the teacher's role in the learning process. Furthermore, the results revealed that learners' attitudes towards learning in technology-enhanced learning environments pose challenges to the instruction of less commonly taught languages. Even though current digital technology offers multiple opportunities for the integration of new media modes into learning activities, the choice of relevant media for the learning context and learners' competences seems to remain one of the teacher's main responsibilities.

Keywords: e-learning, learning environment, Slovak, less commonly taught languages, LCTL, communicative competence.

---

1. Language Centre, University of Jyväskylä, Finland; anna.kyppo@jyu.fi

How to cite this chapter: Kyppö, A. (2015). Virtual Slovak: insight into learning Slovak in an e-learning environment. In J. Jalkanen, E. Jokinen, & P. Taalas (Eds), *Voices of pedagogical development - Expanding, enhancing and exploring higher education language learning* (pp. 57-84). Dublin: Research-publishing.net. doi:10.14705/rpnet.2015.000287

Chapter 4

1. Context of the study

This study offers insight into learning Slovak in an e-learning environment. One of the challenges for teaching in the last decade or so has been the design of new learning environments for language learning and the efficient employment of versatile ICT[2]-enhanced approaches and resources. The development of new course content and learner training modules, as well as of collaborative practices between teachers and students within distance learning programmes focusing on the efficiency and multimodality of learning materials, generated the idea of a new learning environment designed specifically for learning Slovak. The Slovak e-learning course *Virtual Slovak* was designed and piloted in 2008–2010. The pedagogical basis of the course is the socioconstructivist approach to teaching and learning. The main focus is on the development of learners' communicative competence, which is perceived as their linguistic and pragmatic knowledge about a language and their ability to create meaning in the target language. This teaching experiment then led to an investigation of how Slovak is acquired in an e-learning environment. The main focus is on the learners: how they experience their learning in such an environment and what they believe they have or have not learned.

1.1. Slovak

Slovak is an Indo-European language belonging to the group of West Slavic languages, together with Czech, Polish and Lower and Upper Sorbian. In addition to the roughly 4.5 million Slovaks living in Slovakia, Slovak is also spoken in other parts of the world, with altogether about 2.7 million speakers of Slovak outside of Slovakia (Ondrejovič 2009). Slovak is the official language spoken in the Slovak Republic. Due to its regular structure and closeness to all Slavic languages, it is often called the lingua franca of Slavic languages. Together with approximately 30 other languages, Slovak is one of the Less Commonly Taught Languages (LCTL) (Brecht & Walton 1994).

---

[2]. Information and Communications Technology

1.2. Slovak in Finland

Studies of Slovak language and culture are offered by more than 40 universities around the world. In the Nordic countries, however, the only academic institution of higher education that has offered Slovak studies for over 30 years is the University of Jyväskylä. In addition to various projects aimed at the translation of Slovak literature into Finnish and the dissemination of knowledge about Slovakia in Finland, one of the greatest challenges was the design of an open, web-based learning course of Slovak. To meet this challenge, Slovak instruction had to move through several stages of development aimed, first, at the enhancement of self-directed learning, and second, at the integration of ICT into language teaching. In the early 2000s, the instruction of Slovak became more multimodal due to the integration of educational and communication technology into so-called traditional instruction (Kyppö 2007). The next challenge was the design of efficient learning materials for distance learning, and finally, the implementation of the e-learning course, which was piloted with two groups of students in 2008–2010.

2. Slovak e-learning course: pedagogical principles

This section introduces the main concepts and theories supporting the development and implementation of the Slovak e-learning course. These concepts include the socioconstructivist approach to learning; Computer-Assisted Language Learning (CALL), frequently referred to as e-learning; communicative competence, which I consider to be one of the most important objectives of any process of language learning; and learners' agency manifested by an increase in their motivation and language learning awareness as well as the growth of deep and strategic approaches to learning.

2.1. The socioconstructivist approach to learning

In constructivist learning theories, learning is perceived as an active process in which knowledge is constructed on the basis of learner's personal experiences.

Social constructivism emphasises the importance of the cultural and social context (learning environment) and learner-centeredness. The term learning environment evokes an image of a place and a space, that is, "room to move and explore" (Wilson 1996: 4). Thus the learning environment may be determined by various physical and virtual locations. In the context of the current study, the learning environment is the overall context of learning which involves not only the e-learning platform and course setting, but also students' attitudes to learning, their histories and their learning cultures.

The focus of the approach is on student activities and the development of their communicative competence. Problem-based instruction and peer collaboration among the learners as well as between the learners and the teacher are in the foreground. As constructivism allows for flexibility, imagination and creativity, constructivist learning environments are generally designed so that they promote the autonomy, creativity and engagement of the students and the teacher. One of the variations to the constructivist-cognitive learning theories, which emphasise the learner's key role in the learning process, is Johnson's (2004) model of Second Language Acquisition (SLA). This model is based on the dialogical framework of Vygotsky's (1986) sociocultural theory and Bakhtin's (1981) dialogised heteroglossia. In SLA, the focus is on learner's problem-solving cognitive skills and the skills of linking the acquired knowledge and skills to those which have been previously acquired. Second language acquisition is viewed in terms of performance. Learning a new language does not occur in the human brain, but in the interactions conducted in sociocultural settings. Bakhtinian dialogism, which also emphasises the interactional and dynamic aspect of language, has been used to frame language learning as a continuous dialogue between language and the external world, between the language learner and his/her inner world, between the language learners themselves, and between the learners and the teacher (Dufva 1994b). As the constructivist theories of learning emphasise the importance of learning-by-doing, learning tasks – their nature, structure and performance – are central. In accordance with Task-Based Learning (TBL) (Willis 1996), the objective is not only to enhance the learner's current language skills, but also the teacher's imagination and creativity. The teacher is responsible for providing learners with the whole range of tasks which may motivate them to experiment with the language and use it spontaneously, as in so-called real life – hence the origin of second language competence, which, as suggested by Johnson (2004), lies in the interaction between language competence (knowledge of the language) and performance (the skills of using the language in real or almost-real life contexts).

2.2. E-learning: asynchronous, synchronous and blended learning

E-learning has become popular due to its flexibility in terms of time and space as well as for its learner-centeredness. It is generally characterised as less expensive to support and not constrained by geography, and thus it is appropriate in almost all contexts. It may be implemented either asynchronously or synchronously.

Asynchronous e-learning (e.g. emails, discussion boards) is considered to be a key component of efficient e-learning due to its flexibility (freedom from time and space) and thus essential for collaboration. Learners may enter the e-learning environment at any time and then spend longer periods on various learning activities. According to Robert and Dennis (2005), asynchronous communication increases learners' ability to process information and supports their cognitive participation.

On the other hand, synchronous learning (e.g. chat, videoconferencing, face-to-face learning) may be perceived as a more social activity in which learners are participants rather than isolated learners, a status which often results in an increase of commitment and motivation (Kock 2005). Synchronous e-learning primarily supports learners' personal participation.

Furthermore, combining face-to-face classroom instruction and computer-mediated activities, with the aim to form an integrated instructional approach, offers an opportunity to redesign teaching (Vaughan 2010). In blended learning, both modes of e-learning, the asynchronous (e.g. a course management system, e-learning environment) and synchronous learning (virtual classroom) accompanied by face-to-face sessions, may be used. If designed and used meaningfully, the result may be an evident increase in learners' self-directed learning and clear development of communicative competence.

Mayes and de Freitas (2013) proposed a curriculum design model for e-learning that includes the descriptions of the intended learning outcomes, the design of teaching and learning activities, the assessment of achieved outcomes and assessment of the curriculum alignment. Their curriculum design is based on constructive alignment, in which all teaching elements, expected learning outcomes, teaching methods, tasks and assessment procedures are aligned with each other and turned into learning activities (Biggs 2003). As the focus of the constructivist pedagogical approach is always on doing, learning and teaching activities are placed at the centre of the process. One of the implications of this model for teaching is how it reshapes the sociocultural setting of a learning environment into one that is more favourable and motivating. In practice, it means the design of a genuine social context. The interaction in such a context, like in this course, may take various forms, including collaborative or knowledge building dialogues with peers or online resources, or various real-life simulations.

2.3. Communicative competence

Because one of the key questions of this study is learning Slovak in an e-learning environment, a key assumption is that learning, which is expected to result in the acquisition of the four language skills (reading, listening, writing and speaking), is reflected in the level of communicative competence. Communicative competence can be viewed from various perspectives. The Common European Framework of Reference for Languages (CEFR 2001: 9) defines communicative competence as "the sum of knowledge, skills and characteristics that allow a person to perform actions". In the light of this definition, learners' communicative competence includes three types of competence: sociolinguistic, pragmatic (discourse and functional) and linguistic (lexical, grammatical, semantic, phonological, orthographic and orthoepic).

As Johnson (2004) has claimed, the origin of second language competence lies in the language use that takes place in real social contexts. In practice, learners are expected to learn not only the language, but also what to do with the language, that is, how to use it in real-life contexts. To that end, they need to develop their knowledge of the target culture and its practices, and through that enhance their intercultural awareness (Byram, Nichols & Stevens 2001).

2.4. Learner agency, motivation, awareness and approaches to learning

The focus of this section is on learner agency. A number of authors have identified agency as being demonstrated by an increase in learners' motivation, language learning awareness and development of deep or strategic approaches to learning (see Basharina 2009; Entwistle 2001; Kyppö 2014).

2.4.1. Learner agency

Agency and motivation are often intertwined. Both of them are closely related to self-determination, autonomy, responsibility, locus of control and self-efficacy (Brown 2014). Agency may be perceived as one of the key concepts in learning, as a movement, a change of state or direction, or even as "the lack of movement where movement is expected" (van Lier 2010: 4). Drawing on van Lier (2010), agency in the context of this study is perceived through the increase in learners' motivation and in their consciousness of the target language and learning (language learning awareness). Furthermore, agency is reflected in their approaches to learning. Van Lier (2010) sees that the employment of agency significantly depends on the learning environment, including the whole context of learning and an agency-promoting curriculum.

2.4.2. Motivation

One of the most evident manifestations of learner agency is motivation. The main force for engaging in goal-oriented learning (mastery or performance orientation) is constituted by motives (Engeström 1999). They not only affect the outcomes of learning but also determine the conditions under which the learning goals are implemented and directly or indirectly affect the circumstances of learning (learning context) both spatially and temporally (Johnson 2004). Dörnyei (1998: 117) claims that motivation provides "the primary impetus to initiate learning the L2 and later the driving force to sustain the long and often tedious learning process". His model of L2 motivation (Dörnyei 1991) is composed of a set of motivational components that includes, among others, learner's motivational strategies and group cohesiveness. Motivational components involve the level of language, the learner, and learning situations related to various aspects of language learning such as curricula, teaching materials and methods, and learning tasks. However, one important factor that substantially affects the degree of learner motivation is the teacher's enthusiasm and commitment (Dörnyei 1998; Dufva 1994a).

From the viewpoint of technology-enhanced language learning, an interesting issue is the impact of new language learning environments on learner motivation. Ushida (2005), among others, has explored the role of learner attitudes and motivation in L2 learning within an online language course context. Her study provides evidence for the relation between the learners' motivation and the development of their language proficiency. The learners with positive motivation and attitudes managed to control their study in both face-to-face and independent learning sessions. Their results, in other words, corresponded to their effort. Interestingly, the teacher-specific motivational components were considered to be crucial in student evaluations of learning situations in the online courses. This study also points to the relation between learners' motivation and the development of their language proficiency. However, maintaining motivation throughout the course appeared to be one of the teacher's greatest challenges.

2.4.3. Language learning awareness

In this study, awareness means the consciousness of the target language, of its specific features and relations to other languages as well as consciousness of learning the language. This concept includes the knowledge of the culture represented by the target language, what Dufva (1994a) identifies as cultural awareness. In Dufva's (1994a) view, language, interaction and culture are intertwined aspects of language awareness. Language awareness may also be seen as the same as learners' ability to reflect on the learned language, on themselves as learners, and to recognise the similarities and differences between languages. But there are questions of what the learners become aware of and what has an impact on their learning awareness. The answer may be motivation, hence the close relatedness of these concepts. However, most significant is the impact of learners' everyday knowledge, that is, their personal experiences. These may be related to the target language, to their views of the language itself or to learning a language, as well as to so-called common knowledge, the sociocultural views of the target language and culture.

Bilash and Tulasiewicz (1995: 49) perceive language awareness as a key concept in the learner-centred classroom. In their opinion, language awareness is the integration of four elements: "content about language, language skills, attitudinal education and metacognitive opportunities, which allow the student to reflect on the process of language acquisition, learning and language use" (Bilash & Tulasiewicz 1995: 49).

Ellis (2003) believes that one of the most important awareness-raisers is the teacher. The teacher is responsible not only for the design of the curriculum and tasks, but also for raising the learners' language awareness (consciousness) aimed at becoming sensitive to foreign languages. In the context of this course, language awareness was raised implicitly by the teacher, but also explicitly, as learners themselves discovered similarities and differences between their native languages and Slovak, built on their previous linguistic knowledge and developed their own language awareness.

2.4.4. Approaches to learning

Learning Slovak was explored in this study from the learners' viewpoint; from how the learners themselves experience their learning. The framework used to investigate their experiences is based on Entwistle's (2001) model of approaches to learning. According to this model, agency may be manifested through the use of deep, surface or strategic approaches to learning. The deep approach to learning refers to learners' active engagement with the content, which in turn leads to personal understanding of learning material. The surface approach indicates the reproduction, even the memorisation, of the learned matter. These concepts point to the strong impact of intentions and motivation related to learning. The third approach, strategic, is strongly based on the need for achievement (success or getting the best grades). This approach is characterised by the fear of failure.

To explore the role of agency in learning in international online learning environments, Entwistle's (2001) model was adapted by Basharina (2009). She found that students with a deep approach to learning use more effective learning strategies, seek meaning and therefore benefit the most from learning. Students with the strategic approach put consistent effort into learning. They provide themselves with the most favourable conditions for study, find good learning materials and monitor the effectiveness of their learning strategies (Basharina 2009; Thorpe 2002). Due to their good organisational skills, they generally cope well with time pressures and achieve good grades. On the other hand, the students with the surface approach usually have difficulties in making sense of the new ideas presented in a course and typically do not reflect on their purpose of learning, because their intention is mainly to cope with the syllabus requirements. They perceive the course as unrelated bits of knowledge and see little value in learning activities. In addition, they often suffer from the stress caused by the lack of time and planning. Basharina's (2009) model of approaches to learning presents learning as the result of a complex interrelationship between the affordances and constraints of a learning environment (physical or virtual) and the learner's agency.

3. Course design: mountain climbing as metaphor for learning new languages

This section introduces the Slovak e-learning course: its structure, layout and content as well as its ideology, which is based on the metaphor of learning as climbing (Figure 1 and Figure 2).

Figure 1. Layout of the Slovak e-learning course (Kyppö 2014)

The pedagogical purpose of the Slovak e-learning course was to bridge the gaps between self-directed, open and task-based types of learning. Its aim was to increase the development of learners' overall communicative competence and enhance their autonomous learning. The focus was on the learners' activities; on what they could do with the language. While learners at the beginner's level are typically expected to create simple dialogues (e.g. introduce themselves, ask simple questions, and compose lists of items), learners at the intermediate level know how to employ their problem-solving skills and ability to search for required information to perform tasks such as telling as well as retelling a story and expressing their opinion. Learning activities consisted of both tasks with immediate feedback, which were focused primarily on language forms and accuracy, and collaborative practices (peer and group tasks) aimed at increasing communicative competence. The assessment was based on the completion of tasks and learners' active participation.

Figure 2. Structure of a camp webpage[3]

The website of the e-learning course was built around an image of the Slovak High Tatra Mountains, which acted likened the approach to learning Slovak to climbing a mountain. The climbing metaphor also depicted the challenges of teaching Slovak as one of the less commonly taught languages, pointing not only to the difficulty of climbing, but also the various external constraints that may endanger climbing (learning). In this metaphor, the teacher was both climbing guide and climber, one who was also constantly in danger but who also attempted to reach the summit together with the students. The course consisted of 10 camps. In accordance with the CEFR (2009), the curriculum was equivalent to the proficiency levels A1–B2. The starting point was Base Camp, which presented the basics of Slovak – its phonemic, morphological and lexicological system as well as information about its social use. Learning outcomes for respective camps were introduced on the startpage of the camp in the form of *can do / know how to do* statements.

---

3. http://users.jyu.fi/~akyppo/virtuaalislovakki/c7_text2.htm

References to climbing and its symbols were part of the course layout. These included planning, getting familiar with the terrain (course), proceeding from the easiest towards the more difficult, and continuous skill improvement (e-learning skills and strategies). They complied with the idea of spiral learning: with each session learners expanded their skills and learned something new. While the content (i.e. the themes) of various camps varied, the website structure remained the same. Visual symbols corresponded with the metaphor of climbing (Kyppö 2014). For example, a rope symbolised language structures. A good rope was the guarantee of the *best performance*. Task sessions were illustrated by *abseiling* (i.e. a controlled descent), which corresponded with the lesson recaps. Dangerous places (i.e. tricky language issues) were denoted by warning signs. The mountain cabin was a safe place indicating each learner's own space in the Optima online environment.

4. Data collection and analysis

This section introduces the main areas of teacher investigation and provides some information on the collection and analysis of the data. The main questions (Table 1) address the students' experiences of learning Slovak in an e-learning environment, their views on the acquisition of all four language skills and the teacher's role in an e-learning environment. Nevertheless, the focus is on the learners' beliefs: what they believed they learned and/or did not learn, and how they experienced their learning.

Table 1. Research questions

Focus	Question
Learning Slovak in an e-learning environment.	Do the learners of Slovak feel that they learn the language in the e-learning environment?
Learners' views on the acquisition of language skills (speaking, listening, reading and writing) in the e-learning environment.	Can all four language skills be equally acquired in the e-learning environment?
Teacher's role (feedback, evaluation, motivation) in the e-learning environment.	What is the teacher's role as perceived by the learners?

In 2008–2009, 22 students of Slovak at the University of Jyväskylä participated in the study. In 2010, 15 students from the University of Helsinki took part. The demographics of the groups were as follows: at the University of Jyväskylä, 21 students were female, 1 was male; 20 were Finnish and 1 was Polish. At the University of Helsinki, 8 students were male, 7 were female; 13 were Finnish, 1 was French and 1 was Japanese. They were all language students without any previous knowledge of Slovak. In addition to the contact sessions held once every two weeks in Jyväskylä, and once every three weeks in Helsinki, students were expected to learn independently. Their e-learning activities were monitored for the period of one academic term.

The data were collected from three questionnaires, personal interviews, learning journal content, course feedback and teacher reflections. A pre-course personal questionnaire was used to gather information about the personal and professional background of the students. The purpose was to obtain the maximum amount of information about their language learning history.

The data were analysed using thematic analysis (Braun & Clark 2006). Taking a data-led approach, the collected data were initially described and then the items were divided into themes that were grouped as pre-, on- and post-course, and finally, the interpretations were developed.

5. Key themes

This chapter reports the key themes identified during the data analysis. The findings are presented under the pre-course, on-course and post-course themes and are accompanied by excerpts from the students' learning journals (Table 2).

The *pre-course themes* are related to the learners' concept of Slovakia and the Slovak language, their concept of learning with a special focus on e-learning, learners' expectations of the course, as well as their beliefs about themselves as e-learners.

Table 2. Pre-course, on-course and post-course themes

Pre-course themes	On-course themes		Post-course themes
Slovak language and Slovakia	E-learning skills and strategies		E-learning revisited
Students' beliefs of themselves as learners	Language awareness	Learning awareness	Approaches to learning
Students' beliefs of themselves as e-learners	Linguistic issues	Manual vs. digital writing	Course evaluation Self-evaluation
Learners' course expectations	Motivation	Approaches to learning	Teacher's role: teacher & student perspective

5.1. Slovakia and Slovak language

All learners had some knowledge of Slovakia and the Slovak language. For example, they knew that Slovak is a West Slavic language spoken in Slovakia. Slovak was perceived as a new language, which became a motivating factor. Two respondents chose Slovak because they knew it was considered to be a lingua franca of Slavic languages. They believed that the knowledge of Slovak might facilitate their study of other Slavic languages. Even though no specific reasons were given for learning Slovak, all respondents except for one strongly believed that they would be able to use Slovak in the future either for work or leisure purposes, especially when Slovakia joined the Eurozone in 2009.

5.2. Learners' expectations of e-learning and their beliefs of themselves as learners

Table 3 displays results of the thematic analysis aimed at learners' expectations of e-learning and their concept of themselves as learners.

Flexible learning is generally the secret of popularity for e-learning. Due to its novelty, the Slovak e-learning course was attractive for both the students and the teacher. All respondents expected the e-learning to be more flexible and more challenging than traditional classes, but some doubted whether they would be able to acquire all four languages skills. They were most sceptical about speaking. Nevertheless, they believed that the success of e-learning depends on their own efforts, so there was confidence that they might find a way of enhancing their spoken communication. Overall, learners' expectations of the course were high, and their belief in their own learning skills was strong. The use of a new learning environment was perceived as a valuable addition to traditional learning.

Table 3. Learners' expectations of e-learning and learners' concept of themselves as learners

Learners' expectations of e-learning		Learners' concept of themselves as learners	
PROS	CONS	PROS	CONS
Efficiency	Scepticism about learning	Independent learning	Learning alone
Novelty	Teacher's absence	Learning through positive experiences	Superficial learning, memorising
Flexibility	Too much freedom	Learning through sudden insights	Fear of unsuccessful learning
Challenge	Speaking & writing	Task-based learning	Lack of printed text

The students saw themselves as independent learners that learn the most through positive experiences. Some of them believed in learning incidentally. The inherent interest of the content, motivation and the curiosity of learning a new language positively affected their learning. The terms "reasonable learning" – learning a foreign language with the prospect of using it in working life (instrumental motivation) – as well as "learning out of curiosity" occurred several times.

> "I learn most efficiently when the subject is interesting. If the subject is too difficult, I need more time for learning…".

> "If I know that I will be able to use my skills and knowledge in the future, then I get motivated".

Surprisingly, a few students expressed a preference for e-learning over face-to-face sessions. Two learners described themselves as superficial learners who generally learn through memorisation. Learning through a sudden insight occurred as well.

"When learning, I mostly enjoy the moment when I get it, when I understand something that has not been taught directly...The moments when something clicks into place are the rewards for learning" (Student 3).

With the exception of two learners, all of the students perceived themselves as efficient learners if the content was interesting and if they knew that they would be able to apply their knowledge and skills in the future.

The *on-course themes* are related to the development of students' e-learning skills and strategies as well as the development of their language learning awareness. This development was reflected in the awareness of various issues related to the similarities and differences between languages, but also in how they became more conscious of their learning, in particular through writing.

5.3. E-learning skills and strategies

E-learning provides opportunities to employ a variety of learning styles. To ensure success in e-learning, two skills are necessary: the ability to adapt traditional study skills used in the face-to-face environment to online strategies, and the ability to adopt new strategies for learning and communicating in the online environment (Watkins 2007). Clarke (2008) argues that successful e-learning requires a solid foundation in traditional learning skills. In addition, learners are expected to acquire specific skills related to e-learning, such as time management and planning, responsibility for learning, self-assessment, problem solving, coping with stress, self-motivation, reflection, and research skills (e.g. planning, searching for information, assessing the quality of the obtained information). In line with Clarke's (2008) claims, in this course special emphasis was placed on the new e-learning skills. Students recognised self-assessment, self-reflection and collaboration as new and highly important skills for any learning. While only some students recognised their own learning styles and the impact of the e-learning environment on their learning strategies during the course, almost all of the respondents claimed that they benefitted from such new skills as self-assessment, self-reflection and collaboration.

5.4. Motivation

Motivation in language learning is defined as learner's orientation to the goal of learning a second language (Norris-Holt 2001). While motivation theories generally focus on the amount of motivation compared to the results of learning, Guyan (2013) recommends that teachers focus instead on creating the conditions that facilitate the internalisation of learners' motivation in the online and classroom context. As part of Self-Determination Theory (SDT), Ryan and Deci (2008) propose the satisfaction of students' three basic needs: competence (a sense of being able to do something), autonomy (a sense of control and freedom) and relatedness (a sense of being connected to others).

The authors recommend the use of strategies which may be used in both online and classroom situations. Such strategies include, for example, allowing the learners some level of control, providing them with continuous and meaningful feedback, incorporating social elements into the course and giving them opportunities for collaboration. In the current study, learners were provided with continuous feedback and various opportunities for collaborative learning (e.g. simulations and task-based activities). Collaborative learning – sharing experiences and engaging in common tasks – was a new learning experience for most of the students.

Group motivation, perceived as part of group cohesion (Dörnyei 2001), was evident from the beginning of the course. It was reflected in various group activities, the purpose of which was to increase students' motivation by, for example, enriching their knowledge of Slovakia and its culture and meeting Slovak people. Despite the teacher's consistent efforts to maintain the group motivation, students' personal motivation was frequently at risk, especially when they were overwhelmed by stress due to a lack of time or proper planning.

To facilitate their learning and maintain their motivation, the teacher tried to preserve the balance between learning and personal life as well as to create more pleasant conditions for learning (Kyppö 2014).

5.5. Writing and language learning awareness

Awareness plays an important role in the process of learning a new language and serves as an efficient motivator. The learners of Slovak successfully developed their learning awareness through listening and reading, but they failed to internalise the diacritic system of Slovak through digital writing. The problem with searching for the diacritical signs resulted in frustration and a loss of interest in writing. To solve this problem, students had the option to use the computer or to write by hand. Those who wrote by hand generally used the diacritic signs properly. In contrast, those who wrote with the computer either totally or partly ignored the diacritic system. This mix of approaches, making use of the technology and manual writing, often resulted in a compromise: scanning of the hand-written texts. Those who preferred manual writing claimed that writing by hand had a direct, positive impact on their awareness of learning Slovak.

> "When I write in Slovak, it feels like painting. I enjoy it. I cannot get the same feeling on the computer" (Student 4).

These results reflect some of the latest research on manual writing, which suggests that writing by hand strengthens the learning process and that typing on a keyboard may mitigate it (see Saperstein Associates 2012). Studies have shown that when writing by hand, different parts of the brain are activated and the movements of the hand leave a motor memory in the sensorimotor aspect of bodily activity, which facilitates the recognition of the letters.

Other experiments suggest that there is a clear connection between touching, moving and acting, and human perception (Mangen & Velay 2010 cited in Toft 2011). These results support the students' reported increase in language learning awareness for manual writing.

The *post-course themes* are related to learners' approaches to e-learning after the course, their approaches to learning and their evaluation of the course. They also include some reflections on the teacher's role (Table 4).

Table 4. Learners' attitudes, perceptions and approaches to learning after the course

Attitudes towards e-learning	Learners' perceptions of themselves as learners	Approaches to learning
Lack of contact classes	New skills	Deep and strategic
E-learning for advanced levels only	New learning styles and strategies	Language awareness
Time constraints	Identification with the metaphor of climbing	Consciousness of learning
Lack of planning	Increase in motivation	Cultural awareness
Challenge of writing: awareness	Language learning awareness	Increase in motivation
Motivation	Creativity	Increase in communicative competence
Excessive flexibility	Successful learners	Increase in knowledge

5.6. Attitudes towards e-learning revisited

The Slovak e-learning course was generally considered to be appropriate for synchronous and asynchronous learning. Nevertheless, students believed that blended learning was the best option for learning not only Slovak but any less commonly taught language.

> "Learning without the contact classes would have taken me ages! I have learned plenty of small (and big) things in the contact classes, things I wouldn't have noticed when learning completely alone…" (Student 6).

Students claimed that without the regular contact classes they would not have completed the course.

> "Learning a completely new language in the e-learning environment is very difficult. I learn most on the contact lesson. When the teacher is physically present, my motivation to learn Slovak is far stronger" (Student 7).

E-learning was generally perceived to be highly motivating, but it was also seen as highly challenging due to the time constraints. Flexibility was regarded as the highest priority and, at the same, as the greatest obstacle in e-learning. Learning Slovak, as well as any other language at the beginner's level, was considered to be too demanding in this particular learning environment. Nonetheless, the presence of the new skills and specific strategies for e-learning (e.g. self-estimation, self-reflection and collaboration) was recognised.

5.7. Learners' agency: approaches to learning

In line with Entwistle's (2001) model of approaches to learning, all learners made a constant effort to understand Slovak and learn a significant amount. Except for one, all respondents regarded themselves as independent learners with the deep approach to learning. Their participation in the course was based on their personal interest and group commitment, which resulted in deep learning and minimum dropout.

Basharina (2009) suggests that e-learning consists of a complex interrelationship between the affordances and constraints of a learning environment and a learner's agency. Although students with the deep approach to learning generally employ more effective learning strategies, actively seek meaning and benefit the most from learning, the students with the strategic approach to learning put consistent effort into learning, provide themselves with the right conditions for study and good learning materials, and monitor the effectiveness of their learning strategies (Thorpe 2002). In the context of this study, the strategic approach to learning reflects the consistency of effort needed for studying that is expressed in the course's climbing metaphor. During the course, students were constantly building on their previous experience of language learning, comparing the target language to previously acquired languages (see Mayes & de Freitas 2013).

> "I had a great time on the course! This is for me more like a hobby than any 'obligatory' study...When I am learning, I can feel how all that is getting saved deeply somewhere in my mind. That is learning. In the contact class, it is the teacher who generally provides the answers to the questions but on the e-learning course it is the learner who attempts to get the answers..." (Student 8).

Along with the development of their learning awareness, students also became sensitive to Slovak culture, thereby building what Dufva (2004) calls cultural awareness. Learners' reflections revealed an evident increase in learning awareness and a solid belief that they had achieved significant learning gains.

5.8. Teacher's role

The teaching experiment revealed some of the teacher's multiple roles: linguistic and cultural informant, expert and negotiator (Dufva 1994a), facilitator, mentor, student, and participant in the continuous dialogue. The metaphor of teacher as a mountain guide provided a guarantee that the climbers (students) would reach the top (learning objectives). Thus the teacher was seen as a tutor, guide, facilitator and, above all, as a friend.

The students' reflections revealed that their motivation to learn was higher when the teacher was present. This aligns with Kock's (2005) claim that the teacher in the contact class represents a natural medium that may contribute to learners' psychological engagement and promote an increase in motivation. Interestingly, even the teacher's virtual presence may have a significant impact on the learners through the design of the learning environment and through the enhancement of learner interaction (Phillips 2014; Stewart 2014).

5.9. Assessment of the e-learning course

The e-learning course was continuously evaluated and developed by both the learners and the teacher. The course was evaluated from the viewpoint of clarity, authenticity, functionality and relevance. In the students' opinion, a learning environment should not only be practical and easy to navigate, but also pleasant and motivating, especially when the target language is a less commonly taught language and the learning community is small in size. Blended learning was regarded as the best option for learning Slovak, a result that agrees with the results of other studies examining student satisfaction with blended, online and face-to-face courses (Diaz & Entonado 2009; Lim & Morris 2009; Solimeno, Mebane, Tomai & Francescato 2008). The overall organisation of the course, including the teacher's individual and group feedback, was considered to be an inevitable prerequisite not only for successful completion of the course, but also for further Slovak studies.

The metaphor of learning as climbing and the overall layout of the course had a positive impact on students' activities. The course structure and layout was perceived as well organised, functional and visually attractive. Table 5 presents a summary of the students' feedback, including an overall evaluation of the course, the e-learning environment and the course structure.

Table 5. Course evaluation: student perspective

Course evaluation (overall) criteria	e-Learning environment criteria	Course structure (camps, sections)
Clarity	Authenticity	Relevant
Authenticity	Flexibility	Clear
Functionality	Immediate feedback	Appropriate
Relevancy	Time for reflection	Up-to-date
Learner-centeredness	Collaboration	Interesting
Promoting learner agency	Supportive atmosphere	Pleasant
Novelty	Consistent interaction	Challenging
Promoting collaboration	Promoting learner autonomy	Motivating

In addition to the development of students' communicative competence in Slovak, one of the purposes was to inspire learners and arouse their interest in Slovak studies. Based on the students' feedback and reflections, this objective was met.

6. Concluding remarks and implications

The initial research questions of this study were whether and how Slovak is learned in an e-learning environment and to what extent a good command of all four language skills, especially writing and speaking, may be acquired. The findings showed that an e-learning environment may be used for learning less commonly taught languages. However, not all language skills may be acquired at an equal level without contact classes. Furthermore, the results show that this particular learning environment promotes the feeling in students that they have learned Slovak (identifying with the metaphor of learning as if climbing). All of the learners, with the exception of two, believed that they learned a good deal about Slovak. Based on their reflections, the learners showed clear progress in their receptive skills (reading and listening), but had difficulty in developing their productive skills (speaking and writing). The problem of digital writing was resolved with a compromise in which the learners were given the freedom to choose the writing medium. Blended learning – face-to-face classroom tutorials and computer-mediated activities – was used to compensate for the lack of spontaneous speaking. Furthermore, new e-learning skills such as research, content creation and collaboration were adopted and further developed.

This teaching experiment shows that technology-enhanced learning of lesser commonly taught languages can be successful. Nevertheless, from the viewpoint of sustainable learning (i.e. knowledge management and exchange in the target language), the contact classes may be more efficient, particularly at the beginners' level. The greatest challenge in teaching and learning less commonly taught languages in an e-learning environment is the availability of web-learning resources and the development of new pedagogies. While numerous readymade web-learning materials and sophisticated learning spaces for major languages are constantly offered, very few effective web materials may be found for less commonly taught languages. The teacher thus often ends up being the course designer and developer. However, current developments and innovations in language learning and teaching emphasise the use of learner-centred pedagogies in new, personalised learning environments. Rapidly growing mobile technologies and the use of social media offer new learning platforms for the development of all areas of communicative competence. The emergence of social networking tools removes the borders of the traditional concept of a learning environment and opens the gate towards multiple learning spaces, both physical and virtual. New technological opportunities that involve the integration of new media modes such as blogs and wikis into learning activities make use not only of multiple resources and learning environments, but also of the interconnectivity and social participation among the learners (Mcloughlin & Lee 2008). This type of interaction may result in an increase of the learners' communicative competence and motivation.

References

Bakhtin, M. M. 1981. *The dialogic imagination. Four essays*. Austin: University of Texas Press.

Basharina, O. 2009. Student agency and language learning pocesses and outcomes in international online environments. *CALICO Journal, 26* (2), 390–412.

Biggs, J. 2003. *Teaching for quality learning at university – What the student does* (2nd ed.). Buckingham: Open University Press.

Bilash, O. & Tulasiewicz, W. 1995. Language awareness – Its place in the Canadian context. In K. A. McLeod (ed.), *Multicultural education: the state of the art*. Toronto: CASLT.

Braun, V. & Clark, V. 2006. Using thematic analysis in psychology. *Qualitative Research in Psychology, 3* (2), 77–101. doi:10.1191/1478088706qp063oa

Brecht, R. D. & Walton, A. R. 1994. *National strategic planning in the less commonly taught languages*. Washington DC: National Foreign Language Center.

Brown, D. 2014. Agency and motivation to achieve language-learning objectives among learners in an academic environment in France. *APPLES - Journal of Applied Language Studies, 8* (1), 101–126.

Byram, M., Nichols, A. & Stevens, D. 2001. *Developing intercultural competence in practice*. Clevedon: Multilingual Matters.

CEFR 2001. *Common European Framework of Reference for Languages: Learning, teaching, assessment.* Cambridge University Press.

CEFR 2009. *Common European framework of reference for languages : learning, teaching, assessment. A Guide for users*. Strasbourg: Language Policy Division.

Clarke, A. 2008. *eLearning skills*. New York: Palgrave Macmillan.

Diaz, L. A. & Entonado, F. B. 2009. Are the functions of teachers in e-learning and face-to-face learning environments really different? *Educational Technology & Society, 12* (4), 331–343.

Dörnyei, Z. 1991. Motivation in second and foreign language learning. *Language Teaching, 31* (3), 117–135. doi:10.1017/S026144480001315X

Dörnyei, Z. 1998. Motivation in second and foreign language learning. *Language Teaching, 31* (3),117–135. doi:10.1017/S026144480001315X

Dörnyei, Z. 2001. *Teaching and researching motivation*. Harlow: Longman.

Dufva, H. 1994a. *Language awareness and cultural awareness for language learners*. *Hungarologische Beiträge 2, Probleme des Spracherwerbs*. Jyväskylä: Hungarologia.

Dufva, H. 1994b. Everyday knowledge of language: a dialogical approach to awareness. *Finlance, A Finnish Journal of Applied Linguistics, 13* (2), 22–49.

Dufva, H. 2004. Language, thinking and embodiment: Bakhtin, Whorf and Merleau-Ponty. In F. Bostad, C. Brandist, L. S. Evensen & H. C. Faber (eds.), *Bakhtinian perspectives on language and culture: meaning in language, art and new media*. Houndmills, Basingstoke, Hampshire: Palgrave Macmillan, 133–146.

Ellis, R. 2003. *Task-based learning and teaching*. Oxford: Oxford University Press.

Engeström, Y. 1999. Activity theory and individual and social transformation. In Y. Engeström, R. Miettinen & R.-L. Punamäki (eds.), *Perspectives on activity theory*. Cambridge: Cambridge University Press.

Entwistle, N. J. 2001. Styles of learning and approaches to studying in higher education. *Kybernetes, 30* (5/6), 593–602. doi:10.1108/03684920110391823

Guyan, M. 2013. Improving motivation in e-learning. *e-Learn Magazine*, October 2013. Retrieved from http://elearnmag.acm.org/featured.cfm?aid=2527388

Johnson, M. 2004. *A philosophy of second language acquisition*. New York: Yale University Press.

Kock, N. 2005. Media richness or media naturalness? The evolution of our biological communication apparatus and its influence on our behavior toward E-communication tools. *IEEE Transactions on Professional Communication, 48* (2), 117–30. doi:10.1109/TPC.2005.849649

Kyppö, A. 2007. A long way to the top of a mountain. In M. Kalin, A. Räsänen & T. Nurmi (eds.), *Kirjomme kielillä, Jyväskykön yliopiston kielikeskus 30 vuotta. Tapestry of Teaching. University of Jyväskylä Language Centre 30.Year.* Jyväskylä: Univeristy of Jyväskylä, 132–140.

Kyppö, A. 2014. Learning Slovak in an e-learning environment: a case study. *APPLES - Journal of Applied Language Studies, 8* (1), 127–146.

Lim, D. H. & Morris, M. L. 2009. Learner and instructional factors influencing learning outcomes within a blended learning environment. *Educational Technology & Society, 12* (4), 282–293.

Mangen, A. & Velay, J.-L. 2010. Digitizing literacy: reflections on the haptics of writing. In M. H. Zadeh (ed.) *Advances in Haptics*. Intech. doi:10.5772/8710

Mayes, T. & de Freitas, S. 2013. *Review of e-learning theories, frameworks and models.* Joint Information Systems Committee. London. Retrieved from http://www.jisc.ac.uk/whatwedo/programmes/elearningpedagogy/outcomes.aspx

McLoughlin, C. & Lee, M. J.W. 2008. The three P's of pedagogy for the networked society: personalization, participation, and productivity. *International Journal of Teaching and Learning in Higher Education, 20* (1), 10–27.

Norris-Holt, J. 2001. Motivation as a contributing factor in second language acquisition. The Internet TESL Journal. Retrieved from http://iteslj.org/Articles/Norris-Motivation.html

Ondrejovič, S. 2009. *The Slovak language. Languages in Slovakia. Ministry of Foreign Affairs of the Slovak Republic.* Bratislava: Public Diplomacy Department.

Phillips, B. 2014. How technology has affected the learning environment. *brennaphillips.com.* Retrieved from http://www.brennaphillips.com/how-technology-has-affected-the-learning-environment

Robert, L. P. & Dennis, A. R. 2005. Paradox of richness: a cognitive model of media choice. *IEEE Transactions on Professional Communication, 48* (1), 10–21. doi:10.1109/TPC.2004.843292

Ryan, E. L. & Deci, R. M. 2008. Facilitating optimal motivation and psychological well-being across life's domains. *Canadian Psychology, 49* (1), 14–23. doi:10.1037/0708-5591.49.1.14

Saperstein Associates, 2012. *Handwriting in the 21st century? An educational summit.* Retrieved from https://www.hw21summit.com/media/zb/hw21/files/H2948_HW_Summit_White_Paper_eVersion.pdf

Solimeno, A., Mebane, M. E., Tomai, M. & Francescato, D. 2008. The influence of students and teachers characteristics on the efficacy of face-to-face and computer supported collaborative learning. *Computers & Education, 51* (1), 109–128.

Stewart, M. 2014. Designing for emergence: the role of the instructor in student-centered learning. *Hybrid Pedagogy Journal.* Retrieved from http://www.hybridpedagogy.com/journal/designing-emergence-role-instructor-student-centered-learning/

Thorpe, M. 2002. From independent learning to collaborative learning: New communities of practice in open, distance and distributed learning. In M. Lea & K. Nicoll (Eds.), *Distributed learning: Social and cultural approaches to practice.* London: Routledge.

Toft, T. E. 2011. Better learning through handwriting. *ScienceDaily.* Retrieved from www.sciencedaily.com/releases/2011/01/110119095458.htm

Ushida, E. 2005. The role of students' attitudes and motivation in second language learning in online language courses. *CALICO Journal, 23* (1), 49–78.

Van Lier, L. 2010. The ecology of language learning: practice to theory, theory to practice. *Procedia - Social and Behavioral Sciences, 3* (2-6), 1276–1284. doi:10.1016/j.sbspro.2010.07.005

Vaughan, N. D. 2010. Blended learning. In M.F. Cleveland-Innes & D.R. Garrison, *An introduction to distance education: understanding teaching and learning in a new era.* New York: Routledge

Vygotsky, L. S. 1986. *Thought and language*. Cambridge: MIT.

Watkins, R. 2007. E-learning study skills and strategies. *Distance Learning, 1* (3), 24–26.

Willis, J. 1996. *A framework for task-based learning*. London: Longman.

Wilson, B. G. 1996. *Constructivist learning environments: case studies in instructional design*. New Jersey: Educational Technology Publications.

5 Developing a conceptual framework: the case of MAGICC

Teija Natri and Anne Räsänen[1]

Abstract

This paper reports the steps taken to develop the conceptual framework of the MAGICC project (2013), which aimed to provide action-oriented descriptions of multilingual and multicultural academic and professional communication competence, instructional designs to promote these in higher education language teaching, and multidimensional forms of assessment aligned with the learning outcomes established – all presented in an academic ePortfolio that expands the features of the existing European Language Portfolio (ELP) to the higher education level. "Starting with systematic desk research into the existing conceptualisations of multi/plurilingual and multi/intercultural competences as well as lifelong learning and employability skills, the next step was to collect and analyse the data gathered from all partner institutions and existing national and European projects on descriptors already in place for academic level competences, practices and assessment. […] To ensure the social relevance of the framework, the third step was to develop questionnaires for students, faculty, and employers and ask them to rank the synthesised skill and competence descriptors in terms of their importance for the academic and professional competences graduates would need for study purposes as well as for the global labour market. The first draft of the conceptual framework was revised on the basis of this stakeholder consultation and led to the version presented to a new group of selected stakeholders in a consultation seminar" (Räsänen 2014: 66–67).

Keywords: academic language learning, multilingual and multicultural competence, language assessment, Common European Framework of Reference, CEFR.

1. Language Centre, University of Jyväskylä, Finland; teija.natri@jyu.fi; anne.e.rasanen@jyu.fi

How to cite this chapter: Natri, T., & Räsänen, A. (2015). Developing a conceptual framework: the case of MAGICC. In J. Jalkanen, E. Jokinen, & P. Taalas (Eds), *Voices of pedagogical development - Expanding, enhancing and exploring higher education language learning* (pp. 85-102). Dublin: Research-publishing.net. doi:10.14705/rpnet.2015.000288

Chapter 5

1. Introduction

This paper presents the main steps taken to develop the conceptual framework for the project Modularising Multilingual and Multicultural Academic Communication Competence (MAGICC)[2]. The project emphasises the role of languages and communication in the construction of academic expertise and in the process of socialising graduates for international working life. The developed competences constitute transversal key competences and are "vital for living, studying and working in an internationalised knowledge-based society and economy" (Forster Vosicki 2014: 66).

Explicit development of students' multilingual and multicultural academic communication competences is needed as a strategy to contribute to the modernisation agenda of higher education (i.e. the European Higher Education Area (EHEA) and Bologna Process 2020), because these competences have not been sufficiently taken into account in the implementation of the Bologna process.

The European documents related to higher education competences and qualifications as well as to the quality of the Bologna process were used as the initial rationale for the MAGICC project. These documents describe the general core competences and expected learning outcomes for each cycle established during the Bologna process (see e.g. Bologna Working Group 2005). The most important descriptors of graduate achievement from the point of view of the project are the following:

First cycle (BA):

- "have the ability to gather and interpret relevant data [...] to inform judgments;
- can communicate information, ideas, problems and solutions to both specialist and non-specialist audiences;
- have developed those learning skills that are necessary for them to

---

[2]. http://www.magicc.eu: A Lifelong Learning Programme of the European Commission (2011-2014)

continue to undertake further study with a high degree of autonomy" (Bologna Working Group 2005).

Second cycle (MA):

- "have the ability to integrate knowledge and handle complexity, and formulate judgments with incomplete and limited information;
- can communicate their conclusions, and the knowledge and rationale underpinning these, to specialist and non-specialist audiences clearly and unambiguously;
- have the learning skills to allow them to continue to study in a manner that may be largely self-directed or autonomous" (Bologna Working Group 2005).

These qualifications for the European Higher Education Area (EHEA) therefore focus on the graduates' ability to manage information and construct knowledge, to share one's own expertise with various audiences, as well as to have the skills and strategies for continuous independent learning. Further principles of the Bologna implementation documents are concerned with action orientation, maintenance of diversity, transparency and comparability of student achievement, as well as the social relevance of education in terms of, for example, employability and integration in society. However, as was stated above, specific attention in higher education is needed to promote students' multilingual and multicultural competences for managing global contexts of study and work (see EHEA 2012: Bologna Process Implementation Report).

Following the initial rationale above, the main purpose of the MAGICC project was to conceptualise multilingual and multicultural communication competence for the higher education level and in this way complement the Council of Europe's Common European Framework of Reference for Languages (CEFR[3]) in areas that are not addressed in the CEFR. The key difference, however, is that the starting point for MAGICC is not a monolingual

---

3. http://www.coe.int/t/dg4/linguistic/source/framework_en.pdf

view of language and communication competence, but a view where various languages – mother tongue included – are intertwined and appear side by side in constructing the individual's interactive competence and communicative action in various social contexts. The conceptual framework and its learning outcome descriptions of general "academic, discipline-specific, professional, intercultural, and lifelong learning competences" (Räsänen 2014: 67) form the foundation for new types of instructional designs, learning activities and assessment forms. These are manifested by practical tools that were developed in the project, namely, learning tasks in the form of scenarios, transparency tools for assessment and an academic ePortfolio. With these outputs the MAGICC project forms an integrated, online reference tool for various users, from teachers and students to employers and policy- and decision-makers. Nine universities from seven European countries took part in the project:

- Université de Lausanne and Université de Fribourg from Switzerland;
- Universität Bremen and Freie Universität Berlin from Germany;
- Jyväskylän yliopisto from Finland;
- The Open University from the United Kingdom;
- Rijksuniversiteit Groningen from the Netherlands;
- Universidade do Algarve from Portugal;
- Politechnika Poznanska from Poland.

The European Centre for Modern Languages of the Council of Europe participated in the project as an associated partner.

The project tasks were divided into nine different work packages (WP) in order to provide the four envisaged tools: (1) a conceptual framework for multilingual and multicultural communication competence with specific learning outcomes for higher education and aligned assessment criteria and grids (WP1 & WP2); (2) an academic ePortfolio to provide recognition of students' multilingual and multicultural profile and render it visible to third parties (WP3); (3) action-oriented multilingual and multicultural academic or professional communication scenarios (WP4); and (4) transparency tools to enable harmonisation of assessment (WP5). The other four WPs were concerned with dissemination, exploitation, quality assurance, and project coordination and management.

The University of Jyväskylä was in charge of the first two WPs: mapping the field and establishing the state of the art as well as the elaboration of the conceptual framework. This work required much collaboration and evaluation by all partners and external stakeholders who would be the potential users of the framework. The stepwise development processes are explained below. The outcomes of the processes, then, formed the basis for the work done in the other WP.

2. Step 1: Mapping the field and establishing the state of the art

The first task in the project was to map the field and carry out systematic desk research into existing conceptualisations of multi/plurilingual and multi/intercultural competences, lifelong learning skills, and employability skills. Also, in this first part, the existing multilingual and multicultural learning outcome descriptions for the higher education level in use at the participating universities were collected. All this information was collected in a synthesis report for the first work package.

2.1. Defining basic concepts

As the MAGICC project was concerned with describing, conceptualising and integrating competences from a new perspective, an important and necessary task was to reach an agreement among the project partners on what terminology and concepts would be used in the conceptual framework. After mapping the field for existing definitions of the basic concepts, the second partner meeting (in June 2012) included a workshop during which agreements were reached on the basic concepts of the project.

First of all, there are many existing understandings of multilingualism, depending on whether the perspective is sociolinguistics, communication, identity, cognition, translation, learning, or agency and participation. The older conceptualisations saw multilingualism as multiplied monolingualism, where languages were present as bounded entities, each with a defined system of its own, and one language was used at a time. Recent views see languages as resources for social and other actions, in other words, people use their multilingual resources in their local contexts, often simultaneously, interacting with the context. Furthermore, new conceptualisations (for an overview, see Lähteenmäki, Varis & Leppänen 2011) emphasise the fact that multilingualism needs to be seen as language resources that may be heterogeneous and represent independent profiles and that are mobilised by individuals and groups with different effects and outcomes. In addition, recent sociolinguistic research approaches multilingualism as a dynamic repertoire of linguistic and discursive resources an individual may use without experiencing that there are separate languages or varieties within it (heteroglossia, in Leppänen), and that the repertoire never represents whole languages but only those resources which have become accessible through life experience (truncated multilingualism, comprising e.g. certain genres and registers, in Blommaert, Collins & Slembrouck 2005) or which are available and necessary in pursuing certain communicative goals (polylingualism and translanguaging, in Jørgensen 2008, Møller 2008; all references are from Lähteenmäki et al. 2011). In these conceptualisations, the Council of Europe distinction between the terms *multilingual* (about communities) and *plurilingual* (about individuals)[4] is not explicitly made.

If multilingualism has been a complicated concept to handle and define, so has the term *multicultural*. Existing definitions, again depending on the perspective and context, have listed pluricultural, intercultural, multicultural and inter/pluriculturality as related concepts. Because the European Commission uses the term *multilingual/multicultural* to refer to either individual- or community-level usage, we could not adopt the Council of Europe distinction between pluricultural

---

4. The Council of Europe definition of plurilingualism: "lifelong enrichment of the individual's plurilingual repertoire [....] made up of different languages and language varieties at different levels of proficiency, including different types of competence. [...] A person's plurilingual competence changes in its composition throughout one's life. [...] A plurilingual person has a repertoire of languages and language varieties as well as competences of different kinds and levels within the repertoire" (Council of Europe: Language Policy Division 2006, http://www.coe.int/t/dg4/linguistic/division_EN.asp?).

and multicultural directly. However, it was jointly agreed that the definition of the key concepts should accommodate relevant meanings from several existing definitions and be reformulated accordingly. Thus, for example, the term multicultural in the project is defined as a combination of the pluricultural and intercultural profiles of graduates. The jointly agreed definition for the key terms in the title, then, is as follows:

> "**Multilingual and multicultural academic communication competence** is an individual's communicative and interactive repertoire, made up of several languages and language varieties including first language(s) at different levels of proficiency, and various types of competence, which are all interrelated. The repertoire in its entirety represents a resource enabling action in diverse use situations. It evolves across time and experience throughout life, and includes growth in intercultural awareness and ability to cope with, and participate in, multicultural contexts of academic study and working life" (MAGICC Conceptual framework 2013: section 2.1).

General definitions for lifelong/independent/autonomous learning skills and employability/workplace/professional communication skills were also initially agreed upon among the partners. Further specification was then necessary when dealing with the data and deciding on the learning outcome descriptors. All terminological definitions are presented in the conceptual framework.

2.2. Mapping existing learning outcome descriptions

After agreeing on the basic terminology to be used, all partners conducted a survey on existing learning outcome descriptors related to academic, discipline-specific, professional, intercultural and independent learning competences in use at their universities. The CEFR was also consulted for the general descriptors relevant for the academic level. In addition, related projects and good practices were mapped. These mappings provided rich data, which then had to be analysed and presented in a manageable form on the basis of the principles and terms underlying the conceptual framework.

Chapter 5

The survey data on academic competences could have been synthesised and categorised in many ways. For instance, a classification according to *transferable academic skills* or *employability skills* or *critical thinking skills* – all of which can be related to academic communication competences – could have been used. Other terms often used include *soft skills* and *generic skills* or *competences*. However, in the end, the categorisations of academic competences and strategies presented by Adamson (1993) and Cottrell (2003) were adopted, in a slightly adapted form, because they seemed to reflect more directly what the data were showing and because the role of language and study skills was more explicit and added new elements to the CEFR, particularly in terms of the higher education level. Thus, the general, discipline-specific and professional learning outcomes as well as the independent learning outcomes provided by the data were synthesised accordingly. It is important to bear in mind that in real academic situations, the separate skills are developed on an integrated basis, and because of this integration there was significant overlap in the data.

The survey data also included references to and descriptions of intercultural academic communication competence, which is a key element of the MAGICC project endeavour. As was explained in the previous section above, this concept can also be described from different perspectives and includes aspects that are not easy to formulate as learning outcomes, let alone as assessment criteria. However, some categorisation principles were necessary in this case as well, because the CEFR is not very elaborate in its descriptions for the academic level. As the starting point and first reference for dealing with the data, we chose the Council of Europe's publication Assessment in Plurilingual and Intercultural Education (Lenz & Berthele 2010), because it starts with assessment and not with a mere analysis of the abilities, skills and attitudes involved in intercultural encounters. The second framework used was that of the INCA project (2004), on intercultural communicative competence (ICC), which also includes assessment. The plurilingual approach of the CARAP project (2011) was also consulted, because it includes a comprehensive set of descriptors (for Byram's (2008) complete ICC framework, see Lenz & Berthele 2010: 9).

Lenz and Berthele (2010: 6) define intercultural competence as having "to do with the integration of 'otherness' in one's thinking and actions", and continue that this definition is "significantly different from a concept of pluricultural competence, which highlights the plurality of cultures one may identify and is familiar with". The first one, according to them, is not necessarily linked with knowledge of languages, because it could materialise through, for example, a lingua franca. The second concept, on the other hand, represents a default case of plurality and dynamics of languages and cultures. In this context, plurilingual (or in MAGICC terminology, multilingual), communication competence refers to "the ability to mobilise [one's] language repertoire as a whole [and] to use existing competences transversally, [that is], to recombine existing knowledge and skills in any language(s) in order to respond flexibly to needs that arise in a multilingual environment" (Lenz & Berthele 2010: 5–6).

It seems clear, however, that intercultural competence is a prerequisite for plurilingual competence to be materialised, which is why it is treated here separately from the other sets of learning outcomes in the data. Existing learning outcomes for intercultural communication competence in the data were categorised according to the INCA (2004) descriptors, because they relate more explicitly to communication (from Lenz & Berthele 2010: 10):

1st strand: *openness*

- *respect for otherness* (ability to look at all customs and values from a distance, regarding them at the same time as worthwhile in their own right);

- *tolerance of ambiguity* (ability to accept ambiguity and lack of clarity and deal with it constructively).

2nd strand: *knowledge*

- *knowledge discovery* (ability to acquire and actually use cultural knowledge);

- *empathy* (ability to intuitively understand what other people think and how they feel).

3rd strand: *adaptability*

- *behavioural flexibility* (ability to adapt one's own behaviour to different requirements and situations);

- *communicative awareness* (ability to identify and consciously work with communicative conventions) (Lenz & Berthele 2010: 10; cf. INCA project 2004).

Finally, the synthesis report also provided a short overview of good practice samples, scenarios, pilot approaches and assessment forms and criteria in use at the participating universities. The whole was then completed with some relevant data on descriptors already in place for academic level competences, practices and assessment from existing national and European projects (e.g. Bilingue plus[5]; CARAP 2011; LanQua 2010; Profile Deutsch[6]; TNP3[7]).

3. Step 2: Elaboration of the MAGICC conceptual framework

The information collected in the WP1 survey was further elaborated into a descriptive conceptual framework which contains transnationally shared learning outcomes for multilingual and multicultural academic core communication competences. The overall aim for higher education degrees presented in the quality toolkit of the Language Network for Quality Assurance (LanQua 2010) project was adopted as the basis for elaboration. This aim is expressed as follows:

---

5. http://www.unifr.ch/bilingueplus/fr

6. https://www.goethe.de/de/spr/unt/kum/prd.html

7. http://web.fu-berlin.de/tnp3/

"The overall aim for higher education degrees is to ensure solid multilingual mastery of the discipline/field-specific and professional domain with a developed competence in lifelong learning and use of own multilingual and multicultural repertoire for effective communication and interaction as well as for self-directed learning" (MAGICC Conceptual framework 2013: section 10).

The core competences of graduates for global employability were also described in the LanQua (2010) project and they are presented in the conceptual framework. As mentioned by Räsänen (2014: 67),

"[t]he three main action-oriented, multilingual and multicultural competences established through this stepwise process for the BA and MA levels, with some variable focuses, address management of information and knowledge sources, conceptualization and communication of information and expertise, and management of learning from a lifelong perspective. They form the essence of the conceptual framework, detailed further into specific skills and strategies that combine descriptors [in line with e.g. Baume 2009 and Moon 2006] for academic, discipline-specific, professional, intercultural and lifelong learning competences and their aligned assessment".

The whole is completed by assessment criteria for improving reliability, as well as a list of innovative types of activities to scaffold the achievement of expected learning outcomes. Figure 1 below illustrates the integrated approach followed when building the MAGICC conceptual framework (2013).

The conceptual framework includes a comprehensive set of learning outcome descriptions (i.e. the minimum threshold levels to be achieved) and their multidimensional assessment forms, serving as a reference tool for language specialists and curriculum designers. The learning tasks and activities – academic and professional scenarios – are examples of the actual implementation of the framework and adaptable to various situations of developing students' competences and repertoires.

Figure 1. The principle of constructive alignment of learning outcomes, learning tasks and alternative assessment forms and criteria in the MAGICC conceptual framework (2013, adapted from Biggs 1999)

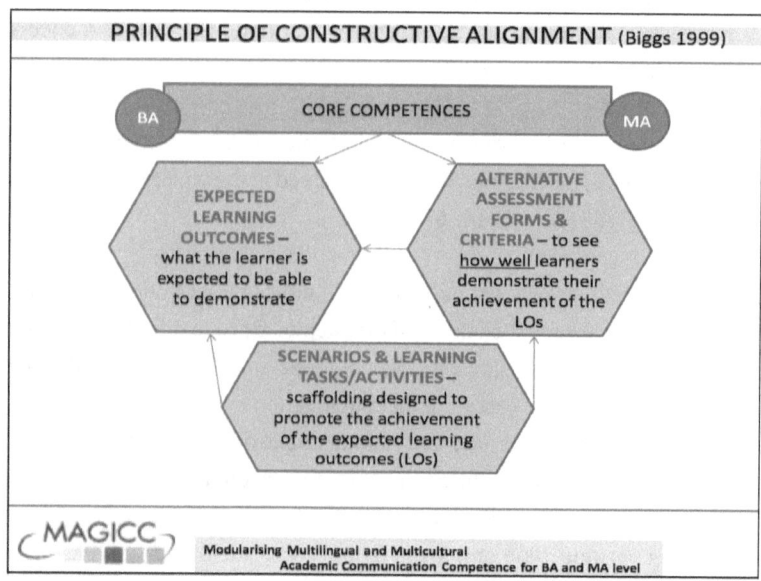

4. Step 3: Checking the social relevance of the conceptual framework

An important element in the implementation of the Bologna Process for EHEA was the social relevance of higher education. The MAGICC project attended to this requirement by conducting two consultations with stakeholders, with an aim to ensuring the relevance of the conceptual framework and the learning outcome descriptions included. Another aim was to communicate the objectives and expected outcomes of the project to a wider circle of potential future users as well as to explore possible ways of implementing its future results.

The first consultation (autumn 2012) took place in all participating universities in the form of guided interviews based on pre-established questionnaires in order to facilitate analysis and allow comparability of the results. Three different questionnaires were designed for three stakeholder groups: students, faculty, and employers. Besides a series of general questions specific to the stakeholder groups, the questionnaires contained the same sets of learning outcome descriptions in the following domains to allow comparison: academic communication competences (receptive and productive skills), employability skills, multilingual and multicultural strategies and competence, lifelong learning skills and work-related language and communication skills. The different stakeholder groups were invited to rate these sets of competences in relation to their importance for study purposes and/or for the global labour market and also indicate in which languages these competences are required. The stakeholders also suggested during which university cycle (BA and/or MA) these competences should be developed.

All learning outcomes listed in the questionnaires were perceived as relevant by the stakeholder groups. Although there was much convergence in the perceptions, receptive skills were in general seen as particularly important for the BA cycle, whereas productive skills (particularly writing) were of greater importance for the MA cycle. This preference was partly due to the disciplinary field, programme requirements, and specific academic cultures, and related in particular to conceptualising and communicating information, knowledge and expertise in a multilingual and multicultural context. According to the student, faculty, and employer representatives interviewed, professional, lifelong learning, and intercultural skills should, therefore, be developed in both cycles. Regardless of the general consensus on the importance of the listed learning outcomes for academic competence building, there were also some differences between the three stakeholder groups in how much emphasis they placed on certain skills and strategies, as exemplified in Figure 2 and Figure 3 below.

As the figures indicate, the employers in the consultation perceived all other skills except lifelong learning as clearly more important than the two other stakeholder groups did. On the other hand, student answers on, for example, the importance of adapting communication may only reflect their inexperience with multilingual and multicultural communication, whereas they saw lifelong

Chapter 5

learning and study skills as very important to develop, as did the faculty representatives interviewed.

Figure 2. Stakeholders' (%) perceived importance of skills development in the management of information, teamwork, intercultural awareness and ability to adapt to communication in multilingual and multicultural contexts

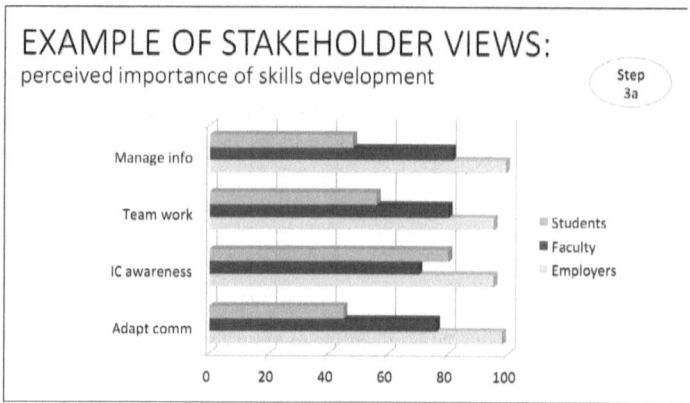

Figure 3. Stakeholders' (%) perceived importance of skills development, lifelong learning, and communication in multilingual and multicultural social situations

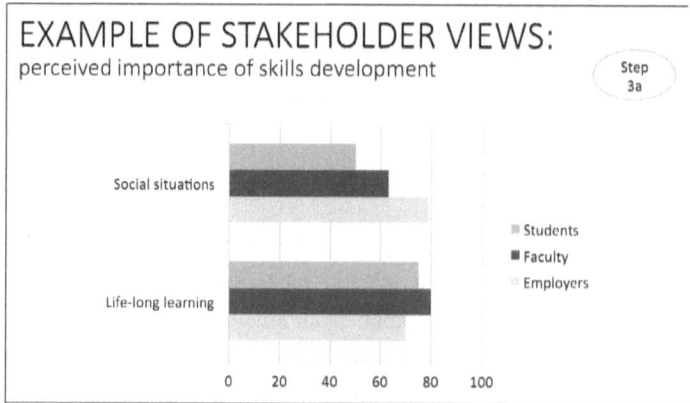

The second stakeholder consultation (February 2013) was organised as a dissemination and feedback event. During the event, two panel discussions with invited guests from all the partner countries were arranged. The first group of panellists comprised specialists in different domains, such as university policy, psychology, international relations and labour market research. The second panel was composed mostly of specialists in the area of languages. Both groups were asked to give feedback on the conceptual framework from the viewpoint of their expertise and experience, as well as to suggest recommendations for implementation.

In general, the panelists saw MAGICC as an important project which raises awareness about the dimensions of multilingual and multicultural competences and the interdependency of languages, thus making the role of languages in mediating and constructing knowledge important and transparent. Moreover, well-developed skills and strategies were seen as a clear competitive edge for graduates' employability. However, for implementation, the conceptual framework needed more concrete and generic examples and guidance for users to concretise the value of developed multilingual and multicultural competences for employers, staff and students.

The conceptual framework was revised on the basis of the two consultations. Some concepts and learning outcome descriptions, for example, were clarified, and some user guidance added. The end result, however, remained: the framework was perceived as socially relevant and potentially useful as a reference document for the higher education level.

5. Concluding remarks

The multilingual and multicultural approach advocated by the project aims at promoting students' use and expansion of their entire multilingual repertoires, thus enabling both wider access to learning and negotiation of meanings in interaction. In addition, it aims at maintenance and respect of diversity as an intrinsic value to full participation in a globalised society.

Achieving these aims requires a mental change in attitudes and practices, a move from a monolingual mindset to appreciating the coexistence of languages in communication and interaction. Moreover, it requires acknowledgment of the significance of individuals' agency and the use of one's repertoire, because they are enabling factors for multilingualism to become manifest and grow (see Blommaert et al. 2005). From the pedagogical point of view, new skills and strategies need to be developed in higher education, including negotiation strategies for meaning, intercomprehension and mediation strategies, code-switching and translanguaging strategies, and other tools to cope with multilingual and multicultural realities. Avoidance of so-called correctness is also an issue, because partial competences are an important element of an individual's communication repertoire. Naturally, in certain situations (e.g. formal writing), accuracy remains an important criterion, but diversification of instructional designs and approaches is equally important. It is to this effect that the MAGICC project has attempted to contribute.

The conceptual framework itself is mainly addressed to language specialists and policy makers. It is an open resource, including learning outcome descriptions and transnational tools for integrating academic, intercultural and lifelong learning dimensions in the graduate's multilingual and multicultural repertoire building in higher education. Moreover, it is operationalised as scenario activities, multidimensional performance assessment and an academic ePortfolio, which expands the features of the Council of Europe's ELP to match new needs in higher education and to improve the visibility and recognition of the specific nature of academic communication competences in relation to employability. Through this operationalisation, the outcomes of the MAGICC project are designed to serve students, teachers, faculties and employers.

The project work is extremely well documented and fully available on the project website, including learning outcome descriptors in English, German and French and their assessment scales presented as an interactive reference as well as templates for building new pedagogical scenarios or adapting and combining existing ones for individual purposes. The consultation questionnaires are available in all partner languages, and all partner universities also made implementation plans and reported on their outcomes. It is only by actively using the project outputs that the potential of the innovative elements designed for higher education language teaching and learning purposes can become manifest for the stakeholders envisaged in the project.

References

Adamson, H. D. 1993. *Academic competence. theory and classroom practice: preparing ESL students for content courses*. London: Longman.

Baume, D. 2009. *Writing and using good learning outcomes*. Leeds: Leeds Metropolitan University. Retrieved from https://www.leedsbeckett.ac.uk/partners/files/Learning_Outcomes.pdf

Biggs, J. 1999. *Teaching for quality learning at university: what the student does*. Buckingham: The Society for Research into Higher Education and Open University Press.

Blommaert, J., Collins, J. & Slembrouck, S. 2005. Spaces of multilingualism. *Language & Communication, 25* (3), 197–216. doi:10.1016/j.langcom.2005.05.002

Bologna Process. 2020. The European higher education area in the new decade. Retrieved from http://www.ehea.info/Uploads/Declarations/Leuven_Louvain-la-Neuve_Communiqu%C3%A9_April_2009.pdf

Bologna Working Group. 2005. *A framework for qualifications of the European higher education area*. Copenhagen: Ministry of Science, Technology and Innovation. Retrieved from http://www.ehea.info/Uploads/qualification/QF-EHEA-May2005.pdf

Byram, M. 2008. *From foreign language education to education for intercultural citizenship: essays and reflections*. Clevedon: Multilingual Matters.

CARAP. 2011. *A framework of reference for pluralistic approaches to languages and cultures*. Retrieved from http://carap.ecml.at

Cottrell, S. 2003. *The Study Skills Handbook*. New York: Palgrave Macmillan.

Council of Europe: Language Policy Division. 2006. *Plurilingual education in Europe. 50 years of international co-operation*. Retrieved from http://www.coe.int/t/dg4/linguistic/source/plurinlingaleducation_en.pdf

EHEA. 2012. *The European higher education area in 2012: Bologna process implementation report*. Brussels: EACEA P9 Eurydice. doi:10.2797/81203

Chapter 5

Forster Vosicki, B. 2014. *Modularising multilingual and multicultural academic communication competence: rationale and purpose of the MAGICC project*. Paper presentation in the 13th International CercleS Conference, programme and abstracts, 4-6 September 2014, Fribourg, Switzerland. Retrieved from http://www.cercles2014.org/docs/programme_and_abstracts.pdf

INCA Assessor Manual. 2004. *Intercultural competence assessment (INCA)*. Retrieved from https://www.yumpu.com/en/document/view/8814059/assessor-manual-inca-project

Jørgensen, J. N. 2008. Polylingual languaging around and among children and adolescents. *International Journal of Multilingualism, 5*(3), 161–176. doi:10.1080/14790710802387562

LanQua quality model 2010. Retrieved from http://speaqproject.files.wordpress.com/2012/02/lanqua-quality-model_eng.pdf

Lenz, P. & Berthele, R. 2010. *Assessment in plurilingual and intercultural education*. Strasbourg: Council of Europe: Language Policy Division. Retrieved from http://doc.rero.ch/record/31422/files/Assessment2010_Lenz_Berthele_EN.pdf

Lähteenmäki, M., Varis, P. & Leppänen, S. 2011. Editorial: The shifting paradigm: towards a re-conceptualisation of multilingualism. *Apples: Special issue on Mediated Multilingualism, 5* (1), 2–11.

MAGICC Conceptual Framework. 2013. Retrieved from http://www.unil.ch/files/live//sites/magicc/files/shared/Revised_Conceptual_Framework_MAGICC.pdf

Møller, J. S. 2008. Polylingual performance among Turkish-Danes in Late-Modern Copenhagen. *International Journal of Multilingualism, 5* (3), 217–236. doi:10.1080/14790710802390178

Moon, J. 2006. *Linking levels, learning outcomes and assessment criteria – EHEA version*. Retrieved from http://spectare.ucl.slu.se/adm/sus/2008/plagiarism_eng/JennyMoonExercise.pdf

Räsänen, A. 2014. *Towards the MAGICC conceptual framework*. Paper presentation in the 13th International CercleS Conference, programme and abstracts, 4-6 September 2014, Fribourg, Switzerland. Retrieved from http://www.cercles2014.org/docs/programme_and_abstracts.pdf

Section 2.
Enhancing practices

6. Feedback on individual academic presentations: exploring Finnish university students' experiences and preferences

Adrienn Károly[1]

Abstract

With an increasing emphasis on measuring the outcomes of learning in higher education, assessment is gaining an ever more prominent role in curriculum design and development as well as in instructional practices. In formative assessment, feedback is regarded as a powerful pedagogical tool driving student engagement and deep learning. The efficacy of feedback, however, depends on a multitude of factors. From a learning cultures perspective (James 2014), assessment strives for an appropriate balance between structural constraints and individual agency. To have a better grasp of how feedback functions in practice, it is useful to investigate students' views and preferences as well as the immediate and wider contexts shaping these constructs. The small-scale research reported in this article explores Finnish university students' prior experiences and initial preconceptions regarding feedback on individual academic presentations with a view to enhancing feedback practices.

Keywords: feedback, higher education language learning, academic expertise, student attitudes and beliefs.

---

1. Language Centre, University of Jyväskylä, Finland; adrienn.karoly@jyu.fi

How to cite this chapter: Károly, A. (2015). Feedback on individual academic presentations: exploring Finnish university students' experiences and preferences. In J. Jalkanen, E. Jokinen, & P. Taalas (Eds), *Voices of pedagogical development - Expanding, enhancing and exploring higher education language learning* (pp. 105-130). Dublin: Research-publishing.net. doi:10.14705/rpnet.2015.000289

Chapter 6

1. Introduction

Higher education is facing a number of challenges worldwide, from changing industry demands and increasing calls for accountability and quality to continuously expanding and diversifying student populations and constraints on funding as well as resources. These trends influence not only the positions and interests of various stakeholders but also the educational experience. Some researchers have voiced deep concerns about the negative consequences of these tendencies, which lead to growing pressures and tensions (Gibbs 2006; Hussey & Smith 2002). For example, due to the intensifying competition, economic interests and market pressures often dominate over educational and professional considerations at multiple levels of decision-making (Amsler & Bolsmann 2012; Chapleo 2005). Others have called for more comprehensive research on the linguistic corollaries of globalisation and internationalisation, particularly as they relate to the spread of English as the language of instruction in non-native contexts (Marginson & van der Wende 2007).

Assessment, often regarded as a central component of teaching and learning (Ashford-Rowe, Herrington & Brown 2014; Boud & Falchikov 2006; Clark 2012; Sambell, McDowell & Montgomery 2013; Wiliam 2011), has been gaining increased research attention in the context of higher education, where the effects of the above-mentioned factors are most directly felt. Assessment practices are influenced not only by dominant educational philosophies but also by supranational policy actors. Since the launch of the European Higher Education Area (EHEA) in 2010, the EU has placed special emphasis on improving the quality of teaching and learning with a view to enhancing mobility and employability. Even though the education policy remains the prerogative of the Member States, EU policies play an important role in informing institutional decision-making.

In the Standards and Guidelines for Quality Assurance in the EHEA (ESG), developed in 2005 and promoted through an EU recommendation, assessment is seen as instrumental in enhancing student learning and evaluating the effectiveness of teaching (ENQA 2009). The ESG represents a milestone in

European higher education policy because it emphasises cooperation and at the same time acknowledges the diversity and autonomy of higher education institutions (Stensaker, Harvey, Huisman, Langfeldt & Westerheijden 2010). On the other hand, it also signals a growing focus on normative conceptions of good practices in higher education. Capturing this tension, the learning cultures approach to assessment (James 2014) suggests that assessment is a complex social practice, shaped by the dialectic relationship between structure and agency. James (2014) argues that in order to enhance assessment practices, it is important to reflect on social interests and influences (including their wider cultural dimensions) and investigate students' and teachers' collective and individual beliefs and views.

The small-scale, localised empirical research reported in this article was conducted within an ongoing project aiming to improve feedback practices at the Language Centre of the University of Jyväskylä. It explores a group of Finnish university students' prior experiences along with their views and preferences regarding feedback related to individual presentations on compulsory academic English courses. Since there can be substantial differences between students in terms of prior experiences and views, exploring these can provide valuable information for teachers. Furthermore, tailoring assessment to the students' individual beliefs and expectations can make students more engaged with their learning. Motivated by these aims, the study addresses the following research questions:

- How much experience do students have making individual oral presentations at the start of the first compulsory academic English course?

- What kind of previous experiences do students have regarding feedback in the case of individual oral presentations?

- What are the students' specific views and expectations concerning various types of feedback related to the preparation and delivery of individual oral presentations?

2. The concepts of *assessment for learning* and *feedback landscape*

Assessment has two main types depending on its primary purpose. *Summative assessment* measures student achievement at the end of the instructional process by comparing it against some standard. A certain level of performance is required for progression or certification, but grades can also serve quality assurance purposes. On the other hand, *formative assessment* aims to enhance student learning and motivation through continuous feedback (e.g. Gardner, Harlen, Hayward & Stobart 2010; Sambell et al. 2013; Wiliam 2011).

Formative assessment helps students to develop into self-regulated learners, so it guides learning in the long term (cf. sustainable assessment, Boud 2000, and authentic assessment, Sambell et al. 2013). The terms feed-forward and feed-up also imply a process-based, formative conceptualisation of assessment, viewing feedback as a means to enhance future learning in educational and workplace contexts (Hounsell, McCune, Hounsell & Litjens 2008). Besides supporting student learning, formative assessment provides valuable information for the teacher about the effectiveness of the instructional process (Bloxham & Boyd 2008).

While the term *assessment of learning* refers solely to summative assessment, *assessment for learning* includes both summative and formative elements, and is based on the idea that all forms of assessment should contribute to student learning. Therefore, it can be considered a holistic model of assessment. According to Sambell et al. (2013: 6–7), it is underpinned by six principles: (1) using authentic and complex assessment tasks, (2) relying on both summative and formative assessment, (3) providing opportunities for practice through a wide range of low-stakes activities, which help to increase students' competence and build their confidence before high-stakes summative assessment takes place, (4) offering different forms of formal feedback from multiple sources, (5) providing opportunities for diverse forms of informal feedback from various sources, and (6) developing students' self-regulatory capacities, which help them become effective lifelong learners.

In contemporary educational research, feedback is regarded as a key dimension of assessment for learning (Biggs & Tang 2011; Hattie & Timperley 2007), and researchers underline its contextual and socially constructed nature (Boud & Falchikov 2006; Evans 2013; James 2014; Wiliam 2011). Evans's (2013) notion of the *feedback landscape* implies that although theoretical principles of effective feedback designs can be identified, their implementation in a given context is not always simple. The way individuals experience and respond to feedback depends on an array of personal and contextual variables. In an attempt to illustrate the complexity of feedback exchanges between students and teacher, Evans (2013: 98) lists the following twelve key factors discussed in the literature: (1) ability/intelligence/levels of understanding of academic content and process, (2) personality, (3) gender, (4) culture/ethnicity, (5) social and cultural capital, (6) previous experiences of learning and schema, (7) attributions/motivation/self-efficacy/resilience, (8) perceived relevance of the task/support, (9) ability to navigate the learning communities and filter relevant information, (10) beliefs about learning and expectations of the learning environment, (11) cognitive styles/approaches to learning, and (12) perceived role(s) within the academic learning communities. Evans (2013) mentions three additional mediators affecting teacher feedback: (13) awareness of other contexts students are working in, (14) alignment with other modules, and (15) knowledge of students and level of adaptation/affordances. Teacher feedback is in the centre, but the author also emphasises the role of alternative sources of feedback.

Unfortunately, teachers typically work under tight constraints of time and resources, and the rationale behind using peer feedback is often simply to shift some of the burden of assessment onto the students to ease heavy teacher workloads (Evans 2013). Another problem can be a mismatch between student and teacher beliefs about the essential role of feedback. Nevertheless, if designed and implemented in an interactive, timely, and integrated manner, feedback can be highly motivational. By using objective and easily accessible criteria, applying clear principles, providing desirable models and guidance, and training students in giving and receiving feedback, teachers can greatly enhance student learning. Ideally, the learning objectives are closely aligned not only with instructional but also with assessment methods (Topping 2010).

With regard to self-assessment, which is an important component of self-regulation, Evans (2013) emphasises that its efficacy also depends on several factors. She suggests moving from subjective self-assessment/self-reflection practices to self-directed assessment utilising external feedback, which can lead to a more objective assessment of one's own abilities. Evans (2013) also stresses that the development of self-assessment skills is a continuous process, requiring instructional scaffolding as well as consideration of the differences in students' abilities and dispositions. While most contemporary research underlines the crucial role of collaboration in promoting self-regulatory capacities, Evans (2013) notes that for more introverted students, tasks based on independent work might be more natural and productive. As Cain (2012) has pointed out, the ideal of the extraverted personality prevails in contemporary education and working life, while introversion is generally associated with shyness and ineffectiveness, and is often considered inferior or even pathological. The importance of group work and collaboration is undeniable, but through the exclusive or uncritical use of such activities (which are more suited for extroverted students), teachers may hinder autonomy and independent thought and unwittingly promote group thinking and conformity. Since using certain types of feedback – such as public group peer feedback or face-to-face teacher feedback – might not be suitable for everyone, teachers should provide options for students based on their individual preferences.

3. Research design

3.1. Setting and participants

The research was conducted at the University of Jyväskylä in the fall semester of the 2014–15 academic year. A questionnaire was sent to 115 students enrolled in the first compulsory English course (Academic Reading or Academic Reading and Communication Skills), of whom 40 returned it (representing a 34.7% response rate), 6 males and 34 females. Their age ranged from 19 to 31 years ($M = 23.1$, $SD = 3.15$). The students were studying at the following faculties (number of students in brackets): social sciences (16), humanities (11), natural sciences (12), and sports and health sciences (1), majoring in psychology (2), sociology (7), social work (4), philosophy (2), social and public policy (1), history (1), ethnology (1), speech communication (1), Swedish (2), literature (2), Finnish (3), art history (1), environmental science and technology (3), physics (4), accounting (2), mathematics (3), and sport medicine (1). They have spent from 1 to 13 years in higher education ($M = 2.9$, mode = 2).

3.2. Data collection and analysis

An online questionnaire was used to collect data. This instrument was chosen over interviews because it enabled the collection of both quantitative and qualitative data from a larger group of participants, it ensured anonymity to the respondents, and it was easier to administer with students studying at different departments. Initially two language versions of the questionnaire were developed, and the first version of the English language questionnaire was piloted during the spring semester with 37 students. The original questions were refined or modified after identifying ambiguities and the range of possible answers. The final version of the questionnaire was sent by e-mail to students registered for the compulsory academic English courses offered in the 2014 autumn semester. Participation in the research was voluntary.

The first four questions elicited background information from the participants (gender, age, number of years spent in higher education, and main subject). The main part of the questionnaire comprised 27 items, including both closed and open-ended questions. Some of the questions were contingency questions, limited to a subset of respondents based on their answers to an earlier filter question. The questionnaire consisted of two sections: the first one (Questions 1–9) focused on students' previous feedback experiences related to individual oral presentations during their university studies, while the second part addressed their views and preferences concerning various types of feedback related to individual presentations. Numerical data were analysed by descriptive statistical methods (calculating frequency distributions and central tendencies), and a thematic analysis was conducted on the qualitative data obtained from the open-ended questions. In the coding, a data-driven perspective was adopted

(Boyatzis 1998), whereby data was first categorised into major themes (based on recurring patterns emerging from the responses), which formed the basis of the subsequent analysis.

4. Results and discussion

4.1. Students' previous feedback experiences

The first question was related to students' prior experiences preparing and delivering an individual academic presentation. Twenty-eight respondents (70%) reported having had experience making such presentations, primarily in courses related to their main subject and/or in other compulsory language courses. 30% of the respondents, however, had no prior experience, suggesting that the individual presentation was a less frequently used activity in some departments during the first and second year, while group presentations seemed to be common.

The results indicating that students started the compulsory English course with varying degrees of experience has important implications for teachers. According to the literature, previous experiences strongly influence motivation, self-efficacy (confidence in one's ability) and resilience (ability to cope with stress) as well as the perceived difficulty of the task (Evans 2013). Students who are inexperienced in making individual presentations will probably require more guidance in the preparation stage and more feedback from multiple sources following the final presentation. It should also be noted that although some students have experience making group presentations, preparing and delivering an individual presentation requires additional competences and different strategies.

Questions 2 and 3 were targeted only at those students who reported having had experience making individual presentations ($n = 28$). They told who they had received feedback from in the preparation stage and after the final performance. The respondents marked the types of feedback they had received (see Figure 1).

Figure 1. Frequency of receiving feedback from different sources *before* and *after* the individual presentation

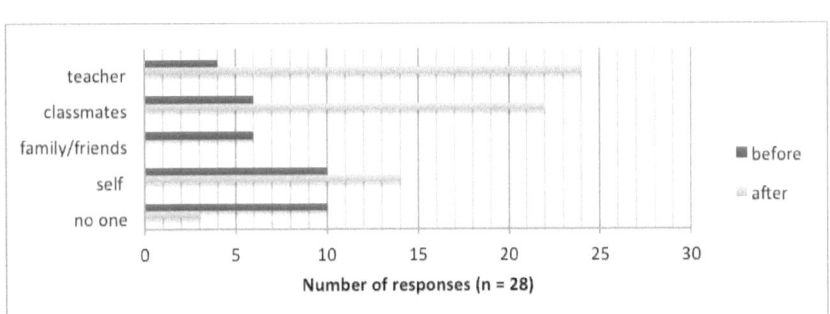

In the preparation stage, feedback seemed to be less common although ten respondents reported having received feedback from peers and family members/ friends respectively. Feedback appeared to be more typical after the presentation, particularly from the teacher (24 students) and peers (22 students), although half of the respondents had also had to reflect on or analyse their own performance. Interestingly, four respondents indicated that they had not received any feedback after delivering the presentation.

Questions 4 and 5 focused more closely on teacher feedback that students received after the presentation. The respondents ($n = 28$) first had to select the forms of feedback they had received from a pre-given list. Feedback was divided into six main types along the following three dimensions: degree of specificity (general vs. more detailed), medium (oral vs. written) and mode (public/open vs. private/individual). Based on the responses, it seems that oral feedback was the most typical from the teacher. General oral feedback given in front of the others appears to be the most frequent (13 students), but oral feedback (both general and more detailed) given face-to-face was also common (marked by ten and nine students respectively). Written teacher feedback seemed to be less typical. Only four students had received general written feedback individually, and only three got more detailed, individual feedback. Teachers' preference for oral feedback might be related to the fact that giving written feedback is more time-consuming. On the other hand, some teachers may perceive oral feedback as more effective due to its interactive nature. Still, as Evans (2013) points out, using a generic 'best-practice' strategy is not always a good idea as some students may find detailed written feedback more useful (as will be shown later in this research as well). Finally, four students reported that they had not received any feedback from the teacher after their presentation. This finding is rather unexpected as researchers emphasise the key role of teacher feedback in student learning.

In Question 6, respondents who received feedback from the teacher after the presentation ($n = 24$) specified what aspects of the presentation were mentioned in the feedback. Teacher comments were mostly related to structure (mentioned by ten students), language (including grammar, vocabulary, and pronunciation; eight students), nonverbal communication (including the use of voice; eight students), topic (eight students), argumentation/reasoning/ criticality (five students), slides (four students), professional background knowledge (two students), and cohesion (one student). Interestingly, argumentation, which is related to critical thinking and is supposed to be a key feature of academic presentations, was only rarely mentioned in the teacher feedback.

The next question focused on students' previous experiences regarding peer feedback after the individual presentation. Students ($n = 28$) selected the forms of feedback they had received on a pre-given list (note: students could mark more than one option). Based on their responses, it seems that teachers used different peer feedback practices. Among those who got feedback from the others, the most common type of feedback was general oral feedback in class (eight students), followed by general written feedback from everyone (seven respondents), more detailed oral feedback in class (five students), and more detailed written feedback from everyone (four students). Interestingly, eight students reported having received no peer feedback at all.

The next two questions were concerned with self-analysis as a type of feedback. In response to the question whether the respondents had to reflect on or analyse their own performance after the individual presentation, 12 students gave a positive answer, while 16 students indicated that they were not required to do this task ($n = 28$). The following question was targeted only at those students who had to analyse themselves ($n = 12$), and aimed to find out whether the self-analysis was based on a video recording of the presentation. Half of these respondents (six students) indicated that their presentations had been video recorded.

Finally, the last question in this section was related to the task of students grading their own performance ($n = 28$). Only five students reported that they had had to do this after the individual presentation, indicating that self-grading was not a common task. Indeed, self-grading is a rather controversial issue, with some researchers emphasising the risk of grade inflation. This means that students tend to give higher grades to themselves, particularly in high-stakes situations (Andrade & Valtcheva 2009). Other researchers, however, argue that if designed and implemented appropriately, self-grading can increase student motivation, responsibility, ownership, and the level of engagement with the assessment criteria, and can help students to improve their ability to judge their own achievement or performance more objectively (Kearney 2013; Strong, Davis & Hawks 2004).

Overall, the results of the first part of the survey indicate that students arrived at the compulsory classes with different feedback experiences, which could have strongly influenced the way they valued, interpreted and responded to various forms and sources of feedback. Sambell et al. (2013) have argued that addressing these diverse needs and preferences can significantly increase student engagement. Students more fully grasp the relevance of different activities and become more aware of the links between courses that often appear to be isolated and unrelated with repetitive activities and assignments. In Evans's (2013) feedback landscape model, the academic learning community includes the immediate academic community (programme of study) as well as wider social (personal and professional) communities. By building on students' previous experiences of feedback exchanges within this complex network, teachers can make students more aware of the continuity and recursive nature of the learning process as well as their own learning progress.

4.2. Students' views and preferences regarding feedback

The second section of the questionnaire focused on students' views and preferences regarding various types of feedback related to individual presentations. The first question aimed to explore students' perceptions about the main purpose of feedback ($n = 40$). The analysis of the responses revealed four main functions for feedback. The first one implies a technical approach and is related to the role of feedback in the development of certain skills (in the case of oral presentations primarily communication and presentation skills). 31 students emphasised this function of feedback. The second general theme emerging from the responses has a psychological orientation. 11 students highlighted the role of feedback in increasing personality traits such as self-confidence and self-esteem. Nine respondents placed the main emphasis on how feedback helped them understand themselves better, as well as see themselves and the world from a different perspective. Finally, two students underlined the importance of feedback as a form of interaction between individuals. According to them, feedback can serve as a useful vehicle for assessing the effects of communication and checking whether the audience has understood the message the way it was intended. Interestingly, two students seemed to be unsure about the main purpose of feedback, which may be linked to previous negative experiences, originating from a lack of clarity and guidance or the methods used by the teacher.

In the next two questions, the respondents had to rate the importance of different types of feedback on a 4-point scale (ranging from very important to not important at all) in the case of feedback from the teacher, peers, self and family members/friends. Figure 2 and Figure 3 summarise students' preferences before and after the presentation, respectively.

In the preparation stage, the majority of the respondents seemed to attach high importance to self-reflection, with 37.5% rating it as very important, and 50% as important. With regard to peer feedback, 65% of the students found it very important or important, while 35% considered it less important. In comparing the responses with those given to the next question, it seems that peer feedback was generally regarded as much more important after the final performance, with 40% rating it as very important and 60% as important. Interestingly, almost 60% of the respondents liked receiving feedback from relatives or friends while preparing for the presentation.

Figure 2. Frequency distribution of students' views on the importance of receiving feedback from different sources *before* the presentation (*n* = 40)

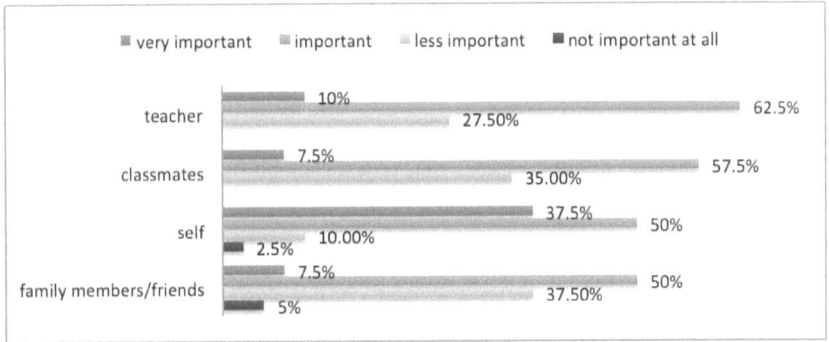

Figure 3. Frequency distribution of students' views on the importance of receiving feedback from different sources *after* the presentation (*n* = 40)

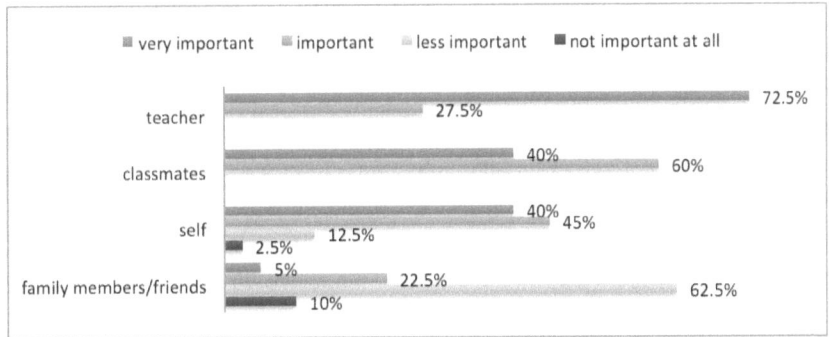

These people did not necessarily have the competence to judge the overall quality of the presentation, but they could easily comment on such aspects as the clarity of the main message, non-verbal communication, interaction, and the design of the slides. Relying on friends and family members as sources of feedback can also help students to overcome their nervousness, particularly if peer feedback is not used before the presentation. Concerning feedback after the presentation, 75% of the respondents attached the highest importance to receiving feedback from the teacher although peer feedback and self-reflection were also seen as very important or important. Students' preference for teacher feedback is somewhat natural although Evans (2013) underlines that for some students, the teacher may not be the most valued source of feedback. Other authors emphasise that trust plays an essential role in teacher–student relationships, which can easily be undermined if 'transmissive-style rituals' dominate teachers' instructional practices, denying the social and iterative nature of feedback (Boud & Molloy 2013). Finally, assessment practices that rely too much on teacher feedback do not reflect real-life settings, so students often regard them as inauthentic and thus demotivating (Sambell et al. 2013). Therefore, students need to realise that since people have different beliefs, values and preferences, in real life different individuals can judge the same performance or interpret the same message differently.

The next item in the questionnaire was an open-ended question, which focused on students' preferences regarding teacher feedback when preparing the presentation. More specifically, it aimed to explore what aspects of the presentation the respondents would like to receive comments on from the teacher. The most common theme emerging from the responses was the structure of the presentation, with 16 students mentioning it. Within this group, three students mentioned that they would prefer to get feedback on how to start the presentation in an effective and interactive way. Nine students reported that they would like to receive feedback on the topic of the presentation beforehand. Other common themes mentioned were related to content (seven students), clarity of focus (four students), planning the length of the presentation (four students) and grammar (three students). Six students, however, indicated that comments from the teacher in the preparation stage were not necessary. One respondent emphasised that he or she prefers working autonomously, while another student stressed the importance of learning from his or her own mistakes. The others seemed to be more concerned with the time and effort that this type of feedback requires from the teacher. The responses suggest that feedback in the preparation stage could work most effectively if it remains optional. It is also clear from the responses that even if the general principles of making a good presentation are covered in class, some students require practical help related to the particular presentation they are working on.

The next question was concerned with teacher feedback after the final presentation. On a pre-given list, the respondents ($n = 40$) rated the importance of receiving teacher feedback regarding various aspects of the presentation. The list contained 22 specific aspects related to structure, content, language, and the delivery of the presentation, each of which had to be rated on a 4-point scale (ranging from very important to not important at all). The responses indicate that students generally considered all these aspects important to some extent, so the response 'not important at all' was extremely rare. The aspects related to structure and content were generally seen as very important or important, while students' attitudes were more mixed regarding the aspects related to language and delivery, with the responses being more evenly distributed across the categories. Students seem to be particularly divided on some of the language-related aspects. For example, pronunciation was seen as very important by seven, important by 16, and less important by 17 students, while grammar was considered to be very important by three, important by 19, less important by 17 students, and not important at all by one student. With regard to general/academic and field-specific vocabulary, the number of students who rated them as very important or important was higher than in the case of pronunciation and grammar although these numbers were still lower than for structure and content-related aspects. The aspect that was considered very important or important by the highest number of students was the overall structure of the presentation (39 students altogether), while comments on the design of the slides were viewed as less important or not important at all by the highest number of the respondents (27 students). These findings seem to confirm arguments that assessment should focus primarily on essential generic and transferable skills, such as critical thinking, innovation, or creativity (Kearney 2013) rather than on technical competence or language, particularly in the case of individual academic presentations.

With regard to students' views on the most useful forms of teacher feedback after the presentation ($n = 40$), the responses indicate a marked preference for detailed feedback given individually – either orally or in writing (40% and 30% respectively) – although general written individual feedback was also marked by six students (15%). At the same time, fewer respondents seemed to like general oral feedback. The most common justification for favouring written feedback was that it is possible to re-read it, reflect on it at leisure, and use it as a point of reference in the future. Students who favoured individual feedback emphasised that they found it more personal. According to some respondents, individual feedback is more effective if given face-to-face as they have the opportunity to ask questions and react to the teacher's comments immediately, making communication more interactive and authentic. Those respondents who preferred general oral feedback given publicly (in front of the others) emphasised that this enables other students to learn from the discussion, regardless of the actual quality of the performance.

The next question was concerned with teacher feedback during the delivery of the presentation. Almost all respondents ($n = 40$) expressed a dislike for any kind of comments during the presentation except for technical issues and problems related to voice and tempo of speech. A few students further pointed out that nonverbal cues (an encouraging smile or gesture) or some motivating words could be helpful for those students who are overly nervous.

Regarding numerical teacher assessment, the responses were rather mixed. Students' views were explored through two questions, one using a 5-point Likert scale (1= not useful…5 = very useful), followed by an open-ended question asking for justification. Out of the 40 respondents, 14 (35%) had a neutral opinion, rating the usefulness of grades in the middle of the scale, six students (15%) marked it as less useful, and 12 students (30%) as somewhat useful. On the two extremes, five students (12.5%) regarded grades as not useful at all, while three students (7.5%) thought that grading was very useful. For justification, the respondents cited various reasons. Highlighting the benefits, students emphasised that grades could serve as a concrete and useful point of reference in determining their own performance and level of competence, and that high grades can be highly motivating, giving them a sense of achievements. On the other hand, one student underlined that performance in a particular situation on a given day is always influenced by a multitude of factors, so it does not necessarily reflect the actual level of competence. Some respondents see grades as rather vague, subjective, and unreliable. Within this group, one student mentioned that grades do not take into account the whole learning process but measure only the outcome, while another student openly criticised the standard numerical grading scale (1–5), suggesting a 3-point qualitative scale. This comment implies that the meaning of grades and the summative evaluation criteria are not always clear for students. Overall, most respondents emphasised that grades should always be accompanied by qualitative feedback, providing more concrete evaluation and guidance. These findings seem to confirm recent criticisms that summative assessment in contemporary higher education is extremely problematic and disorderly, and thus grades can no longer be considered as reliable sources of information about student achievement (e.g. Knight 2002). Knight (2002) also argued that the problems surrounding summative assessment are so deeply rooted that it is difficult to change current practices without touching on philosophical issues.

The next group of questions were related to peer feedback. The first item was an open-ended question exploring students' preferences regarding peer feedback while preparing the presentation. The majority of the respondents ($n = 40$) indicated that they would like to get some general comments on the content and structure of the presentation, particularly concerning the choice of the topic (12 students), the overall logic and clarity of the ideas/argumentation (11 students), and the logic of the structure (nine students). Five students emphasised that they want the others to give constructive feedback with specific suggestions on how to improve the presentation (e.g. ideas to clarify, elaborate on, add or delete). Interestingly, five students also found it important to get peer feedback on aspects related to the delivery of the presentation, such as self-confidence and voice, which suggests that for these students a trial, small-group presentation might be extremely helpful. Other less common (and more specific) themes emerging from the responses were peer comments on the slides (three students) and language use (three students).

With regard to the type of peer feedback after the final presentation, responses show a clear preference for general as opposed to more detailed feedback, mostly because of time constraints and the perceived academic ability of other students. Half of the respondents favoured general oral feedback in class ($n = 40$). General feedback focuses mainly on the overall performance and not so much on specific aspects, so this finding seems to confirm previous research results pointing out that non-directive peer feedback is usually more effective (Cho & MacArthur 2010). According to Topping (2010), peer feedback is closely linked with issues of trust and psychological safety, which can be lower if the feedback is too analytical and directive. The author emphasises that the reception of directive feedback also depends on the differences between the (perceived) level of competence of the feedback giver and receiver. If the difference is perceived to be large, the receiver of the feedback is more likely to interpret directive feedback as interfering and confining, whereas if the difference is seen as small, even specific suggestions might be accepted without evoking negative feelings (Topping 2010). This underlines the importance of training students in giving peer feedback. The most typical reason that the respondents cited for their preference for general oral feedback was that oral feedback leads to a more natural, personal and interactive discussion, from which other students can also benefit. 12 students (30%), however, expressed preference for general written feedback from peers because they saw it as less direct and thus less hurtful, particularly if it included negative criticism. Another typical justification for favouring written feedback was that it could be re-read at home and used in the future. One respondent also highlighted that Finnish students were generally reluctant to provide negative criticism, particularly in face-to-face situations, which makes written feedback more honest, particularly if given anonymously. This is an important comment, pointing to the culturally embedded nature of assessment. It is an important feature of Evans's (2013) feedback landscape model that social interaction can also refer to situations when the other person is not physically present, which implies that written feedback can also be carried out in an interactive way. Finally, one student emphasised the crucial role of the teacher in providing the students with clear criteria in advance and explicit guidance on how to give meaningful feedback.

With regard to specific features of the presentation that the respondents expected their peers to comment on after the presentation, the most commonly mentioned aspects were related to content (including the topic and argumentation, mentioned by 34 students), delivery (30 students) and the structure of the presentation (16 students), with some respondents explicitly mentioning language-related issues and the design of the slides (eight and six students respectively).

Finally, the last four questions were concerned with self-assessment. The first question used a 5-point scale (1 = useful at all…5 = very useful), on which the respondents ($n = 40$) had to rate the usefulness of the activity of watching their videotaped presentation and analyse their own performance. Attitudes towards this activity were rather mixed, and the responses were fairly evenly distributed across the scale, with the same proportion of students rating the usefulness of this activity as 3 and 4 (ten students respectively, 25%). Similarly, the same number of students (seven respectively, 17.5%) chose the two end points of the scale, and six students (15%) marked the usefulness of this activity as a 2. The respondents cited multiple reasons for the high ratings (4 or 5). For example, some of them believed that this activity would promote a deeper self-analysis and allow them to see themselves from the outside, focusing also on aspects of the performance that are less conscious, such as body language, voice and errors related to language use. According to some respondents, watching the video could also help to see themselves more objectively, instead of relying on a subjective and often false (overly positive or negative) picture of their performance. Another advantage mentioned was that a more objective self-image could make the interpretation and acceptance of peer feedback easier. Those respondents who were more critical about the use of video recording were mostly afraid that watching themselves could be a painful, awkward and demotivating experience, in particular if something went wrong during the presentation. Another potential risk reported was that some students might become too critical of themselves and end up overanalysing their own performance. Some students were afraid that the presence of the video camera might negatively affect their performance, particularly when they have to use a foreign language. On the other hand, several students admitted that even though they had never been recorded before, they found the idea exciting.

This openness seems to confirm the idea that new and challenging technology-enhanced assessment tasks that provide opportunities for active engagement and authentic learning can be motivating. However, as it has been pointed out in the literature, the use of technology should be complemented by dialogic teaching methods emphasising such aspects as critical thinking and teachers' cognitive presence (Hosler & Arend 2012), the level of academic challenge, the proportion of collaborative learning, and the amount and quality of interaction between teacher and students (Evans 2013). According to James (2014), assessment practices adopting a humanistic perspective enhance student learning and engagement by emphasising autonomy, critical and independent thinking, creativity, self-reflection and collaboration. This approach advocates holistic assessment strategies, which take into account the complex nature of learning as well as the role of interpersonal relationships and affective factors, most importantly trust.

The last two items in the questionnaire were related to the activity of self-grading. On a 5-point scale ranging from not useful at all to very useful, the respondents had to rate the activity of awarding a grade to themselves followed by a brief justification. Attitudes towards this task were mixed, with the majority of respondents (14 students, 35%) marking this activity as a 3 in the middle of the scale. This implies that they did not have a clear opinion of this activity, or that their opinions were mixed. Eight students (27.5%) rated this activity as a 4, emphasising such benefits as the ability to objectively evaluate themselves and measure their performance against their own expectations, as well as the opportunity of being involved in the final evaluation. These students also mentioned that such empowerment could increase not only motivation but also their need for higher achievement, an idea highlighted also by Sendziuk (2010). A few students pointed out that this activity would allow them to focus not only on their actual performance at a particular time, but also on their overall effort and learning progress. It has been argued that self-grading can enhance students' engagement with the assessment criteria, particularly if the students are involved in the creation of the criteria (Kearney 2013). Many students, however, were sceptical about the usefulness of this activity, emphasising that self-grading can be extremely difficult. One student was concerned about the way the self-awarded grade would count in the final evaluation, and another respondent mentioned that some students might under- or overestimate their skills or their performance. Another typical explanation for the negative response was that awarding a grade, even if it were justified, would not necessarily help them improve. These attitudes might be linked to the general negative perceptions about summative assessment in higher education, which has shifted attention from learning to documentation and criteria compliance (Torrance 2007). Nevertheless, with the help of instructional practices that combine various formative and summative assessment methods, self-grading can have a key role in the overall assessment design. In fact, Hattie's (2009) comprehensive research concluded that self-report grades have the highest positive effect on learning. Finally, an important element of self-grading is the timing of the activity. Ideally, students are asked to do this task after reading the feedback from the teacher and/or peers although one student noted that it would also be interesting to compare the similarities and differences between the self-awarded grade and the received feedback. Fischer (2011) mentioned an interesting initial self-grading activity (combined with self-grading after receiving other forms of feedback), in which she asked students to evaluate their work based on the time and energy invested in the whole task. She concluded that a prior self-evaluation positively affected students' achievement, and encouraged them to pay more attention to quality. On the other hand, because some students tend to overestimate the importance of time and energy invested into a task, the teacher should make it clear that in real-life situations, these kinds of input are typically not taken into account when others assess the overall quality of their performance or achievement. Along the same line, Boud and Falchikov (2006) argued that in order to enhance lifelong learning skills, students should be able to also evaluate their own work without relying too much on other people's judgements.

According to James (2014), the interactionist perspective, which is widely known among sociologists and educational theorists, seems to receive less attention in actual practice. This approach underlines the crucial role of interaction between students and teachers, which is important because students and teachers often hold different individual and collective views about different aspects of assessment. For instance, they can differ in their perceptions of how ability is related to academic achievement, and thus can interpret the function of grades and feedback differently (Becker, Geer & Hughes 1995). Similarly, the messages that teachers want to convey through feedback and the ways students interpret the messages can be different (Hyland 2013). Students' perceptions can sometimes create a 'hidden curriculum', stemming from the differences between the officially declared aims and forms of assessment and the actual assessment practices (Sambell & McDowell 1998: 392). Since the hidden curriculum is thought to have a profound influence on learning, it seems that a more open dialogue is needed between students and teachers in order to better understand each other's values, views and expectations.

5. Conclusions

This article set out to explore students' previous experiences and current preferences regarding feedback on individual academic presentations. The findings suggest that it is useful for teachers to adopt a *learning cultures perspective* (James 2014) and take into account the social nature of assessment, including the wide range of individual and contextual variables as well as the important role of interpersonal relationships and affective factors. Contemporary research has pointed out that despite the diversity of feedback practices, students often fail to engage with and benefit from feedback. This might be related to the dominance of a technical perspective in assessment, which places the main emphasis on such general principles as "fairness, transparency, efficiency, the avoidance of student appeals or litigation, reliability and validity in relation to standards, and coherence between assessment processes and learning outcomes" (James 2014: 156), and advocates analytic assessment schemes. While these principles are undoubtedly crucial, James (2014) argues that problems can arise if there is an overly heavy reliance on the codification of learning and generic, standardised assessment practices without critical reflection. Others have also pointed out that increased transparency may result in instrumentalism and criteria compliance to the detriment of learning (Torrance 2007).

If, however, genuine learning is not the primary concern of teachers, students may not capitalise on feedback. Therefore, there is a pressing need for a better alignment between the officially declared learning objectives and the actual instructional and assessment methods. The research reported here was limited in its scope, but the findings seem to strengthen previous arguments about student feedback experiences. Namely, because students bring different experiences to the classroom and hold heterogeneous views about the nature of effective feedback, teachers should adopt assessment methods that engage students more and provide options regarding the most preferred types of feedback.

References

Amsler, S. S. & Bolsmann, C. 2012. University ranking as social exclusion. *British Journal of Sociology of Education, 33* (2), 283–301. doi:10.1080/01425692.2011.649835

Andrade, H., & Valtcheva, A. 2009. Promoting learning and achievement through self-assessment. *Theory into Practice, 48* (1), 12–19. doi:10.1080/00405840802577544

Ashford-Rowe, K., Herrington, J. & Brown, C. 2014. Establishing the critical elements that determine authentic assessment. *Assessment & Evaluation in Higher Education, 39* (2), 205–222. doi:10.1080/02602938.2013.819566

Becker, H. S., Geer, B., & Hughes, E. C. 1995. *Making the grade: the academic side of college life*. New Brunswick: Transaction Publishers. (Originally published 1968).

Biggs, J. & Tang, C. 2011. *Teaching for quality learning at university: what the student does* (4th ed.). Maidenhead: McGraw-Hill/Society for Research into Higher Education/Open University Press.

Bloxham, S. & Boyd, P. 2008. *Developing effective assessment in higher education: a practical guide*. Maidenhead: Open University Press.

Boud, D. 2000. Sustainable assessment: rethinking assessment for the learning society. *Studies in Continuing Education, 22* (2), 151–167. doi:10.1080/713695728

Boud, D. & Falchikov, N. 2006. Aligning assessment with long-term learning. *Assessment & Evaluation in Higher Education, 31* (4). 399–413. doi:10.1080/02602930600679050

Boud, D. & Molloy, E. (eds.). 2013. *Feedback in higher and professional education*. London: Routledge.

Boyatzis, R. E. 1998. *Transforming qualitative information: thematic analysis and code development.* Thousand Oaks: SAGE Publications.

Cain, S. 2012. *Quiet: the power of introverts in a world that can't stop talking.* New York: Crown Publishers.

Chapleo, C. 2005. Do universities have 'successful' brands? *International Journal of Educational Advancement, 6* (1), 54–64. doi:10.1057/palgrave.ijea.2140233

Cho, K. & MacArthur, C. 2010. Student revision with peer and expert reviewing. *Learning and Instruction, 20* (4), 328–338. doi:10.1016/j.learninstruc.2009.08.006

Clark, I. 2012. Formative assessment: assessment is for self-regulated learning. *Educational Psychology Review, 24*, 205–249. doi:10.1007/s10648-011-9191-6

ENQA (European Association for Quality Assurance in Higher Education). 2009. *Standards and guidelines for quality assurance in the European higher education area* (3rd ed.). Retrieved from http://www.enqa.eu/wp-content/uploads/2013/06/ESG_3edition-2.pdf

Evans, C. 2013. Making sense of assessment feedback in higher education. *Review of Educational Research, 83* (1), 70–120. doi:10.3102/0034654312474350

Fischer, M. 2011. A társas és önértékelés szerepe a fordítás oktatásában [The role of peer- and self-assessment in translation teaching]. In J. Dróth (ed.) *Szaknyelv és Szakfordítás. Tanulmányok a szakfordítás és a fordítóképzés aktuális témáiról.* Gödöllő: Szent István Egyetem GTK. 76–82.

Gardner, J., Harlen, W., Hayward, L. & Stobart, G. 2010. *Developing teacher assessment.* Maidenhead: Open University Press.

Gibbs, G. 2006. Why assessment is changing. In K. Clegg & C. Bryan (Eds.), *Innovative assessment in higher education.* London: Routledge. 11–22.

Hattie, J. 2009. *Visible learning: a synthesis of 800+ meta-analyses on achievement.* London: Routledge.

Hattie, J. & Timperley, H. 2007. The power of feedback. *Review of Educational Research, 77* (1), 81–112. doi:10.3102/003465430298487

Hosler, K. A. & Arend, B. D. 2012. The importance of course design, feedback, and facilitation: student perceptions of the relationship between teaching presence and cognitive presence. *Educational Media International, 49* (3), 217–229. doi:10.1080/09523987.2012.738014

Hounsell, D., McCune, V., Hounsell, J., & Litjens, J. 2008. The quality of guidance and feedback to students. *Higher Education Research and Development, 27* (1), 55–67. doi:10.1080/07294360701658765

Hussey, T. & Smith, P. 2002. The trouble with learning outcomes. *Active Learning in Higher Education, 3* (3), 220–230. doi:10.1177/1469787402003003003

Hyland, K. 2013. Student perceptions of hidden messages in teacher written feedback. *Studies in Educational Evaluation, 39* (3), 180–187. doi:10.1016/j.stueduc.2013.06.003

James, D. 2014. Investigating the curriculum through assessment practice in higher education: the value of 'learning cultures'. *Higher Education, 67* (2), 155–169. doi:10.1007/s10734-013-9652-6

Kearney, S. 2013. Improving engagement: the use of 'Authentic self- and peer-assessment for learning' to enhance the student learning experience. *Assessment & Evaluation in Higher Education, 38* (7), 875–891. doi:10.1080/02602938.2012.751963

Knight, P. T. 2002. Summative assessment in higher education: practices in disarray. *Studies in Higher Education, 27* (3), 275–286. doi:10.1080/03075070220000662

Marginson, S. & van der Wende, M. 2007. To rank or to be ranked: the impact of global rankings in higher education. *Journal of Studies in International Education, 11* (3/4), 306–329. doi:10.1177/1028315307303544

Sambell, K. & McDowell, L. 1998. The construction of the hidden curriculum: messages and meanings in the assessment of student learning. *Assessment & Evaluation in Higher Education, 23* (4), 391–402. doi:10.1080/0260293980230406

Sambell, K., McDowell, L. & Montgomery, C. 2013. *Assessment for learning in higher education*. London: Routledge.

Sendziuk, P. 2010. Sink or swim? Improving student learning through feedback and self-assessment. *International Journal of Teaching and Learning in Higher Education, 22* (3), 320–330.

Stensaker, B., Harvey, L., Huisman, J., Langfeldt, L. & Westerheijden, D. F. 2010. The impact of the European standards and guidelines in agency evaluations. *European Journal of Education, 45* (4), 577–587. doi:10.1111/j.1465-3435.2010.01450.x

Strong, B., Davis, M. & Hawks, V. 2004. Self-grading in large general education classes: a case study. *College Teaching, 52* (2), 52–57. doi:10.3200/CTCH.52.2.52-57

Topping, K. J. 2010. Methodological quandaries in studying process and outcomes in peer assessment. *Learning and Instruction, 20* (4), 339–343. doi:10.1016/j.learninstruc.2009.08.003

Torrance, H. 2007. Assessment as learning? How the use of explicit learning objectives, assessment criteria and feedback in post-secondary education and training can come to dominate learning. *Assessment in Education, 14* (3), 281–294. doi:10.1080/09695940701591867

Chapter 6

Wiliam, D. 2011. What is assessment for learning? *Studies in Educational Evaluation, 37* (1), 3–14. doi:10.1016/j.stueduc.2011.03.001

7 Sharing and promoting disciplinary competences for university teaching in English: voices from the University of Jyväskylä language centre's TACE programme

Kirsi Westerholm[1] and Anne Räsänen[2]

Abstract

The internationalisation of universities often means that the language of learning and teaching needs to be changed – at present most commonly to English. Apart from English-speaking countries, then, most European universities offer their degree programmes in a language that is not the first language of either the students or the teachers. This challenging situation is also the reality in Finland and at the University of Jyväskylä. Many Finnish universities have set up supporting infrastructures to deal with the new challenges, particularly in their international master's programmes. In this article we describe the TACE programme, which has been run by the Language Centre on an annual basis since 2010, and in a modular form since 2005. Starting with the framework, rationale and research-based framework for our TACE programme in intercultural university pedagogy, we then move to describe its content and practices as well as report some 'voices from the floor', that is, perceptions and experiences of the interdisciplinary and international group of teaching staff who have participated in the programme. Finally, some concluding remarks, challenges and benefits are presented.

Keywords: internationalisation, English-medium higher education, staff development, pedagogical development, teaching academic content through English.

1. Language Centre, University of Jyväskylä, Finland; kirsi.westerholm@jyu.fi

2. Language Centre, University of Jyväskylä, Finland; anne.e.rasanen@jyu.fi

How to cite this chapter: Westerholm, K., & Räsänen, A. (2015). Sharing and promoting disciplinary competences for university teaching in English: voices from the University of Jyväskylä language centre's TACE programme. In J. Jalkanen, E. Jokinen, & P. Taalas (Eds), *Voices of pedagogical development - Expanding, enhancing and exploring higher education language learning* (pp. 131-157). Dublin: Research-publishing.net. doi:10.14705/rpnet.2015.000290

Chapter 7

1. Introduction

The internationalisation of higher education (HE) in Finland has been one of the core strategies of national internationalisation policies. According to the Ministry of Education strategy for 2009–2015 regarding internationalisation in HE (Finnish Ministry of Education 2009), internationalisation is needed for societal renewal, for promoting diversity and networking, and for national competitiveness and innovativeness in general. This policy provides the general national guidelines to be implemented at the institutional level. For obvious reasons, promoting Finnish higher education and mobility internationally has resulted in changing the language of instruction from Finnish or Swedish to English. According to the 2012 evaluation of international degree programmes by the Finnish Higher Education Evaluation Council (Välimaa et al. 2013), there were 257 English-medium programmes at universities, with 98% at the master's level. Although there were no major differences in the way that these programmes were launched, implemented, managed or evaluated in comparison to the domestic programmes, English language proficiency and pedagogical skills were emphasised in the evaluation because full degree programmes tend to have higher stakes than do short-term mobility or individual English-medium courses.

A recent ACA study (Wächter & Maiworm 2014) lists Finland as having the highest percentage (82%) of HE institutions in Europe to offer English-medium master's programmes. As in the other Nordic countries, the main reasons behind this are to attract foreign students, to improve the intercultural competence and skills of domestic students, and to promote the international profile of the institution and in this way also foster networking and partnerships in research and education. The main challenges brought by the multilingual and multicultural classroom in institutions with entry requirements in language proficiency relate to students' academic skills, learning styles, level of content knowledge, academic practices, and varying ethical standards. And yet, as Wächter and Maiworm (2014) report, support of either students or of teachers is not common in the other Nordic countries, whereas 78% of Finnish institutions offer language and study support to students and many also provide staff support.

Changing the language of learning and teaching is not a straightforward process, but one that affects all parties involved. For the institutions, it means that new policies and guidelines will be needed to accommodate the new international dimension of the student body, curricula and counselling in order to ensure the quality of the education and the image of the institution. For the teachers, an international classroom requires management of heterogeneous backgrounds and skills in language, content matter and culture, in addition to competence in facilitating and promoting disciplinary learning in a foreign language. The students, then, are required to handle conceptually demanding academic language in a new learning community characterised by new academic practices and demands for increased tolerance of uncertainty and intercultural communication skills. It is to meet these challenges that the support systems at the University of Jyväskylä were established.

The aim of the present article is to give an account of the rationale, content and experiences of the staff development programme in intercultural university pedagogy offered by the University of Jyväskylä Language Centre. The 10/15 ECTS credit TACE programme has been offered on an annual basis since 2010 and in a modular form since 2005. The institutional framework, set up to implement the national strategies concerning, for example, English-medium higher education, is introduced first, followed by an explanation of the research-based rationale of TACE. The content and practices of the programme are then outlined, accompanied with some 'voices from the floor', that is, the perceptions and experiences of the interdisciplinary and international group of teaching staff who have participated in the programme. Finally, some concluding remarks, challenges and benefits are presented.

2. Institutional framework

Two institutional policies of the University of Jyväskylä are behind the staff development programme TACE, namely the University of Jyväskylä (JYU) Language Policy (2004, 2012) and the requirement, as of 2010, for all staff appointed in positions involving teaching to have university pedagogical training within two years of their appointment if they have not previously had it. This latter policy is not specific to teaching in English but to teaching in general. The JYU Language Policy, however, specifies the kinds of pedagogical and English communication and language skills that teaching and counselling staff must have for teaching in international classrooms. It states that

> "Teachers and counsellors of multilingual and multicultural student groups are expected to be proficient in the language of instruction (minimum level C1 in the Common European Framework of Reference for Languages) as well as to have developed intercultural competence" (University of Jyväskylä 2012: 5).

> "Language plays a more prominent role in knowledge and competence building when teaching and learning is done through a foreign language, rather than in the mother tongue. This requires special awareness from the teacher, as well as mastery of intercultural pedagogy and guidance in the language of instruction. ... The communication skills and intercultural competences of both teachers and counsellors will be systematically developed and also taken into account in recruitment and in the appraisal system" (University of Jyväskylä 2012: 8).

The action plans for the JYU Language Policy further state that the quality of teaching in English is systematically ensured, that tailored staff development is provided, and that the language quality of students' English-medium research communication, theses and dissertations is systematically attended to. Similar actions were recommended in the internal evaluation of the master's programmes in 2014.

The policies indirectly acknowledge the fact that language proficiency and pedagogical competence are intertwined in good teaching, and that a mere language test is not sufficient in evaluating the qualifications for teaching in a foreign language – a fact that has been suggested in various studies (see e.g. Airey, Lauridsen, Räsänen, Salö & Schwach Forthcoming; Dafouz & Núñez 2009; Klaassen 2001, 2008; Kling & Staehr 2011, quoted in Unterberger

2012; Pilkinton-Pihko 2013; Räsänen & Klaassen 2006). Nor is a language test alone enough to ensure that the competence of students is adequate for the conceptual academic level of language use in their discipline, although it is necessary for setting the threshold level at entry to a master's programme, for example.

3. Rationale for staff development in English-medium instruction

The challenges that both students and teachers face in a multilingual and multicultural classroom are already well documented. In general, students should graduate as new experts in their fields, and teachers should facilitate their construction of expertise through interactive pedagogical designs and agency. Both these processes are conducted through language (see Wells 2002). However, as indicated by Räsänen & Klaassen (2013) "an international classroom [automatically] implies heterogeneous backgrounds and skills in language, content and culture. Added to this is the awareness (or non-awareness) of the content specialist in terms of the linguistic and cultural characteristics of the discipline being taught as well as of how language choice might affect knowledge building and knowledge structures in that discipline" and how all this could be promoted using appropriate pedagogical approaches and practices. These issues provide the essence of the research-based rationale behind the TACE programme, detailed in this section.

3.1. From student to expert

Academic experts are people who are recognised as such on the basis of how they communicate their expertise to other people – whether within their own disciplinary group, within cross-disciplinary groups or as members of society in general. It is through this communication that their professional status becomes transparent to others, in other words, they are able to use the language of the discipline at the conceptual level that is required in different situations. Hyland (2012) refers to this in stating that "an academic identity is who the individual is when acting as a member of a discipline' and that 'an engineer is an engineer because he or she communicates like one and the same is true for biologists, historians and linguists" (Hyland 2012: 25). They have learned the language of their field through studying and interacting with previous experts in the field. Their teachers have structured the content of the discipline by using various kinds of pedagogical methods, thus engaging them in building their knowledge and expertise in the field. At the same time, they have gradually learned to use the kind of language that is typical of that discipline as well as whether the discipline could be characterised as one with explicit notions and truths or perhaps one with many angles and possible answers, and therefore also more variable and ambiguous in its language (see also Airey 2009). This process of becoming an academic expert is similar regardless of whether the language used is one's mother tongue or some other language. However, in the former case, little attention is usually given to making the necessity of the integration of language and content explicit, because the prerequisites for learning a new communication register and new discourse conventions are assumed to be in place. In the latter case, however, more awareness and attention are needed to facilitate and scaffold learning, which is particularly obvious in an international classroom where the language of instruction may be foreign for both teachers and students.

It is most often the case that the multilingual and multicultural student group is studying in English in a new academic and cultural context. It is possible that they have little experience in using discipline-specific English and, in many cases, no experience in writing academic papers in English. Therefore, the students are "required to transition from everyday language use to conceptually demanding academic language use" (Räsänen 2011: 156, see also Cummins 1984 on the move from basic interactive communicative skills, [BICS] to cognitive academic language proficiency [CALP]).

It is also possible that academic cultures and practices differ greatly between their home environment and the new environment, thus making it necessary "to enter a learning community characterised by demands for increased tolerance of uncertainty and intercultural communication skills" (Räsänen 2011: 156).

However, the expectations of achievement are usually the same for all students regardless of the language of instruction. Across their studies – and in degree programmes in particular – students are expected to have the capacity to combine linguistic, pragmatic and previously gained background knowledge in the understanding and construction of the new knowledge in their disciplinary field and ability to use appropriate strategies in completing the required learning tasks. Furthermore, they need to be able to monitor, assess and direct their own learning in the way needed. They should have the capability to process, analyse and evaluate conceptual-level information and to draw conclusions, solve problems and compile syntheses. Moreover, they are expected to participate in class discussions and seminars, work purposefully in intercultural teams and to give presentations as well as write reports that indicate their progress in disciplinary expertise. All this is what we expect as higher education professionals. The students, on the other hand, expect teachers to be able to make it all possible, without of course detailing it in this way. To fulfil these expectations, both parties need to have certain well-developed and specific skills and abilities, sometimes referred to as 'operational competence' or 'knowing how', as opposed to 'knowing what' (Light & Cox 2001: 8; Räsänen & Klaassen 2006: 256). And the operational competence required has to become manifest in a new language. Regardless of this, language and communication development is seldom included in the expected learning outcomes or curricula of, for example, master's programmes taught in English, but rather, they are seen to grow as incidental learning because of the medium of instruction. There are, however, preconditions to be met for 'picking up the language', which makes the absence of attention to the role of language a serious quality issue in English-medium instruction (see e.g. Hellekjaer 2007; Räsänen & Klaassen 2006; Shaw 2013; Wilkinson 2008).

Discipline specialists (i.e. HE content teachers) at their best are competent in the use of the new instructional language at the conceptual level that is required and often consider the use of a so-called simpler language a sign of watering down the content and not expressing it properly. In other words, they are able to transfer their way of speaking about the discipline to a new language but consider that the discipline requires a certain level of thinking and expression in order to remain a discipline. They might also be able to transfer and adapt their teaching skills to the new situation on the basis of their experience, and provide the kind of scaffolding that the multilingual and multicultural group requires – often intuitively and without explicit attention to, or awareness of, the role of language in the process. Thus, when they notice students having problems, they modify their slides, check comprehension more specifically, use clear structuring, provide more handouts and instructions, change their learning tasks and so on. In this way, the good pedagogical skills compensate for, and complement, the conceptually complex language use of the discipline and facilitate learning in a multilingual and multicultural classroom. However, there are other issues that require attention. Construction of knowledge differs between disciplines and languages, and different disciplines tend to have preferred academic practices that teachers use in their own teaching. In certain cases, specific actions must be taken to make the role of language explicit for both teachers and students in information management, knowledge construction and expression, and professional communication in order to provide the kind of a learning environment that becoming an academic expert requires (see e.g. Airey 2009; Parpala, Lindblom-Ylänne, Komulainen, Litmanen & Hirsto 2010; Shaw 2013; Wells 2002).

3.2. Dimensions of culture in a multilingual and multicultural classroom[3]

Although cultural issues have only become clearly salient features of European academic communities and significant topics for research more recently, multilingual and multicultural classrooms have existed and been studied in other parts of the world for much longer. In addition to numerous studies on ethnic cultures (see e.g. Palfreyman & McBride 2007), Flowerdew and Miller (1995) suggested nearly twenty years ago already there are several cultural issues that tend to cause problems to student understanding in multilingual and multicultural classrooms. As illustrated in Figure 1 below, four dimensions of culture that are present in such a class were identified.

---

3. This section is adapted from Räsänen 2011

Figure 1. Dimensions of culture in a multilingual and multicultural class
(adapted from Flowerdew & Miller 1995 and Räsänen 2011)

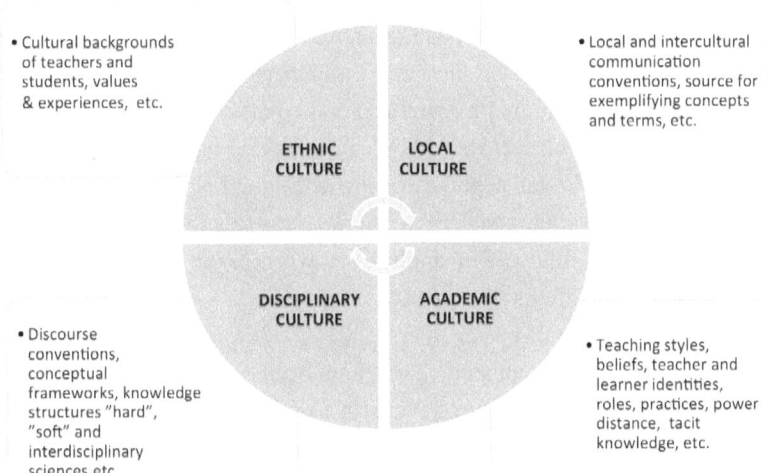

All these dimensions are integrated in the TACE programme on an across- the-curriculum principle. The main focus, however, is on disciplinary culture and its relation to academic culture and academic practices, because it is there that the integration of content, language and discourse needs more specific attention and awareness.

As was indicated above, an academic and disciplinary expert is able to use the discourse conventions which are typical of his/her specific field and profession, whatever the language involved. Räsänen (2011: 158) further mentions that,

> "[a]ccording to some studies (e.g. Hyland 1999) the traditional distinction between 'hard' sciences and 'soft' (or 'interdisciplinary') sciences [also shows] in the ways in which knowledge is structured in these sciences and in which way it is constructed within the social practices of their discourse communities. Thus, following Hyland (1999: 121), communicating as [some academic] professional means 'being able to construct an argument

that meets field-specific standards of these respective disciplines', as well as reflects the kinds of social practices (e.g. academic writing in the first person singular vs. using the passive voice) that [belong to] these disciplinary cultures. [Furthermore,] for the same reason, there tend to be [preferences in the] academic practices and teaching styles [that are followed in those cultures], characterising the basic differences in disciplinary knowledge construction, [namely,] hierarchical and cumulative knowledge building (often with one correct answer based on existing facts and hard evidence) vs. interpretative and negotiated knowledge building (with many answers, classifications, and paradigms). The former tends to prefer transmission-type lecturing followed by application, whereas the latter tends to prefer dialogical and interactive type of teaching".

Along the same lines, Neumann, Parry and Becher (2002) characterise pure hard disciplines (e.g. physics) as having an atomistic knowledge structure and being concerned with universals, whereas pure soft disciplines are individually interpretative with no clear knowledge community. As regards the students of the various disciplines, then, Parpala et al. (2010; see also Parpala, Lindblom-Ylänne & Rytkönen 2011), among others, have reported that students' approaches to, and experiences of, the teaching–learning environments as well as their conceptions of good teaching and the teachers' role in facilitating learning in different disciplines vary accordingly. These studies concerned learning in the mother tongue, not in a foreign language.

Becoming an academic expert necessarily involves knowledge construction and sharing, as well as conceptual-level communication. For these reasons it is essential for content teachers to be aware of the characteristics and preferences of their disciplines so that they are able to act as 'role models' for their students in this respect. Added to this in an international classroom is the fact that the medium of instruction and learning might be a foreign language for all, with its own way of expressing knowledge construction and disciplinary expertise. Therefore, besides being able to analyse and assess the cognitive load of their concepts, teachers should also be aware of whether their discipline in general is linguistically complex or not. Moreover, the lexical range of the discipline potentially affects the kind of discourse competence required from teachers and future experts, for example, in terms of whether the terminology of the discipline can be explicitly defined or vague and culturally loaded. This kind of reflection and sharing with colleagues and students – all part of the practices in the TACE programme – contributes greatly to everybody's understanding of what teaching and learning through a foreign language actually requires (Räsänen 2011).

In the following section, the details of the TACE programme, its module contents and expected learning outcomes are described in the light of the theoretical considerations and rationale above and accompanied by participant voices and reflections. The main practices and assignments for each module are also introduced.

4. TACE modules and participants' voices

As was explained above in the introduction, TACE is a staff development programme in intercultural university pedagogy and English provided by the University of Jyväskylä Language Centre. The programme was designed to meet the needs and challenges of both the domestic and international staff with teaching and guidance responsibilities and possibly no particular pedagogical qualifications. Since the beginning of the present form of TACE in 2010, some 15–20 staff members per year have completed the programme, 20 being the number accepted annually. They have represented all of the seven faculties of the university, and thus the group is each year multidisciplinary, multilingual and multicultural with approximately one third of international and two thirds of Finnish discipline specialists. Three English lecturers of the Language Centre form the permanent team of instructors. The programme is separately funded and part of the University's staff development provision for enhancing the quality of teaching.

Figure 2 below illustrates the TACE programme modules, which are flexible in that they are partially overlapping and adjusted to the needs and wishes of each participant group. The total extent of the programme is 10/15 ECTS credits, depending on the development project that each participant wishes to complete. TACE itself follows an integrated approach of addressing issues specific to both the language and the teaching of the discipline. The programme begins and finishes with an intensive day, with bimonthly contact sessions in between, and in this format runs for approximately eight months. Each teacher is also observed in action, in other words, visited by one of the trainers and provided with individual feedback and consultation. Furthermore, feedback on language and related issues is given on the written distance tasks as well as on, for example, pronunciation based on videoed presentations.

Figure 2. TACE programme modules

The TACE programme is often described in the participants' written work and comments as a journey. Across the programme, the TACE teachers have a variety of distance assignments (e.g. a critical review or a position paper), reflective blog posts after each contact session and a development portfolio where they discuss their experiences, insights and learning process as well as their teaching philosophy. These tasks and activities have been aligned with the expected learning outcomes for both content and language, including, for example, mapping of student needs and experiences, matching pedagogical approaches to student skills, analysing the requirements of one's own discipline, adapting task designs and assessment criteria, revising instructions for assignments, and guiding and giving feedback to students.

In what follows, the content of each module and the expected learning outcomes as well as examples of activities and assignments are presented briefly. This is accompanied by reflections of the participants extracted verbatim from their blog posts and portfolios, both of which are compulsory elements in the programme.

4.1. Module 1: orientation and formulation of learning outcomes

The first thematic module of the TACE programme introduces and explains the expected learning outcomes of the programme as well as establishes a theoretical background to teaching and learning through English in higher education settings. The TACE website and the blogging expected are also introduced. An important expected learning outcome is to understand the special features and requirements of teaching and learning through a foreign language. In the sessions, the TACE context is reflected upon from the perspective of the participants (i.e. their disciplines and backgrounds) and from that of their students' background: who they are, where they come from and what their cognitive, disciplinary and linguistic skills and previous experiences are. The dimensions of four cultures – ethnic, local, academic and disciplinary (Flowerdew & Miller 1995) – are explored in the participants' contexts. The concepts of an academic expert and the role of language in becoming one are discussed. Furthermore, the challenges and impact of English-medium instruction in the non-English context for both teachers and learners as well as for the entire institution are investigated. In the discussions and workshops the TACE participants usually raise such issues as the need for new pedagogical skills, approaches and focuses, and new requirements for intercultural communication competence (i.e. new teacher profiles) as teachers and role models of both content and disciplinary language and discourse.

"Unfortunately the linguistic proficiency aspect is often a secondary concern for the curriculum planners, course designers and teachers who are mainly subject teachers and proficient users – not trained teachers – of a foreign language".

"These [master's level] courses should be designed carefully and keeping the learning objectives in mind and would profit from professional dialogue with language teachers especially when course assignments and tasks are prepared".

"During the TACE module I have updated the learning outcomes I use in my courses so that they include not only content but also language skills".

4.2. Module 2: multilingual and multicultural learning context

As was suggested above, an international classroom with students and teachers from different ethnic, academic and disciplinary cultures requires a set of intercultural competences accompanied by pragmatically correct use of English as a lingua franca for instructional purposes and learning. This module focuses on how to attend to critical incidents, how to use diversity as an asset in a multilingual and multicultural HE classroom, and how to take into account the special needs of international students in promoting their learning. Therefore, the expected learning outcomes designed for this module include managing group dynamics with intercultural students, intercultural communication competence, surveying academic practices in multilingual and multicultural settings and attending to learning styles and study skills (see Joy & Kolb 2009). TACE addresses these issues from several viewpoints. Some of the most prominent theories and definitions of culture are discussed, followed by themes of intercultural communication competence. Barriers to effective small group work are also discussed in the light of ethnic and academic cultures, and understanding one's international students is a key theme. Furthermore, acknowledging the type of language needed in the participants' disciplines is among the expected learning outcomes, as is how learning both content and language can be promoted by choosing suitable methods, assignments and task design. Below are some reflections concerning the module topics covered.

"I have noticed differences in thought patterns and ways of perceiving issues between business students and non-business students...When we add national/societal cultural influences to the same situation, we will find even more variation in thought patterns and perception of issues".

"It is therefore not enough as a teacher to only take into account the different cognitive abilities and knowledge of the students in the group but also the cultural differences and their impact on teaching and learning should be kept in mind in order to interact successfully in the classroom".

"I have never really stopped and considered the different challenges and issues related to teaching a multicultural group and understanding intercultural students".

4.3. Module 3: interactive lecturing and small group teaching methods

The expected learning outcomes for this third module include knowing how to structure and illustrate lectures through an interactive approach, and to guide small group work so that learning becomes possible at various proficiency levels. A number of studies and surveys (e.g. Braine 2002; Shaw 2013) show that teaching through English is an added cognitive and linguistic load for a non-native speaker of the language, and that new pedagogical skills and practices are required to guarantee learning in heterogeneous, multicultural and multilingual classrooms. As one of the goals is to promote learners' academic language competence, it is of the utmost importance that students are indeed given plenty of opportunities to use the language in many meaningful ways and in authentic situations (see e.g. collaborative meaning-making activities suggested by Klaassen 2001; Wells 2002; Wilkinson & Zegers 2006). In other words, new, student-centred and interactive ways to learn and teach need to be discovered and adopted. Furthermore, it is known that appropriate pedagogical choices can compensate for the teachers' perhaps slightly lacking language skills and this increases the need to master several collaborative methods. TACE themes in the module are, for example, designing learning tasks for collaborative learning, cooperative learning and study skills, pragmatic awareness, and teacher talk in the classroom. In terms of the last topic, teachers in fact have to talk a significant amount in any kind of a class session, moving from classroom management and social talk for community building to expert talk and pedagogical talk (see Moate 2011). Pragmatics in our context, then, refer to the ability to adjust one's language for different purposes when using English as a second language and avoiding transfer from one's own mother tongue into English when it might cause communication breakdown (e.g. directness vs. indirectness in feedback situations). The advantages of, and possible barriers to, effective small group work are also analysed, and the TACE participants are encouraged to share their interactive and collaborative tasks and activities at the beginning of contact sessions and for the Wiki activity bank that is collected during the programme.

> "The topic of small group methods on TACE was very relevant and important for me...I was mainly having lectures before".

> "The topic of pragmatics was very interesting. I believe that we usually do not even think of such things as pragmatics and that quite many misunderstandings or misinterpretations could be avoided if both sides – people from different languages/cultures – would understand the pragmatic aspects of other languages from the beginning".

> "During our TACE-sessions I learned to value a lot an interactive technique used by TACE teachers...this method of participation gave us as students the feeling that our experiences are valuable and accurate".

4.4. Module 4: guiding research and academic writing

Academic writing is in a crucial role in higher education and particularly so in international master's programmes. Students who enter these programmes are required from the beginning to be able to complete writing assignments demonstrating higher-order thinking skills of analysing, synthesising, evaluating information and displaying their command of disciplinary academic discourse. According to research (e.g. Braine 2002; Hunter & Tse 2013), subject specialists are not always able to explicitly define what they require and what the assessment criteria are for written assignments. In addition, there is often no clear understanding of the students' earlier educational or academic practices, and this can lead to confusion when assigning written work such as papers, reports or essays without proper definition or instructions. The purpose of this module is to understand the differences between different academic genres of writing in various disciplines and to learn to design and assess flexible learning tasks and assignments that enable both individual and collaborative knowledge construction and active and appropriate language use at the conceptual and formal level needed.

In addition, the aim is to know how to instruct, guide and assess students' academic and research communication and how to give constructive feedback on it. The module deals with conventions and practices of academic writing, giving feedback, attending to plagiarism and most importantly, formulating instructions for assignments. The clarity of writing instructions has even been considered by the participants as a means to decrease the temptation to plagiarise. In this module, the sharing of interdisciplinary differences in research writing and reporting discourse becomes a rewarding experience, because the terms used in assignments are often vague and may have both cultural and disciplinary differences (e.g. the instructions may say 'write an essay', when the actual task is to write a report or a critical review). In addition, a crucial issue is to become aware of the distinction between fluent writing but not-so-solid content as opposed to not-so-fluent writing but solid content, because the distinction is particularly significant for a fair assessment of student achievement.

> "During the meeting about writing tasks I was thinking that it is not so important to me...And now I realised how much guiding writing is actually important".

> "TACE has taught me already earlier that I must be much...more precise when I write my tasks. I showed my tasks to some of my peer students. They told me that they have no idea where to begin or what to do. I was almost shocked".

Guiding critical reading and visual literacy are also topics in this module. It is common to assign heavy reading packages for students without giving them any guidance on reading strategies or advice on critical reading. This is naturally treated in the language centre courses, but the timing is not always the best, and perhaps the content specialists could also incorporate some relevant practices in their courses. After all, being able to read critically and evaluate and synthesise research are prerequisites for good academic writing and knowledge construction.

> "This links also to giving them more varied reading assignments and then linking these to purposeful tasks for students to work on. I wonder if this kind of approach would increase the students' understanding of how reading helps them with their writing".

4.5. Module 5: alignment of teaching and assessment

Alignment of expected learning outcomes, activities and tasks to facilitate their learning and assessment of the outcomes is a topic that is integrated and embedded in each module as a continual process. The participants are asked to bring with them the learning outcome descriptions of their course and analyse and share with their colleagues issues like recognising the linguistic and cognitive requirements of their discipline, providing appropriate tasks to achieve and assess the outcomes, as well as understanding the whole process from expected learning outcomes to assessment criteria. The alignment principle of describing the minimum level of expected learning outcomes that all students should achieve, the activities used to promote them and the assessment forms used to grade students in how well they had achieved the expected learning outcomes was adopted from Biggs (1999) and Moon (2006). In general, the TACE participants seem to actually be implicitly following the principle, but the use of some alternative assessment forms (e.g. learning logs) makes this more explicit. Learner involvement is also an issue often raised during this module.

> "I have never formulated the goals of the course for content and language. As a student, I used to skip the goals of the course when reading a course description. As a teacher, I cared only about those goals which are directly related to the expected outcomes and their evaluation. Thus, trying to formulate the goals for the course was an interesting experience for me".

> "I understand the importance of having the students interact with the course content in different ways so they can develop critical thinking".

4.6. Module 6: using new learning environments

Using new learning environments is also a theme that is integrated in the programme as a whole and exemplified by both teachers and by the participants themselves. During the programme itself, the TACE participants are expected and encouraged to record their reflections on teaching as well as learning processes and on experiences of modules and of sharing issues with the interdisciplinary group by writing blog posts on the platform used for the programme. Blogging is used as a tool for reflection for several reasons. First, it gives the participants a chance to comment and process information and ideas immediately after each session or module, and in this way share their thoughts, experiences and understanding of the topics covered. Second, being a fairly modern form of social media, it gives a good insight into the types of forums their students are familiar with. Finally, the platform is more flexible and interactive than what the university has been using, and therefore it was also new for the participants. Although there are some initial challenges with blogging, mainly with its practicalities, it soon becomes a tool actively employed by the participants.

> "Blogging also fostered the interaction with other peers who could comment on previous reflections".

Chapter 7

> "Blogging was a very new and challenging experience for me. Before this, I thought I liked sharing my reflections on the issues discussed in the class. However, I was surprised about how shy I used to get when it was time to post something on my Wordpress. I think it would be interesting to use blogging in my future teaching!"

> "Especially what you can do with blogs, how powerful this tool can be for learning was very nicely demonstrated by the personal blogs we used".

4.7. Module 7: TACE teaching portfolios

The final module is concerned with creating an individual TACE teaching portfolio including one's own teaching philosophy, course plans with details on expected learning outcomes, implementation and assignment types, course assessment criteria, selected content from blog posts and, finally, the participants' evaluation of their own contribution in the TACE programme

Typically, the group decides together on what the portfolio should contain, but the participants also have much autonomy to decide themselves what they want to include and how it might serve them for example in their future professional development or as a document used to demonstrate their pedagogical merits – required by the University in, for example, staff recruitment. Judging from the outcomes, it seems that our goal of offering the participants a forum for sharing experiences, concerns and practices with colleagues across disciplines, and allocating ample time for discussions and reflections is seen as a relevant and successful approach.

> "I am very happy that there was so much room given to talk with the other TACE colleagues during class. I learned so many valuable lessons from the other participants through all the fruitful discussions".

> "Class discussions were invaluable for sharing practices about how to manage intercultural groups or specific challenges arising from the group

dynamics; how to assess students' progress; how to provide constructive feedback. TACE provided the possibility to learn from the teachers' way of teaching, other participants' experiences, and provoked my own interest in finding information about the topics. I expect all this to have an impact on my future teaching".

"I have never tried to write down my teaching philosophy...It was an interesting and useful experience".

In the final contact session we also had a workshop where the participants are invited to provide feedback and offer possible development ideas and suggestions for future TACE programmes. Some of the development ideas in the past have concerned the linguistic and pedagogical terminology used in the programme. At times, more explaining would have been appreciated. Moreover, our own instructions have at times been seen as somewhat complicated by some participants, particularly at the beginning before the new jargon becomes more familiar. Both of these comments relate to interdisciplinary and intercultural issues and indicate how important it is to explain, justify and engage the students in meaningful negotiation and collaborative knowledge construction. However, the overall feedback on the programme has always been positive.

"At the beginning the English pedagogical terminology and vocabulary to describe learning designs and activities was strange to me and sometimes I even checked terms...from the dictionary and the internet. But it was also valuable because quite often I found some interesting articles and reports about those topics".

"For me TACE was really to learn how to teach, to learn pedagogy...I think my teaching grew with TACE".

"The TACE programme has been a good opportunity for me to think about my way of teaching, re-think my teaching philosophy and share experiences with people dealing with similar challenges in their work".

5. Concluding remarks

Several studies have reported language and communication problems that teachers perceive in teaching their discipline in a new medium. These include such issues as lack of nuance and reduction of idiomatic expressions, lower speaking rate, lack of pragmatic strategies or problems in establishing rapport with students (Airey 2009; Dafouz & Núñez 2009; Shaw 2013; Smit 2010). The TACE participants have only seldom explicitly voiced concerns such as these, although some issues about English communication skills do surface during class discussions. However, because TACE is primarily a programme in intercultural university pedagogy, and not a language programme, our emphasis has been on exemplifying talk types (Moate 2011) used in class and on promoting interactive approaches and student involvement in the teaching–learning situation. This socioconstructivist approach, advocated by Wells (2002) and others, is seen to both enhance teachers' skills in supporting learning and students' opportunity to have access to, and practice in, the use of the language and communication that characterises their discipline. Nevertheless, because discipline specialists also necessarily act as role models for disciplinary discourse, the participants have also received feedback on their academic writing assignments, class management (observations) and pronunciation, and these might become attended to even more closely if the required C1 level of proficiency is more formally assessed in the future.

It is often suggested that teachers teach in the way that they themselves learned in addition to implicitly following the preferences of their discipline. Although some of these preferences seemed to also exist among the TACE participants in that their instructional designs and approaches to teaching and assessment reflected interdisciplinary differences, it was also clear that there were other factors involved. Thus, as research by, for example, Oleson and Hora (2014) shows, the extent of experience of teaching and cultures, reflective practice, professional development and non-academic roles also contribute to the repertoire of teaching methods used. And, as the participant reflections indicate, sharing one's own views with colleagues representing other academic fields was one of the most appreciated aspects of the TACE programme.

The above practice of sharing is worth considering in relation to the concept of academic freedom. It is still customary that discipline specialists, even within the same department, do not cooperate in order to provide a holistic approach to their discipline and its concepts. This means that the students get bits and pieces of the same discipline formulated in idiosyncratic ways by a number of lecturers and professors, because of the various schools of thought and paradigms within the disciplines. The disciplinary culture and discourse presented in this way can be confusing for students, and even more so when presented in a new language. The situation is naturally better in the case of more focused international master's programmes, for example, because there is usually more joint planning involved.

According to Gibbs and Coffey (2000), there is little concrete evidence that training university teachers would have any real impact. This is particularly true if the training is not based on solid conceptual grounds and empirical evidence. They further claim that

> "teachers' repertoire of teaching methods is not simply an indication of their skill but of their reflection, in that if a teacher can notice differences between contexts, or can diagnose problems, then they will also use a wider repertoire of methods to respond to these problems or contexts. Someone who uses a range of methods is likely to be more reflective than someone who does not." (Gibbs & Coffey 2000: 41)

This is certainly a lesson to keep in mind for both us trainers in the TACE programme and the participants, and one way of gathering the evidence needed is systematic documenting of experiences and professional development. In the case of TACE, the challenges and benefits of building knowledge and understanding through sharing and collaboration, accompanied by the reflections reported above, indicate clearly that heightened awareness of, and attention to, certain cultural, linguistic and pedagogical features apparent in multilingual and multicultural classrooms contribute to both student and teacher success, and in this way also to the quality of higher education learning and teaching.

References

Airey, J. 2009. *Science, language and literacy. Case studies of learning in Swedish university physics*. Acta universitatis upsaliensis. Uppsala dissertations from the Faculty of Science and Technology 81. Uppsala Geotryckeriet.

Airey, J., Lauridsen, K. M., Räsänen, A., Salö, L. & Schwach, V. Forthcoming. *The expansion of English-medium instruction in the Nordic countries. Can top-down university language policies encourage bottom-up disciplinary literacy goals?* Higher Education.

Biggs, J. 1999. *Teaching for quality learning at university: what the student does*. Buckingham: The Society for Research into Higher Education and Open University Press.

Braine, G. 2002. Academic literacy and the nonnative speaker graduate student. *Journal of English for Academic Purposes, 1* (1), 59–68. doi:10.1016/S1475-1585(02)00006-1

Cummins, J. 1984. Wanted: a theoretical framework for relating language proficiency to academic achievement among bilingual students. In C. Rivera (ed.), *Language proficiency and academic achievement*. Clevedon: Multilingual Matters, 2–19.

Dafouz, E. & Núñez, B. 2009. CLIL in higher education: devising a new learning landscape. In E. Dafouz & M. Guerrini (eds.), *CLIL across educational levels: experiences from primary, secondary and tertiary contexts*. Madrid/London: Richmond Santillana, 101–112.

Finnish Ministry of Education. 2009. *Strategy for the internationalization of higher education institutions in Finland 2009-2015*. Publications of the Ministry of Education. Retrieved from http://www.okm.fi/export/sites/default/OPM/Julkaisut/2009/liitteet/opm23.pdf

Flowerdew, J. & Miller, L. 1995. On the notion of culture in L2 lectures. *TESOL Quarterly, 29* (2), 345–373. doi:10.2307/3587628

Gibbs, G. & Coffey, M. 2000. Training to teach in higher education: a research agenda. *Teacher Development: An international journal of teachers' professional development, 4* (1), 31–44. doi:10.1080/13664530000200103

Hellekjaer, G. 2007. The implementation of undergraduate level English-medium programs in Norway: an explorative case study. In R. Wilkinson & V. Zegers (eds.), *Researching content and language integration in higher education*. Maastricht: Universiteit Maastricht, 68–81.

Hunter, K. & Tse, H. 2013. Making disciplinary writing and thinking practices an integral part of academic content teaching. *Active Learning in Higher Education, 14* (3), 227–239. doi:10.1177/1469787413498037

Hyland, K. 1999. Disciplinary discourses: writer stance in research articles. In C. N. Candlin & K. Hyland (eds.), *Writing: texts, processes and practices*. New York: Addison Wesley, 99–121.

Hyland, K. 2012. *Disciplinary identities: individuality and community in academic discourse*. Cambridge: Cambridge University Press.

Joy, S. & Kolb, D. A. 2009. Are there cultural differences in learning style? *International Journal of Intercultural Relations, 33* (1), 69–85. doi:10.1016/j.ijintrel.2008.11.002

Klaassen, R. G. 2001. *The international university curriculum: challenges in English-medium engineering education*. Unpublished PhD thesis. Delft University of Technology.

Klaassen, R. G. 2008. Preparing lecturers for English-medium instruction. In R. Wilkinson & V. Zegers (eds.), *Realizing content and language integration in higher education*. Maastricht: Maastricht University, 32–42.

Kling, J. M. & Staehr, L. S. 2011. Assessment and assistance: developing university lecturers' language skills through certification feedback. In R. Cancino, K. Jæger & L. Dam (eds.), *Policies, Principles, Practices: New Directions in Foreign Language Education in the Era of Educational Globalization*. Newcastle upon Tyne: Cambridge Scholars Press, 213–245.

Light, G. & Cox, R. 2001. *Learning and teaching in higher education. The reflective professional*. London: Sage.

Moate, J. 2011. Reconceptualising the role of talk in CLIL. *Apples – Journal of applied language studies, 5* (2), 17–35.

Moon, J. 2006. Linking levels, learning outcomes and assessment criteria – EHEA version. Retrieved from http://spectare.ucl.slu.se/adm/sus/2008/plagiarism_eng/JennyMoonExercise.pdf

Neumann, R., Parry, S. & Becher, T. 2002. Teaching and learning in their disciplinary contexts: a conceptual analysis. *Studies in Higher Education, 27* (4), 405–417. doi:10.1080/0307507022000011525

Oleson, A. & Hora, M. T. 2014. Teaching the way they were taught? Revisiting the sources of teaching knowledge and the role of prior experience in shaping faculty teaching practices. *Higher Education, 68* (1), 29–45. doi:10.1007/s10734-013-9678-9

Palfreyman, D. & Mcbride, D. L. 2007. (eds.). *Learning and teaching across cultures in higher education*. New York: Palgrave Macmillan.

Parpala, A., Lindblom-Ylänne, S., Komulainen, E., Litmanen, T. & Hirsto, L. 2010. Students' approaches to learning and their experiences of the teaching-learning environment in different disciplines. *British Journal of Educational Psychology, 80* (2), 269–282. doi:10.1348/000709909X476946

Parpala, A., Lindblom-Ylänne, S. & Rytkönen, H. 2011. Students' conceptions of good teaching in three different disciplines. *Assessment & Evaluation in Higher Education, 36* (5), 549–563. doi:10.1080/02602930903541023

Pilkinton-Pihko, D. 2013. *English-medium instruction: seeking assessment criteria for spoken professional English.* Doctoral dissertation. Department of Modern Languages, University of Helsinki.

Räsänen, A. 2011. International classrooms, disciplinary cultures and communication conventions. *Quality Assurance Review for Higher Education, 3* (2), 155–161.

Räsänen, A. & Klaassen, R. G. 2006. From learning outcomes to staff competences in integrated content and language instruction at the higher education level. In R. Wilkinson, V. Zegers & C. van Leeuwen (eds.), *Bridging the assessment gap in English-medium higher education.* AKS-Series: Fremdsprachen in Lehre und Forschung. Bochum: AKS-Verlag, 256–280.

Räsänen, A. & Klaassen, R. G. 2013. *Matching student expectations and disciplinary practices - cultures in conflict?* Abstract for the preconference workshop held at the ICLHE 2013 conference, Maastricht, April 10-13, 2013.

Shaw, P. 2013. Adjusting practices to aims in integrated language learning and disciplinary learning. *La pédagogie de l'EMILE en questions. Recherche et pratiques pédagogiques en langues de spécialité – Cahiers de l'APLIUT, 32* (3), 16–29.

Smit, U. 2010. CLIL in an English as a lingua franca (ELF) classroom: on explaining terms and expressions interactively. In C. Dalton-Puffer, T. Nikula & U. Smit (eds.), Language use and language learning in CLIL classrooms. Amsterdam: John Benjamins, 259–277. doi:10.1075/aals.7.13smi

University of Jyväskylä. 2004. Language Policy. Replaced in 2012.

University of Jyväskylä. 2012. University of Jyväskylä Language Policy 2012. Retrieved from http://www.jyu.fi/hallinto/strategia/en/university-of-jyvaskyla-language-policy-2012

Unterberger, B. 2012. English-medium programmes at Austrian business faculties. A status quo survey on national trends and a case study on programme design and delivery. *AILA Review, 25* (1), 80–100. doi:10.1075/aila.25.06unt

Välimaa, J., Fonteyn, K., Garam, I., van den Heuvel, E., Linza, C., Söderqvist, M., Wolff, J. & Kolhinen, J. 2013. *An evaluation of international degree programmes in Finland.* Finnish Higher Education Evaluation Council 2:2013. Retrieved from http://karvi.fi/en/publication/evaluation-international-degree-programmes-finland-2/

Wächter, B. & Maiworm, F. (eds.) 2014. *English-taught programmes in European Higher Education. The state of play in 2014*. ACA papers on international cooperation in education. Bonn: Lemmens Medien GmbH.

Wells, G. 2002. Learning and teaching for understanding: the key role of collaborative knowledge building. In J. Brophy (ed.), *Volume 9 - Social constructivist teaching: affordances and constraints. Book Series: Advances in Research on Teaching*, 1–41. Elsevier Science Ltd. Retrieved from http://people.ucsc.edu/~gwells/Files/Papers_Folder/SC%20Chapter.pdf

Wilkinson, R. 2008. Locating the ESP space in problem-based learning: English-medium degree programmes from a post-Bologna Perspective. In I. Fortanet-Gómes & C.A. Räisänen (eds.), *ESP in European Higher Education: Integrating language and content*. Amsterdam: John Benjamins, 55–73. doi:10.1075/aals.4.05wil

Wilkinson, R. & Zegers, V. 2006. The eclectic nature of assessment issues in content and language integrated higher education. In R. Wilkinson, V. Zegers & C. van Leeuwen (eds.), *Bridging the assessment gap in English-medium higher education*. AKS-Series: Fremdsprachen in Lehre und Forschung. Bochum: AKS-Verlag, 25–39.

8 Enabling the full participation of university students with disabilities: seeking best practices for a barrier-free language centre

Margaret Trotta Tuomi[1] and Camilla Jauhojärvi-Koskelo[2]

Abstract

Recent research has shown that 3.4% of university students in Finland have a diagnosed or observed illness or disability that affects their learning at the university level. The University of Jyväskylä Language Centre embarked on an organised, ongoing research and intervention project to enable appropriate teaching practices to suit the needs of all students. The process, thus far, has shown there is a need to clarify the rights and obligations of students and teachers to enable an atmosphere of mutual trust. A survey of the Language Centre teachers showed that all had taught students with disabilities during their university careers. Teachers wanted more information about disabilities, such as how to recognise disabilities if they have not been diagnosed or if students are not forthcoming with the information. Most importantly, they wanted to know the extent of their obligations as university teachers. Students also needed guidelines. They wanted to know if they could trust that their teachers would take them seriously or if disclosure of their disabilities would cause more difficulties. To date, university students and staff have been involved in the development of two websites, one for teachers and one for students, to clarify key areas for appropriate information and maximum suitability.

Keywords: barrier free language learning, higher education, identifying learning disabilities, support website.

---

1. Language Centre, University of Jyväskylä, Finland; margaret.tuomi@jyu.fi

2. Language Centre, University of Jyväskylä, Finland; camilla.jauhojarvi-koskelo@jyu.fi

How to cite this chapter: Tuomi, M. T., & Jauhojärvi-Koskelo, C. (2015). Enabling the full participation of university students with disabilities: seeking best practices for a barrier-free language centre. In J. Jalkanen, E. Jokinen, & P. Taalas (Eds), *Voices of pedagogical development - Expanding, enhancing and exploring higher education language learning* (pp. 159-170). Dublin: Research-publishing.net. doi:10.14705/rpnet.2015.000291

Chapter 8

1. Introduction

When discussing the needs of elementary school starters, it comes as no surprise that a percentage of the young students require extra support due to learning or other disabilities. It may be a surprise, however, that research conducted by the Finnish Student Health Service survey in 2012 found that 3.4% of university students[3] had a diagnosed learning difficulty or illness/disability that affected their learning (Kunttu & Pesonen 2012). The majority of the 3.4% university students with disabilities, that is, 69.5%, had dyslexia. The Finnish university students with dyslexia were asked if they had received assistance with their disability during their time in higher education; 63.4% said that they had not. In addition to dyslexia, 8.5% had attention deficiency disorders and 4.9% had an autistic spectrum disorder, in these cases Asperger syndrome. Nearly 5% of the students had a hearing disability and 1.2% had a visual disability. In the United Kingdom, Richardson (2009) looked at the impact disabilities had on the studies of university students. The findings showed that the only students impacted by their disabilities were those with so-called hidden disabilities such as dyslexia and Asperger syndrome.

According to the Universities Act of Finland (558/2009), factors relating to the health and functional capacity of a university applicant may not preclude their admission. Admission, however, is not enough. Full participation in university life is also required for students to complete their degrees and to arm them with the skills they need to support themselves and their families (see Tuomi, Lehtomäki & Matonya 2015; Gidley, Hampson, Wheeler & Bereded-Samuel 2010). The Finnish Constitution and the Non-Discrimination Act (21/2004: 2)[4] requires universities to take "reasonable steps" to enable a person with disabilities to gain access to work and training. As of now, however there is no Act or Code of Practice to define just what the "reasonable" adjustments are which Finnish Higher Education Institutions (FHEI) should fulfil to realize equal access and learning for all students.

---

3. The data in the Student Health Survey 2012 (Kunttu & Pesonen 2012) was collected equally from students in universities and universities of applied sciences. For this paper however, only statistics on university students were used, not on students in universities of applied sciences.

4. As amended by several acts, including No. 84/2009, p.2.

There are international initiatives, such as the UN Convention on the Rights of Persons with Disabilities (United Nations 2006) and the European Parliament Proposal for Directive on Accessibility of Public Sector Bodies' websites (COM (2012) 721)[5], that can give FHEIs more detailed directions in the near future.

As an authority supervising compliance with the terms of the Non-Discrimination Act (21/2004), the Finnish Ministry of Education and Culture has conducted surveys and reported on the accessibility of FHEIs in 2005 and 2012. The Ministry Report of 2012 shows that FHEIs have done goal-oriented work but finds that "the work is [...] still unsystematic to a degree and lacks resources [... A]t the institutional level the promotion of accessibility still has a mark of marginality" (Penttilä 2012: 6). According to the report, there seem to be challenges in studies and social participation, especially for "dyslexic students and students that have difficulties with mental health" (Penttilä 2012: 6). The ministry's recommendations for FHEIs include, among other things, work for accessibility in regard to strategic planning and the personnel's pedagogical skills and accessible use of ICT (Universities Act 558/2009[6]).

2. The Barrier-Free workgroup

When university students choose their major subject, they usually gravitate towards those fields in which they have skills and talents. However, the completion of university studies also includes obligatory non-major courses, such as Finnish language composition and foreign language communication skills. These are exactly the courses that are taught by the Language Centre and that can prove to be difficult for students with hidden disabilities. Despite these difficulties, however, the students' skills acquisition in both written and oral communication in their native and foreign languages are needed for their studies and their future occupations.

---

5. http://eur-lex.europa.eu/procedure/EN/202205

6. http://www.finlex.fi/fi/laki/kaannokset/2009/en20090558.pdf

In 2011, the University of Jyväskylä Language Centre embarked on an organised, ongoing action research project with its staff, composed of specialists in language teaching, communication and administration. The goal of this research is to provide a more accessible environment for students with physical, emotional or neurological disabilities to study in so that they can graduate with an academic degree and the skills needed for working life. The process, currently in its fourth year, has shown that there is a need to clarify the rights and obligations of students and teachers and to promote good practices so that it is easier for students to successfully complete their university studies.

The goal was to canvass teachers' experiences about working with the students with disabilities, to collect their best practices in barrier-free teaching and to gather their views on what and how training in barrier-free issues should be conducted. The open-ended questionnaire (see Appendix 1) focused on four main areas: (1) experiences of teachers and staff working with students with disabilities, either diagnosed or not, (2) how the teachers saw their role in teaching their students with disabilities, (3) what strategies the teachers had used in response to the needs of their students with disabilities and (4) what support the university and the Language Centre could offer to enable the teachers to teach their students with disabilities.

During this study, we have also included feedback from other experts working in various faculties and departments. Both teachers and students of special education were included in the development of a website intended for students and another for teachers only.

3. What did we learn?

The teachers' responses were based on their own observations, students' own reports or statements from doctors. The range of disabilities reported by the staff can be seen in Table 1. The results showed that all the Language Centre teachers had taught students with disabilities. The teachers' so-called comfort zones varied according to their experience and educational background. They spoke of the need for more information to appropriately train and evaluate students with physical, sensory, emotional or neurological difficulties. Since many disabilities are undiagnosed and invisible, we are, unaware of the cause, unable to know how many students do succeed without assistance and how many do not.

3.1. What were the experiences of teachers and staff working with students with disabilities, diagnosed or not?

When the staff was asked about what types of students with disabilities they had encountered, all responded that during their careers they had had students with a wide range of neurological, emotional, visual and physicals disabilities that affected their studies or the completion of their assignments.

Table 1. Disabilities encountered by teachers

Disability	Teachers had taught students with the following disabilities during their careers (N = 48)
reading disabilities	41
stage fright or panic disorders	34
mental health problems	29
hearing impairment	26
visual impairment	25
physical impairment	25
communication impairment (e.g. stuttering)	20
attention deficiency disorders (e.g. ADD, ADHD)	19
autistic spectrum disorders (e.g. Asperger syndrome)	14
chronic pain syndrome	2
other[7]	5

The teachers identified the barriers which prevented students with disabilities from studying. They noticed that students needed a wide range of teaching

---

7. Overemotional, schizophrenia, multiple sclerosis, cerebral palsy, drug addiction, cancer

methods and their teaching had to be modified. They gave more guidance, support materials and alternative tasks to students with disabilities. Many students needed such assistance from the teacher to collaborate with other students. Teachers could assist in enabling each student to become a full and equal member of the class despite their disabilities.

3.2. How did the teachers see their role when teaching students with disabilities?

Teachers provided special arrangements, when needed, to better suit the students' needs and to give them support and encouragement. They wanted to refer students with disabilities to professionals in student health services. Teachers were concerned that they were being asked to function in a way that was beyond their capacity. They were trained as adult educators in language, communication and administration of staff. They had not been trained to recognise neurological disabilities. How could they identify students with undiagnosed disabilities when the students themselves were unaware of their own disabilities? Was it the teacher's duty to bring up the subject that students' difficulties in studying might be caused by disabilities? Some mentioned that such a discussion was both outside their range of expertise and their job mandate.

3.3. What strategies did the teachers use in response to the needs of their students with disabilities?

The teachers had tailored their methods of teaching and student evaluation. They had provided extra materials, advice, tips and instructions. Different types of feedback and self-study tasks were implemented. One teacher even mentioned that she had learned sign language to enable good communication with students with hearing impairment. Several teachers mentioned that they had had many private discussions with the students, paid attention to the teaching arrangements, booked more accessible classrooms, provided a computer for tasks, took interpreters into account, sent materials in advance and gave teaching materials in a variety of formats.

3.4. What support did the teachers need when teaching students with disabilities?

Across the board, the teachers requested training. They requested information on what professionals they could refer their students to so that their students could learn study strategies, on how to discuss with students about their disabilities and on how to identify students with undiagnosed disabilities. In addition, training was requested on how to take the whole class into consideration when one or more students in the class had disabilities that disrupted other students. The teachers wanted to know what their rights and obligations as teachers were, that is, what was included and not included in their role as teachers of students with disabilities. Training sessions where teachers discuss where the rights and obligations of teachers lie in the realisation of a barrier-free Language Centre. For example, a traffic light could symbolically be used to differentiate what tasks were clearly within their obligations as teachers to fulfill, that is, a "green light", what was definitely not within their obligations to fulfill, a "red light", and finally, what areas are unclear, a "yellow light" (Eerola 2014). This type of training can help to clarify the role of teachers in various situations. Most of all the teachers wanted to know where they could turn to when support was needed. The teachers requested written instructions about barrier-free teaching and basic information about various learning barriers. Some, especially part-time teachers, asked about remuneration, wondering if they would be paid for the time spent in the adaptation of materials for students with disabilities.

4. What has been done so far?

As requested by the Language Centre staff, a series of training sessions on a range of topics was offered by a number of professionals on:

- different types of disabilities and how teachers could better help students who have such disabilities by the principal lecturer in special education at the Jyväskylä University of Applied Sciences;

Chapter 8

- the rights and obligations of teachers and students by the university planner responsible for students with disabilities;

- what teachers should do if a crisis situation should occur in their classes by the Head of Safety and Security at the University of Jyväskylä;

- the training of a network of university staff members in each department to promote a barrier-free learning environment by two leaders of the Student Life programme, in the context of a meeting with the Language Centre director and the Barrier-Free workgroup;

- how teachers can guide their students to a professional who can assist them in the development of learning strategies by the psychologist of the University Health Services;

- assisting the staff to identify the perimeter of their roles as teachers, the content of their job descriptions and the setting of boundaries in their roles as teachers.

Additionally, both students and teachers have collaborated on the development of two websites, one for Language Centre staff and one for students. The website for staff includes valuable information on a variety of disabilities and training links. The site for students has been prepared, in a style that is suitable for all, to assist students who may have questions on how to proceed to study in collaboration with their teacher if they believe that they themselves may have a disability. Most of all, both websites clearly state the rights and obligations of university teachers and students.

5. Barrier-free website for language teachers: fear is NOT part of a teacher's work

The materials provided on the website reinforce professional development training. The teachers were concerned that they were being asked to fulfil a task for which they had no training. The website emphasises that teachers are not being asked to act as psychologists, doctors or special education teachers. Rather, it presents basic information included on learning disabilities which affect adults, such as ADHD, autistic spectrum disorder, panic attacks and social anxiety. Case studies on each of these disabilities are also included. The teachers are instructed not to condone physical or emotional abuse from their students, no matter what the cause. The most important advice is, of course, to seek assistance from one's colleagues, university staff and health services. What is stressed is that there is no need for teachers to feel alone, a work environment based on consultation and collaboration being an important step forward (see Tuomi 2004).

6. Barrier-free website for students[8]

The website for students provides instructions concerning students' rights and obligations. Encouraging statements from the Language Centre teachers are also included, pointing out, for example, that all students can complete courses with the same level of difficulty but in different ways, such flexibility making it fair for all. Questions from students with various learning disabilities, such as dyslexia, are answered and guidance is provided. There is also information on students' well-being, performance anxiety and self-direction, among other things. University students are adults responsible for their own studies, development and decisions. Data are now being collected from students with disabilities on their experiences in Language Centre studies.

7. Conclusions

When one considers that 3.4% of university students have disabilities which affect their studies (see Kunttu & Pesonen 2012), it comes as no surprise that all of the University Language Centre staff had taught students with disabilities. What is a surprise, however, is that so little is taught in the pedagogical studies

---

8. https://kielikeskus.jyu.fi/esteeton (in Finnish)

of teachers of adults in higher education and how little it is discussed in the university environment. Perhaps university students, being adults, are mistakenly assumed to have overcome any disabilities, as if they were a matter of concern for elementary school children only. This assumption is obviously false.

The education of each and every individual is necessary for the continued progress of society. We must not allow barriers to stand in their way. The Barrier-Free Language Centre is just a start, but it is a good start, based on research and the practical experiences of teachers and students, with disabilities or not. Furthermore, in the university milieu, students are not the only ones with disabilities; recent research has examined tertiary teachers with dyslexia, their "professional identity negotiation" (Burns 2015: 16) and their success with their different palette of talents. More research in this and other areas is needed. It is only through openness, research and experience that this process can and will move forward.

Acknowledgments

The Barrier Free Language Centre working group would like to thank University of Jyväskylä Planning Coordinator Hannu Puupponen for his support and comments in the production of this article.

References

Burns, E. 2015. *Tertiary teachers with dyslexia as narrators of their professional life and identity*. Jyväskylä: University of Jyväskylä.

Eerola, S. 2014. *Haastavat ohjaustilanteet ja puheeksi ottaminen* [Introducing difficult subjects and other challenging situations when guiding Ssudents]. From a training session given by Eerola for the Language Centre of the University of Jyväskylä.

Gidley, J. M., Hampson, G. P., Wheeler, L. & Bereded-Samuel, E. 2010. From access to success: an integrated approach to quality higher education informed by social inclusion theory and practice. *Higher Education Policy, 23* (1), 123–147. doi:10.1057/hep.2009.24

Kunttu, K. & Pesonen, T. 2012. *Student health survey 2012: a national survey among Finnish university students*. Helsinki: Yliopilaiden terveydenhoitosäätiö.

Non-Discrimination Act (21/2004). Retrieved from https://www.finlex.fi/fi/laki/kaannokset/2004/en20040021.pdf

Penttilä, J. 2012. Hitaasti, mutta varmasti? Saavutettavuuden edistyminen yliopistoissa ja ammattikorkeakouluissa 2000-luvulla [Slowly but surely? Progress in the accessibility of university and polytechnic education in the 2000s]. Helsinki: Opetus- ja kulttuuriministeriön julkaisuja. Retrieved from http://www.minedu.fi/export/sites/default/OPM/Julkaisut/2012/liitteet/okm10.pdf?lang=fi

Richardson, J. T. E. 2009. The academic attainment of students with disabilities in UK higher education. *Studies in Higher Education*, 34 (2), 123–137. doi:10.1080/03075070802596996

Tuomi, M. T. 2004. Planning teachers' professional development for global education. *Journal of Intercultural Education*, 15 (3), 295–306.

Tuomi, M. T., Lehtomäki, E. & Matonya, M. 2015. As capable as other students: Tanzanian women with disabilities in higher education. *International Journal of Disability, Development and Education*, 62 (2), 202–214. doi:10.1080/1034912X.2014.998178

United Nations. 2006. *Convention on the rights of persons with disabilities*. New York: United Nations.

Appendix 1

Barrier-Free Language Centre Learning Environment
Questionnaire for the staff of Jyväskylä University Language Centre

Respondent_____

1) What types of students with disabilities have you encountered in your work? How many of your students have had disabilities which affected their studies or assignments? Circle the appropriate choices using the following scale:

0 = none
1 = very few, a few students during the past few years
2 = few, a few during the past year

Chapter 8

3 = more than five students during the past year
4 = more than ten students in the past year
5 = more than fifteen students in the past year

    a) Visual disability[9]   0 1 2 3 4 5
    b) Hearing disability   0 1 2 3 4 5
    c) Physical disability   0 1 2 3 4 5
    d) Communication disability, e.g. stuttering   0 1 2 3 4 5
    e) Reading disabilities   0 1 2 3 4 5
    f) Stage fright or panic disorders   0 1 2 3 4 5
    g) Autistic spectrum disorders, e.g. Asperger Syndrome 0 1 2 3 4 5
    h) Attention deficiency disorders, e.g. ADD, ADHD   0 1 2 3 4 5
    i) Mental health problems   0 1 2 3 4 5
    j) Chronic pain syndrome   0 1 2 3 4 5
    k) Other, describe_____ 0 1 2 3 4 5

2) What, in your opinion, is your role as a teacher/facilitator when teaching students with disabilities?

3) With those students who have disabilities:

    a) What types of barriers have you noticed which prevent your students from studying?

    b) How have you responded to these barriers? (For example, different materials, discussion with student/class, developed a new teaching method – what kind?)

    c) What type of support or training would you have needed? How could the University Language Centre support you? What other types of support could you use from the university?

---

9. The original questionnaire (a, b, c) used the word "impaired" rather than disability.

Doing what we teach: promoting digital literacies for professional development through personal learning environments and participation

Ilona Laakkonen[1]

Abstract

Despite the proliferation of social media, few learners make effective use of digital technology to support their learning or graduate with the skills necessary for developing and communicating their expertise in the knowledge-driven networked society of the digital age. This article makes use of the concept of Personal Learning Environments (PLE) to approach the question of how digital literacies for learning can be taught and learned in the context of higher education. It presents a model of a PLE course, the overall goal of which was to equip the learners with the skills and competences needed to create their own digital environments that would enable them to tap the online networks and resources relevant for their professional and personal lives. From the viewpoint of Design-Based Research (DBR), the article lays out the design principles, pedagogical choices and activities on the course, and explains how these contributed to the creation of a learning culture. Furthermore, the design and its outcomes are reflected upon in the light of student feedback and reactions. The article argues that through the personalised, dialogic and networked approach inherent in PLE ideology, students with diverse goals, backgrounds and skills can explore practices and learn digital literacies that help them progress toward their professional goals.

Keywords: digital literacies, PLE, DBR, participatory culture, pedagogical design.

---

1. University services, University of Jyväskylä, Finland; ilona.laakkonen@jyu.fi

How to cite this chapter: Laakkonen, I. (2015). Doing what we teach: promoting digital literacies for professional development through personal learning environments and participation. In J. Jalkanen, E. Jokinen, & P. Taalas (Eds), *Voices of pedagogical development - Expanding, enhancing and exploring higher education language learning* (pp. 171-195). Dublin: Research-publishing.net. doi:10.14705/rpnet.2015.000292

Chapter 9

1. Introduction

Providing students with the skills and knowledge they need for their future professional lives is and has always been the core task of higher education. The work increasingly relies on knowledge-driven practices and production, as work problems are becoming complex and require continuous updating of expertise and building of new knowledge, and many workplaces model themselves as highly networked and distributed environments (Littlejohn, Beetham & McGill 2012). Being a professional in this networked field of work requires capabilities for lifelong learning, managing distributed expertise and learning across sites (Ludvigsen, Lund, Rasmussen & Säljö 2011), participation (Jenkins et al. 2005) and effective communication in environments mediated by technology. These skills and competences have been mapped out in several models and classifications, under such titles as 21st-century skills (e.g. ATC21S[2]), digital or new literacies (e.g. Beetham & Sharpe 2010; Lankshear & Knobel 2007) and participatory culture (Jenkins et al. 2005). Because the development in the ways information is distributed and produced is a relatively recent and rapid phenomenon, formal education is faced with the challenge of developing pedagogies that would serve the various needs of students today and help them in developing the skills, literacies and identities they need in their future as professionals.

This article approaches digital literacies for learning through the concept of the Personal Learning Environment (PLE). This concept was used as both a practice-oriented description of the digital environments students use and may use for learning purposes (see e.g. Drexler 2010; Guth 2009), and as an ideological concept that entails and presumes certain pedagogical choices (see Attwell 2007). These choices involve ideas such as student involvement in the design of learning, building a learning community or affinity space (Gee 2007) in which people gather around a common interest and which allows for various levels of participation, expertise and involvement. They also include premises inherent to the idea of connectivism (Siemens 2005) and the presumption that

---

2. Assessment and teaching of 21st century skills. http://atc21s.org/

learning these skills should happen in relation to students' identity building and wider personal goals. The question in the focus of this article is how the skills needed for professional learning and communication in digital environments can be taught and learned in the context of higher education. The article builds around a teaching experiment that took the form of an elective course provided as part of the offering of language and communication studies at the University of Jyväskylä Language Centre. It was designed for a group of Finnish university students with diverse backgrounds, stages of studies, technological skills and attitudes toward social networks.

The research presented in this article builds on a body of work conducted in a larger research and development project, Future space for shared and personal learning and working (F-SHAPE), of which the context, research strategy and methods are introduced in section 2. Design-Based Research (DBR), which seeks to contribute to the theory of learning through a practice-oriented, iterative and holistic approach, was used as a general research strategy for the project and had implications on the design and outcomes of the study at hand. The theoretical background for the teaching experiment and the concept of PLE are presented in section 3. Sections 4 and 5 present and discuss findings from the study. Section 4 presents the teacher perspective by outlining the design principles of the experiment and describing the course participants as well as the working modes of the course. Section 5, in turn, extracts the viewpoint of the students through qualitative content analysis of the students' reflections on their own learning and the pedagogical choices made by the researcher-teachers. Finally, section 6 concludes the article and provides some implications of the research.

2. The research design

2.1. The research context

The research reported in this article was initiated as part of the F-SHAPE project (2010–2012). The overall goal of the project was to develop and research flexible learning solutions to fit the needs of adult learners and working life. The project was funded by Tekes (the Finnish Funding Agency for Innovation) and combined research teams from two universities with business partners to explore the possibilities of and interplay between various spaces for learning: social media applications, 3D virtual environments, personal and collaborative learning environments, and informal and formal learning contexts. The PLE perspective was employed as an alternative to traditional approaches to the organisation of learning: the aim was to develop solutions that would center around the individual needs of the learner, yet still support networked and community-based learning and goals of the organisation.

The part of the project reported in the article at hand was conducted at the University of Jyväskylä Language Centre, where researchers collaborated with teachers in ethnographic and experimental modes. In Finnish higher education, language and communication courses are compulsory in all degree programmes. In addition, the University of Jyväskylä Language Centre offers a range of elective courses in various languages and modes of communication. The institution has a tradition of pedagogical development and of nourishing a culture of inquiry and renewal. Goals such as multiliteracy, ICT skills and transferable, lifelong, independent learning skills are cited as focal points in the teaching. To help its students, drawn from various academic backgrounds, become effective and convincing communicators in their specific professional fields, the Language Centre applies multimodal pedagogy, which, as mentioned by Laakkonen (2011: 20), "links meaningful communication to real-life situations, supports individual and peer processes, and encourages creativity and self-regulation". This pedagogical approach, the general teaching goals, and the organisational culture were seen as supportive of the PLE experiments.

The experiment presented in this article was designed by two researchers with backgrounds in pedagogy, ICT, linguistics and communication studies. The experiment was based on observations at the Language Centre and earlier experiments with PLEs (see section 2.2) that had called the researchers' attention to the potential of PLEs and the constraints of its implementation (see Laakkonen & Taalas 2015).

2.2. Design-based research as an iterative approach

DBR was employed as a general research strategy in the project. It "involves a goal-oriented, pragmatic and iterative view of research and proposes [means] for developing learning practices through empirical research" (Laakkonen 2011: 19, see also Reinking & Bradley 2007). DBR mediates a dialogue between research, theory and practice by its dual objectives: it aims at responding to local needs through developing new practices and environments, yet strives to increase the general understanding of learning (Barab & Squire 2004).

DBR is not a method as such, but employs a wide array of mixed methods and approaches. In practice, the research often takes an ethnographic form, because it fits well with an ecological view of learning. This research project was partly autoethnographic due to the close interaction with the setting and the learning position taken by the teacher-designers, who reflected throughout on their pedagogical choices. DBR usually involves a collection of an extensive body of data through multiple means of inquiry, including interviews, observation, artefacts, classroom recordings and field notes, among other methods. During its three-year duration, the F-SHAPE project involved gathering data in various contexts and by various means: the PLE tools developed for and in workshops organised for participants at an ICT conference, and for university students and staff over the span of the project; an ethnographic study on the possibilities for implementing PLEs at the Language Centre; and theoretical and practical conceptualisations of PLEs by the researchers. All of this work formed the basis for the design of the course that this article focuses on and which has been reported on in Laakkonen (2011), Laakkonen and Taalas (2015) and Juntunen and Laakkonen (2014, in Finnish).

2.3. The research questions, data and analysis

This article presents a sub-study that addressed the question of how digital literacies useful in the professional lives of the students today can be taught and learned. In other words, the focus is on finding the pedagogical qualities that help to cater for a group of learners with various backgrounds, attitudes and experiences as learners, experts and internet users. The research approach is qualitative. The answers to the research questions were sought by designing and conducting a teaching experiment – or more precisely, providing organically developing conditions for learning – in the form of an elective communication course, and then pinpointing the pedagogical choices in the course design (section 4) and evaluating the student reactions (section 5). The course was organised at the University of Jyväskylä Language Centre in the spring of 2012.

The course design is a lens for the research (Joseph 2004) and helps to target questions that are relevant to the implementation of the design itself. The course was designed and taught by two researchers, the author of this article and her colleague, both of whom have a research focus on PLEs. The researcher-teachers' notes, observations and materials served as a resource for connecting the pedagogical ideas and theories with their implementation on the course.

The student data (see Table 1) were gathered in course enrolment, during the course and shortly after the final session. They provide insights into the student perspective, including their reactions to the course design and culture and reflections on their personal learning experience.

Defining a certain starting point for the analysis would be illusory, because in practice, the dialogic and co-design principles of the course already entail continual cycles of analysis, adjustment, response and re-modification, and, furthermore, because the research approach in general implies dialogue between theory and practice. Keeping this in mind, the transcript of the final course meeting can be defined as the starting point of analysis in this article, because it contained presentations of student projects (their PLEs), their reflections on their learning journeys, feedback on the course in general and a possibility to observe group interaction and conversational patterns. These data were supported with the final assignment, a written self-reflection by the students on their learning and on the course in general.

In the first round of analysis, the data were arranged around the themes outlined in the research questions. Excerpts concerning two themes were systematically selected: what the students considered they had learned during the course and what aspects of the pedagogical design had contributed to this learning. The following round of analysis then allowed for typing within the themes. Although each student had a unique approach to the questions, certain topics and themes evoked similar responses.

Table 1. Types of student data gathered on the course

	Type of data	Data	Time	In focus of analysis	Background/ triangulation
Learning outcomes	Observed	Activity on the course, activity in social media, questions, interaction, assignments, course retention	During the course	(X)	X
	Reported	Transcript of the final session (6 students), reflection paper	At the end/after the course	X	
	Reported	Questionnaire upon enrolment: characteristics as a digital learner, expectations	Before the course		X
	Other evidence	Reported transformations and changes in behaviour, newspaper articles of two students	During/ after the course		X
Student reactions to the course pedagogy & culture	Observed	Participation F2F & online, interaction, assignments	During the course		X
	Reported	Final session (6 students), reflection paper	During/ after the course	X	

The citations selected for this article are more than comments of individual students. They represent the typical responses to the pedagogical choices and learning design as shared by the students in general, or they illustrate the range of approaches reported by students. The qualitative analysis is thus used to produce a representative image of the student reflections. The data excerpts provided in section 5 come from the six students who were present at the final session, and the students are referred to with pseudonyms in order maintain their privacy.

3. Background: personal learning goals in connected environments

3.1. Personal learning environments and networks

The concept of the PLE is prominently used to describe the collections of (digital) tools and environments that individual learners use, whether in formal or informal contexts, to promote their learning. The idea that it is the learners who should focus on designing their own learning environments challenges the tradition according to which Learning Management Systems (LMS) or Virtual Learning Environments (VLE) have been designed. The latter environments, typically owned and controlled by the teacher, usually centre on a specific course in a particular context, with the main focus on the management and administration of learning, not on learning itself. A PLE arranges itself around an individual student, who selects the tools and practices that best suit their needs and preferences, and in which both the ownership and control belong to the learner (see van Harmelen 2008).

In the e-learning community, the concept of PLE emerged soon after the proliferation of Web 2.0. Its conceptualisation, theorisation and implementation were motivated by the potential of social media for both personal and social aspects of learning, and as its transformative impact on knowledge and communication practices began to emerge. Sykes, Ozkoz and Thorne (2008) see that the culture and practices of Web 2.0 changes the positions of learners from consumers to producers and creators, and their role in the educational community towards co-builders and contributors. Downes (2007) formulates that the values of Web 2.0 and the idea of the PLE are essentially the same, namely "the fostering of social networks and communities, the emphasis on creation rather than consumption, and the decentralisation of content and control" (Downes 2007: 19).

Despite its vague definition and the rapid increase (and subsequent decline) in its popularity in the e-learning domain, PLE is more than a buzzword. It provides a useful lens for understanding what learner-centred educational design can be and how learning processes can be supported by technology (Attwell 2007). Thus, PLE in this study is first and foremost a concept that establishes certain premises and principles for how learning and teaching should be organised. The PLE is usually linked with sociocultural, constructivist and connectivist theories of learning. Connectivism, as proposed by Siemens (2005), has not been widely accepted as a learning theory, but it provides some significant insights into learning in networks. The principles of connectivism lie on the process of connecting information sources (including non-human appliances) from a variety of opinions and views, and learning and acquiring the skills and connections that help to maintain learning are more important than knowledge. Furthermore, connectivism emphasises the ability to perceive connections between ideas and concepts as a core skill, and it sees decision-making in choosing what to learn as a mode of learning within the shifting reality. These principles are also prerequisites for learners' ability to use, maintain and develop their PLEs and networks.

The model presented in Figure 1 is the result of iterative development and continuous interplay between the theory and practice of PLE in the F-SHAPE project. The model has been used in various presentations during the project and has undergone several changes and adaptations as the understanding has evolved. The model breaks the concept of PLE into its constituent parts and explicates what the personal, learning and environment components mean in relation to the learning process.

The model has a fourth component, the network, because this is in essence one of the most powerful possibilities of learning on the internet. The PLE is often used interchangeably or complemented with the concept of personal learning networks, that is, organic structures arranged around a learner and comprised of a practically infinite number of people the learner has access to through contacts or through internet communities and the media. The model therefore encompasses both the personal and networked aspects of digital learning.

Figure 1. Components of the PLE model

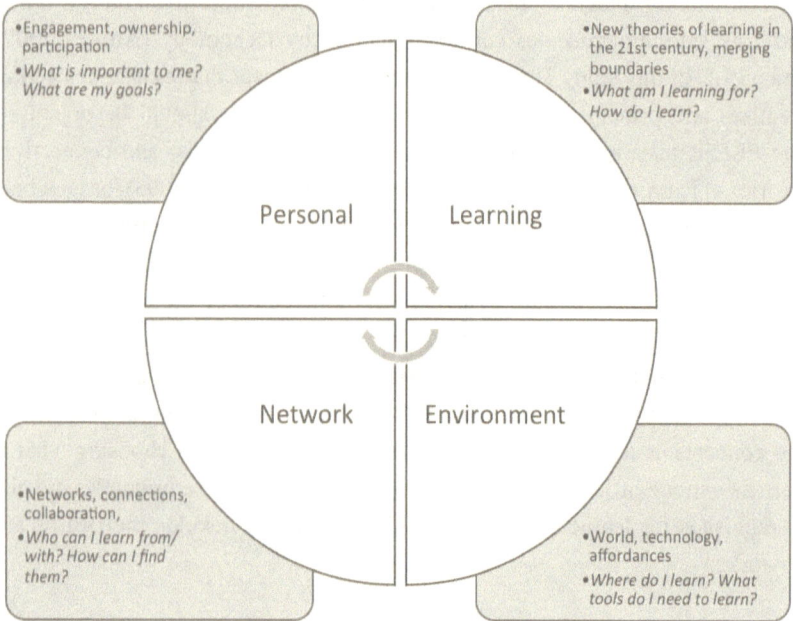

3.2. Digital literacies as skill needed for PLE

Jenkins et al. (2005) emphasise the participatory aspects of digital literacies, which encompass the personal, technological, social and intellectual skills that are needed to live, participate and be involved in the digitally networked world of today. As digital technology becomes increasingly central for full participation in society and the media use shifts from consumption to production and new possibilities for participation emerge, the significance of competences and skills related to social and personal aspects of digital use expand. At the same time, digital literacy encompasses many practical competences related to self-expression, professional and personal learning and working in the knowledge economy.

Being able to build and maintain one's PLE requires various skills in the use of ICT environments, in regulating one's learning process, and in knowledge of the culture and practices of social networks. These capabilities, presented in Figure 1 above, are similar to the areas defined in the digital literacies for learning development framework (Beetham & Sharpe 2010). The digital literacies development framework distinguishes three areas of capabilities relevant to digital literacy: *ICT capabilities* are related to the technical skills and practices built on them as well as to the capacity to choose and appropriate technologies for personal goals and self-expression. *Academic and learning capabilities* are seen as more consistent, but also as more slowly changing in response to the networked technologies that have transformed professional practices. *Information and media capabilities*, in turn, are seen in the intersection of the two previous areas, and they involve the forms, both technological and cultural, in which academic meaning is communicated. According to the model, the development progresses from access and awareness, through skills and practices, to the level of identity and attributes. At that topmost level, students are able to create learning environments suited for their needs and preferences, plan their learning journey, use ICT to "access opportunity, showcase achievements and reflect on the outcomes", design original and meaningful projects as well as be critical users of digital technologies, resources and environments (Beetham & Sharpe 2010). Complemented with the need for managing learning across sites and environments, and a deep understanding of the cultural aspects of networks, the model adequately sums up the skills needed for building a PLE and using it for learning. Consequently, using PLE building as a starting point might provide the students with the opportunity to learn these literacies in a meaningful way.

Selwyn (2010: 67) argues that educators need to address "educational technology as a profoundly social, cultural and political concern". The challenge of the course design presented in this article was twofold: first, to create a course design that would help the students in understanding, building and using their PLEs for the purpose of supporting their professional development; and second, to accomplish this in a manner that would itself reflect the pedagogical ideals of participatory, personalised and networked learning and distributed expertise associated with the PLE.

4. The course design

4.1. Design principles

The overall goal of the course was to equip the learners with the skills and competencies needed to create their own PLEs that would enable them to tap the networks and resources online for learning purposes, and to understand and seize the multiple affordances of technology and the internet in their professional and personal lives. The framework of PLE/N (see Figure 1 above in section 3) translated to the learning goals of the course as follows

- Personal: developing an understanding of one's own strengths and areas of development; setting larger professional and personal goals.

- Learning: setting short-term goals for the course; directing one's learning; grasping the affordances for learning on the internet.

- Environment: understanding one's PLE; seeing beyond it (how it can be developed, what the possibilities for developing it are, how to deal with the constant change); understanding the technologies and their functions.

- Network: understanding the principles of networked learning, understanding the cultural and communicational practices on the web.

Accordingly, the core goals for the course, as stated in the course syllabus, were set as follows:

"After the course the students will understand their personal learning (and communication) environments and be able to develop them according to their needs; understand discursive and communicative practices of various networks and environments; be aware of their personal strengths and expertise and know how to communicate them on the internet; be able to plan their learning and professional development; know how to use digital resources and networks for their own learning in the future".

These general goals served as a starting point for the preliminary design of the course structure and content. In addition, to ensure the implementation of learner-centred pedagogy, the researcher-teachers created a set of principles for the learning culture on the course. Co-design was applied as a form of increasing student engagement and empowerment, and it was also seen as a means for being able to meet the diverse needs of the students. To achieve this and to encourage participation and interaction, students should be encouraged to take initiative, discuss and participate actively, and teachers should ensure that the hierarchy on the course is low and that they are perceived as learners themselves.

Merging the boundaries between informal and formal learning, learning as happening everywhere (serendipity) was seen as an important factor, and meaningfulness and real-life relevance were sought by closely intertwining the learning with students' personal projects. The principles of "backward design" (Wiggins 1998, in Fink 2003) were applied in how the design process and goal-setting for the course began from the desired long-term outcomes of the course, that is, from how it was envisioned that the course participants would be using the internet for their learning long after the course ended. The next step was designing the structure, contents and assignments. On top of these considerations, and as an ideological premise, the course principles should be made transparent and spelled out to the students, from the learning culture and students' responsibility for their learning to expectations of active participation and the co-design principle.

4.2. Participants, timeframe and contents

The experiment was organised as a pop-up course at the Language Centre. It was an elective communication studies course available to all students irrespective of their faculty or stage of studies. There were only a few weeks from the announcement of the course to its opening for enrolment. The ideal group size for the experiment was considered to be 12, with a maximum of 18 students. This is a relatively small number of students, but for experimenting with the pedagogical ideas, working modes and methods it was considered to be optimal. Students could earn only 2 ECTS credits for the course, an amount that was not in proportion to the ideal workload for meeting the course objectives but that was sufficient to cover the minimum workload. However, the small number of credits had an effect on the course's official rate of student retention, as is explained later in section 5.

One of the core questions in designing the course was how to have a design that would not detract from meeting the learning goals but which would provide a sense of organisation and structure and still allow for student participation in its design, personalised learning goals and working modes. To explore this, the designers started with something that might be called a best guess of the goals, contents and timeframe. They also realised that it would be important to spell out the culture of learning involved in the PLE as an educational ideology. That the course syllabus was considered to be a guess is important, and it means that the teacher should be flexible with contents. The course design was set to be open in order to incorporate principles of co-design, dialogue and learner engagement, all of which were seen as premises for student-centred design and learning about PLEs. For more about the co-design principle and its impact, see section 5.

The face-to-face meetings were set to take place over four consecutive weeks. The following month was set for working on the personal projects, after which the projects were presented in class. Figure 2 presents the final timeframe of the course and the main contents of the class meetings.

Figure 2. Course timeframe and contents

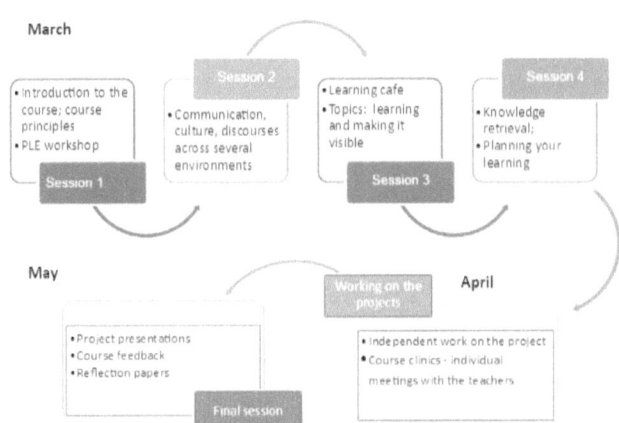

The course had a strong communicative and cultural focus, because this was also the gap identified in the ICT education of the students.

University's IT services offer courses on basic ICT skills, the university library organises courses on information retrieval and databases, and university students are at least assumed to have acquired the skills needed for critical thinking, lifelong learning and the evaluation of information. The design of the course thus filled a gap in the education of students in the skills they need for full professional lives in the digital world. In line with Beetham and Sharpe's (2010) digital literacies development framework, the course was targeted at the level of *attributes/identities* and *practices* (ways of thinking and acting), which would be best learned through project work tied closely to a student's personal development goals, and through the encouragement of participatory, networked and individual learning, respectively.

4.3. Modes of work and assignments

Technological skills (the *skills* and *access* levels in Beetham & Sharpe 2010 framework) were not taught on the course as such. The learners were to build their PLEs using the platforms and environments of their choice. The possible

Chapter 9

need for support was fulfilled through clinics which the students were encouraged to attend individually with their questions and problems of any level. As an additional goal stemming from the core ideology of PLEs, clear connections were needed between the recreational use of digital media and its capacity for developing and performing professional and academic identities. The core of the course was the individual project of building some aspect of one's PLE on the internet for a specific purpose, and the assignments were designed and structured to support this specific goal throughout the course. Furthermore, the assignments were designed to familiarise the students with the digital networks central to their professional development, and at the same time the practices and modes of communication on several platforms and environments were analysed. The individual work was then discussed together in class and in the online environment. The online environment Yammer was used to support the sense of the course as a continuum, because it served as a place to meet and be present between the course meetings and during the individual work. The assignments were designed in a way that they both prepared for the forthcoming class meeting and continued the work on a specific theme afterwards in the online environment.

5. The student perspective

5.1. Student retention

In spite of the short enrolment time, 16 students from four faculties enrolled, and 14 answered the pre-course questionnaire. Twelve were present for the first two class meetings, after which one student left the course with the explanation that other tasks were taking so much time that she would not have the time for the course. Another student simply stopped attending. Her fellow student reported that she had explained that the course did not offer what she was expecting. The remaining 10 students participated actively in the course, both in class and online, and the quality of the student assignments and work was high. However, only seven students finished their personal project and received credit for the course. The three who attended the course but did not finish their project, however, all showed commitment to the course group and to the learning content. The staff member who participated in the in-class sessions later used the ideas and concepts from the course in his own work. The two first-year students announced that they did not particularly need the credits and did not have time for the project at that moment, but announced their willingness to complete the self-reflection assignment for the research, and one of them contacted the teachers a couple of months later to introduce the blog project he had started on collecting people's dreams about their future. The student's project was later expanded to an exposition and it received external funding.

The teachers concluded that the student behaviour and the observations on the course retention tell three things about the effects of tying learning and content to a learner's own identity-building and personal goals and of creating a learning community that also involves the teachers. One is that this seems to increase the commitment to the group and to the purpose of supporting the personal goals of its individual members. The students were willing to contribute to the teachers' research project even when they were not rewarded with credits. Another conclusion is that the significance and urgency of the larger goals beyond the course had a direct impact on the course outcomes. The closer the students were to their graduation or the more pressing their needs for seeking employment were, the more eager they were to finish their project. Finally, these two conclusions build into a question on the relationship between internal and external motivation in formal education. The two credits granted for the course were not important to the students as such, and did not encourage them to finish their projects when they did not feel that it was timely regarding their stage of studies. However, the learning community and course contents seemed to provide sufficient motivation for most of these students to actively participate in all of the classes.

5.2. Enactment of co-design

The analysis of field notes and actualised course practices and activities reveals that engaging the students in the design of the course took shape in several direct and indirect ways.

Upon enrolment the students were asked to fill in a questionnaire that consisted of open-ended questions on the use of the internet and also on the students' expectations of the course. The answers to these questions were used to map the students' needs and helped to fine-tune the first design of the course.

In class the teachers aimed at creating a dialogue with the learners. The students were encouraged to ask questions, interrupt and participate actively. This approach also had perceivable effects and meant that occasionally the topics designed for class were not covered to the extent that was originally planned. From teachers, this requires an internalised belief that dialogue and interaction produce better learning outcomes and help to focus the course contents according to the learners' needs. This dialogue, ultimately, is more valuable than any planned contents. In addition, confidence in one's expertise and willingness to admit its limits are needed, and the answers to students' questions can often be found within the learning community in class or through participants' personal learning networks. Students also had an impact on the methods used in class. The third of the four in-class sessions was organised in the form of a group discussion and utilised the learning café method, which was not in the original course design but was requested by students.

The Yammer online environment was used when planning for the next in-class session. The teachers introduced the main topic of the session a few days earlier and asked the students for ideas, questions and particular sub-topics that they would want to have discussed in class. In addition, the online environment provided possibilities for expanding learning and discussing topics that were of interest to the students, sharing their work and creating interaction in the group. In addition, students were encouraged to familiarise themselves with the learning networks, platforms and environments they found to be of interest.

5.3. Personalised learning on the course

The choice of the shared online environment Yammer was initiated by the teachers as one option among others, such as Facebook and Twitter, but negotiated with the group during the first meeting. However, the students designed their own learning environments, tools and networks for the course as they worked on the assignments that encouraged them to familiarise themselves with the networks and people of interest on the internet. This meant that the social networks, platforms and connections were explicitly also part of the course's learning environment, and selected and designed by the students themselves.

The central form of directing the learning during the course was the personal project. Creating a course in which students design and build projects, in this case their PLEs, cannot be considered an innovative practice because it has been customary in many fields of study and domains of learning. However, this type of a project is almost a prerequisite for meeting the general goals set for the course. The project provided the learners with a chance to approach the use of the internet for learning and communication from an individually meaningful perspective and to pursue their learning goals and seek assistance and guidance in forms that best suit their needs. The various interests and focuses of the students also nurtured distribution of information in class, which supported the social learning processes as well.

To support the personal learning goals and project work, the students had the possibility to meet the teachers privately and to seek assistance on any topic they felt they needed help with. Because the meetings were voluntary, only half of the students booked a session with the teachers. At the time of the clinics, 10 students were still enrolled on the course, with an equal number of males and females. The teachers were unsure of whether it was a question of gender, but all of the students that came to the personal meetings were female. The topics addressed varied from practical help with environments such as LinkedIn and Blogger to more general and even theoretical discussion on using the internet for professional development and on cultural and discursive practices in the social networks.

5.4. Reflections of personal learning and course culture

During the presentation of the course projects, discussion on the way the course was designed emerged. One student expressed having experienced frustration at

Chapter 9

the beginning of the course because of the learner-centred pedagogical approach, a feeling that the rest of group seemed to mainly share:

> "After the first meeting I was frustrated because you sort of got a lot and yet nothing out of it. Maybe after a while, as the course proceeded, you started to like the idea of the course and notice that it is useful. What was frustrating was that you knew that you had to find it yourself from there, that it is not served to you on a plate" (Mary, at the final course meeting).

In general, however, the approach was greeted positively, but regarding the rate of students quitting the course after the first session, this may be an issue that should be addressed. Especially the students that reported having fears and feeling incompetent in digital environments appreciated the open discussion.

> "When I came back to study I thought that what I need is discussing things but you don't have the time for that at lectures and the lecturers put on a little pressure. But here we have had the time to discuss freely and say that 'I don't get it' and get insights from others into that issue" (Miriam, discussion at the final course meeting).

> "I agree...There are others, that I am not the only one who thinks 'Hey, how do I do this, can I press this button?' In this sense it has been really nice and I have learned a lot" (Eva, in response to Miriam at the final course meeting).

The extent and especially the depth to which the students engaged in their development process varied greatly, as can be inferred from the analysis of the reflections at the end of the course. Around half of the students, in their final presentations and their reflective papers, stated mainly that they had had new ideas or learned about new tools. Technology and the PLE were seen as a set of instruments. However, these students also reported on the need to reflect upon one's expertise in another way:

"When it comes to this course, forcing myself to think about and evaluate my professional expertise and to put it in words has been as important as creating a tool that helps me in job-hunting" (Miriam, project presentation at the final course meeting).

The other half of the students reported various changes, revelations or transformations related to themselves, their identity and future goals. These students had also shown more interest in the levels of culture and practice in social networks, and tended to take their learning on this course to a deep level. For example, Nina, a PhD student, reported how her project had brought her earlier thoughts on entrepreneurship to the surface, and how this, in turn, had brought a whole new meaning to the learning during the course:

"So this brought a whole new meaning to this activity (in the social networks). That I am not joining Twitter or creating a blog just for the sake of having done that, but it has a point and may help me in telling what I can do and in finding employment" (Nina, project presentation at the final course meeting).

John, a master's degree student, had thorough plans for his future and for the project, and at the beginning of the course he already had a good knowledge of the internet and social networks. He designed his PLE in a systematic way to serve his well-defined professional goals. However, the dialogue within the group also seemed to serve him, but in a different way than it did the others:

"In short, the consequences have been serendipitous, huge and very positive. I have gathered ideas and insights on this course and others during this spring. Although I often felt that the issue in focus was not relevant to me, some sidetrack or subordinate clause blew my mind. On this course this happened almost on every session, so I got exactly what was promised: insights. As a consequence my master's thesis developed towards a direction that when I had a work interview on Monday, on Tuesday we shook hands and agreed that I will start my new job next Monday" (John, reflection paper).

By aligning the student feedback with information they provided upon enrolment and their personal goals for the project (an assignment at the beginning of the course), it can be concluded that what students learned from the course varied according to the stage of the studies they were at, their experience and attitudes toward ICT, and the goals they currently found meaningful at present. In sum, based on the feedback, reflections and observations, the PLE project allowed for personalised learning paths that meant, on one hand, that what the students reported to have learned varied a great deal (on the Beetham & Sharpe 2010 framework from the awareness and access stages to practices and identities), but on the other, it may have increased both the meaningfulness and depth of learning. The low hierarchy and the positioning of teachers as learners themselves received direct compliments from the students. Based on the student reports and on a few newspaper articles published about the course participants, the course appeared to provide meaningful, in-depth experiences, and perhaps even to initiate transformations beyond the course scope.

6.   Conclusions

Although this study does not offer a conclusive answer to the complex question of how digital literacies for personal professional learning are learned, it does offer insight into the pedagogical choices that may support a student's journey as a digital learner toward competences and skills that are needed in the networked society. It also sheds light on the multiple transformations that take effect in students' thinking and professional development. The question of how these complex and intertwined competences can be taught is perhaps not relevant on the level of individual skills. The more relevant question, then, is how to promote the personal learning process of students who have diverse backgrounds, experiences and attitudes as well as varying needs for support, goals for development and stages of studies. The dialogue on the course seems to enable this, at least to a certain degree, and point the learners towards pursuing their goals and developing their skills and knowledge further, according to their needs. In addition, modelling the course culture more after an affinity space (Gee 2007) than after a community of practice (Lave & Wenger 1991) may be a potential solution that allows for various levels of participation and engagement from the students.

However, the pedagogies of dialogical, networked and personal learning are different from the prevalent pedagogical settings in formal education. Spelling out the rules and expectations for students may be a starting point, but without true opportunities for asking questions, expressing insecurities and directing the discussion towards areas of interest to the students, it may not be enough. From teachers, this approach demands willingness to release control and power, letting go of the planning mentality, and adopting the position of a co-learner. The principle of co-design was implemented with relatively simple means. The way the course environment was used created possibilities for sharing and networked learning, but also provided the course members with an arena for participation in the course design. This indicates that creating a learning culture that offers true possibilities for personal development and deep learning does not require specific tools or methods, but presumes a learning culture that encourages participation and offers possibilities for individuality and personalisation. In other words, organising the teaching and learning in alignment with the values that are inherent in the participatory, networked culture and in the student-centred idea of learning.

References

Attwell, G. 2007. Personal learning environments – the future of eLearning? *eLearning papers, 2* (1). Retrieved from http://www.openeducationeuropa.eu/en/article/Personal-Learning-Environments---the-future-of-eLearning%3F?paper=57211

Barab, S. & Squire, K. 2004. Design-Based Research: putting a stake in the ground. *The Journal of the Learning Sciences, 13* (1), 1–14. doi:10.1207/s15327809jls1301_1

Beetham, H. & Sharpe, R. 2010. Digital literacy framework. *JISC - The Design Studio*. Retrieved from http://jiscdesignstudio.pbworks.com/w/page/46740204/Digital%20literacy%20framework

Downes, S. 2007. Learning networks in practice. *Emerging technologies for learning, 2*. Retrieved from http://www.downes.ca/files/Learning_Networks_In_Practice.pdf

Drexler, W. 2010. The networked student model for construction of personal learning environments: Balancing teacher control and student autonomy. *Australasian Journal of Educational Technology, 26* (3), 369–385.

Fink, L. D. 2003. *Creating significant learning experiences: an integrative approach to designing college courses.* San Francisco: Jossey-Bass. 63–64.

Gee, J. P. 2007. Affinity spaces: from age of mythology to today's schools. *Good Video Games and Good Learning: Collected Essays on Video Games, Learning and Literacy.* Peter Lang: New York, 87–103.

Guth, S. 2009. Personal learning environments for language learning. In S. Thomas (ed.), *Handbook of research on Web 2.0 and Second Language Learning.* London: IGI Global. doi:10.4018/978-1-60566-190-2.ch024

Jenkins, H., Purushotma, R., Clinton, K., Weigel, M. & Robison, A. J. 2005. Confronting the challenges of participatory culture: media education for the 21st Century. *Building the field of digital media and learning.* Chicago: MacArthur Foundation. Retrieved from http://www.newmedialiteracies.org/wp-content/uploads/pdfs/NMLWhitePaper.pdf

Joseph, D. 2004. The practice of Design-Based Research: uncovering the interplay between design, research, and the real-world context. *Educational Psychologist, 39* (4), 235–242. doi:10.1207/s15326985ep3904_5

Juntunen, M. & Laakkonen, I. 2014. PLE – tapa oppia [PLE - a way to learn]. In P. Häkkinen & J. Viteli (eds.), *Pilvilinnoja ja palomuureja – Tulevaisuuden oppimisen ja työnteon tilat. F-SHAPE-projektin satoa* [Clouds and firewalls. Findings from the F-SHAPE project]. Jyväskylä: Finnish Institute for Educational Research, 59–81. Retrieved from https://ktl.jyu.fi/julkaisut/julkaisuluettelo/julkaisut/2014/D109.pdf

Laakkonen, I. 2011. Personal learning environments in higher education language courses: an informal and learner-centred approach. In S. Thouësny & L. Bradley (eds.), *Second language teaching and learning with technology: views of emergent researchers.* Dublin: Research-publishing.net, 9–28. doi:10.14705/rpnet.2011.000004

Laakkonen, I. & Taalas, P. 2015. Towards new cultures of learning: personal learning environments as a developmental perspective for improving higher education language courses. *Language Learning in Higher Education, 5* (1), 223–241. doi:10.1515/cercles-2015-0011

Lankshear, C. & Knobel, M. 2007. Sampling "the new" in new literacies. In M. Knobel, C. Lankshear, C. Bigum, & M. Peters (eds.), *A New Literacies Sampler.* New York: Peter Lang, 1–24.

Lave, J. & Wenger, E. 1991. *Situated learning: legitimate peripheral participation*. Cambridge: Cambridge University Press. doi:10.1017/CBO9780511815355

Littlejohn, A., Beetham, H. & McGill, L. 2012. Learning at the digital frontier: a review of digital literacies in theory and in practice. *Journal of Computer Assisted Learning, 28*, 547–556.

Ludvigsen, S., Lund, A., Rasmussen, I. & Säljö, R. 2011. Learning across sites. *Learning across sites: new tools, infrastructures and practices*. New York: Routledge.

Selwyn, N. 2010. Looking beyond learning: notes towards the critical study of educational technology. *Journal of Computer Assisted Learning, 26* (1), 65–73.

Siemens, G. 2005. Connectivism: a learning theory for the digital age. *International Journal of Instructional Technology and Distance Learning, 2* (1), 3–10.

Sykes, J., Ozkoz, A. & Thorne, S. 2008. Web 2.0, synthetic immersive environments, and mobile resources for language education. *CALICO Journal, 25* (3), 528–546.

Reinking, D. & Bradley, B. A. 2007. *On formative and design experiments: approaches to language and literacy research*. New York: Teachers' College.

van Harmelen, M. 2008. Design trajectories: four experiments in PLE implementation. *Interactive Learning Environments - Special Issue: Personal Learning Environments, 16* (1), 35–46. doi:10.1080/10494820701772686

Wiggins, G. 1998. *Educative assessment: designing assessments to inform and improve student performance*. San Francisco: Jossey Bass.

10. Learner agency within the design of an EAP course

Riina Seppälä[1]

Abstract

To meet the demands of today's society and working life, higher education should support the development of learner agency. How the agency of individual learners emerges in university courses and what kind of agency empowers the learners to face new challenges should be considered. In this article, the focus is on learner agency enabled and expressed on a higher education language course. One learner's experiences of a blended English for Academic Purposes (EAP) course are explored and used to examine the design of the course. The data reveal that the learner's views of language-use categories and of herself as a language user emerged as central parts of her agency. Although the learner was, in many respects, an active agent on the course, she seemed to be restricted by the assumed expectations of academic language use. Thus, empowering agency was not expressed within the course design. The Design-Based Research (DBR) approach employed in the study enables changes to the learning design to better support the development of empowering agency. Examples of such changes include discussing different learner positions on academic courses and supporting learners' reflections on the relevance of the course. DBR as a strategy to support teachers' agency is also discussed.

Keywords: agency, design, design-based research, English for academic purposes.

---

1. Language Centre, Aalto University, Finland; riina.seppala@aalto.fi

How to cite this chapter: Seppälä, R. (2015). Learner agency within the design of an EAP course. In J. Jalkanen, E. Jokinen, & P. Taalas (Eds), *Voices of pedagogical development - Expanding, enhancing and exploring higher education language learning* (pp. 197-222). Dublin: Research-publishing.net. doi:10.14705/rpnet.2015.000293

Chapter 10

1. Introduction

Constant changes and developments in today's society and working life require skills and resources different from those needed before (Conole 2012; Kalantzis & Cope 2001, 2004; Sawyer 2006; Taalas, Tarnanen & Huhta 2007; Tynjälä 2011). It is increasingly important for individuals to be able to adjust to and learn in novel situations and contexts throughout their lives (Kalantzis & Cope 2001, 2004; Sawyer 2006; Tynjälä 2011). This need is also reflected in the requirements placed on the education system, particularly on higher education, because students proceed to the labour market during or after their studies.

Higher education students, preparing to work as experts in their own field, should be able to exercise their agency to meet new challenges and to undertake the responsibility of maintaining their own expertise. Agency to construct one's own learning and expertise should therefore be supported and promoted during university studies. The question then arises of how the agency of individual learners emerges in university courses and what kind of agency empowers learners to face new challenges. In this article, the focus is on one learner's agency on a higher education language course and the way it relates to the notion of life-long learning. The research questions are as follows: (1) What kind of learner agency is enabled and expressed within the design of an EAP course from the point of view of one learner? (2) How does the learning design support or restrict the development of the type of agency needed to maintain and expand learners' expertise? It should be noted, however, that this article examines learner agency from a limited, single-learner perspective. To further develop tertiary level studies, large-scale, in-depth research on learner experiences is needed.

2. Dimensions of agency

The conception of learners' intentional action to develop their skills and to discover the best ways to achieve that development are embedded in the concept of agency, which can be briefly described as the individual's "socioculturally mediated capacity to act" (Ahearn 2001: 112). Extensive research has been conducted on agency in different fields and with different emphases in the interrelationship between individuals and their environment. Some schools of thought place more stress on the environment and structures, and others concentrate on the inner processes of an individual in the emergence of agency. Due to the complexity of the concept, forming a thorough understanding of agency as well as grasping and benefiting from the significance of the research results in other contexts has been difficult. Even the brief definition by Ahearn (2001) extends in many directions and implies various processes that cannot be defined decisively. However, uncovering the concept of agency and its different forms and manifestations is crucial to be able to support life-long learning in education. So rather than providing a fixed definition of agency, constructing an understanding of agency based on its various dimensions could better illustrate the concept.

Drawing on previous studies, the central dimensions of agency include the initiative or intentional action (e.g. Hunter & Cooke 2007; van Lier 2008) of individuals to reach personal goals (Kalaja, Alanen, Palviainen & Dufva 2011). In addition, the accountability of individuals for their actions and the way in which these individuals are credited for their accomplishments could be viewed as another dimension of agency (Lipponen & Kumpulainen 2011). Agency is also often seen as dynamic, emerging and shaped in and by interaction (e.g. van Lier 2008). In that sense, agency has been described by a number of authors (Ahearn 2001; Hunter & Cooke 2007; Lantolf & Thorne 2006; van Lier 2008; Wertsch 1991; Wertsch, Tulviste & Hagstrom 1993) as being mediated by, for example, structures and tools. In addition, closely connected to the concept is individuals' sense of their own agency (see Bandura 1997 and 2001 on self-efficacy; van Lier 2008), that is, the way individuals feel they are able to "make a difference" (Mercer 2012: 41) in their own learning in a particular context. Mercer (2011, 2012) argues that agency consists of two components: the deliberate, agentic behaviour of the learners and their sense of agency. This would suggest that when exploring agency, observational and reflective data should be combined to capture these different components.

Given the dynamic nature of agency, certain dimensions might emerge as central to individual learners in different learning contexts. In-depth case studies then become necessary to uncover how agency unfolds in specific situations. Moreover, taking into account the need for the new types of participation and individual development mentioned earlier, it is essential to explore what kind of agency would be truly empowering for learners to function in society and what kind of agency should, therefore, be supported through pedagogical choices and decisions for individual courses.

One specific change should be promoted across all educational levels. Following the notion of life-long and life-wide learning, crossing the boundaries between and connecting formal and informal contexts for learning should be encouraged (e.g. Luukka et al. 2008; Kalantzis & Cope 2012). In this era of ubiquitous information and new literacies (e.g. Lankshear & Knobel 2003; Cazden et al. 1996), learners should be able to draw on learning contexts from outside of formal education, and this ability should also be acknowledged by the educational system. In this way, focusing on the development of each individual would make learning more personalised and meaningful. Although attempts have been made to achieve this personalisation, the implementation is challenging. One reason might be that learners have usually been socialised into a certain type of a culture of learning for several years, and transforming that familiar and established culture is a lengthy process. Uncovering the roots underlying this difficulty, therefore, requires a more thorough understanding of the personalisation process. The current article is based on one higher education language teacher's design-based research process, aimed at understanding individual learners' experiences during university studies and contributing to the development of teaching practices. In this respect, two perspectives are adopted; that of an individual learner on an academic English course and that of the design.

3. Design-based research strategy

When considering supporting learners' agency from the perspective of a higher education language teacher, the design of courses is the main tool in the process. In this article, design is defined as the way in which the pedagogical course plan unfolds in the interaction between the learners and the teacher – in other words, how the design is "enacted" (Lund & Hauge 2011: 262) in the course. Through this enactment, learner agency is contextualised and situated within the design.

One research strategy to support practitioners in this type of exploration is DBR, which aims at changing educational practices by researching learning in real-life contexts and developing learning designs through cycles of data collection, analysis and development (Barab & Squire 2004; Design-Based Research Collective 2003; Edelson 2002; Sandoval & Bell 2004; Wang & Hannafin 2005). This cyclical approach allows researching how agency is enabled on an individual course but also immediately making changes in the learning design to better support learners. This might also facilitate implementation of significant changes in higher education.

As mentioned above, although the need for development in the education system has been recognised, implementing the change in, for example, language teaching, has been slow and difficult (Conole 2012; Ruohotie-Lyhty 2011a). One reason for this difficulty is that educational structures and the decision-making within them are usually complex. Another reason might be that if the terms of the change have been prescribed from above, practitioners might not have ownership of how the change should be brought about. Therefore, research conducted from within the system by, for example, teachers, would be particularly valuable: how individual teachers struggle with the new demands, how these themes materialise on individual courses and how they could best be tackled. Through DBR, these questions can be addressed. In addition, due to the combination of research, development and implementation, DBR allows new types of researcher profiles to emerge, as the dual role of a teacher-researcher is recognised and valued. Furthermore, teachers' experience and ethnographic data are often a natural part of DBR. Therefore, this type of research could support individual teachers' agency by giving them the opportunity to explore and raise new themes that are relevant for discussion from their perspective and by giving an example of a different career path of a teacher-researcher.

4. Finnish higher education as research context

The research context in the current article is unique in the research on agency to date. For example, recent research on agency in language learning has largely focused on high school students (Wassell, Fernández Hawrylak & LaVan 2010), language majors (Kalaja et al. 2011; Mercer 2011, 2012) and English as a Second Language (ESL) learners (Flowerdew & Miller 2008). Skinnari (2012) has investigated the agency (and language learner identity construction) of primary school pupils in the fifth and sixth grade in Finland. Alanen et al. (2011) studied the agency of pre-service teachers majoring in languages during a Language Technology for Language Teachers programme, focusing on multimodal pedagogy. In the current article, the learner is not a language major but attends a university-level English course as a part of her studies. Blin and Jalkanen (2014) have explored university students' agency in a Finnish literacy skills course, taking a design perspective on language learning. University students' agency related to learning English has been studied by Basharina (2009, with a focus on online environments) and Murphey and Carpenter (2008). In Finland, language and communication studies are included in all higher education degrees. This means that all university students attend pre-determined language courses during their studies, in addition to the major and minor subject studies that they have chosen themselves. These courses are either compulsory ones tailored for students of a particular field or elective courses with different focuses (e.g. writing). This background offers a research setting to explore and increase understanding of the relationship students have with the focus of the courses and how that focus as well as course content could be better connected with their "life-world" (e.g. Kalantzis & Cope 2004).

5. Data and methods

The course in question was an elective EAP course taught by a teacher-researcher. University students from all faculties could take the course as a part of the language and communication requirements of their degree. The course combined contact lessons (16 hours) with distance work, facilitated by a virtual learning environment. The course focused on academic writing as well as on learners' personal language learning beliefs and experiences. More specifically, factors affecting language learning were discussed on the course and the learners reflected on their own learning, strengths and weaknesses and their proficiency level in English. The course themes were discussed in academic papers written by the students, feedback was given on them and academic writing was discussed in class. Other course assignments included an independent learning project planned and implemented by the learners themselves as well as an oral presentation.

Following the typical features of DBR, various types of data were collected from the course in order to document it as thoroughly as possible from different perspectives. The data consist of all the course materials in the learning environment, the teacher's course and lesson plans and a reflective diary during the course, students' course assignments (including a reflective blog, academic texts, materials related to the independent learning project, videoed oral presentations), teacher and peer feedback on them, questionnaire answers collected during the course, emails related to the course, videoed contact lessons and learner interviews. First, qualitative content analysis (Dörnyei 2007) was conducted on the questionnaire and interview data in order to identify themes that emerged as relevant for learning. After that, one learner's data were scrutinised to truly get to the core of the dimensions of agency that emerged as central for the learner in question. As the learner attended a university course, these types of data can be seen as a kind of performance (a performance to the teacher-researcher, to the other learners). However, this has been acknowledged in the research process, because, to some extent, the learner probably builds a picture of the ideal learner through her answers. Even so, the data can still shed light on the learner's actions and views on the type of learning she assumes is aimed at in university studies and in this way they reveal some of the main challenges of higher education language education.

The learner focused on, in this article, is 'Katri' (a pseudonym). At the time of attending the course, she was finishing her bachelor's degree and later continued with her master's studies. She had earlier completed one compulsory English course and her proficiency level was approximately B2 based on the Common European Framework of Reference for Languages (Council of Europe 2013). Based on questionnaire and interview data as well as learner documents, Katri had clear career plans for herself and already had work experience in her field. She was chosen for a more detailed analysis, because her data clearly revealed her views on language use in different contexts. Her views are illustrative of some crucial contradictions learners on this course and other EAP courses might experience. In addition, she was able to reflect on her own views and experiences extensively during and after the course. As such, Katri's data provided a fertile ground for exploring the dimensions of her agency. Focusing on one learner also allows her experiences to be responded to in the design decisions in more detail.

6. Language use categories underlying learner agency

What became central in Katri's course experience were her descriptions of two language use categories: everyday language use and academic language use. More specifically, what seemed to define her experience was her relationship with those language use categories and, particularly, academic writing as the focus of the course. Her views were made explicit in various data types before, during and after the course. For example, in a questionnaire completed before the course's contact lessons began, Katri writes about her preferred ways of learning languages. In one of her replies, she clearly refers to a class environment: "I learn best by listening to others and taking notes. It's also good to talk with other students who are trying to learn the same things"[2]. However, in the answer to the question "Describe yourself as a language learner" she highlights her preference for other types of learning situations: "I think I learn best in practice, for example during holidays when I have to use the language in everyday life. Too many assignments at school kill my motivation".

---

2. All examples taken from the learner's questionnaire answers and blog entries are direct quotations. Spelling errors have been corrected.

Here, Katri emphasises being an everyday language user and suggests that the institutional, formal way of learning ("too many assignments at school") is not ideal for her. Similarly, when asked about how writing in English makes her feel, her answer is neutral: "It's quite normal. I don't feel anything special". However, when she is asked specifically about the kind of academic writer she thinks she is at the moment, she again stresses the difference between various contexts of language use: "Not so much an academic writer I guess, I have ways to go around the words I don't know in everyday life texts".

In a comparison to her skills in writing everyday life texts, Katri does not consider academic writing to be her strength. This dichotomy seemed to set the tone for her whole course experience, and it was also illustrated in her course goals, which learners were asked to record during or after the first contact meeting of the course. At this point, the learners had more specific information about the content and focuses of the course. Katri wrote that she would like to learn to write in a more formal style, know more academic vocabulary and cite sources appropriately. In addition, she wanted to change her attitude towards academic writing, so that it would stop feeling so stressful and difficult that it would "show in the text".

Based on these examples, Katri is aware of her own views and constructs her course experience around the premise that she does not identify with the focus of the course. This approach is also illustrated later when, in a reflective task, she was asked to assess her proficiency in English and write the self-assessment in her blog. She described the following situations and characteristics as some of her strengths in using English:

> "Natural conversations…natural perspective towards English; I am not much of an academic English user, but I enjoy using the language in natural settings in school, work, and with my friends, I am not nervous in those situations at all and I am the one who always has something to say".

In addition, as her weaknesses she names not having the "occupational or personal need" to learn academic English because she already manages different everyday language use situations. In these comments, Katri again refers to academic English as something that does not feel relevant to her and she contrasts it with "natural settings". However, in those "natural settings" she also includes school and work. The comments seem, therefore, to highlight the conception that she does not see academic language use as a part of her life in any way – even her university studies or future work – and that, in this sense, it is not authentic language use for her. She described similar views in two semi-structured interviews as well (Dörnyei 2007), which were conducted at the end of the course and six months later. In the interviews, she describes her own abilities in language use in the following ways:

> [Katri answers a question on what kind of situations she uses English in at the moment]: "Speaking in English if I don't need any specific vocabulary – that I do best – if I don't remember a word I can always say it in another way[3].
>
> I don't really regard myself as an academic writer – when I write it is difficult for me not to express my own opinion – I would just like to bring my own point of view into it".

Here, Katri gives reasons for enjoying speaking English in everyday situations: the communication is natural in the sense that she is able to express her own opinion and she does not have to be concerned about mistakes. The ideal topics would be related to something deeper than, for example, work. In those discussions, she would be able to exchange experiences and impressions with another person as well as describe her feelings. Some of the language learning goals described by her were connected with these views: for example, learning new vocabulary in order to express her feelings and opinions using rich language.

At the same time, Katri's descriptions shed some light on why academic language use makes her anxious. She implies that more formal language use situations

---

[3]. All examples taken from the interviews were originally in Finnish and have been paraphrased in English by the researcher.

have stricter rules and norms that she is perhaps not able to follow. These include situations in which "specific vocabulary" is needed, accuracy is expected, and in which making a mistake would be a cause for embarrassment. In addition, she sees that requirements related to references and even the use of commas are imposed on language users, and expressing one's own opinions is not allowed.

What is interesting is that although academic writing is not relevant in Katri's life, she still set goals for herself to change her way of thinking. Here Katri describes her course goals:

> "The last two [goals] were intertwined so that the use of sources would just become like 'I'll just search for a source and put it there' – and that it wouldn't be like 'oh no, not the bibliography again, how do I do this, how about commas, how about dates' – and if we talk about essays, research proposals, theses, academic texts, that I wouldn't feel like 'this is the difficult task again' but I would just start to write instead – and that I would just do that and that's it – a kind of change in my attitude – that I do not have to stress about it".

As her answer shows, it is clearly the formal context of language use that is focused on in this university course, so Katri needs to adjust to it by changing her attitude.

7. Attitude to language use categories as a means to construct learner identity

In addition to defining her own preferences and goals in relation to these different categories of language use, Katri also presents and defines herself in relation to the same categories in the interviews, questionnaire answers and blog texts. This type of reflective data (e.g. interviews, questionnaires, diaries) has been made use of in earlier agency research (e.g. Flowerdew & Miller 2008; Lasky 2005; Murphey & Carpenter 2008; Ruohotie-Lyhty 2011a, 2011b; Vähäsantanen, Saarinen & Eteläpelto 2009) in order to gain insight into how the individuals, in their own words, describe their personal experience and the way in which they perceive the situation. This emphasises agency as being constructed through an individual's own experiences and perceptions (e.g. Ruohotie-Lyhty 2011a). It also aligns with Dufva and Aro's (2014) dialogical view on agency in language learning. Drawing on, for example, Sullivan and McCarthy (2004), Dufva and Aro (2014) have discussed a dialogical perspective on agency in learning English, placing importance on the personal stories and lived experiences of an individual and focusing on the fluidity of agency of those individuals in time and space. This type of emphasis on the personal experiences sheds light on learner agency in Katri's case as well.

From this perspective, agency is closely connected to identity construction, especially if identity is defined according to Norton's (2000) view, in which it consists of the way an individual sees and constructs the relationship between oneself and the world, and one's possibilities for the future. This relationship is dynamic as it is reshaped, for example, during the learning process (Norton 2000; Norton Peirce 1995; see also Lave 1993). The view is shared by van Lier (2007), who defines identity as new ways of relating the self to the world. Individuals perceive situations, decide on their own actions and interpret experiences in their own way. Similarly, in the interviews, questionnaire answers and blog texts, Katri was describing her relationship to using English.

Ruohotie-Lyhty (2009) has conducted similar research using interview data on newly qualified teachers and their agency during the first years in working life. According to Ruohotie-Lyhty (2009), teachers acted in different work-related situations based on how they, from the perspective of their own backgrounds, saw and understood those situations. This approach, in turn, shaped their agency. Ruohotie-Lyhty (2009, 2011b) connects this finding to Bandura's (1997) as well as Holland, Lachicotte, Skinner & Cain's (1998) views. For example, Holland et al. (1998) suggest that agency is rooted in individuals' expertise and how they identify themselves with the expert community. How individuals view themselves and their expertise determines how different situations are perceived and, as a consequence, how those situations are addressed. This is closely connected to Bandura's (1997, 2001) views on self-efficacy. Although Ruohotie-

Lyhty's (2009, 2011b) study focused on teachers instead of learners, a similar situation emerged in the present study, as Katri's own perceptions seemed to shape her actions and experiences on the course. Based on the data excerpts, Katri described herself as someone clearly belonging to the group of everyday language users and, at the same time, excluded herself from the expert group of academic language users. What she saw as the focus of the course contradicted her ideal language use and the identity and expertise she associated with herself.

7.1. Assumptions of preferred agency

Despite the perceived contradiction, Katri clearly tried to make sense of academic language use when working on the course assignments. She expressed some uncertainty about the proper way to complete the assignments. For example, after the second contact meeting of the course, Katri went to talk to the teacher. She explained that she felt some of the instructions for the written assignments were not always clear regarding language use and style. She mentioned that based on what she knew about academic writing – having even consulted a friend about it – the use of passive voice is often recommended. Katri did not know whether to write the texts using the first person pronoun (I) or if more objective language use was preferable. The teacher tried to guide Katri in class by explaining that as the topics of the written assignments were related to the students' own experiences in language learning, the style of the texts could reflect that.

When writing the third assignment, a synthesis, Katri contacted the teacher via email, asking for advice on how to write such a text. The text type seemed to be unfamiliar to her and she wanted to know how to correctly incorporate the different sources of information. In this way, Katri seemed to find it important to ensure that she followed the instructions of the assignment thoroughly and fulfilled the expectations for academic writers. Based on the questionnaire answers of all students, the text type was unfamiliar to most of them, but Katri was still the only one who asked for more detailed instructions. Considering that she did not see the relevance of academic writing in her life, she still made attempts to complete the academic writing assignments as carefully as possible, suggesting some type of investment in and intentional action for completing the assignments well. This effort highlights the type and complexity of Katri's agency on the course. It is possible that she assumed that merely following the rules to complete the assignments was the preferred type of agency for the learners.

7.2. New positioning: learner agency in mastering academic writing

Katri's views on these different types of language use and her efforts to figure out the features of the more distant language use category were also illustrated in her descriptions of her successes and accomplishments in the course. For example, in the questionnaire filled in during the final contact meeting of the course, she replied:

> "My views related to reading and writing academic texts and incorporating sources have changed in the way I hoped: they are like any other texts, and it is not so stressful anymore, because I have gained new tools and good feedback".

Here Katri describes how her view of academic texts has changed. In the interviews, she went into more detail on how she viewed them and how she felt when completing academic reading or writing assignments:

> "If I had to start writing something – a thesis, a research paper – I have an idea of what the paragraphs are *supposed* [emphasis by author] to be, what kind of vocabulary I *should* use and not use – what the bibliography looks like – maybe some kind of models in my head – I already have some kind of an idea of what is *expected* of me.
>
> Well I really did learn what I was *supposed* to learn – that I do not have to stress about them [academic texts] – that even if someone says 'academic something' and talks about references and certain formats and how something should be done then fine, I just write it and that's it (laughs)".

Katri describes succeeding in adjusting her language use to meet the requirements of a different genre. She, in a way, describes being able to gain access to the group of academic language users to the extent that she needed to in order to complete the course assignments and to write her thesis later on. In that sense, she was extending her own language use repertoire as she gained resources for academic writing.

What Katri described was a change in the relationship between herself and the focus of the course: as she became better able than before to manage academic language use situations, she was able to relate herself to the world in a new way (Norton 2000; Norton Peirce 1995; van Lier 2007). She saw those situations as ones with predetermined rules with little room for adjustments, but once she mastered them, she felt less stress. The introduction to concrete rules and guidelines became central to Katri's agency on the course. Through her own perception, she reported new ways to function in that context (the world of academic writing) and described herself as someone who knows what she is supposed to do (illustrated in the use of words such as supposed, should, expected), for example, when engaged in the process of writing her thesis.

8. The frames set for learner agency through the design

Despite the new ways in which Katri described her own actions, she still explained the focus of the course itself (academic writing) through its rules and restrictions. In that sense, her agency could be seen as rather limited, because her writing was directed by those restraints. Because this view emerged from other learners' data as well, these learner experiences gave reason to explore the design of the course and how the focus of the course is presented through it. In this exploration, the following questions were considered: Was there some aspect in the design that emphasised academic language use in this way and formed a basis for those learner descriptions? Did the design of the course restrict other views?

Chapter 10

When considering this interrelationship between the design of an individual course and learner experiences in it, the idea of positioning could be applied. According to Harré and van Langenhove (1999), positioning refers to the way in which we assign certain dynamic "roles" or "parts" to ourselves and others in, for example, a conversation. Individuals can position themselves in relation to others, or in relation to the "action" one is engaged in. Language learning and language use could be examples of such action. An individual can also be given certain positions by others, which can be assumed or rejected. This idea of positioning in relation to agency has been employed earlier by, for example, Lipponen and Kumpulainen (2011). They stress that instead of being stable, positions are constructed and reconstructed. Following this, Lipponen and Kumpulainen (2011) conducted research on positions that pre-service teachers took and were given and how those positions were created and transformed in situated discourse practices on a course related to their studies. For example, teachers may give authority to students by positioning them as experts in a conversation and by positioning themselves as belonging to the same group as the students.

Here, the notion was first utilised in exploring the way in which Katri positioned herself as a language learner and language user in relation to the focus of the course. Another way to employ the theory is to examine the positions that are available or given to the learners on the course through its design – in the course materials and feedback given to them on the course assignments. On this EAP course, academic writing as the main focus of the four contact meetings was made explicit through the course materials (e.g. lesson plans, the teacher's slides and other materials saved in the learning environment). For example, academic writing was defined at the beginning of the course through its features, and the assessment criteria for the course assignments were introduced then. Many of the features were discussed during the course through concrete examples in texts and short writing tasks given to the learners. For example, in the first two contact meetings, academic text types and their structures as well as citation practices were introduced, while the second meeting focused on formal style as well as on online dictionaries and thesauruses as tools in editing texts. The writer's voice, hedging, coherence and cohesion were also discussed on the course. Although the purpose of these themes was to make the genre of academic writing more concrete and accessible for the learners, it could also have been perceived as a list of requirements on how the course assignments should be completed appropriately, following all the guidelines. This is what the teacher also noticed during the course. The purpose of academic writing was returned to in the third meeting, because the teacher felt that the purpose behind the writing process had been overlooked. Therefore, the learning design was changed so that the topic was returned to halfway through the course.

When giving feedback on the written assignments, the teacher tried to focus on various elements of academic writing introduced in class. For example, based on analysis of the feedback given on Katri's academic texts, the feedback focused not only on, for example, the style and the structure of the texts and grammar but also the progression of ideas and the way in which conclusions were drawn at the end of the paper. The teacher acknowledged the critical approach that Katri had adopted on one topic and pointed out her strengths in writing an argumentative text. The teacher also commented on Katri's ability to make use of the feedback given to her in the earlier assignments. The teacher encouraged her to view the comments as recognition of her hard work.

Although the feedback was intended to help the learner consider various aspects of academic writing, it did not seem to have an effect on Katri's views. Actually, what was alarming for the teacher was that Katri did not once describe academic writing or academic language use as communication. Despite efforts to portray academic writing as a way to express one's views and to present one's arguments in a specific context, it was not seen or, rather, was not described as such by Katri. It might be that her earlier views on the nature of academic writing were too strongly ingrained to be changed during one course. However, considering the actual course content (e.g. themes of the contact lessons and the instructions given for the writing assignments), much of that might still have been perceived as restrictions on writing at the expense of the idea of communication.

These ideas on the nature of language and communication should have been discussed, because the academic context was not the most relevant one for all learners. As Katri's case shows, for those outsiders, this perhaps presented problems in terms of learner agency: how to connect one's identity and one's views of the course focus so that the course experience would be meaningful.

Although the research setting was different, Lasky's (2005) observations in a study on the interaction of reform mandates with teacher identity resemble those in Katri's case. In survey and interview data of experienced teachers in the midst of educational reform, Lasky (2005) observed a "disjuncture" between the teachers' identity and the assumptions that were embedded for their role in the mandates for reform. This restricted teachers' agency in the reform context. Still, despite the new expectations related to the reform, their sense of identity as teachers, which had developed over the years, was not altered. In one sense, a similar situation seemed to occur with Katri on the EAP course in how she experienced a disjuncture between her own identity and the expectations embedded in academic writing assignments.

9. Insights into agency within the design of the EAP course

This individual learner's experience provides important insights into the type of agency expressed on this EAP course and the type of empowering agency that should be supported on other higher education language courses. First, Katri's experience highlights the complexity of the learning situation and of the interrelationship between individual learners' agency and design. The design of the course carries certain expectations and assumptions related to the focuses of the course as well as the learners. There is potential for meaningful learning to take place, but, at the same time, the assumptions are not always verbalised, made explicit or challenged. In addition, those expectations are not necessarily realised when the design is enacted on the course. Through the design, the teacher did not want to portray academic writing – or any language use on her courses – in the way that Katri saw it, but it was still Katri's experience. She most likely had these views of everyday and academic language use also before the course, but the design of the course did not succeed in highlighting the underlying purpose of communication in different contexts: conveying one's own views. To support the development of higher education language teaching, the course design should, at the very least, enable and afford the emergence of empowering agency, not hinder or restrict it.

However, considering the dimensions of agency presented earlier, Katri was in many respects an active agent on the course: she completed extensive independent assignments, initiated interaction with the teacher on several occasions, set her own goals at the beginning of the course, worked purposefully to reach them and described having reached most of those goals (e.g. Kalaja et al. 2011). She also described her sense of agency (e.g. Mercer 2012) when she explained her course experience, and, for example, listed several features of a specific genre that she had apprehended. Nevertheless, the learning that Katri described was based on a view of academic language use as following specific rules even at the level of individual words. Her agency seemed to emerge through having concrete guidelines for language use that she could then adjust to, but the goal of that action merely seemed to be to complete the course assignments and it did not seem to be particularly meaningful outside the context of the course. Agency emerged and was operationalised within certain frames and it was limited by this mismatch of one's own skills and aspirations in relation to those perceived as the focus of the course. The design of the course did not therefore offer Katri possibilities for a different type of empowering agency. On the other hand, Katri, in her own way, gained access to academic language use. Although she did not see further use for it other than writing her thesis for graduation, that access might eventually become meaningful and more closely connected to her future life-world. Due to that possibility, longitudinal studies on learners' agency could shed light on the long-term development of learning paths (see Dufva & Aro 2014).

One reason why the course focus failed to become meaningful for Katri might be that the formal and informal contexts of learning remained separate, and the boundaries between them were too clear and limiting. Drawing on the learners' own experiences and life-world was utilised when language learning experiences, views and needs were discussed on the course and were given as the topics of most of the writing assignments. However, it is possible that Katri perceived the main focus of the course to have been presented as only being related to formal contexts of language use, which alienated her and prevented her from constructing something meaningful within that context. In Katri's case, connecting her known life-world to the new in a meaningful way (Kalantzis & Cope 2004) did not happen, with the result that her identity was not engaged (Kalantzis & Cope 2004) in learning. One explanation for this might be that Katri, through years of being a part of a certain type of a culture of learning, had been strongly socialised into that way of studying, learning and using languages (see "school chronotype" in Dufva & Aro 2014). Katri herself maintained this division in her own questionnaire answers, interviews and blog texts, because she might have thought that it was expected. Still, even in terms of the design of the course, the position the learners perceived as being offered by the course was probably too limiting. They did not view being positioned as academic writers without clear connections to their life-world as empowering.

10. Implications for the design of higher education language courses

Although this article focused on one learner's experiences on an EAP course, Katri's views on academic communication might be common among higher education students. Therefore, if teachers are aware of the language use categories that learners might have before attending an EAP course, it could help them avoid assigning learners to any predetermined positions from the start. For example, in the case of academic communication, different registers and language use situations certainly need to be focused on, as an expert of any field should be able to adjust one's language use based on the audience and context. However, those registers and language use situations should also be explicitly presented as possibilities and resources to extend the learners' language use repertoire instead of presenting merely the requirements of those situations. In addition, the design should challenge learners' existing views and any positions they might have already given themselves and which might limit their experience. One concrete way could be to negotiate with learners about the contents of a course and their own learning goals. The learners then become accountable for and capable of participating in the design of their own learning. This approach could promote a new type of learning culture. Learners could draw on their own life-worlds and exercise the type of agency that is needed today: to negotiate and construct a meaningful learning path for themselves. On the other hand, considering Katri's own interests in life and in language learning, the course was probably not the best choice for her. Timely study guidance could have supported her in finding an elective course which would have better fulfilled her ambitions. From the broader perspective of developing higher education language teaching, the course selection should include options with various focuses and cater for learners with diverse career plans.

Various ways to blur the boundaries of formal and informal contexts should also be explored, especially on courses that learners might initially see as formal or outside of their life-worlds (e.g. compulsory language courses). This shift needs to be made explicit and visible by, for example, offering anchors for reflection at various stages of a course, thereby helping learners localise themselves on their learning paths. Understanding the role or significance of, for example, an individual course on that path would support learners' life-long learning and help them better comprehend and articulate their own expertise. This could also strengthen the learners' sense of agency and their ability to adjust to rapid changes as well as help them make use of the situations that unavoidably come their way, such as compulsory studies. This is the form of agency that is needed in diverse contexts today.

This study contributes to the research on developing higher education teachers' expertise because, as a study conducted by a practitioner, it also supports individual teacher's agency by providing new tools for research-based development of one's work. In addition, the experience provided important insights into evaluating the suitability of the design-based research strategy in general. First of all, DBR allowed focusing on the learner experiences more thoroughly than regular collection of course feedback and observations in class would have. In fact, without in-depth research, Katri's struggle with the perceived contradictions in different types of language use might have gone unnoticed. In addition, DBR enabled quick changes to the design even during the course (e.g. discussing the purpose of academic writing), which aligns with the teacher's day-to-day work. The critical points that emerged from the data were also selected as focus points when developing the learning design. However, what is important is that the insights and development ideas need to be integrated into pedagogical discussion of the organisation. As a result, the research has the potential to inform and contribute to the expected learning outcomes and the content of higher education language and communication courses, higher education in general and to carry over into supporting students' life-long learning. In addition, DBR as a research strategy could support teachers' own agency in constructing their teacher identities by doing research related to their work, becoming aware of the challenges learners might face during their studies and developing learning designs to respond to those challenges.

References

Ahearn, L. M. 2001. Language and agency. *Annual Review of Anthropology, 30*, 109–137. doi:10.1146/annurev.anthro.30.1.109

Alanen, R., Huhta, A., Taalas, P., Tarnanen, M. & Ylönen, S. 2011. Toimijuus ja asiantuntijaksi kasvaminen monimediaisessa kielenopettamisessa [Developing agency and expertise for multimodal language teaching]. In E. Lehtinen, S. Aaltonen, M. Koskela, E. Nevasaari & M. Skog-Södersved (eds.), *Kielenkäyttö verkossa ja verkostoissa* [Language use in networks and on the net], AFinLA vuosikirja 69, AFinLA Yearbook 2011. Jyväskylä, Finland: AFinLa, 23–39.

Bandura, A. 1997. *Self-efficacy: The exercise of control.* New York, NY: W. H. Freeman.

Bandura, A. 2001. Social cognitive theory: an agentic perspective. *Annual Review of Psychology, 52*, 1–26. doi:10.1146/annurev.psych.52.1.1

Barab, S. & Squire, K. 2004. Introduction: design-based research: putting a stake in the ground. *The Journal of the Learning Sciences, 13* (1), 1–14. doi:10.1207/s15327809jls1301_1

Basharina, O. 2009. Student agency and language-learning processes and outcomes in international online environments. *CALICO Journal, 26* (2), 390–412.

Blin, F. & Jalkanen, J. 2014. Designing for language learning: agency and languaging in hybrid environments. *Apples – Journal of Applied Language Studies, 8* (1), 147–170.

Cazden, C., Cope, B., Fairclough, N., Gee, J., Kalantzis, M., Kress, G., Luke, A., ... Nakata, M. 1996. A pedagogy of multiliteracies: designing social futures. *Harvard Educational Review, 66* (1), 60–92. doi:10.17763/haer.66.1.17370n67v22j160u

Conole, G. 2012. *Designing for learning in an open world: explorations in the learning sciences, instructional systems and performance technologies* (Vol. 4). New York, NY: Springer.

Council of Europe. 2013. *Common European Framework of Reference for Languages: Learning, Teaching, Assessment (CEFR)*. Retrieved from http://www.coe.int/t/dg4/linguistic/cadre1_en.asp

Design-Based Research Collective. 2003. Design-based research: an emerging paradigm for educational inquiry. *Educational Researcher, 32* (1), 5–8. doi:10.3102/0013189X032001005

Dörnyei, Z. 2007. *Research methods in applied linguistics*. Oxford: Oxford University Press.

Dufva, H. & Aro, M. 2014. Dialogical view on language learners' agency: connecting intrapersonal with interpersonal. In P. Deters, X. Gao, E. R. Miller & G. Vitanova (eds.), *Theorizing and Analyzing Agency in Second Language Learning – Interdisciplinary Approaches*. Bristol: Multilingual Matters, 37–53.

Edelson, D. C. 2002. Design Research: what we learn when we engage in design. *The Journal of the Learning Sciences, 11* (1), 105–121. doi:10.1207/S15327809JLS1101_4

Flowerdew, J. & Miller, L. 2008. Social structure and individual agency in second language learning: evidence from three life histories. *Critical Inquiry in Language Studies, 5* (4), 201–224. doi:10.1080/15427580802286173

Harré, R. & van Langenhove, L. (eds.). 1999. *Positioning theory: moral contexts of intentional action*. Oxford: Blackwell.

Holland, D., Lachicotte, W., Skinner, D. & Cain, C. 1998. *Identity and agency in cultural worlds*. Cambridge, MA: Harvard University Press.

Hunter, J. & Cooke, D. 2007. Through autonomy to agency: giving power to language learners. *Prospect, 22* (2), 72–88.

Kalaja, P., Alanen, R., Palviainen, Å. & Dufva, H. 2011. From milk cartons to English roommates: context and agency in L2 learning beyond the classroom. In P. Benson & H. Reinders (eds.), *Beyond the language classroom*. Basingstoke: Palgrave Macmillan, 47–58.

Kalantzis, M. & Cope, B. 2001. *New Learning: a charter for Australian education*. Canberra: Australian Council of Deans on Education.

Kalantzis, M. & Cope, B. 2004. Designs for learning. *E-Learning, 1* (1), 38–93. doi:10.2304/elea.2004.1.1.7

Kalantzis, M. & Cope, B. 2012. *New learning: elements of a science of education* (2nd ed.). Cambridge: Cambridge University Press. doi:10.1017/CBO9781139248532

Lankshear, C. & Knobel, M. 2003. *New literacies: changing knowledge and classroom practice*. Buckingham: Open University Press.

Lantolf, J. P. & Thorne, S. 2006. *Sociocultural theory and the genesis of second language development*. Oxford: Oxford University Press.

Lasky, S. 2005. A sociocultural approach to understanding teacher identity, agency and professional vulnerability in a context of secondary school reform. *Teaching and Teacher Education, 21*, 899–916. doi:10.1016/j.tate.2005.06.003

Lave, J. 1993. Situated learning in communities of practice. In L. B. Resnick, J. M. Levine & S. D. Teasley (eds.), *Perspectives on socially shared cognition* (2nd ed.). Washington, D.C.: American Psychological Association, 63–82.

Lipponen, L. & Kumpulainen, K. 2011. Acting as accountable authors: creating interactional spaces for agency work in teacher education. T*eaching and Teacher Education 27*, 812–819. doi:10.1016/j.tate.2011.01.001

Lund, A. & Hauge, T. E. 2011. Designs for teaching and learning in technology-rich learning environments. *Nordic Journal of Digital Literacy 6* (4), 258–272.

Luukka, M.-R., Pöyhönen, S., Huhta, A., Taalas, P., Tarnanen, M. & Keränen, A. 2008. *Maailma muuttuu, mitä tekee koulu?: Äidinkielen ja vieraiden kielten tekstikäytänteet koulussa ja vapaa-ajalla* [The world changes – how does the school respond? Mother tongue and foreign language literacy practices in school and in free-time.]. Jyväskylä: Jyväskylän yliopisto.

Mercer, S. 2011. Understanding learner agency as a complex dynamic system. *System 39*, 427–436. doi:10.1016/j.system.2011.08.001

Mercer, S. 2012. The complexity of learner agency. *Apples – Journal of Applied Language Studies, 6* (2), 41–59.

Murphey, T. & Carpenter, C. 2008. The Seeds of Agency in Language Learning Histories. In P. Kalaja, V. Menezes & A. M. Barcelos (eds.), *Narratives of Learning and Teaching EFL*. New York, NY: Palgrave Macmillan, 17–34.

Norton, B. 2000. *Identity and language learning: gender, ethnicity and educational change*. Harlow: Longman.

Norton Peirce, B. 1995. Social identity, investment, and language learning. *TESOL Quarterly, 29* (1), 9–31. doi:10.2307/3587803

Ruohotie-Lyhty, M. 2009. Newly qualified language teachers' agency and professional development during the first years at work. In R. Kantelinen & P. Pollari (eds.), *Language education and lifelong learning*. Joensuu: University Press of Joensuu, 279–303.

Ruohotie-Lyhty, M. 2011a. Constructing practical knowledge of teaching: eleven newly qualified language teachers' discursive agency. *The Language Learning Journal, 39* (3), 365–379. doi:10.1080/09571736.2010.544750

Ruohotie-Lyhty, M. 2011b. *Opettajuuden alkutaival – Vastavalmistuneen vieraan kielen opettajan toimijuus ja ammatillinen kehittyminen* [First steps on the path of teacherhood. Newly qualified foreign language teachers' agency and professional development]. Doctoral dissertation. University of Jyväskylä, Jyväskylä.

Sandoval, W. A. & Bell, P. 2004. Design-based research methods for studying learning in context: introduction. *Educational Psychologist, 39* (4), 199–201. doi:10.1207/s15326985ep3904_1

Sawyer, R. K. 2006. Introduction: the new science of learning. In R. K. Sawyer (ed.), *Cambridge Handbook of the Learning Sciences*. New York, NY: Cambridge University Press, 1–16

Skinnari, K. 2012. *"Tässä ryhmässä olen aika hyvä": ekologinen näkökulma kielenoppijaidentiteetteihin peruskoulun viidennen ja kuudennen luokan englannin opetuksessa* [I'm quite good in this group". An ecological view to fifth and sixth graders' language learner identities in elementary school English language learning]. Doctoral dissertation. Jyväskylä studies in humanities 188. University of Jyväskylä, Jyväskylä.

Sullivan, P. & McCarthy, J. 2004. Toward a Dialogical Perspective on Agency. *Journal for the Theory of Social Behaviour, 34* (3), 291–309. doi:10.1111/j.0021-8308.2004.00249.x

Taalas, P., Tarnanen, M. & Huhta, A. 2007. Oppilaat ja opettajat kielten ja tekstien käyttäjinä koulussa ja vapaa-ajalla – kartoitustutkimuksen suunnittelu ja toteutus [Pupils and teachers as users of languages and texts in school and out-of-school contexts – the planning and implementation of a survey]. In O.-P. Salo, T. Nikula & P. Kalaja (eds.), *Kieli oppimisessa – Language in Learning*. Jyväskylä: Suomen soveltavan kielitieteen yhdistys AFinLA, 75–91.

Tynjälä, P. 2011. Asiantuntijuuden kehittämisen pedagogiikkaa [Pedagogy of developing expertise]. In K. Collin, S. Paloniemi, H. Rasku-Puttonen & P. Tynjälä (eds.), *Luovuus, oppiminen ja asiantuntijuus* [Creativity, learning and expertise](1st–2nd ed.). Helsinki: WSOYpro, 79–95.

Vähäsantanen, K., Saarinen, J. & Eteläpelto, A. 2009. Between school and working life: vocational teachers' agency in boundary-crossing settings. *International Journal of Educational Research, 48*, 395–404. doi:10.1016/j.ijer.2010.04.003

van Lier, L. 2007. Action-based Teaching, Autonomy and Identity. *Innovation in Language Learning and Teaching, 1* (1), 46–65. doi:10.2167/illt42.0

van Lier, L. 2008. Agency in the classroom. In J. P. Lantolf & M. E. Poehner (Eds.), *Sociocultural Theory and the Teaching of Second Languages*. London: Equinox, 163–18.

Wang, F. & Hannafin, M. J. 2005. Design-based research and technology-enhanced learning environments. *Educational Technology Research and Development, 53* (4), 5–23. doi:10.1007/BF02504682

Wassell, B. A., Fernández Hawrylak, M. & LaVan, S.-K. 2010. Examining the structures that impact English language learners' agency in urban high schools: resources and roadblocks in the classroom. *Education and Urban Society, 42* (5), 599–619. doi:10.1177/0013124510375598

Wertsch, J. V. 1991. *Voices of the mind: a sociocultural approach to mediated action*. Cambridge, MA: Harvard University Press.

Wertsch, J. V., Tulviste, P. & Hagstrom, F. 1993. A sociocultural approach to agency. In E. A. Forman, N. Minick & A. S. Stone (eds.), *Contexts for learning: sociocultural dynamics in children's development*. New York, NY: Oxford University Press, 336–356.

Section 3.
Exploring perceptions

11. Learning paths on elementary university courses in Finnish as a second language

Johanna Eloranta[1] and Juha Jalkanen[2]

Abstract

Along with the growing degree of internationalisation, Finnish university education needs to address issues related to learning and teaching Finnish as a second language. From the perspective of teaching Finnish and related pedagogical development, it is essential to recognise when, where and for which purposes learners need Finnish at the various stages of the language acquisition process. This article focuses on the learning paths of three international students who studied Finnish on a one-term elementary course at the University of Jyväskylä Language Centre. The article is based on a socio-cultural and ecological view on language learning and teaching. The data consist of learning diary texts written by the students during the course. Through these texts, university students' language usage situations and views on the Finnish language and its acquisition are explored. The learners' narratives conveyed their ideas related to languages and language acquisition, which appeared to be central background factors for different language usage and study practices. The three learner paths represented different forms and degrees of integration. The learners' goals were closely related to the environments in which they led their daily lives.

Keywords: Finnish, second language learning, higher education, internationalisation, university students, interaction.

---

1. Language Centre, University of Jyväskylä, Finland; johanna.eloranta@jyu.fi

2. Language Centre, University of Jyväskylä, Finland; juha.jalkanen@jyu.fi

How to cite this chapter: Eloranta, J., & Jalkanen, J. (2015). Learning paths on elementary university courses in Finnish as a second language. In J. Jalkanen, E. Jokinen, & P. Taalas (Eds), *Voices of pedagogical development - Expanding, enhancing and exploring higher education language learning* (pp. 225-240). Dublin: Research-publishing.net. doi:10.14705/rpnet.2015.000294

Chapter 11

1. Introduction

Increasing internationalisation has also challenged Finnish university education to consider questions related to learning and teaching Finnish as a second language (F2). As a result of international recruitment, universities employ a growing number of teaching and research staff for whom learning Finnish is an important channel for integration into the university community and Finnish society. To some extent, the international students enrolled in master's degree programmes and doctoral programmes share similar needs. Many exchange students, who usually spend either one or two terms in Finland, also want and need to learn some Finnish. Matching the diverse needs and goals is one of the key challenges for teaching Finnish as a second language at university today.

From the perspective of teaching Finnish and related pedagogical development, it is essential to recognise when, where and for which purposes learners need Finnish at the various stages of the language acquisition process. Even though there is relatively abundant research on the integration of immigrants into Finnish society, this research has primarily focused on daily and working life contexts (see e.g. Pöyhönen, Rynkänen, Tarnanen & Hoffman 2013; Suni 2008). The integration of international students into the academic community and the Finnish language community has not been studied from the perspective of learning Finnish. Research into second language (L2) pedagogy, particularly at the university level, has as yet also been scarce in Finland (however, see Aalto & Taalas 2005 and Jalkanen & Vaarala 2013).

In this article we explore the learning paths of three international students who studied Finnish on a one-term elementary course at the University of Jyväskylä Language Centre. The focus is on events that are significant for the learning process and on the role of language in them. The following research questions will be answered:

- How do the learners describe their F2 learning paths?
- How do the learners' descriptions portray the Finnish language and learning Finnish?

First, we present some current research trends in L2 learning, concentrating on a pedagogical viewpoint. Thereafter, we describe the data used in the article as well as the analysis results divided into three sections. Finally, we discuss what the learners' descriptions reveal about university students' initial F2 learning paths and what guidelines the results offer for developing F2 university pedagogy.

2. Learning L2 in interaction

Recent research into second-language acquisition highlights that language is learned in interaction, not for it (e.g. Suni 2008). This seemingly small distinction is visible, in particular, in viewing language skills as situational (Dufva & Aro 2012; Gee 2004; Pennycook 2010). The approach implies that interaction is the starting point for learning, not its terminal point. Practice is still needed, but structures and vocabulary are approached by examining the situations in which they are typically used. The linguistic environment is thus highly significant for the learning process. Teaching should help learners to analyse different interaction situations at school and in their leisure time as well as the surrounding linguistic environment.

Language is today actually regarded as an activity in which linguistic resources are utilised. These resources vary from one situation and modality to the next. This approach basically includes the spatial variation and temporal regeneration of language (Dufva & Aro 2012). From the language acquisition point of view, this means that language proficiency is not demonstrated as mastery of grammar but as a strategic ability to use different multimodal meaning-making tools in a goal-oriented way (Canagarajah 2008; Pennycook 2010).

Within L2 learning, ground has been particularly gained by holistic theories that aim at explaining the complex and dynamic nature of the language acquisition process. Complexity theory (Larsen-Freeman & Cameron 2008) and an ecological approach (van Lier 2004) share a systemic approach to language acquisition and highlight the need to understand the connections between processes occurring at different levels. Larsen-Freeman and Cameron (2008) also emphasise that it is essential to see language as a dynamic system that is constantly shaped in human interaction. From a pedagogical viewpoint, the idea of dynamic language usage implies that, for example, the discussions recorded in learning materials are always in a certain sense frozen and static. On the other hand, teaching should also provide safe possibilities to test the application of language systems (see also Gee 2005).

Even though teaching plays a central role in L2 acquisition, its primary purpose is to support and structure the learning process rather than to define or control learning sequences based on assumed language difficulty levels (Larsen-Freeman & Cameron 2008; Suni 2008). By following the learners' progress, pedagogical support can be targeted at different process stages at the right time. This is how the learners' orienteering on their learning paths can be guided toward the next control point, whereby they can structure a part of the linguistic system as a meaningful and intelligible whole (Larsen-Freeman & Cameron 2008).

3. The context and data

Students who attend F2 courses at, for instance, Finnish university language centres have very different backgrounds and starting points. They come from different parts of the world, with different school and learning cultures, and speak different languages. Furthermore, it is typical for these courses that the groups consist of exchange students, international master's degree programme students and postgraduate students. As a consequence of this heterogeneity and differing personal plans and goals, the participants' expectations for their learning outcomes also vary. Exchange students who stay in Finland for four months may be motivated to study Finnish in order to facilitate everyday situations, or some of them are interested in knowing an exotic language. On the other hand, master's degree students who intend to pursue a career and remain permanently in Finland may aim at applying for a job in Finnish within a few years. Naturally, in addition to these extreme cases, there are a large number of students with no clear plans and hopes for the future yet. At the initial stage, teaching therefore involves finding a balance between students' diverse interests and learning paths.

The data for this study were collected on an initial F2 course in the autumn of 2014 (target level: CEFR A1 / basic user). Instead of a presumed hierarchical learning sequence, the course was designed based on language usage situations that are meaningful for the learners. A common starting point for initial teaching is the idea of a basic language proficiency that must be acquired before language can be used in interaction. This approach influences learning materials so that the spectrum of texts and language usage situations becomes narrow and irrelevant for the needs of the user. In order to avoid this disadvantage, we mapped the learners' language usage situations via an inquiry before designing the course. The situations chosen for the course included different types of linguistic resources, which the students either analysed or learned to identify. All the situations also entailed linguistic resources that were beyond the learners' comprehension abilities. The aim was to direct their focus to the development of strategic skills and discovery of core content. The course was organised for the first time in its new format while collecting the resources, and the new approach was piloted with one student group.

Students with varying countries of origin, mother tongues and student statuses were selected for the study. The aim was to cast light on learner paths that had different individual starting points. According to these criteria, three participants were chosen: Julie, Naoto and Daniel (the names are pseudonyms).

The research data consist of the learning diaries written by the participants in the course online learning environment. The diary entries were written approximately once a month. The narrative nature of the data links our study to a narrative research approach, which according to Webster and Mertova (2007) is optimally suited for analysing the complex and nuanced experiences that learning and teaching involve. In narrative research, individual experiences are recorded through the construction and reconstruction of personal stories, which makes it possible to record and retell events that have been the most influential for participants. Therefore, the narrative approach allows researchers to portray experiences holistically, in all their complexity and richness, trying to illustrate the temporal notion of experience, which is based on the idea that an individual's understanding of people and events changes (Webster & Mertova 2007).

The objective of narrative analysis is to discover in the data those stories that represent the phenomenon. Narrative analysis yields generalisations about thinking, activity, meanings and attitudes that are related to the phenomenon. In this study, we read the students' learning diaries first alone and then compared our observations and interpretations. Even though the aim in interpreting the diaries was to convey each learner's personal voice, the interpretation involved retelling the stories. The students wrote their diaries in English, and their diverse language skills may have affected the way they verbalised their experiences. The aim was also to take this into account in analysing the texts.

The following sections present the participants' learning paths, first by introducing their backgrounds. The learners' reasons for studying Finnish and set learning outcomes are described thereafter. Then we characterise how language and its learning are manifested in the learners' narratives, as well as potential turning points that appear as meaningful for the learning process. Finally, the focus will be on the learners' retrospective thoughts about learning Finnish. The structure of the descriptions is chronological, that is, they proceed as the course progresses.

4. Three beginners' learning paths

4.1. Path 1: the language enthusiast

Julie was an exchange student from Central Europe. Her mother tongue was French and her major subject during the six-month exchange period was political science.

According to Julie, learning Finnish was an essential part of a relatively long stay in Finland. She found that in addition to the practical functions of language, such as going to shops and talking to people, it also opens a window to the Finnish mindset and culture. Moreover, Julie mentioned that for her learning languages was a hobby.

Julie's aim was that after living four months in Finland she would be able to speak Finnish, as she described it, 'at the basic level'. She also wanted to know some Finnish grammar. Julie specified the means of achieving her learning outcomes on a general level by using passive constructions. She regarded the Finnish course as the primary step in learning the language and mentioned daily life language usage situations, such as going to shops and cafes and using public transport, in this context. Julie noted that conversations with native speakers of Finnish were a good way to learn the language, particularly vocabulary. However, she suspected that the language she would learn from Finns would mainly be slang and vulgar vocabulary. Because of the general nature of her description, it was difficult to conclude which of the aforementioned language usage situations Julie intended to utilise in her learning.

As the course progressed, Julie frequently reflected on the differences and similarities between Finnish and the other languages she knew (French, Italian, English and Russian), trying to define her relationship to the structural system of the language. Julie explained that her Russian skills helped her perceive the structures of Finnish, even though she generally found the differences between Finnish and the Indo-European languages challenging. Nonetheless, she remarked that she enjoyed learning a new linguistic system.

Julie seemed to have a relatively structure-oriented approach to Finnish, which was manifested distinctly as a conflict between her interests (verbs, tenses, suffixes) and the situational approach applied in the course (forming questions, asking for directions, agreeing on appointments). In addition to structures, Julie frequently mentioned wanting to expand her vocabulary, yet without specifying the type of vocabulary she needed. She also regarded speaking and writing as individual subareas to be developed separately.

Julie defined language usage as a game of two levels: on the first level, one learns and uses language in the closed, safe and undisturbed course environment, whereas the second level involves language usage in more challenging contexts characterised by time pressures and external distractions. According to Julie, practising on the first level, that is, in the classroom, prepares students for the second level.

The turning point in Julie's language learning process can be dated to the final stage of the course, at which her language usage environments expanded to meaningful extramural situations. She mentioned reading Moomin books and buying tickets on the internet as examples of these situations. When comparing her achieved learning outcomes to her initial goals, she noted having obtained the keys to speaking and understanding Finnish at the basic level. Julie found that the course had been useful for living in Finland even though its major benefit for her was the opportunity to explore Finnish language and culture, in compliance with her attitude toward languages as a hobby.

4.2. Path 2: the persistent labourer

Naoto was an exchange student of biological and environmental science, whose mother tongue was Japanese. He lived in Finland for approximately nine months during his studies.

Naoto told that he chiefly attended the Finnish course in order to master everyday situations, which he described as 'a quiz game'. For example, figuring out the content of food packages and prices in supermarkets presented great challenges to him in spite of contextual clues. Furthermore, he regarded studying Finnish as an opportunity to learn more about Finnish culture.

At the beginning of the course, Naoto's only objectives were knowledge of grammar and fluency of speech. He said that he studied Finnish in order to be able to use it; such simple phrases as *yksi kahvi* (one coffee) he mentioned having already adopted in his everyday usage. The initial situation for learning Finnish differed from what he had expected: his social network included mainly other exchange students. The role of strong emotions was visible in Naoto's attitude toward language acquisition and usage already at an early stage. He found it irritating having to be involved in the daily quiz game, but tried to change his attitude toward the issue.

As the course progressed, Naoto found that he mastered daily language usage situations relatively fluently as long as they did not include excessive variation. However, particularly challenging for him were situations that required finding essential information from texts and deducing meanings. One of the reasons for this, as mentioned by Naoto himself, was the dissimilarity of languages. Naoto's learning targets had been specified at this stage: he highlighted basic vocabulary and, in particular, verbs as the focus of his learning.

The first significant event in Naoto's language acquisition process occurred as he was halfway through the course. He explained how he had tried to make himself understood in Finnish by a cafeteria attendant but had begun to speak English because of time pressure and the other party's problems in understanding. He found that Finns' generally good English skills allow changing the language in challenging situations. Emotions were strongly present in this situation: the attendant's confusion and insecurity made Naoto feel uncomfortable.

A turning point in Naoto's Finnish studies occurred at the final stage of the course. Naoto still highlighted his lexical challenges related to recalling and recognising words. Therefore, reading was difficult for him and a dictionary was constantly needed while writing. He experienced that the texts became increasingly difficult but his reading skills did not develop at the same pace. Naoto also found listening comprehension challenging because he did not understand all he heard and had to guess some meanings. He was ashamed when speaking Finnish. These extremely strong emotions weakened his motivation to study and his willingness to attend the lessons. However, he was not willing to terminate his Finnish studies. According to Naoto, the challenges related to studies resulted from working method differences as well as limited time resources and English skills.

The next turning point followed right at the end of the course. Naoto explained that he had reflected on his own class participation and noticed that he had avoided interaction with the other students: instead of participating in class, he had only been 'attending' it. According to him, this passiveness had been affected by his incapability of expressing his thoughts fluently, which had posed emotional challenges for him. Nevertheless, supported by a peer and encouraged by positive interaction situations, Naoto's ultimate experience of the course was positive.

4.3. Path 3: the passionate adventurer

Daniel was a North American student enrolled in an English-medium master's degree programme in sport sciences at the University of Jyväskylä. Master's degree programmes are usually completed in two to three years. Daniel had just begun his studies in Finland when he came to the F2 course.

Daniel's initial target was to acquire a language proficiency level that would allow him to communicate in ordinary everyday situations and to continue studying Finnish in the future. He defined the target situation also as a personal feeling of being able to say that he knew some Finnish. On the other hand, he also wished to acquire a language proficiency level appreciated by native Finnish speakers. Daniel's attitude to studying Finnish was extremely positive, and he expressed having enjoyed the first classes.

Daniel retained his positive attitude as his studies progressed: learning Finnish was fun, and he was confident that the interconnections between the things learned would become clearer in the course of time. Daniel also told about his willingness to throw himself into new situations based on an experimental approach in order to see what would happen. He believed that the desire to learn, sufficient practice, immersion in the language, and patience would result in achieving the set targets, irrespective of how loud the social networks echoed the impossibility of learning Finnish. In addition to his confidence, Daniel's learning process was supported by his prior linguistics studies and the lexical similarities between Finnish and English.

On the other hand, Daniel found the differences in pronunciation and particularly in morphological identification to be challenging. Even though he experienced a need to have more practice in all areas, he explained having noticed how much easier speaking Finnish had already become. Halfway through the course, Daniel still emphasised the importance of practising.

The first significant event on Daniel's learning path was an interaction situation in a cafe. The event was significant because of the presence of a native Finnish speaker whom Daniel wanted to impress. Daniel narrated having placed an order in Finnish and having been satisfied with his own performance in a challenging situation. In addition to ordering, Daniel said he had tried to use the everyday phrases he knew in order to create a conversation. The native Finnish speaker occasionally corrected Daniel's pronunciation, which Daniel interpreted as assistance for his attempt to use Finnish. However, Daniel felt uncomfortable and insecure when talking to a native speaker in a particularly significant interaction situation.

The turning point on Daniel's learning path occurred towards the end of the course. Daniel's earlier enthusiasm and positive attitude had disappeared and given way to an attitude that highlighted the importance of practice. Daniel said that he was partly rather satisfied and partly dissatisfied with the development of his language skills. He focused on describing the areas that needed improvement and felt that his insufficient language proficiency resulted from a lack of independent studying and practice.

At the final stage of the course, Daniel analysed his achieved learning outcomes and development targets in various ways. Relying on his linguistics student background, he felt he discerned Finnish as a language system but found situational and idiomatic language usage challenging, in particular, in interaction with native Finnish speakers. Daniel also reflected on his own initial targets in relation to the present situation. He felt he was now able to communicate relatively well in everyday situations as well as being allowed to say that he knew some Finnish. Nevertheless, Daniel did not feel his language skills were good enough to be appreciated by native speakers. He intended to enhance his proficiency by speaking Finnish with native speakers and by independently practising grammar and vocabulary (Table 1).

Table 1. Dimensions of learning paths

	Starting point	Experience in the learner role	Form and degree of integration
Julie	Interest in learning another language	Feels comfortable	Access to Finnish culture through cultural products
Naoto	Surviving daily life in Finland	Feels anxious	Integrated into the exchange student community but only loosely into the Finnish-speaking community
Daniel	Building and maintaining interaction relationships	Enjoys at first but gets frustrated during the learning process	Aims at attachment to Finnish society and wants to establish social relationships with Finns

5. Discussion

Guided by our two research questions, we have explored in this article three students' descriptions of their paths to learning Finnish. We have focused on how language and language learning were manifested in the learners' texts and what the texts revealed about the learning paths of university students attending elementary Finnish courses.

The learners' narratives conveyed their ideas related to languages and language acquisition, which appeared to be central background factors for different language usage and study practices. Julie's starting point – her interest in learning another language – was demonstrated by the way she observed her learning and further development targets through linguistic structures and vocabulary. She regarded the Finnish course as the principal language learning setting, from which language usage and learning would later expand to interaction outside of the course context. Naoto's point of departure was more closely related to everyday language usage situations, even though for him also language appeared as mastery of structures and vocabulary. Daniel's motivation for learning Finnish was associated with the social function of language: language is used for building and maintaining interaction relationships. Daniel experienced practising Finnish as a means to prepare for future interaction situations. In light of these three cases, language is significant primarily because it enables interaction and functioning in Finnish society. Language learning appears as a chiefly individual in-class activity that serves to enable interaction.

The learners' narratives highlighted a variety of emotions involved in the learning process. Julie seemed to enjoy adopting a learner role, in which she felt safe, whereas Naoto felt anxious in the same role and was unable to adjust his emotions to the learning process. Daniel first felt comfortable in the learner role and had an analytical attitude toward his learning-related emotions. However, his understanding attitude began to give way to impatience during the course. One of the reasons for deciding to use learning diaries in the course was actually our aim to observe the learners' attitudes and emotions during the learning process. Participants often reflected on their experiences more openly in the diaries than in the group sessions. Moreover, the opportunity to concentrate on listening to the experiences of individual learners allowed us to provide targeted feedback on the learning process as well as on linguistic questions.

The three learner paths represented different forms and degrees of integration. Naoto identified the exchange student community as his main social setting. Daniel's aim was attachment to Finnish society, which was demonstrated by his plans to continue studying Finnish and establish social relationships with Finns. Julie, instead, wished to access Finnish culture chiefly through cultural products, not so much through social interaction.

The students' narratives about their learning paths can be crystallised in two key questions: why and how is language learned. The learners' goals were closely related to the environments in which they led their daily lives, yet they focused on different aspects within these environments. From a pedagogical viewpoint, it is challenging to reconcile the diverse goals of language acquisition and social integration. This makes us consider whether it is, overall, meaningful to pursue the goals of these student groups within the framework of one single course.

The idea of learning in interaction currently prevailing in research on L2 acquisition was not visible in our students' notions (see Partanen 2013). This may partly result from Finns not being used to speaking Finnish with non-native speakers and supporting their initially insecure language usage. In addition, the learners may have lacked the ability to utilise interaction situations as learning situations. Based on our data, however, encounters with native Finnish speakers seem to be significant for the learners of Finnish. Their experiences of genuine interaction situations also seem to have an impact on their conceptions of themselves as language users. In this light, learning a second language in interaction implies throwing ourselves collaboratively into a discomfort zone: native Finnish speakers should recognise their role as support providers and the learners of Finnish as utilisers of this support. Neither of these skills emerges spontaneously but requires conscious and systematic development (on the forms of pedagogical support, see van Lier 2007) This is a challenge that should be addressed in developing pedagogies for both Finnish as a second language and Finnish as mother tongue. Questions related to the contexts in which different language registers are learned must be constantly and actively discussed at the various stages of teaching and learning. The purpose of teaching is also to shape students' conceptions of learning, not only to echo them.

Acknowledgement

This article has been translated from Finnish by Sirpa Vehviläinen.

References

Aalto, E. & Taalas, P. 2005. Tavoitteelliseksi opiskelijaksi monimuotoisella ja –mediaisella kurssilla. In L. Kuure, E. Kärkkäinen, M. Saarenkunnas (eds.), *Kieli ja sosiaalinen toiminta – Language and Social Action.* AFinLA Yearbook. Publications de l'association finlandaise de linquistique appliquée 63, 349–362.

Canagarajah, A. S. 2008. Foreword. In A. Clemente & M. Higgins (eds.), *Performing English with a post-colonial accent: ethnographic narratives from Mexico*. London: The Tufnell Press, 9–13.

Dufva, H. & Aro, M. 2012. Oppimisen kronotooppisuus: aika, paikka ja kielenkäyttäjä. In L. Meriläinen, L. Kolehmainen & T. Nieminen (eds.) *AFinLA-e: soveltavan kielitieteen tutkimuksia 4*. Jyväskylä: AFinLA, 7–21.

Gee, J. P. 2004. *Situated language and learning: a critique of traditional schooling*. New York: Routledge.

Gee, J. P. 2005. Learning by design: good video games as learning machines. *E-Learning, 2* (1), 5–16. doi:10.2304/elea.2005.2.1.5

Jalkanen, J. & Vaarala, H. 2013. Digital texts for learning Finnish: shared resources and emerging practices. *Language Learning & Technology, 17* (1), 107–124.

Larsen-Freeman, D. & Cameron, L. 2008. *Complex systems and applied linguistics*. Oxford: Oxford University Press.

Partanen, M. 2013. Kieli tulee kielen päälle: kansainvälisten opiskelijoiden käsityksiä suomen kielen oppimisesta. In M. Eronen & M. Rodi-Risberg (eds.), *Haasteena näkökulma, Perspektivet som utmaning, Point of view as challenge, Perspektivität als Herausforderung*. Vaasa: VAKKI Publications 2, 257–268.

Pennycook, A. 2010. *Language as a local practice*. New York: Routledge.

Pöyhönen, S., Rynkänen, T., Tarnanen, M. & Hoffman, D. 2013. Venäjänkiliset IT-alan asiantuntijat työyhteisöissä – monikieliset käytänteet, identiteetit ja osallisuuden kokemukset integroitumisessa. In T. Keisanen, E. Kärkkäinen, M. Rauniomaa, P. Siitonen & M. Siromaa (eds.), *Osallistumisen multimodaaliset diskurssit. Multimodal discourses of participation*. Jyväskylä: AFinLAn vuosikirja. Suomen soveltavan kielitieteen yhdistyksen julkaisuja, 77–102.

Suni, M. 2008. *Toista kieltä vuorovaikutuksessa. Kielellisten resurssien jakaminen toisen kielen omaksumisen alkuvaiheessa* [Second language in interaction: sharing linguistic resources in the early stage of second language acquisition]. Jyväskylä: Doctoral dissertation, University of Jyväskylä. Retrieved from http://urn.fi/URN:ISBN:978-951-39-3209-1

van Lier, L. 2004. *The ecology and semiotics of language learning: a sociocultural perspective*. Boston: Kluwer Academic. doi:10.1007/1-4020-7912-5

van Lier, L. 2007. Action-based teaching, autonomy and identity. *Innovation in Language Learning and Teaching, 1*(1), 46–65.

Chapter 11

Webster, L. & Mertova, P. 2007. *Using narrative inquiry as a research method: an introduction to using critical event narrative analysis in research on learning and teaching.* London: Routledge.

12 From canon to chaos management: blogging as a learning tool in a modern Finnish literature course

Elina Jokinen[1] and Heidi Vaarala[2]

Abstract

This article is based on the teaching experiment implemented in summer 2013 in a modern Finnish literature course organised by the Centre for International Mobility (CIMO) and the University of Jyväskylä Language Centre. In order to break away from the traditional conception of literature and text, students' independent blogging was chosen as the final course assignment instead of a traditional final project. Our aim has been to determine what blogging as an activity can add to second-language learning (i.e. learning the language in a country where it is spoken as a native language) in the context of modern Finnish literature. Our special interest is how new learning environments and approaches broaden the conception of literature held by students of Finnish as a foreign language. The 22 participants of the modern literature course were university students from different European countries. They had studied Finnish language and literature in their own countries, in other words, Finnish as a foreign language. The focus of this article is on the blogging process, which we observe from the perspective of process stages as well as student output. The article demonstrates that a teaching method that opens up new learning environments and learning modes – such as blogging – contributes to broadening students' conception of literature and is particularly suitable for analysing phenomena in modern literature.

Keywords: second language learning, modern literature, social media, new writing.

1. Language Centre, University of Jyväskylä, Finland; elina.k.jokinen@jyu.fi

2. Centre for Applied Language Studies, University of Jyväskylä, Finland; heidi.vaarala@jyu.fi

How to cite this chapter: Jokinen, E., & Vaarala, H. (2015). From canon to chaos management: blogging as a learning tool in a modern Finnish literature course. In J. Jalkanen, E. Jokinen, & P. Taalas (Eds), *Voices of pedagogical development - Expanding, enhancing and exploring higher education language learning* (pp. 241-278). Dublin: Research-publishing.net. doi:10.14705/rpnet.2015.000295

1. Introduction

Students study Finnish language and culture at about a hundred universities in over thirty countries. For these university students, the Centre for International Mobility (CIMO) offers a special course on modern Finnish literature. The objective of the course is to deepen the participants' knowledge and understanding of modern literature, to make them reflect on the main characteristics of modern literature and to enhance their language skills in a genuine environment. The first course was provided in 2012 by the University of Helsinki; in 2013 and 2014 the organiser was the University of Jyväskylä Language Centre. This article is based on the teaching experiment implemented in the modern literature course of summer 2013 in Jyväskylä.

The 22 participants of the modern literature course were university students from different European countries. They were students of Finnish as either a major or minor subject at universities in Russia, Hungary, Poland, the Czech Republic, Denmark, Estonia, Latvia, Lithuania and Germany. Four of the participants were men and 18 women. According to the Common European Frame of Reference for Languages, their language proficiency levels varied between B2 and C1. In other words, everyone's language skills were at least at a good average level. At this proficiency level, language users understand speech and different texts, are able to produce texts, and speak good Finnish.

In the pre-assignment and initial interview, students described their own conceptions of literature. As the course started, their conceptions of Finnish literature seemed to be traditional, with a National Romantic emphasis: they were familiar with the national literary canon, and many of them were able to name the classics of Finnish literature history. Literature published in the 1990s and 2000s was occasionally named.

The course was implemented by integrating thematic entities with blogging. The main thematic contents were nature, fantasy, humour, comic strips, multicultural literature, the various forms of modern prose, and children's and young adult literature. In addition, the characteristics of the Finnish literature institution, such as modern writers' different roles and their status on the book market, were also analysed in the joint meetings.

Independent blog writing was chosen as the course assignment instead of the final project traditionally used in summer courses. This was done because the participants found that writing a long report in three weeks would have made the course too fast-paced. However, we do not deal here with the problematics of the blog concept. *Blog* here refers to a webpage written in diary format or otherwise chronologically, whose posts are closely related to the author's personal life or are of special interest to the author (e.g. Jalkanen & Pudas 2013).

In this article we explore the significance of blogging for broadening learners' conception of literature and strengthening their language proficiency. Our principal research question is: What can blogging as an activity add to second-language learning in the context of Finnish contemporary literature? Our special interest is how new learning environments and approaches can broaden the literature conception of students of Finnish as a foreign language.

The relationship between learners of Finnish as a foreign or second language and modern Finnish literature has been studied relatively little from a pedagogical perspective. This is true even though introducing Finnish literature is an important part of teaching in nearly all units in the world in which Finnish is taught. Internationally, literature has been handled from a variety of perspectives in the context of language teaching. The following are recent examples from the 2000s, from both Finland and abroad. The *Journal of Literature in Language Teaching* has published articles on using literature in the context of second/foreign language teaching, for example, about audio books as a tool for second-language learning (Husson Isozaki 2014). Another interesting study reveals that literature circles offer students opportunities for meaningful and motivating literature discussions (Myonghee 2004). Hvistendahl (2000) has studied the role of literature in immigrant instruction, specifically how the integration of immigrant students into Norwegian society was promoted through discussions on the classics of Norwegian literature. In Vaarala (2009), the ways in which advanced learners of Finnish understand and interpret Finnish literary texts have been examined. Apart from this, there have mainly been empirical descriptions of the different ways of teaching Finnish literature for both university students studying Finnish outside of Finland and for learners of Finnish as a second language in Finland (Malm 2006; Mela & Mikkonen 2007; Parente-Čapková 2009). The topic has also been addressed in a number of master's theses (e.g. Lounavaara 2004; Smolander 2012). Furthermore, in the national core curriculum for basic education (Perusopetuksen opetussuunnitelman perusteet 2014), literature is more visible in the instruction of Finnish as a second language – in both the subject name and its contents. The present article provides new research data for this research gap as well as presents a viable pedagogical approach for deepening students' knowledge of Finnish literature from the 2000s.

The data for our study comprise the diverse material collected during the teaching experiment: all students' written outputs and our observations on the group's activities. The most significant texts are the students' pre-assignments, the blog texts written during the course, and their feedback on the course. Due to the approach and limited scope of this article, we concentrate on the blogging process, observing it from the perspective of process stages and student output.

For the blogging task – presented in more detail in Section 2 – the students wrote three blog posts on a literary topic of their choosing on a shared online learning platform. We proceeded by looking for answers to the following questions in (a) students' blog posts and comments and (b) the notes we made on their working process:

- How do students act when they work on the blogging task? What actually happens?
- What forms of activity does each pair have in the blogging?
- What dimensions does blogging offer for work?
- What choices do students make in order to demonstrate their expertise and competence in this learning task?

The primary focus of examination was student activity. After analysing the data, we look at blogging through four stages that are loosely based on the model of inquiry-based learning. We present and examine in more detail the working processes of three blogger teams.

This study assumes an ethnographic approach as part of its methodology. The aim is to understand and describe the subject holistically and to observe people and the environment in a multifaceted way. Rantala (2006), among others, suggests that observing also implies physical presence in people's environments and concrete interaction situations with the participants in the study. We are personally present in the study as researchers who create meanings but, as the two teachers of the course, we are also part of the group we analyse. One of us has a background in literary research (Jokinen 2010) and written communication, the other has studied how learners of Finnish interpret and understand literature (Vaarala 2009) and taught Finnish both as a second and a foreign language.

2. Background of the teaching experiment: how to teach #literature?

Until a few decades ago, literature teaching in schools and universities was dominated by the literary canon that serves the purposes of classical education (Ahvenjärvi & Kirstinä 2013). In practice, literature education meant presenting the major classics of domestic literature and so-called national writers, in addition to reading text excerpts.

Assigning value to literature and naming significant national pieces of work was – at least in principle – possible as long as the amount of published literature was somehow manageable and the literary elite shared an idea of what was counted as high or elite literature (Niemi 2010). However, this is not the case anymore. In the 2010s, the literary canon has been replaced by chaos: the amount of published literature has exploded (Ekholm & Repo 2010; Jokinen 2010), and literary researchers do not even agree on what is meant by *literature*, let alone how its different manifestations should be valued (Jokinen 2010; Lehtonen 2001). On the other hand, the ubiquity of technology has changed our conceptions of both reading and writing (Ekholm & Repo 2010; Saarinen, Joensuu & Koskimaa 2003).

Instead of aesthetic schools or ideological groups, modern literature seems to be defined by a new independence of time and place (Lehtonen 2001), the creation of a meaning network through, for instance, sound, image, videos, different visual elements and hyperlinks. In other words, this modern conception is a break from the traditional idea of text. As a whole, the role of literature in the thoroughly media-integrated culture of the 2010s is anything but unambiguous.

'The book is now #thebook' – this lightly provocative statement comes from the website kirja.fi, launched in 2014 by Finland's largest publishers. In reality, the literary taste and reading habits of the general public change slowly, which is demonstrated, for example, by the fact that e-books accounted for less than one percent of overall literature sales in Finland in 2014 (The Finnish Book Publishers Association 2015). Nevertheless, it is clear that the internet and particularly social media shape our social, technological and cultural practices related to reading (Kallionpää 2014a, 2014b). In our daily textual practices, in how we read and write, the change has already taken place: reading linear texts on paper is more and more uncommon, and writing rarely involves scribbling text on paper (e.g. Coiro, Knobel, Lankshear & Leu 2014; Jenkins, Ford & Green 2013; Taipale 2013).

The broad spectrum of texts and styles in modern literature is most typically structured (e.g. in general upper secondary school textbooks) using the concept of postmodern literature. However, the most typical characteristic of postmodern literature paradoxically seems to be precisely the avoidance of definitions: in an upper secondary school textbook, the most recent literature is aptly described as 'constantly moving carnival of diversity' and the works as 'luscious constructions, often built of intertextual loans and different historical and fictive elements' (in Hakulinen, Kivelä & Ranta 2006). These kinds of definitions are challenging to adopt – and understand – for anyone. For non-Finnish students of Finnish language and literature, tracing these intertextual loans and fictive elements is particularly demanding.

It is clear that when literature changes, literature education must look for new forms as well. For teachers, modern literature has become #literature. In this new form, a text is no longer just a book filled with writing. Instead, #literature is a phenomenon encompassing the entire discussion around a text and all the forms it takes, where a text's images, videos, links and strings of special characters, such as smileys, are all integral parts of it. These new elements have transformed reading and writing so that they no longer occur between the individual and the text only but are connected to various new activities, such as designing and producing videos and integrating them into the text. Indeed, reading and writing can now be discussed as social activities that are more than cognition occurring inside one individual's head.

Just like in the Finnish school context, a typical approach in teaching literature for learners of Finnish as a second or foreign language has involved concentrating on the various phases, trends and classics of literary history (e.g. Staršova 2007). When designing this modern literature course, we wanted to look beyond the canon and devote ourselves to enhancing students' abilities to master the 'chaos of modern literature'.

Because of modern literature's chaotic nature, with its dynamic themes and forms, we decided not to offer any ready-made explanation or model of what modern literature is. Instead, a central starting point in designing the course was our interest in modern literature as a phenomenon – its manifold texts often detached from the traditional book form, but also the functioning of the literary institution and the field of Finnish literature. The aim of this approach was to promote understanding and enable a conceptual change in students' thinking – not so much to increase the amount of scattered knowledge.

Similarly, because of the changed conception of text and the technologisation and multimodality of literature, we found it important to emphasise learning-by-doing in our course. From our perspective, learning does not occur by passively receiving information given from outside. Instead, the learner is an active participant who learns by comparing the new to existing conceptions and experiences. We also wanted to apply the idea of inquiry-based learning in a technologically advanced environment: if literature lives in a symbiosis with media and, in particular, information networks, isn't it also important that learners study it in an authentic learning environment? Our teaching experiment was essentially about putting this insight into practice. The new learning environments also challenge the ideas of where and how learning occurs. As the ubiquity of technology grows, the pen and paper are gaining competitors that must be taken into account in learning situations. Young people can use technology in their free time, but applying it to learning situations is a new challenge for both teachers and students. Modern literature is far from being the only theme that requires language and literature teachers to take a stand on how to integrate a pedagogical approach that emphasises students' active participation with technology-enabled learning environments (e.g. Cope & Kalantzis 2009).

In designing teaching, one should take into account the nature of the phenomenon to be taught, students' backgrounds and preliminary data, and the teaching objectives. Based on these premises, we formed the principal theme and objective of our modern literature course for international students learning Finnish: make the students' conception of literature as a unified entity collide with the reality of what modern literature can, in fact, be.

Using blogging as the pedagogical medium for teaching modern Finnish literature, in particular, was justified, because book blogs are a typical component of Finland's literary landscape. Even though the internet has not yet become a dominant publishing channel for literature, the technological revolution is visible precisely in the changed environment of how literature is received. Discussion forums, blogs and social media have brought a new, interactive dimension to literary publicity. In the 2010s, literature is discussed online (Niemi-Pynttäri 2013). There are about 150 active book blogs in Finland, with tens of thousands of monthly readers (Jalkanen & Pudas 2013). Blogs are written by both authors and readers. In their blogs, authors discuss their life and work, and literary criticism, after having almost totally disappeared from print media, lives and flourishes in readers' blogs. Heated literature debates are an essential feature of these blogs. The blogs not only help overwhelmed readers navigate the vast amount of available books but they also offer new forms of commentary and activities promoting reading (Jalkanen & Pudas 2013; Niemi-Pynttäri 2013). This is the culture of literary discussion we aimed to introduce to our students through the course.

3. Implementing the teaching experiment

Our aim in the course was not to offer a ready-made explanation or model of what modern literature is. Instead, the starting point was the idea emphasised in, for example, a new publication on literary history (Hallila et al. 2013), which suggests the field of modern literature is so fragmented that creating a holistic picture of it is not possible. We also applied Hallila et al.'s (2013) notion of how to create an idea of modern literature: analyse its individual elements, different works, themes and phenomena, and then try to form a holistic picture.

This approach to modern literature optimally suited our pedagogical thinking. Throughout the course, the emphasis was on understanding students as active participants who learn by reflecting on the new ideas they encounter and comparing them to existing conceptions and their own experiences. We chose independent blogging as the main working method because it supported our idea of modern literature and meaningful learning.

In this section we describe the progress of blogging based on the model of inquiry-based learning. Inquiry-based learning is a pedagogical model according to which the acquisition and adoption of new knowledge is most efficient when the learning process imitates the process of scientific research. This view is based on the idea that learning is a constructive process which, in a cognitive sense, strongly resembles the research process. Correspondingly, the research process can be understood as a learning process for the researcher and the academic community. (See also: Hakkarainen, Bollström-Huttunen, Pyysalo & Lonka 2005; Hakkarainen, Lonka & Lipponen 2005; Tynjälä 2004).

An essential element of the inquiry-based learning process is students' role as active participants and so-called shared expertise. Students become a sort of research group that jointly looks for a solution to a meaningful research problem. New knowledge on the topic is collaboratively constructed in the group, but data is also searched for individually – or as in our case, in pairs.

The model of inquiry-based learning optimally suits a study in which the aim is to understand a relatively ambiguous phenomenon (Hakkarainen, Lonka & Lipponen 2005). In the case of this teaching experiment, the multifaceted phenomenon of modern literature required an innovative pedagogical method.

Figure 1. Blogging as a learning process

We analyse blogging in the modern literature course through four perspectives loosely based on the stages of inquiry-based learning. These perspectives are (1) creating a context and defining a problem, (2) agreeing on the research task and working method, (3) data collection, editing, documentation, and publishing, and (4) sharing expertise and continuing the process (see Figure 1). Stage 1 is about defining the assignment, in which both teachers and students participate. Students' independent activities start at Stage 2.

3.1. Defining the assignment (stage 1)

The planning and implementation of the course began by mapping what students already knew about modern Finnish literature and what they found interesting and perhaps strange in it.

The participants' preconceptions were analysed based on essays titled 'Literature and Me', which were a part of the course application. The applicants wrote these essays in their own countries and attached them to the applications. The essays provided advance information as to what Finnish literature courses they had potentially attended, what Finnish literature they had read, and what they knew about the history and present state of Finnish literature. It was also essential to find out what the students wanted to know about Finnish literature.

We approached the essays through a number of questions, such as the following: What do the students write about when they are assigned to write about literature? What is the students' conception of modern literature like? What kind of a personal relationship with literature do the students have?

The course began with a joint introductory lecture intended to make the students realise how they could broaden their way of structuring the characteristics of modern literature. At the beginning of this lecture, the teacher summarised – based on the pre-assignment and the initial interviews – the aspects that the participants were already familiar with, for example, the history of Finnish literature and the great significance of Finnish-language literature in the history of Finland. Then she highlighted some seemingly paradoxical features that the students had mentioned, for example, that modern literature is "gloomy and difficult" and contains "original humour".

The next step – in compliance with the model of inquiry-based learning – was to make the new information conflict with existing conceptions. The students were told about, for instance, the different roles writers have in modern Finland and that the traditional conception of literature based on a uniform national culture has reached the end of its road in the country (Jokinen 2013).

The key issues of modern literature were illustrated through cases and personal examples on such themes as how the boundary between so-called low and high literature has been erased and the co-existence, alongside the realistic narrative, of the fantasy narrative and poetry that searches for the limits of literature in the information network (Hallila et al. 2013).

Chapter 12

In the first meeting, the idea of the course was explained explicitly: owing to the manifold characteristics of modern literature and the transformation that literary culture has experienced, the main focus in this course would not be on studying writers' names, works or styles in the way the students might have expected. Their accustomed study methods would probably also change, because the aim was not to study the characteristics of literature or texts as such but to personally observe and reflect on phenomena in modern literature.

The course assignment – blogging in pairs, or co-blogging – was next presented to the participants. The assignment provided them with the opportunity to explore any phenomena related to modern Finnish literature and to write on it in the course blog collaboratively with another participant. We discussed with the students how a blog post, in addition to text, includes images, videos, links and colours, and challenged everyone to choose a research question that genuinely engaged them.

At this stage, the expectations for the blogging were defined. It was not important that the students produce some specific output or answer to a question. Instead, the aim was for each pair to produce at least three texts about the process stages for the course blog (see instructions for the blog task, Appendix 1).

It was emphasised that the text should be an online one and not written in a traditional research format. A number of important elements were highlighted: (a) their own independent thinking and personal experiences, (b) multifaceted utilisation of different textual resources (including image and video material) and online resources, and (c) consideration of interaction and the recipient. The blog's primary target group was identified as students in this course and other international learners of Finnish interested in Finnish literature. The students could thus design their blog projects rather freely. Blog posts were made in the joint lessons and marked in the course programme approximately every other day. In addition, the participants were expected to contribute to the assignment in their free time. Finally, the pairs presented their projects on the last day of the course.

3.2. The blogging process (stages 2–4)

3.2.1. Stage 2

The second essential stage of the learning process in blogging included agreeing on the research task and creating a working method. The course's open-ended instructions provided students with the opportunity to implement the blogs in different ways. At this stage, students themselves became responsible for the activities: the rather loose assignment gave them the freedom but also the responsibility to think about the studied phenomenon itself – modern literature – and to choose an authentic problem or perspective that they found meaningful to explore.

For the blogging activity, this stage was significant. This was when the students began to choose their topics and discuss their conceptions of literature with people whose reading history differed from theirs. The pairs were formed and preliminary topics chosen at the beginning of the course, after the introductory lecture. Thereafter, the students began to plan their working schedules and create ideas for the content of their blogs.

The students could form pairs based on their own interests. The only restriction was that the partners should not have the same mother tongue, thereby ensuring that they spoke as much Finnish as possible at the different stages of the working process. Topic choice was also free, which resulted in a range of topics, from poetry slams as a phenomenon to detailed analyses of fictional texts.

In practice, as the students further specified their topic, they also discussed their conceptions of literature and starting points. Because the pairs themselves defined the assignment for their blog project, they also had to define the focus of their study, the implementation of the research and working processes, and the target of their work. Choosing the approach and writing style provided interesting insights on the learning process. Students had to agree on many points, for example, what to address or start with – the genre, a specific writer, an institution or something else. The writing also required agreement on aspects such as what style the blog was to be written in. Although online digital writing offers great potential for bloggers to have their voices heard, working in pairs meant a negotiation of what one's own voice is.

3.2.2. Stage 3

At Stage 3, students carried out the actual research, in other words, material collection, editing, documentation, and publishing. An essential feature of the blogging, however, was constant movement between the stages. In the same way, shared expertise was present throughout the process. After having defined the assignment for themselves, the pairs started to search for information on the internet and in books. Questionnaires, internet inquiries and interviews with Finnish people and foreigners were other important methods for collecting data. Interviews were filmed with mobile devices and edited to suit the blog posts. The visual material also included photographs taken by the students or found on the internet. Material was collected using a number of different channels.

An essential feature of the working process, however, was that the stages of the study occurred in parallel. The research problem was processed constantly, and for each pair, the essence was specifically what was done around the theme, not what was achieved. The final product in the blogging differed in an essential way from writing a traditional final report, though, because in such reports the work process usually remains invisible.

The students worked on the blogs for about three weeks, and the process could be described and documented from the beginning. All the stages of the learning process were shared between the members of the learning community. Through the students' reciprocal interaction, everyone's competence could be utilised to enhance the research process.

3.2.3. Stage 4

At Stage 4, the focus was on sharing expertise and continuing the process. It was essential to note that in blogging, the last stage of the inquiry-based learning process – the publication of results – was not the final step of the process. Instead, publishing the results of the substages was part of the blogging. Nevertheless, it was important to provide a joint opportunity for sharing expertise and returning to the research task given at the beginning of the course. After publishing the texts, the students presented their blogs orally and were given feedback by peers and teachers. However, the working process continued in various ways, especially for some pairs, and may still continue.

In this process, the aim went beyond publishing research results, and they were not the main criteria in evaluating the project's success. It was crucial, instead, to examine the results in relation to the common problem and to reflect on learning (Figure 2).

Figure 2.   Blogging as a learning process:
               activities at the various stages

4.   Student blogs: three cases

In the following sections, we analyse three cases that represent different ways of carrying out the blogging. In practice, we describe the activities of each pair at Stages 2 to 4.

Chapter 12

4.1. Pair 1: blogging as social activity

"It's raining. We are sitting in the best cafe in Jyväskylä. We found the cafe, called Lounge, near the university. Here you can drink a perfect espresso and chai latte, and the prices are also friendly. Just like the cafe's cute barista boy. We visited this cafe looking for inspiration, and we found it. There is an old second-hand bookshop next to the cafe, and even at the coffee table we can smell old books through the wall. Suddenly we knew what we should write about. We saw a small, old copy of *The Unknown Soldier* in the bookshop window.

We were taught at the university that all Finns have read those great classics. Have Finns really read them? If yes, did they read them only because they had to? Do even adults want to read them? Or do they all just read modern literature?

We'd like to look into this topic a bit, and we should find the best experts. We're planning to go to second-hand bookshops and Suomalainen Kirjakauppa ('The Finnish Bookshop', a national chain of bookshops) in Jyväskylä and ask the shop assistants what their experiences are. Then we can ask young Finns what they read" (Translated Blog text entry 19 August 2013[3]).

4.1.1. *Agreeing on the research task and working method*

Anna and Kata did not know each other at all before their team work began. However, guided by their shared interests, they decided to form a team. They

---

3. Photos taken by Anna and Kata, reproduced with kind permissions of the authors.

chose a cafe in which they could more closely discuss the topic they wanted to choose for their blog. Their personal experience – the cafe, the smells and the barista – were described at the beginning of the blog as the starting point for their work. Anna had been blogging before and thus knew the features of its style. A beginning like this is characteristic of blogs. The most typical blogs are internet diaries in which individuals or groups focus on a specific theme. Here, as Anna and Kata openly reflected on their research problem, they arrived at their theme: they wanted to test and question the truthfulness of what they had been taught about Finnish literature.

In this pair's first blog post, there was a conflict between the past and the present: the modern reality of the cafe was contrasted with the second-hand bookshop full of old books. In addition, what had been learned at the home university and the truth about the present state of affairs collided with each other. Through their study, the students later revealed the present state of affairs. The post also described the students' working process as they planned their activities, that is, whom they needed to approach in order to find answers to their research problem.

4.1.2. Data collection, editing, documentation, and publishing

This blogger pair's second post also began with a personal approach – the authors retained their chosen blogging style:

> "The sun is shining outside. At last. But we are again sitting in the same cafe after a hard day of work. The smell of coffee gives you new energy. Our notes are on the table together with the small *The Unknown Soldier*" (Translated Totta ja tarua blog entry, 23 August 2013).

The bloggers continued their post by discussing their interview with the second-hand bookshop keeper. An answer to the research question was part of the blog text and personal story of the interviewee:

> "He also told us about his own experiences. We wanted to know if he had read, for example, *The Unknown Soldier*. He said he had read all

the Finnish classics, but only at school, when it was compulsory. Maybe he would like to read some of them again when he gets a little older or middle-aged, but it does not feel like that yet. However, he said that **many people buy all the old classics because they should have them on their bookshelves** [emphasis added]" (Translated Totta ja tarua blog entry, 23 August 2013).

Here was one answer to the pair's research question: classics have been read at school because it was required, and Finns buy classics to have them on their bookshelves, not to read them. The students did not point at their results nor tell the reader they had found at least partial answers to their research questions. Instead, the answers were embedded in a light and chatty blogging style.

Data collection continued in the pair's third post, titled '*The Unknown Soldier* is rather unknown'. In it, the students described a visit to the Suomalainen kirjakauppa bookshop in their search for the classics of Finnish literature.

"With the help of the Top 10 list, we easily familiarised ourselves with new books, but we also wanted to look for classics. Even after ten minutes, we found nothing by Väinö Linna [the author of *The Unknown Soldier*]; we were almost certain that no classics were even sold here. Fortunately a friendly shop assistant asked if any help was needed. He showed us where the works of Linna, Waltari and Kivi were. But there weren't many, only two or three copies. Compared to this, contemporary literature sells rather well, because about 30 copies of [Sofi] Oksanen's new book were found. There were even two versions of it, a basic one for 30 euro and a deluxe edition 50 euro" (Translated Totta ja tarua blog entry, 27 August 2013).

The pair found individual copies of classics at the bookshop only after a long search and with the help of a shop assistant. They stated that that it seems Finns really do not read their classics in the way the students had been taught. The student pair concluded the blog post by saying: "*The Unknown Soldier* was so difficult to find that if you want to buy it at Suomalainen Kirjakauppa, it may remain unknown forever".

All the posts of this pair included photos taken by the students themselves to document their activities. They mostly described the second-hand bookshop, the cafe and the bookshop, which were the central scenes of the posts. The main research findings were presented, seemingly unnoticed, as headings for the posts: 1) The smell of books through the wall, 2) Classics to be put on the shelf, and 3) *The Unknown Soldier* is rather unknown.

In this team's work, data collection, editing, documentation, and publishing merged. In the blog, the pair described and documented the interviews and search for classics through the medium in which they published.

4.1.3. Sharing expertise and continuing the process

The students presented their blog in a joint course meeting. They emphasised that it was useful to work together with someone they did not know. However, blogging did not end with the presentation. After the course, Anna posted a link to their video for the course Facebook group. The video was not created by just one individual. First the pair asked various people – from the course as well as outsiders – to write on post-it notes nice wishes that they would say to other people. Then they brought the notes to the second-hand bookshop described at the beginning of their blog, filmed the entire process, and made a video of it. Finally they posted the video on YouTube and linked it to the course Facebook site. In this way, the video became a public text, able to be viewed and shared by many people.

This process of sharing shows how writing is by no means a solitary activity anymore. In this new mode of writing, multimodal text is created through social activities (e.g. post-it notes + taking them to the bookshop + video + video editing + linking the video to the group's website). In the 'new writing' (Jenkins et al. 2013), the emphasis is on technical and social skills combined with a creative approach and the willingness of authors to publish their texts.

Anna commented on the video by saying that it was produced in their free time, while studying Finnish. In such a comment, she distinguished between activities related to leisure and those related to studying. She was probably not used to integrating leisure writing and study writing. Despite her prior blogging experience, she continued to see video making as something different from so-called actual studying. In the blog-writing process, however, the boundaries between leisure time and learning are erased and daily activities are incorporated into learning.

Overall, this pair's posts demonstrated how the bloggers worked seamlessly together and produced stylistically uniform text. Anna's conception of literature was traditional, but her conception of writing was modern – she was a skilled and experienced blogger able to create dialogue between the blog posts. Kata, on the other hand, had a more modern conception of literature but no experience of blogging. The conceptions of literature and writing collided with each other in a way that furthered the thinking of both of these learners.

During the process, the students modified the conception of literature they had adopted in their prior studies. Working on blogs included documenting the change that has occurred in their mindset. The old mental construction did not work because the modern Finnish conception of literature is, after all, not what they had previously learned and thought about it. Because the students had to broaden their view of the literary canon, a change in mindset occurred.

Characteristics of Anna and Kata's blogging:
- strong digital literacy (photography, making and posting videos on YouTube, editing, etc.);
- awareness of the text type used in blogs, experience of blogging;
- writing as a social activity, co-writing.

4.2. Pair 2: writing a blog as a remixing of voices

The first blog post of this student team, Anita and Veiko, began as follows:

> "*It surely did gripe us when* we had to write a blog post on a Monday morning. But as we have to, so be it. It was you who wanted it!!!

Nowadays everybody blogs, even writers – to mention an example, Jääskeläinen! They surely have forgotten what they should be doing, instead of sitting at the computer. Everything used to be clear – when you got a good idea, you took paper and a pen and wrote it down. Then you sent a letter to the newspaper agency, and the newspaper agency published it – so that everybody could read about it in the paper. But now everybody sits at the computer writing nonsense and publishing it, thinking that everybody will read what they've been writing. They surely do not read. Who in the world would manage to read all those blog posts? Nobody! Listen to me, you person – instead of sitting in front of the computer all evening and night long, you should be doing proper work. Our ancestors did real work ever since the Stone Age, and even the human body is used to it. Now the last couple of years it's been so that people just sit in front of the computer and move their fingers. So no wonder they've become weak and fat and don't even manage to do proper work. Especially young people are quite lost because of computers – they only laze around and loiter all the time" (Translated Totta ja tarua blog entry, 19 August 2013).

4.2.1. Agreeing on the research task and work method

Anita and Veiko knew each other from a previous Finnish course and formed a Hungarian-Estonian team, whose differences were related to their prior knowledge of Finnish literature. Anita was familiar with the classics and some modern literature, and she had already read books in Finnish. She had her own special perspective on Finnish literature: "A good thing about Finnish literature is that one can write about anything (immigrants, gay relationships, history, politics...) without having to be afraid of punishments from different parties or a negative reception from the audience". Veiko, on the other hand, had read Finnish literature in Estonian and wrote: "I still would like to know much more because I am really interested in Finnish culture as a whole".

Anita was also aware that by reading literature in the original language one can learn the language, develop one's own writing style and learn to know Finnish culture and "the soul of Finns". Besides, for her it was "a way of escaping everyday Hungarian life". The concept of soul was present in the excerpt, just like it is often highlighted in literary discussions with people from Eastern Europe. The concept is associated with classical literature analysis, and it can be connected to the cultural literacy mentioned earlier in this article. It was, indeed, interesting to see if the student would return to the concept later.

This blogger team shared an interest in societal affairs, and both of them were to some extent familiar with Tuomas Kyrö's bestseller *Mielensäpahoittaja* (translated as *Griped* by Douglas Robinson). Furthermore, they did not approach their topic too seriously but instead wanted to have fun. They were also interested in practising writing:

> "Our aim is to investigate, through Tuomas Kyrö's bestseller, what gripes Finnish people. Tuomas Kyrö has already done great work and written about forty possible reasons. We want to continue Kyrö's work and ask ordinary Finns if they are also upset for the reasons Kyrö mentions. That is how we intend to find out how much the reasons invented by Kyrö are connected to reality, in other words, to Finns' everyday experiences" (Translated Totta ja tarua blog entry, 19 August 2013).

This team ideated and planned the work process thoroughly. Using ten of the forty reasons described by Kyrö for the grumpy old man to be griped, they created a statement-based questionnaire intended for the ordinary Finn. Respondents answered the ten statements (e.g. *mailed advertisements*) on a 5-point scale: 1 = does not annoy or annoys only a little, 2 = annoys a little, 3 = annoys to an average extent, 4 = annoys a lot, 5 = annoys thoroughly.

4.2.2. Data collection, editing, documentation, and publishing

In their data collection process, Anita and Veiko interviewed ten people on the streets of Jyväskylä. They found that four of these interviewees had not read *Mielensäpahoittaja*, which made the pair wonder about the cultural knowledge of the local people. They processed the responses to the questionnaire and stated that the reasons that upset the grumpy old man were similar to those that upset the people in Jyväskylä in general. The reason that received the highest score was *jumping the queue*. An essential characteristic of this blogger pair's text was remixing, in other words, combining and editing (Lankshear & Knobel 2011). Anita and Veiko imitated Kyrö's style, beginning all their posts with the grumpy old man's signature phrase: "*Kyllä minä niin mieleni pahoitin, kun...*" (It surely did gripe me when...). They also imitated the writer's style but modified the reasons for being upset to suit their own daily lives, for example, "I surely would like to complain about Kata leaving the bar early last night" (Totta ja tarua blog, 23 August 2013).

In addition to a young student's perspective, the bloggers imitated Kyrö from the perspective of an imaginary old man: "There surely are too many choices today, and especially young people have too big dreams" (Totta ja tarua blog, 23 August 2013). The text received extra nuance from the continuously advancing language skills of the advanced learners of Finnish. Combining and editing different voices – polyphony – is a typical feature of postmodern literature.

This team went beyond polyphony, however, and actively utilised multimodality in their posts, including images found on the internet with their source information, a link to Kyrö's Facebook site, videos in which Kyrö reads his work, and remixed and edited images. This team made a picture collage in which they remixed images and text, placing the reader in the centre of activity. Different writers fight for the reader's time and interest, equipped with swords. On the left, two serious writers – the poet Olli-Pekka Tennilä and magical realism writer Pasi Jääskeläinen – call for the reader's attention, and on the right, the humorist Tuomas Kyrö. The students' knowledge of Finnish literature had grown, and they demonstrated it in a multimodal way, through images. They generated authorship by combining and editing existing artefacts in a creative way.

4.2.3. Sharing expertise and continuing the process

An analysis of the students' conceptions of literature clearly showed that Veiko's conception of Finnish literature had broadened. Together with his co-blogger, he had become able to sort modern Finnish writers into temporal and thematic categories. Anita's serious approach to literature, on the other hand, seemed to have become lighter – her earlier cultural literacy related to literature had been transformed, her reflections on the concept of the soul receded, and she was able to assume a playful attitude toward literature. A completely different approach joined her 'literature is the soul of a nation' thinking.

Characteristics of Anita and Veiko's blogging:
- the ability to produce multimodal text: editing and combining existing artefacts (images), that is, remixing;
- creativity, play and humour;
- breaking the boundaries between formal and fictive writing, innovative authorship.

4.3. Pair 3: blogging as metadiscourse on literature

An excerpt from the beginning of Giedre and Johanna's first blog post:

> "Both of us are interested in literary metadiscourse, literary criticism, and we have also written reviews in journals. That's why we would now like to study how Finnish literary criticism is doing.
>
>
> In her lecture, Elina told us that when studying literature one should also pay attention to the institution of literature. This institutionality is also important in criticism. Already at the turn of the millennium, people spoke about Finnish press criticism becoming more journalistic, in other words, more superficial (see e.g. Markku Ihonen's essay 'Mitä on hyvä kritiikki' [What is good criticism?, link included in original blog post]). But nowadays perhaps most criticism is not officially published in magazines but, instead, in blogs, where nobody edits the texts and people can write whatever.

Or can they? To find out more on this, for our next post we decided to compare reviews of Kari Hotakainen's novel *Juoksuhaudantie* [The Trench Road] (2002) from official reviews and from blogs.

We chose this book because it is a recognised, provocative and modern work that has received important prizes" (Translated Totta ja tarua blog, 19 August 2013[4]).

4.3.1. Agreeing on the research task and work method

Even the blog title, 'Discourse on metadiscourse', highlighted the bloggers' expertise in literary research. What the two bloggers – Johanna from Estonia and Giedre from Lithuania – had in common was expertise, the writing of literary reviews, and an inquiry-based approach to literature. The bloggers' own self-ironic definition of themselves in the title, 'Johanna and Giedre LTD', portrayed them as competent content producers.

Johanna was writing her literature dissertation in Estonia. She had also studied literature outside of her home country and worked in literature-related museum and media positions. Giedre had studied in Finland for a year and was particularly interested in Finnish literature. She had completed various literature courses and studied both comparative literature and Finnish literature. Giedre had long been writing a fashion, style and culture blog in Lithuanian, so she was an experienced user of social media. Additionally, she wrote about music and had started to read modern fiction in Finnish as well.

These bloggers' research question focused on the relationship between official literary criticism and literature blogs. They chose Kari Hotakainen's novel *Juoksuhaudantie* [The Trench Road] as their example of Finnish literature. Their hypothesis was that literature blogs were simple and too personal, whereas literary reviews in newspapers and literary magazines were complex

---

4. A sculpture portraying a critic at the Jyväskylä University Library (Leena Turpeinen-Kitula: The Critic, 1975. Photo taken by Giedre; reproduced with kind permissions of the author.

and impartial. They began to test their hypothesis using the means of literary research.

4.3.2. Data collection, editing, documentation, and publishing

The first reference in the bloggers' post told its own tale of expertise: the bloggers referred to literary researcher Markku Ihonen's essay 'Mitä on hyvä kritiikki' [What is good criticism?]. These kinds of references to literary researchers were not included in the blog texts examined earlier.

This blogger team formulated research questions that were used to search for certain features in reviews and literature blogs. The questions concerned the who, what, where, and central ideas of the material. They also considered whether or not the language in the book should be handled or why it might be interesting. Next the team created tables based on the four literary reviews and six literature blogs that were used. Finally, the research process was made transparent by the publication of the tables in their blog posts.

The bloggers used lots of images in their posts, ranging from ready-made internet stock photos and comics to the students' own photos. The ready-made online artefacts and self-produced ones formed a fluctuating whole. In addition to text, the students posted a screenshot of the literature blogs and reviews used as sources.

The visual element of the blog started with a photo of a sculpture called *The Critic*, which portrays a beetle rolling a ball of manure. The students also photographed their source materials, that is, the bound yearbooks of the Finnish literary magazine *Parnasso*.

An interesting feature of one blog post was the use of the hashtag (#) with keywords:
#Johanna&GiedreOY #nykykirjallisuus #friikki #löyly #CIMO #Anna Karenina #Raskolnikov #Juoksuhaudantie #kotiäiti #parnasso #hipsterit (Totta ja tarua blog, 26 August 2013).

The bloggers condensed their message and flagged it in the way they would on Twitter. Was this a new way of condensing? Was it a new form of language, #Finnish? In any case, the authors emphasised their cooperation, which implied that their writing was a social activity. Moreover, they were creative, played with the language, and produced public text. In these aspects, the blog post displayed a number of essential features of the 'new writing' (see Jenkins et al. 2009; Kallionpää 2014a, 2014b).

The hypothesis the bloggers set for their research turned out to be wrong; in other words, their conception of literature changed. Based on their study, they concluded that some literature blogs were of a high level, and that language and style were considered in nearly all of them. Literary reviews in magazines, instead, were sometimes 'personal and chaotic'. The team further stated that good texts could be found from various sources and that the opinions of both bloggers and literary researchers should be taken into account in order to get to know a book. Johanna and Giedre adopted the conception of literature experts according to which literature can be discussed in relevant ways also by those outside of the literary elite. Since the 1990s, this issue has been a central one in literary research, namely, a debate about what high literature is and who is entitled to talk about it (Jokinen 2010).

4.3.3. Sharing expertise and continuing the process

The bloggers were familiar with the scientific research report genre and began to experiment with broadening it in their blog texts. The genre received new dimensions in the online environment, in this case at least by making the research process visible. Images and comics provided an ironic, playful perspective on the literary research process, however, without parodying the assignment. Publicity is also a new feature of literary research – formerly, scholarly texts were bound in leather covers and forgotten on library shelves. This blogger team explicitly highlighted the change that took place in their conception of literature.

Characteristics of Johanna and Giedre's blogging:
- creativity, play, humour, irony;

Chapter 12

- experimenting with a new form of expression, #Finnish;
- self-direction and initiative: literary researchers conduct research because they are able to;
- both participants' conception of literature changes due to their research.

5. Results and discussion

Literature provides readers with a window to the textual culture it represents – or to the cultural context in which it has been written. Reading modern Finnish literature constructs a mental picture of Finnish people and society in the minds of foreign language learners, in addition to profoundly developing their language skills and cultural literacy.

In the Finland of the 2010s, the cultural context of literature is strongly mediated: the sanctity of literature has been shaken, and a textual as well as technological transformation is affecting even the structures of the publishing industry. If students are to have a realistic picture of the cultural context of Finnish literature, the teaching of literature must cover the texts, images and media that are essential for modern culture.

Book blogs and other websites are presently the dominant channels of Finnish literature discussion. In our teaching experiment, we aimed to introduce students to this environment of literary debate and offer them an innovative opportunity to take possession of the field of modern literature.

The purpose of this article was to investigate what kinds of new dimensions blogging can add to second-language learning in the context of modern Finnish literature. We also wanted to find out how new learning environments and approaches can be applied to broaden the literature conception of students of Finnish as a second or foreign language. Our practical aim was to present a potential pedagogical solution to the following question: What should we talk about or teach when our mission is to deepen students' knowledge of Finnish contemporary literature in the 2000s?

In this concluding section, we summarise our findings on how blogging supports the learning process by broadening the participants' conception of literature and enhancing their language skills.

5.1. Characteristics and benefits of blogging

The analysis of blogging as an activity shows that the working process includes various stages, during which students practise a range of skills in diverse ways, and their in-depth understanding of the phenomenon being taught increases. In creating multimodal texts, students disengage from the production of traditional, linear text, and it is clear that their conception of what a text is changes during this process. This implies that the production of text is interactive instead of being one-way, linear writing for the reader. Observations made at the various stages of the activities also show that it is not the final output that is significant in blogging (e.g. a traditional research report) but the shared learning process that, at its best, continues even after the learning event.

Students' blogging complies with the principles of new writing: existing artefacts (videos, digital texts, images, colours) are combined and edited (i.e. remixed) into a new format. New authorship self-consciously utilises creativity, play and humour. It also embeds new features into older text types, which may generate the text types of the future. For new authorship, it is important to experience one's own output as significant and to share it (Jenkins et al. 2013).

In the teaching experiment, we observed that the chosen working method and assignment motivate students to adopt an active role in their learning process. Agency activates students' thinking. At the same time that the assignment encourages active and independent agency, it also encourages independent thinking and new, creative solutions, which they experience as meaningful.

Language learners often remain even for long periods in a 'learner's niche', in which they are not in contact with the target-language community. Writing blogs facilitates participation: because blog texts are multimodal, readers pay more attention to the blog as a whole than to potential individual language errors. Bloggers have the opportunity to demonstrate their competence in various ways, not just by producing linear text.

Blogging shows that it is fruitful and mutually beneficial to integrate second or foreign language learning with the understanding and production of factual texts. Language need not – and actually should not – be taught separately from the context of the surrounding society and its texts. The integration of language and literature study is beneficial for the learner.

It is also worth emphasising that blogging provides an excellent language and culture learning opportunity even for students whose language skills are not of the same level. Our starting point was not to group students into pairs based on equal language skills levels. Instead, we let them form pairs taking into account all human dimensions, not just their level of language skills assessed through a specific method. This pair work succeeded excellently, and language proficiency was only one feature among many.

5.2. Broadening the conception of literature

Our study shows that blogging by applying the basic idea of inquiry-based learning suits the teaching of modern literature ideally: blogging allowed us to integrate pedagogical needs with the content.

Blogging is suitable for teaching modern literature in a cultural situation where literature education can no longer be based on the literary canon emphasised in traditional teaching. It is difficult to identify the canon of modern literature because, first, the identification of classics and their features would require distance from the era that is being evaluated. Second, the number of published books has exploded, and so many conceptions of literature exist side by side that reaching a consensus is impossible.

Therefore, when it comes to assigning value to literature, the present emphasis is on the view that the evaluation of artistic quality is relative, subjective and context dependent. In this sense subjective experientiality is the main element of quality measurement (Jokinen 2010). Literary discussion has, overall, become more democratic. It is natural that literature blogs are extremely popular in a time when an individual approach is appreciated – in both modern literature and blogs, room is given to deep, personal feelings.

Based on the pair work examples examined here, it can be stated that students' blog projects highlighted relevant perspectives on modern literature. The work process – particularly students' own digital writing – provided experiences of modern literature that could not have been conveyed through a teacher-centred approach.

An unexpected finding in our teaching experiment was that learning and the broadening of the conception of literature were visible, in addition to topic and perspective choices, also in the way students in the multimodal environment independently adopted the role of a modern writer and expressed in their blog texts (in a surprising way) the essence of modern literature.

The activities of the first blogger pair highlighted the social dimension of writing and the expansion of writing beyond digital texts and the so-called official teaching context. In contemporary writing, the process no longer ends when the text is etched on paper – its life continues in, for example, video format.

The role that the second pair of students adopted in relation to Tuomas Kyrö's *Mielensäpahoittaja* concretely manifests postmodern authorship: literature is intertextual, and every new voice is, in practice, a combination edited from different existing voices, which makes the result creative.

The third pair assumed a position on the way in which a new cultural situation generates new metadiscourse on literature. The handling of traditional literary criticism and digital texts side by side is an argument for the necessity to question established roles of discussing and assigning value to literature. In any case, we are facing a situation in which the old and new literary discourse can coexist: new features are embedded into older text types, which may generate new text types and forms of expression.

All the student pairs looked for and implemented new ways to discuss literature. The blog posts often focused on themselves, a typical approach for postmodern literature. They are self-conscious and interpret themselves, explaining 'what we wanted to say with this'.

The work of the student pairs also demonstrated in practice the break-up of the sanctity of literature: new authorship is based on creativity, play and humour – and, as a whole, does not take its role too seriously. The change in students' conception of literature became visible, above all, through the new ways of discussing literature that emerged in their blogs. This postmodern conception of literature, which highlights the features of the 'new writing,' clearly differs from the traditional idea of literature expressed in the preassignments.

Among various pedagogical methods, precisely blogging is exceptionally suitable for teaching modern literature because multimodal digital writing embodies, in an optimal way, the characteristics of postmodern literature. Based on the implementation and analysis of our pedagogical experiment in the modern literature course of CIMO, we found that it is pedagogically justified to use blogging to support second-language teaching. At its best, blogging is a method that opens up new learning environments and learning modes as well as helps broaden students' conception of literature. It seems particularly suitable for the examination of phenomena in modern literature.

5.3. Critical reflection on the teaching experiment and its applicability

Teachers should take into account that the 'new writing,' as part of new media literacies, is a challenge for teaching as well. They should discuss with students their conceptions of writing and start to practise and implement digital, multimodal texts: 'new writing'. These actions will inevitably lead to new questions, such as how to assess multimodal text produced with a peer. Because there are no ready-made assessment tools for these texts, teachers should agree on them together with students before they begin to write. This is a way of genuinely involving students in the entire writing process.

Even though this article focuses on the skills development of second-language learners, the process and results can be applied to any form of literature education, ranging from basic education to literature classes at general upper secondary school and comparative literature studies at universities.

Acknowledgement

This article has been translated from Finnish by Sirpa Vehviläinen.

References

Ahvenjärvi, K. & Kirstinä L. 2013. *Kirjallisuuden opetuksen käsikirja. Tietolipas 239.* Helsinki: Finnish Literature Society.
Coiro, J., Knobel, M., Lankshear, C. & Leu, D. (eds.). 2014. *Handbook of research on new literacies.* London: Routledge.
Cope, B. & Kalantzis, M. 2009. Multiliteracies: new literacies, new learning. *Pedagogies: An International Journal, 4* (3), 164–195. doi:10.1080/15544800903076044
Ekholm, K. & Repo, Y. 2010. *Kirja tienhaarassa vuonna 2020.* Helsinki: Gaudeamus.
Hakulinen, A. Kivelä, R. & Ranta, T. 2006. *Lukiolaisen äidinkieli ja kirjallisuus.* Helsinki: WSOY.
Hakkarainen, K., Bollström-Huttunen, M., Pyysalo, R. & Lonka, K. 2005. *Tutkiva oppiminen käytännössä. Matkaopas opettajille.* Helsinki: WSOY.
Hakkarainen, K., Lonka, K. & Lipponen, L. 2005. *Tutkiva oppiminen. Järki, tunteet ja kulttuuri oppimisen sytyttäjinä.* Helsinki: WSOY.
Hallila, M., Hosiaisluoma, Y., Karkulehto, S., Kirstinä, L. & Ojajärvi, J. 2013. *Suomen nykykirjallisuus 1–2.* Helsinki: Finnish Literature Society.
Husson Isozaki, A. 2014. Flowing towards solutions: literature listening and L2 literacy. *The Journal of Literature in Language Teaching, 3* (2). Retrieved from http://liltsig.org/wp-content/uploads/2014/12/LiLT-3_2-Isozaki.pdf

Hvistendahl, R. E. 2000. *"Så langt 'vår' diktning tenner sinn i brann..." En studie av fire minoritetsspråklige elevers arbeid med norsklitteratur fra perioden1860–1900.* Acta humaniora 70. Oslo: University of Oslo.

Jalkanen, K. & Pudas, H. 2013. *Rivien välissä. Kirjablogikirja.* Helsinki: Avain.

Jenkins, H., Clinton, K., Purushotma, R., Robison, A. J. & Weigel, M. 2009. *Confronting the challenges of participatory culture: media education for the 21st century.* MacArthur Foundation.

Jenkins, H., Ford, S. & Green, J. 2013. *Spreadable Media. Creating value and meaning in a networked culture.* New York: New York University Press.

Jokinen, E. 2010. *Vallan kirjailijat. Valtion apurahoituksen merkitys kirjailijoille vuosituhannen vaihteen Suomessa.* Helsinki: Avain.

Jokinen, E. 2013. Kirjailijoiden yhteiskunnallinen asema. In M. Hallila, Y. Hosiaisluoma, S. Karkulehto, L. Kirstinä & J. Ojajärvi (eds.), *Suomen nykykirjallisuus 2.* Helsinki: Finnish Literature Society, 159–176.

Kallionpää, O. 2014a. Monilukutaidon opetus on ennen kaikkea uusien kirjoitustaitojen opetusta. *Language, Education and Society e-journal.* Retrieved from http://www.kieliverkosto.fi/journals/kieli-koulutus-ja-yhteiskunta-lokakuu-2014/

Kallionpää, O. 2014b. Mitä on uusi kirjoittaminen? Uusien mediakirjoitustaitojen merkitys. *Media & viestintä, 37* (4), 60–78. Retrieved from http://www.mediaviestinta.fi/arkisto/index.php/mv/article/view/54/43

Lankshear, C. & Knobel, M. 2011. *New literacies: everyday practices and social learning* (3rd ed.). Maidenhead: Open University Press.

Lehtonen, M. 2001. *Post scriptum – Kirja medioitumisen aikakaudella.* Tampere: Vastapaino.

Lounavaara, M.-T. 2004. *Näytelmän lukupiiri suomi toisena kielenä -opetuksessa. Integraation tukeminen kaunokirjallisuuden avulla.* Master's thesis in Finnish. Helsinki: University of Helsinki Department of Finnish.

Malm, R. 2006. Kirjallisuuden opettamisesta Vilnan yliopistossa – kun teoria ja käytäntö eivät kohtaa. In S. Pöyhönen & K. Hiltula (eds.), *Opettajana vieraalla maalla. Opetuskulttuurien kohtaamisia.* Jyväskylä: University of Jyväskylä Centre for Applied Language Studies, 97–109.

Mela, M. & Mikkonen, P. (eds.). 2007. *Suomi kakkonen ja kirjallisuudenopetus. Tietolipas 216.* Helsinki: Finnish Literature Society.

Myonghee, K. 2004. Literature discussions in adult L2 learning. *Language and Education, 18* (2), 145–166. doi:10.1080/09500780408666872

Niemi, J. 2010. Kaanon ja kirjallisuuden opetus 2000-luvulla. In S. Häppölä & T. Peltonen (eds.), *Kuutamokeikka ja muita teitä tekstien kiehtovaan maailmaan*. Helsinki: Äidinkielen opettajain liitto, 45–55.

Niemi-Pynttäri, R. 2013. Verkkokirjallisuus hakee muotoaan. In M. Hallila, Y. Hosiaisluoma, S. Karkulehto, L. Kirstinä & J. Ojajärvi (eds.). *Suomen nykykirjallisuus 1*. Helsinki: Finnish Literature Society, 349–363.

Parente-Čapková, V. 2009. Mietteitä kielestä, kirjallisuudesta, oppimisesta ja opettamisesta. In Vehkanen, M. (ed.), *Karjalanpaistista kaksoiskonsonanttiin*. Suomen kielen ja kulttuurin vaikuttajat maailmalla. Centre for International Mobility CIMO. Erweko, 197–202.

Perusopetuksen opetussuunnitelman perusteet 2014 [National core curriculum for basic education 2014]. Retrieved from http://www.oph.fi/download/163777_perusopetuksen_ opetussuunnitelman_perusteet_2014.pdf

Rantala, T. 2006. Etnografisen tutkimuksen perusteet. In J. Metsämuuronen (ed.), *Laadullisen tutkimuksen käsikirja*. Helsinki: International Methelp.

Saarinen, L., Joensuu, J. & Koskimaa, R. (eds.). 2003. *BOOK 2010. Development trends in the book trade - summary*. Jyväskylä: University of Jyväskylä. Retrieved from http://urn. fi/URN:ISBN:951-39-1559-X

Smolander, J. 2012. *Runoja ja merkityksiä: runous lukion suomi toisena kielenä -opetuksessa*. Master's thesis. Jyväskylä. Retrieved from http://urn.fi/ URN:NBN:fi:jyu-201202011111

Staršova, T. 2007. Kirjallisuuden opetuksesta Petroskoin valtionyliopiston itämerensuomalaisten kielten ja kulttuurin tiedekunnassa. In M. Mela & P. Mikkonen (eds.), *Suomi kakkonen ja kirjallisuuden opetus*. Helsinki: Suomalaisen Kirjallisuuden Seura.

The Finnish Book Publishers Association. 2015. *Statistics*. Retrieved from http://www.kustantajat.fi/pages/k9/tilastot/

Taipale, S. 2013. The affordances of reading/writing on paper and digitally in Finland. *Telematics and Informatics, 31* (4), 532–542. doi:10.1016/j.tele.2013.11.003

Tynjälä, P. 2004. *Oppiminen tiedon rakentamisena: konstruktivistisen oppimiskäsityksen perusteita*. Helsinki: Kirjayhtymä.

Vaarala, H. 2009. *Oudosta omaksi. Miten suomenoppijat keskustelevat nykynovellista? [From strange to familiar: how do learners of Finnish discuss the modern short story?]* Doctoral dissertation. Jyväskylä: Jyväskylä studies in humanities 129. Retrieved from https://jyx.jyu.fi/dspace/bitstream/handle/123456789/22654/9789513937737.pdf?sequence=1

Chapter 12

Website

Totta ja tarua blog http://tosijataru.blogspot.fi

Appendix 1. Student assignment

Assignment. Modern Finnish literature is a broad concept. It is said that the literary field is fragmented, in other words, broken into small parts. That's why we cannot define modern Finnish literature in just a sentence or two. So, if you want to get an idea of modern literature, the best way is to analyse its individual parts, different works, themes and phenomena, and then try to form an overall picture based on them.

In this course, together with another course participant, you will choose a phenomenon in modern Finnish literature that interests you. Then you will **look for information** on this topic and **write** about your thoughts and experiences in the course blog. (Blogs naturally also include images, videos, links, etc., in addition to text.) In the course blog, you can follow and comment on the other pairs' blog texts, which will complement your overall idea of modern literature.

Choosing a topic. Find an interesting perspective that you want to share with the others. You can focus on an individual book or writer, but first discuss from which perspective you will explore the topic. You can also find new books at the course library.

The topic can be any phenomenon related to literature:

- Translating literature, e-books, literary prizes, writer blogs, writers from Jyväskylä...

- A good start could be to define a research question on the topic and then look for an answer to it. For example: What do Finns read? How are books advertised in Finland?

- How has *Harjukaupungin salakäytävät* / book X been handled in literature blogs?

Blog posts are made in the joint lessons, but it's good to prepare them also in your free time. Supervised work on the blogs is arranged about every two days. The pairs are formed and topics chosen on Wednesday 14 August and Thursday 15 August. After that you can independently schedule your work and start to create ideas for the blog content.

Blog posts. Every pair produces at least **three blog posts** and comments on at least three other posts. If you get a comment, it's naturally nice if you also respond to it.

In your first post (written during the first week), you present your topic and explain why you are interested in it.

In your second post (written during the second week), you report on the progress of your research project and how you've been looking for an answer to your question. What have you discovered on the topic? Has something unexpected happened during your journey?

In your third post (written at the beginning of the third week), you share what you have discovered on the topic and what thoughts working on the topic has evoked in you.

Things to remember when writing the blogs:

- a fresh and personal viewpoint (your own thinking and personal experiences);

- the utilisation of text, images, video material, etc. and their suitability for the blog as a whole;

- an interactive approach, i.e. how the recipient has been considered.

Chapter 12

Also remember:

The blog's primary target group consists of students in this course and other international learners of Finnish interested in Finnish literature.

However, remember that the blog is public and accessible for anyone, so you should choose the content accordingly. When you attach photos and videos to the blog, always remember to ask for the permission of the people in them. If you copy an image from the internet, indicate the source.

All the student pairs will present their projects on the last day of the course.

13. Grammar is the heart of language: grammar and its role in language learning among Finnish university students

Pekka Saaristo[1]

Abstract

This article presents and discusses views on grammar and its role in formal language learning amongst Finnish university students. The results are based on a questionnaire which was distributed to students at the University of Jyväskylä as part of institutional action research. The background to the project was a feeling amongst some teachers of increased divergence between student respectively language teacher understandings of the role of grammar in language teaching. This concern raised the need to find out how students view grammar. The knowledge about thoughts on grammar amongst students would then help teachers to adjust and adept the way grammar is used in language teaching. The main finding of the questionnaire was that a majority of the students think of grammar as a valuable asset in language learning, but at the same time have somewhat different understandings of grammar. In this context grammar is understood as a metalinguistic set of (also normative) statements of regularities in language which is the way most students think of grammar. Three different student perspectives on grammar are distinguished. These include a normative, functional and structural perspective. Since all answers in the questionnaire couldn't be placed within these categories, a fourth category, "other" was also included.

keywords: grammar, language learning, folk linguistics/sociolinguistics, emic/etic, written language, normativity, functionality.

---

1. Language Centre, University of Jyväskylä, Finland; pekka.c.saaristo@jyu.fi

How to cite this chapter: Saaristo, P. (2015). Grammar is the heart of language: grammar and its role in language learning among Finnish university students. In J. Jalkanen, E. Jokinen, & P. Taalas (Eds), *Voices of pedagogical development - Expanding, enhancing and exploring higher education language learning* (pp. 279-318). Dublin: Research-publishing.net. doi:10.14705/rpnet.2015.000296

Chapter 13

1. Introduction

During the 2008–2009 semester, a group of teachers at the Language Centre at the University of Jyväskylä in Finland decided to learn something more about how university students look at formal grammar and grammar instruction in language learning and teaching. We shared a concern about a possible widening conceptual and terminological gap between the pre-understandings of teachers and students regarding language teaching and learning. Discrepancies between teacher and student understandings of language learning cannot be beneficial for learning outcomes (see Brown 2009; Horwitz 1988; Jean & Simard 2011; Rättyä 2014; Schulz 2001). It is, of course, not possible or even necessary for learners' and teachers' views on language learning and, for example, the role of grammar to match completely (see Jean & Simard 2011). However, a fairly common understanding of the rationale behind teaching and the concepts utilised seems to benefit learning.

To learn more about the students' views on grammar in language learning, our group of teachers developed a questionnaire. As the title of this article suggests, I do not present all the questions and results from the survey. Instead, my focus is on a single two-part open-ended question: "Briefly describe what you understand by the word *grammar* and what role grammar has in language teaching and learning." The general idea with this question was to find out what kind of pre-understandings the students have about grammar and how they see it as a part of language teaching and learning. One practical aim was to use the results to adapt the use of grammar in our teaching to better match the students' understandings and points of departure. The answers to this question also created a framework for understanding other answers in the questionnaire.

The article begins with a short description of the respondents. This is followed by a discussion of some preliminary issues. The concepts of *grammar* and *teaching method* are discussed in brief and some premises for the study are presented. As expected, the opinions on grammar varied (see Mori 1999) and the answers in the questionnaire are presented under four headings, each expressing a different perspective: *normative*, *functional*, *structural* and *other*. Before discussion of the *other* category, I present the views on the role of grammar in language teaching and learning. The aim with these categorisations is to organise the answers according to salient factors expressed in the answers. The basis for the categorisations is also explained. Since written language seems to have a special role in many formulations in the answers, this modality is also briefly discussed, especially when presenting the more normative or prescriptive views on grammar. The answers are exemplified through more or less prototypical answers. I end the article with some reflections on the role grammar can play in teaching and learning.

2. The data

The results which are presented are based on written answers ($N = 189$) to the question of how students define grammar and relate it to language learning and teaching. The respondents consist of students from all of the different faculties at the University of Jyväskylä (see Table 1).

Table 1. Questionnaire respondents by faculty[2]

Faculty	n
Faculty of Humanities	28
Faculty of Information Technology	17
Faculty of Education	10
Faculty of Sport and Health Sciences	21
Faculty of Mathematics and Science	38
Jyväskylä University School of Business and Economics	39
Faculty of Social Sciences	36
	189

The answers have not been correlated for background factors such as faculty membership or, for example, gender. (For more on the relationship between gender and grammar in language learning, see Rieger 2009 and Jean & Simard 2011). The aim is to present the ways the students understand grammar and its

---

2. The number of respondents from the different faculties is not representative of the number of students in each faculty

role in language learning and teaching on a general level. For the sake of brevity I have left out information regarding faculty membership, sex and age. The sexes were distributed evenly and the average age among the respondents was 26 years. Students who study a language as their major subject were excluded from the sample. In the next section I discuss grammar and teaching methods in order to make some pre-understandings of the subject more explicit.

3. Grammars and teaching methods

Grammar is a key concept in general linguistic theory, but a more thorough discussion of how the concept of grammar has been, and can be, understood is beyond the scope of this article. Writers on the subject usually make different distinctions between theoretical, (traditional) descriptive/reference and (traditional) pedagogical grammars (Aarts 2006; Kachru 2010; Leech 1994; Odlin 1994; Tonkyn 1994). In general, pedagogical grammars (Chalker 1994; Corder 1988; Taylor 2008) seem to be about "usefulness rather than the theory of adequacy or simplicity postulated for pure grammars" (Spolsky 1978: 5).

In other words, grammars function as aids to learning instead of being an object for knowledge per se (Corder 1988; Kachru 2010; Rutherford 1987, 1988 for more on grammars written for other practical purposes, see Leitner & Graustein 1989)[3]. The role of the descriptive linguist is to describe and analyse structures and rules without any consideration of didactic or pedagogical matters (see Achard 2004; Kachru 2010; Nikula 2003; Rutherford 1987; Wilkins 1974). Furthermore, theoretical grammars often aim to prove or support a certain theoretical view on language and/or grammar or a descriptive ideal, whereas pedagogical grammars can afford to be more eclectic and utilise insights from different types of grammatical description according to the practical goals of learning and on the basis of practical experience (Corder 1988; Rutherford 1988; Taylor 2008).

---

3. There is also a tradition advocating almost no explicit use of grammar in language teaching. This tradition has occurred under different labels (Krashen 1982, 1999; Prahbu 1987; see Kachru 2010; Littlewood 2012; Rutherford 1987; Tonkyn 1994; Trappes-Lomax 2002; Yip 1994). The anti-grammar reaction (probably meaning reaction of a certain way of using grammar in teaching) was then followed by a counterstrike in the 1980s and 1990s (Joseph 2002; Tonkyn 1994; Trappes-Lomax 2002).

Although pedagogical grammars are planned for different purposes than theoretical grammars are, it seems that the substance of pedagogical grammars are or should be informed by developments in general linguistic description and that at least some teachers are aware of developments within linguistics. They cannot, of course, be atheoretical either and pedagogical grammars are also descriptive in some sense of the word (see Dirven 1989; Hasan & Perrett 1994; Leech 1994; Leitner & Graustein 1989; Tomlin 1994; Westney 1994; Wilkins 1974).

If, as suggested by Leech (1994), "teacher's grammar" is located somewhere between "academic grammar" (theoretical and descriptive) and "grammar for the learner" (practical, selective, task-oriented etc.), there seems to be at least an indirect connection between folk and expert views on language (see Coupland & Jaworski 2004). Nevertheless, it seems reasonable to assume that, from a folk linguistic (i.e. a non-linguist) perspective, grammar or grammars usually are understood as normative formal rules codified in books and/or presented by teachers (see Odlin 1994). Grammar is, in other words, understood to be an explicit metalinguistic description of a languages, which themselves are understood as imagined singularities such as "Spanish", "Russian", "Norwegian Bokmål" and so on.

It seems likely that people often equate grammar with grammar books and institutional language learning. The opinions of the usefulness of an explicit focus on grammar vary and some students prefer 'communicating' as a way of learning. Obviously one can make oneself understood without applying existing structural features in a language (see Cook 1989; Nikula 2003; Tonkyn 1994). The view that you can communicate without grammar may stem from a perceived dichotomy between lexis and grammar, where grammar is given a lesser communicative and interactional role. From a linguistic point of view, on the other hand, lexis and grammar share communicative responsibilities and should not be seen as separate entities (see Boers & Lindstromberg 2006; Broccias 2008; Langacker 2008; Widdowson 1988). Words and structural elements form dynamic and parallel semiotic resources for performing communicative pragmatic functions and constructing meanings in specific languages, dialects, sociolects and ethnolects. Therefore so-called grammarless methods can only be seen as idealised abstractions and to separate grammar from communicative competence seems odd (see Achard 2004). In line with Widdowson (1988), one could actually claim that language learning essentially is grammar learning, but stating that grammar is unavoidable in language use and learning does not, of course, imply a certain view on language learning or that grammatical phenomena should be focused on explicitly (see Liamkina & Ryshina-Pankova 2012; Spada 2011; Spada & Lightbown 2008; Taylor 2008; Yip 1994). The topic-related choices made in teaching (e.g. semantic topics, communicative functions) also obviously affect the grammatical structures used in meaning construction (Nikula 2003; Rutherford 1988).

As stated, a specific view on grammar in language learning does not mechanistically correspond to a view of a specific preference of learning strategies or teaching methods. Even those who would see an explicit focus on grammar as of little or no value for successful language learning would probably not deny that form, as such, also carries meaning and has communicative and interactional functions (Rutherford 1988). In broader terms, this means that a view on language and metalinguistic knowledge in general does not necessarily imply a specific view of language learning (see Andrews 1999; Corder 1988). From the teacher's point of view, this may be seen as a truism in a "postmethod" era (Kumaravadivelu 1994; for other views of language teachers and learners, cf. Bell 2003, 2007; Block 2001) when the search for *the* method seems pointless and varying learning strategies are acknowledged (Adamson 2004; Ellis 2004; Joseph 2002; Leech 1994; Prahbu 1990; Rutherford 1987).

My personal experience is that most language teachers tend to be pragmatic towards the fads and trends in language teaching, successfully using old practices – never mind how old – and at the same time showing willingness to try new methods, often reconstructing these for specific purposes. In other words, teachers have effectively always been, as Bell (2007: 143) suggests, "beyond methods". I certainly hope that language teachers are not affected by "monotheistic approaches", following fashionable teaching methods while "demonising others" (see Adamson 2004: 611). In general, methods may not be as coherent packages as sometimes thought but rather they may be seen as general characterisations, and the concept of a teaching method itself might have a range of different meanings (Brumfit 1991). The role of canonical teaching methods in practical teaching seems to be exaggerated (see the teacher comments in Bell 2007; see also Bell 2003). Whether we like to consider teaching habits to be methods or not might be a matter of taste, but going beyond method does not, of course, equal lacking a systematic approach (Bell 2007). Most teachers have probably rid themselves of the Cartesian fear (Bernstein 1983) of not having absolute certainty about the best method or, for that matter, that we should throw out method altogether as the principle to follow.

4. Some other premises

The present study could be seen as belonging to the sociolinguistic field known as folk linguistics (Hoenigswald 1966; Niedzielski & Preston 2003; Pasquale 2011; Preston 2006) and sociolinguistic research on language related opinions and attitudes (see Edwards 2006; Garrett, Coupland & Williams 2003) in general. Folk linguistics also forms a natural perspective within applied linguistics, because it often deals with practical linguistic issues and problems. It seems evident that language education can benefit from the knowledge of learner views in specific speech communities (Niedzielski & Preston 2003; Preston 2004, 2006; Wilton & Stegu 2011). If the long tradition of prescriptive school grammar has led to a view that language learning essentially is about separating 'wrong' from 'right' and learning rules, and this tradition has prevailed throughout the 20th century (Harjunen & Korhonen 2008; Odlin 1994; Paunonen 2006; Preston 2006; Vattovaara & Soininen-Stojanov 2006; Wilkins 1974), it seems likely that this would affect the layperson's understandings of language and how it should be learned (see Harris 1996; Hiidenmaa 2007; Niedzielski & Preston 2003). As can be expected, the issue of right vs. wrong was mentioned in the answers in the questionnaire. This is in line with a widespread traditional idea of linguistic entities having a single 'correct' form (Harris 1996; see also Preston 2004, 2006).

Chapter 13

The question about grammar was formulated in a fairly open way and lacked theoretical (apart from grammar) concepts that could steer the answers in a certain direction. The aim was, in other words, to avoid using overly specific formulations expressing certain theoretical views on the subject, which might undermine the folk linguistic objective of learning about common views (Vattovaara 2012).

In terminology stemming from Pike (1967) and often used in other disciplines such as anthropology and ethnography, we can also conceptualise the situation as a dialogue between theoretically generated etic-concepts and user-based emic-conceptions in which the emic-views are seen as an important part in the research on social reality (see Hymes 1964; Saville-Troike 2003). An emic-approach is, naturally, also a part of many studies on beliefs about language learning (Barcelos & Kalaja 2003, 2011). The answers about grammar presented in this study seem to represent a mix of more 'autonomous' views together with more institutionally informed opinions on the matter, the latter views probably echoing an etic-perspective within the institutions of language education as they are encountered in concrete learning situations. If we imagined a dialogue between a linguist and a layperson, the conversation would show diverging as well as converging views on grammar and language in general (see Coupland & Jaworski 2009; Lillis 2013; Vattovaara 2012).

The study might also be anchored in the discipline of applied linguistics because it deals with a 'problem', especially one concerning language learning (see Brown 2004; Davies & Elder 2004). More specifically, the present article deals with beliefs about language learning (see Horwitz 1987; Wesely 2012). One rationale within studies on learning beliefs among language learners is that beliefs affect learning and that it is beneficial for learning outcomes to be aware of pre-understandings, beliefs, expectations and goals among students (see Benson & Lor 1999; Cotterall 1999; Horwitz 1988; Mercer 2011; Mori 1999; Rifkin 2000; Wenden 1998, 1999).

The remit of this article does not allow a further discussion on the concept of belief. However, in this context I would describe it as socioculturally emerged and dynamic metacognitive knowledge and/or a representational state of consciousness recognised by the individual (see Barcelos & Kalaja 2003; Mercer 2011; Negueruela-Azarola 2011; Wenden 1998, 1999; for more on representationalist theories of consciousness and on the connection between consciousness and intentionality, see Siewert 2011 and van Gulick 2014).

The students' answers concerning their thoughts on grammar are semiotic representations of beliefs in this sense. It is important to stress that expressed beliefs do not necessarily correlate with actual behaviour and they are obviously not static. Instead, they are dynamic entities that are affected but not determined by situational, personal and micro- as well as macrocontextual factors (see Barcelos & Kalaja 2011; Benson & Lor 1999; Negueruela-Azarola 2011; Rifkin 2000).

This observation is in line with the findings that expressed language attitudes do not always equal linguistic behaviour (Bainbridge 2001a, 2001b; Edwards 1985, 1994; Garrett et al. 2003; Giles & Billings 2004; Lewis 1981; Niedzielski & Preston 2003; Potter 1999; Potter & Edwards 2001; Potter & Wetherell 1987; Shotter 1993; Zanna & Rempel 1988). In other words, I do not assume a simple correlation between an expressed view on grammar and actual learning preferences or behaviour in language classes.

5. Grounds for classifications: prototypicality in answers

In this chapter I present a short metatheoretical basis for my categorisation of the views on grammar into four classes: *normative, functional, structural* and *other*. The *other* category consists of answers that could not easily be grouped under the three other headings. I also want to emphasise that I have placed the answers in the different categories according to the most salient aspects in the answers. A structural view on language and grammar can be found in most of the answers, but in some answers there seems to be a stronger emphasis on functionality and normativity. My categorisation is, in other words, based on the idea of prototypicality as it is outlined in prototype theory. I should stress here, however, that I do not use prototype theory as an established method of analysis. Prototype theory in this context only describes how categorisation is possible in the first place.

Prototype theory (associated foremost with Eleanor Rosch) is based upon a model of 'best examples'. Categories and general conceptions emerge from the fact that individual cases seem to have enough in common with a prototypical case. The prototype functions as an a priori model to which other cases are compared. The idea can be expressed as "a robin is more birdy than a guinea fowl" (Bolinger 1979: 404). Correspondences between instantiations and the prototype exist as a continuum. In other words, categories and concepts are not seen to be discrete entities. (For more see Gibbs 1994; Hampton 2006; Holme 2010; Hopper & Thompson 1985; Joseph 2002; McCloskey & Glucksberg 1978; Mervis & Rosch 1981; Rosch 1975, 1987, 1999; Winters 1990). Prototypes are conceived as abstractions in relation to concrete instantiations. The a priori and abstract nature of prototypes does not imply that they are autonomous in relation to human social life. Categorisations and classifications are influenced by biological, anthropocentric, cultural and contextual factors that are expressed, passed on and also transformed in language. This means that prototypes are changeable and negotiable (Brown 1990; Dupré 1981; Hampton 2006; Janicki 1990; McCloskey & Glucksberg 1978; Medin 1989; Rosch 1978, 1999; Wikforss 2009; see also Brown 1985). From the point of view of communication, the capability to generalise and the identification of sameness and categories seems to be a practical and even necessary condition (Medin & Atran 2004; for criticism of prototype theory, cf. Fodor 1998, Fodor & LePore 1994 and Margolis 1994).

My aim in this article is to use prototype theory only as a legitimisation for the possibility to identify sameness in the given answers, not to discuss the (dis) advantages of prototype theory. Since none of the answers are identical, I have organised them under the four headings according to the idea of prototypicality. In other words, I base my classification of the answers on prototypical formulations where one aspect seems to be salient. The vantage point is an interpretative one and I make no claims to know what the students actually intended by their answers.

6. Normative attitudes and the role of written language

Instead of *normative* I could have chosen *prescriptive* as a name for this category of attitudes towards grammar in language learning. Any language use is characterised by community-based norms which emerge in linguistic habits and behaviour. The community-based norms are not determinative (Figueroa 1994), but failing to act according to norms may lead to different sanctions or even ridicule. These kinds of norms could be called descriptive norms, as described by sociolinguists, and compared with pedagogical norms, which often reflect an idealised linguistic form (Bowerman 2006). The normatively flavoured comments given in the answers seem to reflect an attitude which could be identified as a prescriptivist one in which the idea of formal correctness is strong. The respondents most often use the word norm, however, and therefore the concept is used throughout.

Implicit or explicit normativity (in all senses) seem to have a long tradition in linguistics (and among laypeople), partly showing as the phenomena which Linell (1982, 2005a) describes as the "written language bias". The bias means the tradition of looking at language and analysing it in its written form, which reproduces language as a visual, stabile, atomistic and regular entity. As a certain type of modality, written language has come to affect our views on language even if the prevailing paradigm within linguistics from the early 19th century onwards has promoted spoken language as 'authentic language' and therefore the primary form. The primacy of spoken language has also been motivated by both phylogenetic as well as ontogenetic reasons. Spoken language is, in other words, primary in human development on both a community and individual level. Language change also mostly happens in spoken language (Bucholtz 2003; Harris & Taylor 1989; Lillis 2013; Toolan 1996; Wilkins 1974). Nevertheless, there seems to have been a tendency to look at spoken language with the written form as a default.

In most formal language learning contexts, grammatical well-formedness seems to equal well-formedness according to the codified norms of written standardised national languages. Obviously, the stability of the written modality also lends itself more easily to being the form focused on (for further discussion, see Bittner 2011; Bowerman 2006; Davies 2006; Linell 2001; Wilkins 1974). Language beliefs are in other words affected by political developments also manifested as language and educational ideologies as well as the general sociolinguistic situation in particular societies and communities (Barcelos & Kalaja 2011; Borg 2003; Kelly 1969; Rifkin 2000). It is not surprising, then, that quite a few of the respondents (47 of 189) express some kind of normative attitude towards grammar and, at the same time, transmit an old tradition. Greek *grammatiké* is explicitly about understanding letters, which echoes the intimate relation between grammar and writing, and in ancient Rome classical writing became the ideal for other language uses as well (Harris & Taylor 1989; Hudson 2006)[4]. The later criteria for 'good language' codified by European Academies for their national languages were based on the literary canon, with an explicit distancing from spoken language use (Edwards 1985; Haarman 1995; Lillis 2013; Lo Bianco 2004; Wilkins 1974).

The respondents expressing normative views on grammar seem to think, importantly, that norms are about one single form of language, a belief which is understandable in the light of Western educational history and the role of written language in this history. In educational institutions and among the general public as well, the ideology of what 'good language' should be is strong and can be seen in a number of public contexts, such as in letters to the editor (see Alho & Kauppinen 2008; Davies 2006; Harjunen & Korhonen 2008; Svensson 1990; Turner 1996; Wilkins 1974). Therefore it is not surprising that grammar is seen as normative for so-called proper language and this proper language is represented in written form.

Of all the answers received (N = 189), approximately 25% (n = 47) expressed a view on grammar as a set of normative rules for correct language use. In the

---

[4]. In the classical tradition of rhetoric and grammar instruction, however, oral and conversational skills were also important factors. These skills were exercised in natural situations and the idea of accommodation to specific contexts was emphasised. When Latin was taken out of the curriculum and mother tongue became an important subject, exercises in speech and conversation disappeared in many European schools for a long time and the status of writing grew even stronger (see Johannesson 1992).

following I present some examples of prototypical answers within this category (all translations from Finnish are by the author):

> "Without grammar one cannot write or speak correctly".

As indicated before many of the answers in this category included references to written language:

> "Grammar includes the rules for correct writing and speaking. An important part of learning, but to learn how to speak is more important".

> "Grammar guides how language should be written/spoken in a correct way. An important part [in learning] but speech should be focused on more, like it is at the university".

> "The correct way of writing/talking, grammatical correctness, the correct way of forming sentences. More important in writing than in speech".

The emphasis on written language might reflect awareness among university students of the demands for formal correctness in academic written genres. In the following answer, the use of *instruction* may express a more reflective attitude. This answer, nevertheless, voices a clear normative view:

> "Grammar includes the instructions for how language should be used correctly. I think it has an important role because it is a prerequisite for good language use".

Some of the normatively framed answers also reflected a purist view:

> "The basic structure of language. Language as pure and grammatically correct".

This formulation does not necessarily reflect a conscious purist ideology, but can also be interpreted as reflecting the idea of purity from norm-breaking. The following formulation can be said to echo a more conscious ideology:

"The grammatically correct form of language and the preservation of this".

It seems that grammar also functions as a protection against unwanted changes. Some of the answers included explicit reference to normativity and also relativised the norms:

"Grammar is the official understanding of how a mother tongue should be written and how to use its structures".

"Grammar equals the agreed upon rules and norms of language. Mostly these are shown in written language".

In the latter answer the role of written language is again emphasised. The phrase *agreed upon* probably reflects the fact that the question of formal grammatical correctness (in one's strongest language/languages) mostly occurs in connection with written language. All in all, the formulations expressing some kind of normative perspective on grammar include the idea of proper and less proper language. Approximately half of the normatively formed answers refer to written language in particular.

7. Functional perspectives

Functions in language, linguistic structure and/or language use can refer to different aspects. A classical grammatical function would be, for example, that a word functions as a subject or an object or that lexical and grammatical entities show functional interdependence (see Martinet 1960; Nichols 1984).

A broader view of the functionality of all linguistic entities has been expressed by Halliday (1978: 19): "Language is as it is because of what it has to do". The answers I have interpreted as expressing a functional view of grammar (22 of 189, 12%) reflect the idea of grammar as a functional tool for communication – it describes how to communicate in specific languages. This view comes close to the basic functionalist idea. Many of the answers emphasise grammar as a practical tool for effective language *use*. Some of the formulations also express grammar as a resource in adapting language use to specific contexts and situations, echoing an idea of grammar as one factor of pragmatic, discourse and sociolinguistic competencies (see Trappes-Lomax 2004). If the normative view emphasised formal correctness, the functional perspectives seem to focus more on pragmatic communicative needs. In fact, it would have been possible to label this category of answers as *pragmatic perspectives*.

Although the word *functional* can have many dimensions and meanings, it was nevertheless possible to identify a category of answers representing a functional attitude towards grammar. Some of the answers seem to look upon grammar as a manual of practical language use designed for communicative purposes. The students with a more functional view of grammar also seem to be less worried about formal correctness, but adherence to formal norms can also fulfil the function of communicative needs. From this point of view, it is problematic to dichotomise between fluency and formal correctness. Depending on the context and situation, formal correctness can be what guarantees fluency.

In comparison to the normatively framed answers, the 'functionalists' do not specifically emphasise the role of grammar in written grammar. As mentioned, reoccurring terms include *use* and *language use*:

> "Rules and instructions of language use for both spoken and written language. I feel that some kind of command of grammar fastens the learning of other areas in language".

> "Includes the rules for language use".

The concept of rules is used in some formulations but, as noted, in connection to use. In some of the answers there were also references to contextual aspects:

> "I think that grammar is the right way of using words, phrases and sentence structures according to the demands of the context".

Chapter 13

There might be a normative aspect in the use of the word *right* in this answer, but the mentioning of contextual appropriateness seems to imply a more functional view and less emphasis on one correct form. In the wording of the next answer, a kind of a meta-perspective can be identified:

> "Knowledge on the structure and use of language which has an important role in the mastering of language, but practical language knowledge is affected by many other things (for example, mastering of the lexicon)".

This answer reflects the idea that a reflexive competence supports a procedural one (see Lehmann 2007). Other formulations view grammar as a tool:

> "Important from a communicative perspective but shouldn't be emphasised too much. The function of language is to be an instrument for communication and expression, not an end in itself".

Here, some important functions of language are mentioned and grammar is given some role in fulfilling these functions. Actually, the formulation is close to others used for pedagogical grammars. The final example of this category expresses a certain need for grammar:

> "Without grammar one cannot know language or, in my mind, even use language".

It is difficult to say what the students have meant by *use*, but it appears that the 'functional' answers view grammar more as something practical facilitating better language use.

Functional views seem to imply that autonomous grammars would not be a practical starting point for pedagogical grammar and for learning purposes in general but that structural aspects should be explained by or related to semantic, pragmatic, discourse and other external factors (Croft 1995; James

1994; Mitchell 1994; Rutherford 1987; Tomlin 1994; Williams 2005). The functional views expressed in the replies seem to support the view of the usefulness of grammar in teaching and learning when it is used as a meaningful resource for communication and interaction and is compatible with usage-based functional and discourse-oriented views on language (see Chalker 1994; Glisan & Drescher 1993; Leech 1994; Tomlin 1994).

8. Structuralist attitudes

A vast majority of the answers (97 of 189) seemed to reflect some kind of structural view on grammar. *Structural* here means the role of grammar as a description of the structures in language. This view is common among non-linguists for, as Niedzielski and Preston (2003: 243) report, there exists a wide "concern...for linguistic structure in language learning". Some of the answers emphasised the metalinguistic aspects of grammar, and others mentioned grammar as a descriptive tool and/or as a list of linguistic conventions. Some of the answers include normative and functional dimensions but the differences in emphasis were clear enough to motivate a separate category.

In the student answers, the term *structure* seems to be understood as a stable trunk onto which miscellaneous content is placed. Grammars try to generalise as much as possible and therefore structure may be conceived as an unchanging thing.

In the structurally framed answers, the relation between structure and use/instantiation are mostly left out, reflecting perhaps a more autonomous view of language. The question of written vs. spoken language also emerges in some of the structure-focused answers:

> "Grammar is sentence structures. Grammar is the basis for writing".

> "Word order, inflection, verbs and nouns are an important basis, but one should emphasise speech more".

Chapter 13

As shown, some of the answer explicitly mentioned different structural aspects of language. Not all of the answers, however, make a distinction between writing and speech:

> "It means the structure of language. It has a pretty important role because it structures writing and speaking".

Many formulations include a similar idea of grammar as a basis for language. This way of thinking is often represented with different metaphorical expressions:

> "Grammar is the basic structure of language which everything is based on".

> "Grammar is the foundation of language, on which one starts to build language".

This idea of grammars as a foundation is, as can be seen, represented with a number of metaphorical expressions. Grammar as a tree is another commonly used metaphor:

> "If language would be a tree, grammar would be its trunk and branches, and words are the leaves. In other words, the whole base for language teaching".

Many of the answers in the structural category express a view on grammar as a separate but important aspect to which other things (e.g. words) are added. Some of the formulations even come close to a more linguistic, theoretical view:

> "Describes the structure of language".

> "The theory of language, structure".

> "The trunk of language, the analytical part of language where strict regularities operate".

The last formulation may not be the view of all linguists, and as Sapir (1921: 38) suggested, "all grammar leaks". Some of the answers focus on learning:

> "Grammar is learning of the structure of language. The basis for spoken and written language".

> "Grammar means learning of the structures and rule of language".

These formulations seem understandable as grammar is most often used for language learning among non-linguists. The last example shows a more reflective and conscious view of grammar:

> "Grammar includes the comprehension of sentence structures like predicates etc. and subordinate clauses".

Many of the respondents also mention *rules*. However, the relation of these rules to language use is not commented on. Another type of question formulation would have yielded such answers, but the aim was, as previously mentioned, to keep the wording of the question fairly open. Answers given in this category do variously indicate how structure is understood and what it actually means to acquire linguistic structure. More light was shed on these issues in the comments concerning the role of grammar in learning, which is the subject of the next section.

9. The role of grammar in language teaching and learning

The latter part of the question concerning grammar in the questionnaire concerned the role of grammar in language teaching and learning. In many of the answers such adjectives as *important* and *central* were used when describing the role of grammar in teaching and learning. As could be expected, some of the respondents gave grammar a less central meaning in language studies. Some gave more detailed specifications regarding the parts of language in which grammar was considered to be especially important.

On the basis of how centrally grammar in language teaching and learning was considered to be by the respondents, I identified roughly four categories. The no-answer category represents answers which did not include a clear view on the matter in question. The distribution of the answers is presented in Table 2.

Table 2. The role of grammar in language teaching and learning

Role of grammar in language teaching and learning	No answer	Not very important	Fairly important	Very important
N =189	66	5	53	65
% ≈	35	3	28	34

It is worth pointing out that many answers explicitly mentioned *learning*. This means that the answers do not reflect only how much formal grammar is used by teachers. Not a single answer implied that grammar would not have any meaning whatsoever.

Over one half of the students (62%) expressed the view that grammar had a fairly or very important role in language studies. When grammar was given a fairly important role, the answers often included explanatory reservations of different sorts. These reservations included, for example, mentions of overemphasis of grammar and, typically, the lesser role played by grammar in learning to speak. The following prototypical answers reflect some of these different understandings. Some of the students have clearly experienced an overemphasis on grammar:

> "To know grammar is fairly important, but without words it [grammar] is of no use, so it alone shouldn't be emphasised too much".

> "Grammar should be learned in parallel with language use itself, not alone as such".

> "Yes, grammar is important, but it is more important to encourage one to use language. Grammar teaching should be made clearer".

These formulations express an experience of grammar as something separate and not always integrated for interactional and communicative uses[5]. The first example also makes a distinction between lexis and grammar, which might be based on how these notions are, unfortunately, often presented as independent entities (see Trappes-Lomax 2004).

Some answers give explicit reference to the situation in Finland:

> "An important part of language studies but in Finland the position of grammar is TOTALLY overemphasised; because people are afraid of making grammatical errors, they don't dare to USE language, which for me is the function of language learning".

> "Important to know, but I think it is overemphasised in Finland. Especially in speech".

These answers may reflect experiences from language teaching where formal correctness has been stressed at the expense of a more tolerant attitude. It is unfortunate, of course, if grammar teaching discourages people from using a specific language altogether. It is sometimes felt that too much emphasis is placed on details and communication should be focused on more:

> "Without grammar it's hard to make oneself understood, but when speaking a foreign language every comma doesn't matter that much".

> "One should be encouraged to learn basic level grammar but otherwise the emphasis should be on encouraging communication".

One could argue that speech also has its own forms of commas that serve to structure dialogues (e.g. different discourse markers and conversational conventions), that is, it too has grammatical features with semantic, pragmatic

---

5. I don't know whether this also can be due to practices of orthodox "communicative language teaching" (for an historical overview see Littlewood 2012) where (formal) grammar not only was separated but also treated with some kind of suspicion or even hostility.

and interactional functions (see Auer 2007; Couper-Kuhlen & Selting 2001; Franck 1980; Fried & Östman 2005; Lindström 2008, 2014; Linell 2003, 2005b; Selting 2000; Weinert, Basterrechea & del Pilar García Mayo 2013). 'Basic grammar' is naturally important but within, for example, academic genres the demands for formal correctness may be greater or even essential. Even if styles, registers or lects other than the codified variant would do equally well as means of communication, it is not always a case where anything goes. To diverge from the norm is usually, at least for students, a risky endeavour, but, of course this does not imply that students should not be made aware of linguistic variation and the relative and ideological basis for standardised norms (see Canagarajah 2011; Celce-Murcia 1991; Davies 2006; Odlin 1994; Wilkins 1974; Ziegler 2011).

Students, of course, also have preconceived views on demands for accuracy depending on, among other things, the specific language to be learned, contexts of language use and beliefs about factors affecting setting of grades (see Chavez 2007). Sometimes students actually wish for more emphasis on formal correctness than teachers do (see Brown 2009; Ellis 2004; Horwitz 1988; Schulz 2001; Sharwood Smith 1988). As before, the difference between spoken and written language was mentioned in a number of answers:

> "An important part of learning but to learn how to speak is more important".

> "An important part of knowing a language but it has overridden speaking and pronunciation in teaching".

It is hard to say whether the second example represents some kind of naturalistic/communicative view on language learning or if the idea is that grammar simply matters less in speech. From a linguistic point of view, the latter seems to be wrong but maybe language teaching could also focus more on structural regularities specific to spoken language and in order to make it more dialogic and cooperative. The relation between metalinguistic grammatical knowledge and practical language use was seen to be problematic in some of the answers:

"The role is important but can't be applied in practice (how many adults know/need the intransitive?)".

Here the question of grammatical terminology also seems to be an issue. The case is, of course, that both children and adults 'know' the use of intransitive verbs in, for example, at least one language, but maybe the formulation is based on a feeling of disconnectedness between practical communication and grammar as it has been taught. The ability to apply a grammatical rule does not, of course, mean the ability to formulate the rule with metalinguistic terminology (Roehr 2007; cf. Borg 1999: 96-99 for different views on using terminology in language teaching).

The question of the role of grammar in mother tongue teaching and, on the other hand, foreign language teaching is also raised in some of the answers:

"Most important in mother tongue studies. Very much overemphasised in the teaching of foreign languages".

This is a somewhat surprising formulation because, from the point of linguistics, everyone has a 'complete grammar' in their mother tongue (or their first/ strongest/most used languages). The answer might be due to the fact that some of the courses in written communication in Finnish (as a mother tongue) at Finnish universities focus on formal grammatical correctness. Other respondents highlight the role of grammar in foreign language learning:

"An important role especially in foreign language studies, it is good to master the basics also in the mother tongue".

"A very important role, one cannot make oneself understood in foreign languages otherwise".

These answers may reflect the idea that grammar becomes prominent in a different way when studying foreign languages. The following statement may strike one as contradictory and/or reflecting a normative attitude:

> "Without grammar one can't know a language. On the other hand also mother tongue speakers make grammatical errors".

Grammar is, in other words, a vital part of communicative competence, but mother tongue speech can also lack grammar. How an 'error' should be interpreted is uncertain but may be based on prescriptive principles. The views on grammar in language teaching and learning depend, of course, on many things, such as personal experiences and specific preferences of language learning. As mentioned, some of the students express unconditional support for grammar in language learning and teaching:

> "An important part of teaching, perhaps there could be more of it".

> "The basis of high-quality language learning".

> "The role of grammar in language learning is very important".

Those who valued grammar high in language studies often completed the answers with practically framed explanations:

> "Mastering grammar helps one to know language comprehensively, for example understanding, speaking, writing".

> "It is important in language teaching and learning because otherwise one cannot use language in an understandable way".

> "Knowing grammar makes talking and writing more fluent".

One may notice that these answers do not make a distinction between speech and writing. The majority of the answers mention *learning*, which was also mentioned in the question. A few answers only talked about *teaching*, which means that it is uncertain how grammar was valued as a learning tool:

> "A central role in language teaching".

"Very essential; 'the Bible' of language teaching".

Nevertheless, my impression is that these types of answers reflect, at the least, an appreciative attitude towards grammar, although the Bible metaphor can be interpreted in many ways depending on one's leanings. As previously stated, less positive opinions on grammar in language studies were also voiced:

"Its role in language teaching should be smaller. One cannot learn language only through grammar-based teaching (the use of communicative methods)".

The answer seems to echo the idea that grammar would have a smaller role in 'communicative methods'. From a linguistic point of view a 'communicative' approach does not imply a lesser role for grammar (Widdowson 1988), but the answer probably reflects the feeling of too much explicit focus on formal grammar. Some of the respondents felt that grammar might be important but that it is difficult and unpopular:

"Important, yes, but in general tedious and in school too much emphasis is put on it".

"I associate "grammar" with the dull, numbing and dominating – although mandatory – side of language studies".

The answers showing a negative attitude towards grammar might, nevertheless, see a point in practicing it (see Jean & Simard 2011). Teaching and learning do not have to be fun all the time, but the goal should be to present or use grammar in a way that seems relevant for learners and in ways which are connected to communicative and interactional needs. A couple of answers did assign grammar a fairly small role without any reservations, of which the following is one example:

"I don't think the role is very big, you can learn grammar without its being taught".

One can, of course, agree with this statement. The formulation seems to express the view that formal grammar teaching is not needed in language teaching, which is, depending on circumstances and resources, a fact. Taken together, then, grammar is given a fairly important role in language learning and teaching. Many respondents see grammar as an essential part of communication. Others experience grammar as potentially important but somehow as a separate entity. If this separateness is seen as a problem, one approach would be to relate the learning of grammatical constructions even more closely to communicative needs and situations.

10. Other views

As expected, some answers could not easily be placed in one of the categories presented above. These answers often included some aspects which imply, for example, a normative view, but not in a clear enough manner. Some respondents preferred to use the adjective *sensible* in their answers:

> "A manual for constructing sensible sentences".

> "Enables a sensible use of the words of a language, including word order, use of tense".

Sensible could possibly be read to mean *understandable*, thus equalling a practical and functional view. In the following formulations, the meaning of the word *technical* can also be interpreted in different ways:

> "Technically correct writing/speech".

> "For me it [grammar] means the "technical" part of language and a basic tool kit and rules".

Without going into deeper conceptual and philosophical issues on classical distinctions of knowledge such as phronēsis, epistēmē and technē (see Bernstein

1983), the last two formulations seem to reflect the idea of grammar as a description of suitable technical know-how about language use. *Technically correct*, on the other hand, also implies a normative component. Memorising is also mentioned in a few answers along with specific grammatical aspects:

> "Mnemonics and word order in sentences".

> "Grammar is like a small jigsaw puzzle which one, little by little, learns (to remember) to assemble in a better way".

In the following case the answer seems to express both a normative and descriptive view at the same time:

> "Grammar is "rules" about how language should be used, or, actually, it tells how mother tongue speakers use language".

The formulation is not contradictory, though, since formally codified prescriptive rules are ultimately derived from community-based language use.

11. Some final reflections

> "Grammar is the heart of language, its role is important".

On the basis of the answers presented in this article, Finnish university students seem to view grammar, if not as "the heart of language", then at least as a fairly important aspect of language learning and teaching. Similar results have been reported in, for example, Schulz's (2001) discussion of Colombian and American students. The views are in all likelihood also an expression of the fact that grammar has been such a self-evident part of language teaching.

My impression is, nevertheless, that the majority still genuinely feels that grammar offers genuine benefits for language learning and language use. To gain a better understanding of the thoughts and feelings behind these attitudes, more qualitative methods should be used, such as interviews and ethnographic observation (see Barcelos 2003; Benson & Lor 1999; Cotterall 1999).

The attitudes towards grammar expressed among the majority of the students should receive a positive reception among teachers who feel that using grammar facilitates more effective language learning. Still, it seems that grammar needs a bit of demythologising and should be approached as just another semiotic resource for communication. If it is indeed the case that, as Littlewood (2004: 513) argues, there is "overwhelming evidence [...] that explicit focus on formal aspects of language is helpful and produces lasting improvement of performance"[6], teachers must offer grammatical knowledge in a way which makes sense to as many learners as possible and to avoid presenting grammar as a separate abstraction with weak connections to pragmatic and interactional needs (see Ellis 1994 for relations between individual learners and types of suitable instruction; see Turula 2011 for learning styles and personality traits in relation to types of instruction). This practice can, of course, be carried out in many different ways (Borg & Burns 2008; Rutherford 1987; Spada & Lightbown 2008).

An open-minded and continuing dialogue between teachers and learners is recommended, but at the same time, teachers' professional integrity must be preserved. This article is but a modest attempt to carry on with such a dialogue.

Acknowledgments

I would like to thank my colleagues Joachim Böger, Timo Nurmi, Maaria Oksala and Margarita Pietarinen for taking part in the action research group and for interesting discussions on the topic. I am, of course, solely responsible for the interpretations and views expressed in this article.

---

[6]. See also Batstone 1994; Borg & Burns 2008; Celce-Murcia 1991; Ellis 1990, 2006; Kachru 2010; Master 1994; Norris & Ortega 2000; Odlin 1994; Rutherford 1987; Schmidt 1990; Skehan 2006; Taylor 2008; Turula 2011; Yip 1994.

References

Aarts, B. 2006. Grammar. In R. Brown (ed.), *Encyclopaedia of Language and Linguistics*. Amsterdam: Elsevier, 113–115. doi:10.1016/b0-08-044854-2/04775-1

Achard, M. 2004. Grammatical instruction in the natural approach: a cognitive grammar view. In M. Achard & S. Niemeier (eds.), *Cognitive Linguistics, Second Language Acquisition, and Foreign Language Teaching*. Berlin: Mouton de Gruyter, 165–194. doi:10.1515/9783110199857.165

Adamson, B. 2004. Fashions in language teaching methodology. In A. Davies & C. Elder (eds.), *The Handbook of Applied Linguistics*. Malden: Blackwell Publishing, 604–622.

Alho, I. & Kauppinen, A. 2008. *Käyttökielioppi*. Helsinki:Suomalaisen kirjallisuuden seura.

Andrews, S. 1999. Why do L2 teachers need to 'know about language'? Teacher metalinguistic awareness and input for learning. *Language and Education, 13* (3), 161–177. doi:10.1080/09500789908666766

Auer, P. 2007. Syntax als Prozess. In H. Hausendorf (Hg.), *Gespräch als Prozess. Linguistische Aspekte der Zeitlichkeit verbaler Interaktion*. Tübingen: Narr, 95–142.

Bainbridge, W. 2001a. Attitudes and behavior. In R. Mesthrie (ed.), *Concise Encyclopedia of Sociolinguistics*. Oxford: Elsevier, 6–10.

Bainbridge, W. 2001b. Social psychology. In R. Mesthrie (ed.), *Concise Encyclopedia of Sociolinguistics*. Oxford: Elsevier, 80–86

Barcelos, A. 2003. Researching beliefs about SLA: a critical review. In P. Kalaja & A. Barcelos (eds.), *Beliefs about SLA. New Research Approaches*. New York: Springer, 7–33. doi:10.1007/978-1-4020-4751-0_1

Barcelos, A. & Kalaja, P. 2003. Conclusion: exploring possibilities for future research on beliefs about SLA. In P. Kalaja & A. Barcelos (eds.), *Beliefs about SLA. New Research Approaches*. New York: Springer, 231–238. doi:10.1007/978-1-4020-4751-0_10

Barcelos, A. & Kalaja, P. 2011. Introduction to beliefs about SLA revisited. *System, 39* (3), 281–289. doi:10.1016/j.system.2011.07.001

Batstone, R. 1994. Product and process: grammar in the second language classroom. In M. Bygate, A. Tonkyn & E. Williams. (eds.), *Grammar and the Language Teacher*. New York: Prentice Hall, 224–236.

Bell, D. 2003. Method and postmethod: are they really so incompatible? *TESOL Quarterly, 37* (2), 325–336. doi:10.2307/3588507

Bell, D. 2007. Do teachers think that methods are dead? *ELT Journal, 61* (2), 135–143.

Benson, P. & Lor, W. 1999. Conceptions of language and language learning. *System, 27* (4), 459–472. doi:10.1016/S0346-251X(99)00045-7

Bernstein, R. 1983. *Beyond objectivism and relativism: science, hermeneutics and praxis.* Oxford: Basil Blackwell.

Bittner, A. 2011. Das Implizite ‚explizieren' – Überlegungen zum Wissen über Grammatik und zum Gegenstand des Grammatikunterrichts. In K. Köpke & A. Ziegler (hrsg.), *Grammatik - Lehren, Lernen, Verstehen. Zugänge zur Grammatik des Gegenwartsdeutschen.* Berlin: De Gruyter, 17–36. doi:10.1515/9783110263183.17

Block, D. 2001. An exploration of the art and science debate in language education. In M. Bax and J.-W. Zwart (eds.), *Reflections on Language and Language Learning: In Honour of Arthur van Essen.* Amsterdam: John Benjamins, 63–74. doi:10.1075/z.109.11blo

Boers, F. & Lindstromberg, S. 2006. Cognitive linguistic applications in second or foreign language instruction: rationale, proposals, and evaluation. In G. Kristiansen, M. Achard, R. Dirven, I. Ruiz de Mendoza & J. Francisco (eds.), *Cognitive Linguistics: Current Applications and Future Perspectives.* Berlin: Mouton de Gruyter, 305–358. doi:10.1515/9783110197761.4.305

Bolinger, D. 1979. The socially-minded linguist. T*he Modern Language Journal, 63* (8), 404–407. doi:10.1111/j.1540-4781.1979.tb02479.x

Borg, S. 1999. The use of grammatical terminology in the second language classroom: a qualitative study of teachers' practices and cognitions. *Applied Linguistics, 20* (1), 95–126.

Borg, S. 2003. Teacher cognition in language teaching: a review of research on what language teachers think, know, believe, and do. *Language Teaching, 36* (2), 81–109.

Borg, S. & Burns, A. 2008. Integrating grammar in adult TESOL classrooms. *Applied Linguistics, 29* (3), 456–482. doi:10.1093/applin/amn020

Bowerman, S. 2006. Norms and correctness. In R. Brown (ed.), *Encyclopaedia of Language and Linguistics.* Amsterdam: Elsevier, 701–703. doi:10.1016/b0-08-044854-2/01299-2

Broccias, C. 2008. Cognitive linguistic theories of grammar and grammar teaching. In. S. De Knop & T. De Rycker (eds.), *Cognitive Approaches to Pedagogical Grammar. A Volume in Honour of René Dirven.* Berlin: Mouton de Gruyter, 67–90.

Brown, A. 2009. Students' and teachers' perceptions of effective foreign language teaching: a comparison of ideals. *The Modern Language Journal, 93* (1), 46–60.

Brown, C. 1985. Mode of subsistence and folk Biological categories. *Current Anthropology, 26* (1), 43–64. doi:10.1086/203224

Brown, C. 1990. A survey of category types in natural language. In S. Tsohatzidis (ed.), *Meanings and Prototypes*. London: Routledge, 17–47.

Brown, J. 2004. Research methods for applied linguistics: scope, characteristics, and standards. In A. Davies & C. Elder (eds.), *The Handbook of Applied Linguistics*. Malden: Blackwell Publishing, 476–500. doi:10.1002/9780470757000.ch19

Brumfit, C. 1991. Problems in defining instructional methodologies. In K. de Bot et al. (eds.), *Foreign Language Research in Cross-Cultural Perspective*. Amsterdam: John Benjamins Publishing Company, 133–144. doi:10.1075/sibil.2.14bru

Bucholtz, M. 2003. Sociolinguistic nostalgia and the authentication of identity. *Journal of Sociolinguistics, 7* (3), 398–416. doi:10.1111/1467-9481.00232

Canagarajah, A. S. 2011. Translanguaging in the classroom: emerging issues for research and pedagogy. In. L. Wei (ed.), *Applied Linguistics Review 2*. Berlin: De Gruyter Mouton. 1–28. doi:10.1515/9783110239331.1

Celce-Murcia, M. 1991. Grammar pedagogy in second and foreign language teaching. *TESOL Quarterly, 25* (3), 459–480. doi:10.2307/3586980

Chalker, S. 1994. Pedagogical grammar: principles and problems. In M. Bygate et al. (eds.), *Grammar and the Language Teacher*. New York: Prentice Hall. 31–44.

Chavez, M. 2007. Students' and teachers' assessments of the need for accuracy in the oral production of german as a foreign language. *The Modern Language Journal, 9* (4), 537–563. doi:10.1111/j.1540-4781.2007.00622.x

Cook, V. 1989. The relevance of grammar in the applied linguistics of language teaching. *Trinity College Dublin Occasional Papers 22*. Retrieved from http://homepage.ntlworld.com/vivian.c/Writings/Papers/TCD89.htm

Corder, S. P. 1988 [1973]. Pedagogic grammars. In W. Rutherford & M. Sharwood Smith (eds.), *Grammar and Second Language Teaching. A Book of Readings*. New York: Newbury House Publishers, 123–145.

Cotterall, S. 1999. Key variables in language learning: what do learners believe about them? *System, 27*, 493–513. doi:10.1016/S0346-251X(99)00047-0

Couper-Kuhlen, E. & Selting, M. 2001. Introducing interactional linguistics. In M. Selting & E. Couper-Kuhlen (eds.), *Studies in Interactional Linguistics*. Amsterdam: Benjamins, 1–22. doi:10.1075/sidag.10.02cou

Coupland, N. & Jaworski, A. 2004. Sociolinguistic perspectives on metalanguage: reflexivity, evaluation and ideology. In A. Jaworski et al. (eds.), *Metalanguage. Social and Ideological Perspectives*. Berlin: Mouton de Gruyter, 15–51. doi:10.1515/9783110907377.15

Chapter 13

Coupland, N. & Jaworski, A. 2009. Social worlds through language. In N. Coupland & A. Jaworski (eds.), *The New Sociolinguistics Reader*. London: Palgrave Macmillan, 1–21

Croft, W. 1995. Autonomy and functional linguistics. *Language, 71* (3), 490–532. doi:10.2307/416218

Davies, A. & Elder, C. 2004. General introduction. Applied linguistics: subject to discipline? In A. Davies & C. Elder (eds.), T*he Handbook of Applied Linguistics*. Malden: Blackwell Publishing, 1–15. doi:10.1002/9780470757000.ch

Davies, W. 2006. Language education: correctness and purism. In R. Brown (ed.), *Encyclopaedia of Language and Linguistics*. Amsterdam: Elsevier, 470–477. doi:10.1016/b0-08-044854-2/00681-7

Dirven, R. 1989. Cognitive linguistics and pedagogic grammar. In G. Graustein & G. Leitner (eds.), *Reference Grammars and Modern Linguistic Theory*. Tübingen: Max Niemeyer Verlag, 56–75. doi:10.1515/9783111354590.56

Dupré, J. 1981. Natural kinds and biological taxa. *The Philosophical Review, 90* (1), 66–90. doi:10.2307/2184373

Edwards, J. 1985. *Language, society and identity.* Oxford: Basil Blackwell.

Edwards, J. 1994. *Multilingualism*. London: Routledge.

Edwards, J. 2006. Language attitudes. In R. Brown (ed.), *Encyclopaedia of Language and Linguistics*. Amsterdam: Elsevier, 324–331. doi:10.1016/b0-08-044854-2/01286-4

Ellis, R. 1990. *Instructed second language acquisition. Learning in the classroom*. Oxford: Basil Blackwell.

Ellis, R. 1994. *The study of second language acquisition.* Oxford: Oxford University Press.

Ellis, R. 2004. Individual differences in second language learning. In A. Davies & C. Elder (eds.), *The Handbook of Applied Linguistics*. Malden: Blackwell Publishing, 525–551. doi:10.1002/9780470757000.ch21

Ellis, R. 2006. Current issues in the teaching of grammar: an SLA perspective. *Tesol Quarterly, 40* (1), 83–107. doi:10.2307/40264512

Figueroa, E. 1994. *Sociolinguistic metatheory.* Oxford: Pergamon.

Fodor, J. 1998. *Concepts. Where cognitive science went wrong*. Oxford: Clarendon Press.

Fodor, J. & LePore, E. 1994. The red herring and the pet fish: why concepts can't be prototypes. *Cognition, 58*, 253–70. doi:10.1016/0010-0277(95)00694-X

Franck, D. 1980. *Grammatik und Konversation*. Königstein: Cornelsen Verlag.

Fried, M. & Östman, J-O. 2005. Construction grammar and spoken language: the case of pragmatic particles. I: *Journal of Pragmatics,* 1755–1778. doi:10.1016/j.pragma.2005.03.013

Garrett, P., Coupland, N. & Williams, A. 2003. *Investigating language attitudes: social meanings of dialect, ethnicity and performance*. Cardiff: University of Wales Press.

Gibbs, R. Jr. 1994. *The poetics of mind. Figurative thought, language, and understanding.* Cambridge: Cambridge University Press.

Giles, H. & Billings, A. 2004. Assessing language attitudes: speaker evaluation studies. In A. Davies & C. Elder (eds.), *The Handbook of Applied Linguistics*. Malden: Blackwell Publishing, 187–209. doi:10.1002/9780470757000.ch7

Glisan, E. & Drescher, V. 1993. Textbook grammar: does it reflect native speaker speech? *The Modern Language Journal, 77* (1), 23–33. doi:10.1111/j.1540-4781.1993.tb01941.x

Haarman, H. 1995. Europeaness, European identity and the role of language – Giving profile to an anthropological infrastructure. In U. Ammon et al. (hrsg.), *Sociolinguistica 9. Europäische Identität und Sprachenvielfalt*. Tübingen: Max Niemeyer Verlag, 1–55.

Halliday, M. A. K. 1978. *Language as a social semiotic: the social interpretation of language and meaning*. Maryland: University Park Press.

Hampton, J. 2006. Concepts as prototypes. *The Psychology of Learning and Motivation, 46*, 79–113. doi:10.1016/S0079-7421(06)46003-5

Harjunen, E. & Korhonen, R. 2008. Äidinkielen kielioppi – sydämmen asia! In M. Garant et al. (toim.), *Kieli ja Globalisaatio – Language and Globalization*. Jyväskylä: Suomen soveltavan kielitieteen yhdistys AFinLA, 125–151.

Harris, R. 1996. *Signs, language and communication. Integrational and segregational approaches*. London: Routledge.

Harris, R. & Taylor, T. J. 1989. *Landmarks in linguistic thought. The Western tradition from socrates to saussure*. London: Routledge.

Hasan, R. & Perrett, G. 1994. Learning to function with the other tongue: a systemic functional perspective on second language teaching. In T. Odlin (ed.), *Perspectives on Pedagogical Grammar*. Cambridge: Cambridge University Press, 179–226.

Hiidenmaa, P. 2007. Ei vain luonnonlahjoilla: ohjailua, opetusta, apuneuvoja kielenkäytön tueksi. In S. Pöyhönen & M-R. Luukka (toim.), *Kohti tulevaisuuden kielikoulutusta. Kielikoulutuspoliittisen projektin loppuraportti*. Jyväskylä: Jyväskylän yliopisto. Soveltavan kielentutkimuksen keskus, 431–450.

Hoenigswald, H. 1966. A proposal for the study of folk linguistics. In W. Bright (ed.), *Sociolinguistics*. The Hague: Mouton, 16–26.

Holme, R. 2010. Construction grammars. Towards a pedagocical Model. *AILA Review, 23*, 115–133. doi:10.1075/aila.23.07hol

Chapter 13

Hopper, P. & Thompson, S. 1985. The iconicity of the universal categories "Noun" and "Verb". In J. Haiman (ed.), *Iconicity in Syntax. Proceedings of a Symposium on Iconicity in Syntax, Stanford, June 24–6, 1983*. Amsterdam: Benjamins, 151–183. doi:10.1075/tsl.6.08hop

Horwitz, E. 1987. Surveying student beliefs about language learning. In A.Wenden & J. Rubin (eds.), *Learner strategies in language learning*. Englewood Cliffs: Prentice-Hall, 119–129.

Horwitz, E. 1988. The beliefs about language learning of beginning university foreign language students. *The Modern Language Journal, 72* (3), 283–294. doi:10.1111/j.1540-4781.1988.tb04190.x

Hudson, R. 2006. Language education: grammar. In R. Brown (ed.), *Encyclopaedia of Language and Linguistics*. Amsterdam: Elsevier, 477–480. doi:10.1016/b0-08-044854-2/00679-9

Hymes, D. 1964. Introduction: toward ethnographies of communication. *American Anthropologist, 66* (6/2), 1–34. doi:10.1525/aa.1964.66.suppl_3.02a00010

James, C. 1994. Explaining grammar to its learners. In M. Bygate et al. (eds.), *Grammar and the Language Teacher*. New York: Prentice Hall, 203–214.

Janicki, K. 1990. *Toward non-essential sociolinguistics*. Berlin: Mouton de Gruyter.

Jean, G. & Simard, D. 2011. Grammar teaching and learning in L2: necessary, but boring? *Foreign Language Annals, 44* (3), 467–494. doi:10.1111/j.1944-9720.2011.01143.x

Johannesson, K. 1992. Retorik. In S. Strömquist (red.), *Tal och samtal*. Lund: Studentlitteratur, 15–34.

Joseph, J. E. 2002. Is Language a verb? - Conceptual change in linguistics and language teaching. In H. Trappes-Lomax & G. Ferguson (eds.), *Language in Language Teacher Education*. Amsterdam: John Benjamins Publishning Company, 29–47. doi:10.1075/lllt.4.03jos

Kachru, Y. 2010. Pedagogical grammars for second language learning. In M. Berns (ed.), *Concise Encyclopedia of Applied Linguistics*. Amsterdam: Elsevier, 172–178

Kelly, L. G. 1969. *25 centuries of language teaching*. Rowley: Newbury House Publishers.

Krashen, S. D. 1982. *Principles and practice in second language acquisition*. Oxford: Pergamon.

Krashen, S. D. 1999. Seeking a role for grammar: a review of some recent studies. *Foreign Language Annals*, 32 (2), 245–254. doi:10.1111/j.1944-9720.1999.tb02395.x

Kumaravadivelu, B. 1994. The postmethod condition: (e)merging strategies for second/foreign language teaching. *TESOL Quarterly, 28* (1), 27–48. doi:10.2307/3587197

Langacker, R. 2008. The relevance of cognitive grammar for language pedagogy. In S. De Knop & T. De Rycker (eds.), *Cognitive Approaches to Pedagogical Grammar. A Volume in Honour of René Dirven*. Berlin: Mouton de Gruyter, 7–35.

Leech, G. N. 1994. Students' grammar – teachers' grammar – learners' grammar. In M. Bygate et al. (eds.), *Grammar and the Language Teacher*. New York: Prentice Hall, 17–30.

Lehmann, C. 2007. Linguistic competence: theory and empiry. *Folia Linguistica, 41* (3/4), 223–278. doi:10.1515/flin.41.3-4.223

Leitner, G. & Graustein, G. 1989. Grammars at the interface of language, linguistics, and users. In G. Graustein & G. Leitner (eds.), *Reference Grammars and Modern Linguistic Theory*. Tübingen: Max Niemeyer Verlag, 1–20. doi:10.1515/9783111354590.1

Lewis, E. G. 1981. *Bilingualism and bilingual education*. Oxford: Pergamon Press.

Liamkina, O. & Ryshina-Pankova, M. 2012. Grammar dilemma: teaching grammar as a resource for making meaning. T*he Modern Language Journal, 96* (2), 270–289. doi:10.1111/j.1540-4781.2012.01333_1.x

Lillis, T. 2013. The sociolinguistics of writing. Edinburgh: Edinburgh University Press.

Lindström, J. 2008. *Tur och ordning: introduktion till svensk samtalsgrammatik*. Stockholm: Nordstedts Akademiska Förlag.

Lindström, J. 2014. Interaktionell lingvistik: procedurer, teman och analyser. In H. Lehti-Eklund et al. (utg.), *Folkmålsstudier LII*. Helsingfors: Meddelanden från Föreningen för nordisk filologi, 31–55.

Linell, P. 1982. *The written language bias in linguistics*. Linköping: The University of Linköping.

Linell, P. 2001. Dynamics of discourse or stability of structure: sociolinguistics and the legacy from linguistics. In N. Coupland et al. (eds.), *Sociolinguistics and Social Theory.* Harlow: Longman, 107–126.

Linell, P. 2003. Grammatiska konstruktioner i samtalspraktiken. In B. Nordberg et al. (utg.), *Grammatik och samtal. Studier till minne av Mats Eriksson*. Uppsala: Institutionen för nordiska språk vid Uppsala universitet, 161–171.

Linell, P. 2005a. *Written language bias in linguistics: its nature, origins and transformations*. Abingdon: Routledge. doi:10.4324/9780203342763

Linell, P. 2005b. En dialogisk grammatik? In J. Anward & B. Nordberg, Bengt (red.), *Samtal och grammatik. Studier i svenskt samtalsspråk*. Lund.: Studentlitteratur, 231–328.

Littlewood, W. 2004. Second language learning. In A. Davies & C. Elder (eds.), *The Handbook of Applied Linguistics*. Malden: Blackwell Publishing, 501–524. doi:10.1002/9780470757000.ch20

Littlewood, W. 2012. Communication-oriented language teaching: where are we now? Where do we go from here? *Language Teaching, 47* (3), 349–362. doi:10.1017/S0261444812000134

Lo Bianco, J. 2004. Language planning as applied linguistics. In A. Davies & C. Elder (eds.), *The Handbook of Applied Linguistics*. Malden: Blackwell Publishing, 738–762. doi:10.1002/9780470757000.ch30

Margolis, E. 1994. A reassessment of the shift from the classical theory of concepts to prototype theory. *Cognition, 51*, 73–89. doi:10.1016/0010-0277(94)90009-4

Martinet, A. 1960. Elements of a functional syntax. *Word, 16*, 1–10.

Master, P. 1994. The effect of systematic instruction on learning the English article system. In T. Odlin (ed.), *Perspectives on Pedagogical Grammar*. Cambridge: Cambridge University Press, 229–252. doi:10.1017/CBO9781139524605.011

McCloskey, M. E. & Glucksberg, S. 1978. Natural categories: well defined or fuzzy sets? *Memory & Cognition, 6* (4), 462–472. doi:10.3758/BF03197480

Medin, D. 1989. Concepts and conceptual structure. *American Psychologist, 44* (12), 1469–1481. doi:10.1037/0003-066X.44.12.1469

Medin, D. & Atran, S. 2004. The native mind: biological categorization and reasoning in development and across cultures. *Psychological Review, 111* (4), 960–983. doi:10.1037/0033-295X.111.4.960

Mercer, S. 2011. Language learner self-concept: complexity, continuity and change. *System, 39*, 335–346. doi:10.1016/j.system.2011.07.006

Mervis, C. & Rosch, E. 1981. Categorization of natural objects. *Annual Review of Psychology, 32*, 89–115. doi:10.1146/annurev.ps.32.020181.000513

Mitchell, R. 1994. Grammar and teaching. In M. Bygate et al. (eds.), *Grammar and the Language Teacher*. New York: Prentice Hall, 215–223.

Mori, Y. 1999. Epistemological beliefs and language learning beliefs: what do language learners believe about their learning? *Language Learning, 49* (3), 377–415. doi:10.1111/0023-8333.00094

Negueruela-Azarola, E. 2011. Beliefs as conceptualizing activity: a dialectical approach for the second language classroom. *System, 39*, 359–369. doi:10.1016/j.system.2011.07.008

Nichols, J. 1984. Functional theories of grammar. *Annual Review of Anthropology, 13*, 97–117. doi:10.1146/annurev.an.13.100184.000525

Niedzielski, N. & Preston, D. 2003. *Folk Linguistics*. Berlin: Mouton de Gruyter.

Nikula, H. 2003. Är grammatik onödigt? Eller: Är tyska svårt? In S. Björklund et al. (red.) *Språk som formar vär(l)den. Festskrift till Christer Laurén på 60-årsdagen*. Vaasa: Vaasan yliopiston julkaisuja, 190–198.

Norris, J. & Ortega, L. 2000. Effectiveness of L2 instruction. A research synthesis and quantitative meta-analysis. *Language Learning, 50* (3), 417–528. doi:10.1111/0023-8333.00136

Odlin, T. 1994. Introduction. In T. Odlin (ed.), *Perspectives on Pedagogical Grammar.* Cambridge: Cambridge University Press, 1–22. doi:10.1017/CBO9781139524605.003

Pasquale, M. 2011. Folk beliefs about second language learning and teaching. *AILA Review, 24* (1), 88–99. doi:10.1075/aila.24.07pas

Paunonen, H. 2006. Vähemmistökielestä varioivaksi valtakieleksi. In K. Juusela & K. Nisula (toim.), *Helsinki kieliyhteisönä. Helsingin yliopisto. Helsinki*: Suomen kielen ja kirjallisuuden laitos, 13–99.

Pike, K. 1967. *Language in relation to a unified theory of the structure of human behavior* (2nd rev ed.). The Hague: Mouton. doi:10.1515/9783111657158

Potter, J. 1999. Beyond cognitivism. *Research on Language and Social Interaction, 32* (1&2), 119–127. doi:10.1080/08351813.1999.9683615

Potter, J. & Edwards, D. 2001. Socilinguistics, cognitivism, and discursive psychology. In N. Coupland et al. (eds.), *Sociolinguistics and Social Theory*. Harlow: Longman, 88–103.

Potter, J. & Wetherell, M. 1987. *Discourse and social psychology: beyond attitudes and behaviour*. London: Sage.

Prahbu, N. 1987. *Second language pedagogy*. Oxford: Oxford University Press.

Prahbu, N. 1990. There is no best method – why? *TESOL Quarterly, 24* (2), 161–176. doi:10.2307/3586897

Preston, D. 2004. Folk metalanguage. In A. Jaworski et al. (eds.), *Metalanguage. Social and Ideological Perspectives*. Berlin: Mouton de Gruyter, 75–101. doi:10.1515/9783110907377.75

Preston, D. 2006. Folk Linguistics. In R. Brown (ed.), *Encyclopaedia of Language and Linguistics*. Amsterdam: Elsevier, 521–533. doi:10.1016/b0-08-044854-2/01501-7

Rättyä, K. 2014. Opettajan pedagoginen sisältötieto kielitiedon opetuksen näkökulmasta. *Kieli, koulutus ja yhteiskunta*. Retrieved from http://www.kieliverkosto.fi/article/opettajan-pedagoginen-sisaltotieto-kielitiedon-opetuksen-nakokulmasta/

Rieger, B. 2009. Hungarian university students' beliefs about language learning: a questionnaire study. *WoPaLP, 3*, 97–113.

Rifkin, B. 2000. Revisiting beliefs about foreign language learning. *Foreign Language Annals, 35* (4), 394–408. doi:10.1111/j.1944-9720.2000.tb00621.x

Roehr, K. 2007. Metalinguistic knowledge and language ability in university level L2 learners. *Applied Linguistics, 29* (2), 173–199. doi:10.1093/applin/amm037

Rosch, E. 1975. Cognitive representations of semantic categories. *Journal of Experimental Psychology: General, 104* (3), 192–233. doi:10.1037/0096-3445.104.3.192

Rosch, E. 1978. Principles of categorization. In E. Rosch & B. Lloyd (eds.), *Cognition and Categorization*. Hillsdale: Lawrence Erlbaum, 27–48.

Rosch, E. 1987. Wittgenstein and categorization research in cognitive psychology. In M. Champman & R. Dixon (eds.), *Meaning and the Growth of Understanding. Wittgenstein's Significance for Developmental Psychology.* Berlin: Springer-Verlag, 151–166. doi:10.1007/978-3-642-83023-5_9

Rosch, E. 1999. Reclaiming concepts. *Journal of Consciousness Studies, 6* (11&12), 61–77.

Rutherford, W. 1987. *Second language grammar: learning and teaching.* London: Longman.

Rutherford, W. 1988 [1980]. Aspects of pedagogical grammar. In W. Rutherford & M. Sharwood Smith (eds.), *Grammar and Second Language Teaching. A Book of Readings.* New York: Newbury House Publishers, 171–185.

Sapir, E. 1921. *Language: an introduction to the study of speech.* New York: New York: Harcourt, Brace and company.

Saville-Troike, M. 2003. *The ethnography of communication: an introduction* (3rd ed.). Oxford: Blackwell. doi:10.1002/9780470758373

Schmidt, R. 1990. The role of consciousness in second language learning. *Applied Linguistics, 11*, 129–158. doi:10.1093/applin/11.2.129

Schulz, R. 2001. Cultural differences in student and teacher perceptions concerning the role of grammar instruction and corrective feedback: USA: Colombia. *The Modern Language Journal, 85* (2), 244–258. doi:10.1111/0026-7902.00107

Selting, M. 2000. The construction of units in conversational talk. *I: Language in Society, 29*, 477–517. doi:10.1017/S0047404500004012

Sharwood Smith, M. 1988 [1981]. Consciousness raising and the second language learner. In W. Rutherford & M. Sharwood Smith (eds.), *Grammar and Second Language Teaching. A Book of Readings.* New York: Newbury House Publishers, 51–60. doi:10.1093/applin/II.2.159

Shotter, J. 1993. *Conversational realities.* London: Sage.

Siewert, C. 2011. Consciousness and intentionality. In E. N. Zalta (ed.), *The Stanford Encyclopedia of Philosophy.* Stanford. Retrieved from http://plato.stanford.edu/archives/fall2011/entries/consciousness-intentionality/

Skehan, P. 2006. Second and foreign language learning and teaching. In R. Brown (ed.), *Encyclopaedia of Language and Linguistics.* Amsterdam: Elsevier, 51–59. doi:10.1016/b0-08-044854-2/00684-2

Spada, N. 2011. Beyond form-focused instruction: Reflections on past, present and future research. *Language Teaching, 44* (2), 225–236. doi:10.1017/S0261444810000224

Spada, N. & Lightbown, P. 2008. Form-focused instruction: isolated or integrated? *Tesol Quarterly, 42* (2), 181–207. doi:10.1002/j.1545-7249.2008.tb00115.x

Spolsky, B. 1978. *Educational linguistics. An introduction.* Rowley: Newbury House Publishers.

Svensson, J. 1990. Språkriktighetsföreställningar som uttryck för makt och vanmakt. In B. Bergh & U. Teleman (red.), *Språkets makt.* Lund: Lund University Press, 127–134.

Taylor J. 2008. Some pedagogical implications of cognitive linguistics. In. S. De Knop & T. De Rycker (eds.), *Cognitive Approaches to Pedagogical Grammar. A Volume in Honour of René Dirven.* Berlin: Mouton de Gruyter, 38–65.

Tomlin, R. 1994. Functional grammars, pedagogical grammars, and communicative language teaching. In T. Odlin (ed.), *Perspectives on Pedagogical Grammar.* Cambridge: Cambridge University Press, 140–178. doi:10.1017/CBO9781139524605.009

Tonkyn, A. 1994. Introduction: grammar and the language teacher. In M. Bygate et al. (eds.), *Grammar and the Language Teacher.* New York: Prentice Hall, 1–14.

Toolan, M. 1996. *Total speech. An integrational linguistic approach to language.* Durham: Duke University Press.

Trappes-Lomax, H. 2002. Language in language teacher education – A discourse perspective. In H. Trappes-Lomax & G. Ferguson (eds.), *Language in language teacher education.* Amsterdam: John Benjamins Publishing Company, 1–21

Trappes-Lomax, H. 2004. Discourse analysis. In A. Davies & C. Elder (eds.), *The Handbook of Applied Linguistics.* Malden: Blackwell Publishing, 133–165. doi:10.1002/9780470757000.ch5

Turner, J. 1996. *Language in the academy. Cultural reflexivity and intercultural dynamics.* Bristol: Multilingual Matters.

Turula, A. 2011. *Form-focused instruction and the advanced language learner. On the importance of the semantics of grammar.* Frankfurt am Main: Peter Lang.

Vattovaara, J. 2012. Spatial concerns for the study of social meaning of linguistic variables – an experimental approach. In H. Lehti-Eklund et al. (utg.), *Folkmålsstudier 50.* Helsingfors: Meddelanden från Föreningen för nordisk filologi, 175–209

Vattovaara, J. & Soininen-Stojanov, H. 2006. Pääkaupunkiseudulla kasvaneiden kotiseuturajaukset ja kielelliset asenteet. In K. Juusela & K. Nisula (toim.), *Helsinki kieliyhteisönä.* Helsinki: Suomen kielen ja kirjallisuuden laitos, 223–254.

Van Gulick, R. 2014. Consciousness. In E. N. Zalta (ed.), *The Stanford Encyclopedia of Philosophy.* Stanford. Retrieved from http://plato.stanford.edu/archives/spr2014/entries/consciousness.

Weinert, R., Basterrechea, M. & del Pilar García Mayo, M. 2013. Investigating L2 spoken syntax. A usage-based perspective. In M. del Pilar García Mayo et al (eds.), *Contemporary Approaches to Second Language Acquistion*. Amsterdam: John Benjamins Publishing Company, 153–176. doi:10.1075/aals.9.11ch8

Wenden, A. 1998. Metacognitive knowledge and language learning. *Applied Linguistics, 19* (4), 515–537. doi:10.1093/applin/19.4.515

Wenden, A. 1999. An introduction to metacognitive knowledge and beliefs in language learning: beyond the basics. *System, 27*, 435–441. doi:10.1016/S0346-251X(99)00043-3

Wesely, P. 2012. Language attitudes, perceptions and beliefs in language learning. *Foreign Language Annals, 45* (1), 98–117. doi:10.1111/j.1944-9720.2012.01181.x

Westney, P. 1994. Rules and pedagogical grammar. In T. Odlin (ed.), *Perspectives on Pedagogical Grammar*. Cambridge: Cambridge University Press, 72–96.

Widdowson, G. 1988 [1985]. Grammar, and nonsense, and learning. In W. Rutherford & M. Sharwood Smith (eds.), *Grammar and second language teaching. A book of readings*. New York: Newbury House Publishers, 146–155.

Wikforss, Å. 2009. Om termer för naturliga sorter. *Filosofisk tidskrift, 1*, 1–19.

Wilkins, D.A. 1974. *Linguistics in language teaching*. London: Edward Arnold.

Williams, G. 2005. Grammatics in schools. In R. Hasan et al. (eds.), *Continuing discourse on language. A functional perspective*. London: Equinox, 281–310.

Wilton, A. & Stegu M. 2011. Bringing the 'folk' into applied linguistics. An introduction. *AILA Review, 24*, 1–14. doi:10.1075/aila.24.01wil

Winters, M. 1990. Toward a theory of syntactic prototypes. In S. Tsohatzidis (ed.), *Meanings and Prototypes. Studies in Linguistic Categorization*. London: Routledge, 285–306.

Yip, V. 1994. Grammatical consciousness-raising and learnability. In T. Odlin (ed.), *Perspectives on pedagogical grammar*. Cambridge: Cambridge University Press, 123–139.

Zanna, M. & Rempel, J. 1988. Attitudes: a new look at an old concept. In D. Bar-Tal, & A. Kruglanski (eds.), *The Social Psychology of Knowledge*. Cambridge. Cambridge University Press, 315–334.

Ziegler, A. 2011. Standardsprachliche Variation als Ausgangspunkt grammatischer Reflexion. In: K. Köpke & A. Ziegler (hrsg.), *Grammatik – Lehren, Lernen, Verstehen. Zugänge zur Grammatik des Gegenwartsdeutschen*. Berlin: De Gruyter, 245-264. doi:10.1515/9783110263183.245

14 Use your languages! From monolingual to multilingual interaction in a language class

Anna Kyppö, Teija Natri, Margarita Pietarinen and Pekka Saaristo[1]

Abstract

This reflective paper presents a new course concept for multilingual interaction, which was piloted at the University of Jyväskylä Language Centre in the spring of 2014. The course, implemented as part of the centre's action research, is the result of a development process aimed at enhancing students' multilingual and multicultural academic communication competences along with promoting use of their entire linguistic repertoire. The course concept was inspired by the EU project Modularising Multilingual and Multicultural Academic Communication Competence (MAGICC), whose main intent is "to integrate multilingual and multicultural academic communication competences as graduate learning outcomes at [the] BA and MA level" (http://www.unil.ch/magicc/home/menuinst/objectifs.html). The main focus of the pilot course was on teachers' approach to multilingual teaching, teachers' interaction with each other and with students as well as students' approach to communication in a simulated multilingual and multicultural environment. Students' employment of their entire linguistic repertoire resulted in an evident increase of their intercultural awareness, enhancement of their intercultural communication competences and of their skills in mediating information in multilingual and multicultural contexts.

Keywords: multilingual interaction, multicultural communication, multilingual multicultural academic communication competence, intercultural awareness.

---

1. Language Centre, University of Jyväskylä, Finland; anna.kyppo@jyu.fi; teija.natri@jyu.fi; margarita.pietarinen@jyu.fi; pekka.c.saaristo@jyu.fi

How to cite this chapter: Kyppö, A., Natri, T., Pietarinen, M., & Saaristo, P. (2015). Use your languages! From monolingual to multilingual interaction in a language class. In J. Jalkanen, E. Jokinen, & P. Taalas (Eds), *Voices of pedagogical development - Expanding, enhancing and exploring higher education language learning* (pp. 319-335). Dublin: Research-publishing.net. doi:10.14705/rpnet.2015.000297

Chapter 14

1. Introduction

This study introduces a pilot course aimed at the enhancement of students' skills in multilingual and multicultural communication. The course Multilingual Interaction: Use Your Languages was offered by the University of Jyväskylä Language Centre in the spring of 2014. Teachers' interest in multilingual and multicultural issues and a concern for the increase of multilingualism and multiculturalism in workplace communication were important motivations for implementing such a course. However, the project Modularising Multilingual and Multicultural Academic Communication Competence for BA and MA levels (MAGICC 2011–2014; see Natri & Räsänen in this volume) served as a major source of inspiration. The project is part of the European Union Lifelong Learning Programme and aims to conceptualise multilingual and multicultural communication competences for higher education and thus to complement the Council of Europe's Common European Framework of Reference for Languages. The MAGICC project emphasises the role of languages and communication as part of academic expertise. The project, in the underlying principles and concepts of its conceptual framework, says that multilingual and multicultural academic communication competence

> "is an individual's communicative and interactive repertoire, made up of several languages and language varieties including first language(s) at different levels of proficiency, and various types of competence, which are all interrelated. The repertoire in its entirety represents a resource enabling action in diverse use situations. It evolves across time and experience throughout life, and includes growth in intercultural awareness and ability to cope with, and participate in, multicultural contexts of academic study and working life" (Räsänen, Natri & Foster Vosicki 2013: 5).

The pilot course was implemented as part of the Language Centre's institutional action research. The main focus was on the development of multilingual and multicultural competences, which involve not only a good command of an individual's L1 and L2, but also efficient use of one's overall language repertoire, that is, one's partial competences in various languages. When competences are perceived in this way, successful multilingual communication means, first of all, the abilities to switch and mediate from one language to another as well as to use one or more languages for the purpose of retrieving, managing, conceptualising and communicating the information in another language. Furthermore, multicultural communication and interaction foregrounds negotiations of meanings, attitudes towards otherness, tolerance of ambiguity and an awareness of multicultural settings.

2. Context of the study

This section introduces the concepts that supported the development and implementation of the course. A brief introduction of translanguaging and transculturation is followed by a presentation of the course's main objectives: raising the awareness of multilingual and multicultural communication and the development of multilingual competence. Culture, competence and communication, which form the main conceptual threads of the course, are in focus.

In the field of applied linguistics, the concepts of translanguaging and transculturation (Garcia 2009; Garcia & Sylvan 2011; Lewis, Jones & Baker 2012a, 2012b) are known as dynamic processes that involve meaning-making and knowledge-shaping through language and thus learning the language (Swain & Watanabe 2012). When two or more languages are systematically combined within the same learning activity, translanguaging may contribute to using one's linguistic repertoire more freely and flexibly, as well as to creating a social space for speakers through their personal histories and experiences, so that they can benefit from mediating and meaning-making across languages (Park 2013). From this perspective, multilingualism is perceived as a complex of specific semiotic resources and a repertoire of varying language abilities rather than as collections of separate languages (see Blommaert 2010).

One of the main objectives of the pilot course was to help students become aware of the factors that may affect multilingual and multicultural communication, and through that to develop their skills and competences for successful participation in such contexts. This involves the readiness to make use of one's own linguistic repertoire by, for example, switching fluently from one language to another or by mediating messages between the interactants who are otherwise unable to understand each other. In order to encourage the students to reflect on various contextual and attitudinal factors which affect different communicative events and circumstances, the concepts of language, culture and communication as well as some specific features influencing multicultural communication were introduced at the beginning of the course. Moreover, some fundamental views from sociolinguistics and the sociology of language, intercultural pragmatics, communication studies and different social sciences were also presented.

The concept of culture given in the course was in line with Spencer-Oatey's (2009: 3) definition, which views culture as "a fuzzy set of basic assumptions and values, orientations to life, beliefs, policies, procedures and behavioural conventions [...] shared by a group of people, [which] influence (but do not determine) each member's behaviour and his/her interpretations of the 'meaning' of other people's behaviour". The concept of communicative competence was based on Figueroa's (1994: 65) idea that an individual's competence means being able "to judge the consequences of actions, to plan strategies, to have expectations as to what is supposed to happen or what might happen or what is expected, in short, to make sense of the situation and act accordingly". Finally, the concept of communication was viewed as a cooperative and interactive process where the meanings are constructed and negotiated within different sociohistorical and cultural circumstances. It is more than transforming the propositional information concerning the state of affairs of external objects. As Mey (2001: 10) claims, "messages are not just 'signals', relayed through impersonal channels; the human expression functions as an appeal to other users and as means of social togetherness".

Among other issues related to the functions and implementation of communication, the inevitability of communication was also discussed. As Watzlawick, Beavin Bavelas & Jackson (1967) point out, making an effort to avoid communication is also a form of communication. Practical issues arising from this aspect are related to such modalities as clothing, non-linguistic gestures or silence as a resource for the construction of meaning or as a communicative practice.

Students were also briefly introduced to some traditional and frequently discussed issues present in the intercultural communication studies, such as the concept of politeness and face, addressivity, self-presentation, conflict management practices, directness/indirectness, stylistic aspects and the use and tolerance of silence in interaction (for more on these issues, see Brown & Levinson 1978, 1987; Goffman 1972; Gudykunst & Ting-Toomey 1988; Nakane 2007; Sajavaara & Lehtonen 1997; Ting-Toomey 1988; Ting-Toomey & Kurogi 1998; Ting-Toomey & Oetzel 2003).

Finally, the spectrum of communicative competences was explored as semiotic wholes or aggregates which may facilitate communication in multilingual situations when one or more languages are used. From the viewpoint of pragmatics, specific and individual competences referring to the dynamic capacity to carry out different kinds of communicative acts in different circumstances were introduced. An individual's overall linguistic competence is to be perceived as a facilitator rather than as a barrier to interpersonal communication (e.g. fear of imperfectness, shortcomings in languages).

3. Course information

This section provides basic demographics and information about the content, modes and expected outcomes of the course.

3.1. Course demographics

Out of 19 students, 14 were Finnish including one Swedish-Finnish bilingual. Russia, Kazakhstan, Greece, the Czech Republic and Macedonia were represented by one student each. Most of the participants were degree students in the humanities, mainly in linguistics, journalism, communication, history and art education. The disciplines of special education, IT, business and economics were also represented.

In addition to a participant's mother tongue, partial competence in at least two languages was expected, but no language pre-tests were required. The students' levels of language proficiency were instead based on self-assessments. All students spoke at least two languages in addition to their mother tongue; in the case of the Finnish students, even three additional languages were spoken. Interestingly, English was not the strongest language for all the Finnish students, with some assessing their English competence as poor. The group's linguistic repertoire (receptive skills) was as follows: English (17), Finnish (15), Swedish (10), Spanish (10), German (9), French (8), Russian (8), Slovak (4), Italian (4), Danish (2), Norwegian (2), Finnish sign language (2), Portuguese (2), Chinese (2) and furthermore, Czech, Greek, Japanese, Kazakh, Macedonian, Polish, Serbian, Cantonese and Swiss German (one speaker per language).

3.2. Expected learning outcomes

Students were expected to participate in multilingual communication, that is, to effectively employ their own linguistic repertoire. As could be expected, most of them showed genuine interest in languages and cultures and welcomed the opportunity to practice their multilingual agility[2].

Apart from the opportunity to use multiple languages, the focus was also on the development of their cultural awareness, in other words, on understanding the impact of culture on overall communication and interaction, including the interpretation and mediation of information and analysing one's own communication from a cultural perspective. Students were also expected to specify their personal learning needs.

---

2. Teachers and students shared a positive view and ideology towards multilingualism and multiculturalism, which is not uncommon among sociolinguists and language teachers. Regarding negative effects, ineffectiveness has been mentioned as one example. However, multilingualism is not viewed as positive in all political-institutional contexts (cf. Blommaert, Leppänen. & Spotti 2012; Lo Bianco 2004).

3.3. Course curriculum and schedule

The course was offered in four- to six-hour weekly contact sessions. In addition, the web-based learning platform Optima was used for various out-of-class activities and course interaction as well as for sharing course resources such as students' personal folders and learner logs, the course schedule and programme.

The focus of every session was on different aspects of multilingual and multicultural communication. After getting familiar with the course content, course participants introduced themselves in various languages. To get familiar with the basic concepts of multilingualism and multiculturalism, a lecture on the fundamental insights into language use, culture and communication was offered.

The purpose of the introductory theoretical background and key concepts was to establish some grounds and tools for reflection and further discussions. The purpose was not only to raise students' awareness of these issues during the course, but also to be able to link them with their personal communication experiences, recognising some of the factors as dominant.

Course participants shared their personal experiences of intercultural communication, such as their knowledge of the world and culture-bound cues of nonverbal communication, such as extralingual elements, body-language and gestures. To demonstrate these concepts, excerpts from two films were used. While the language spoken in the first film was not understood at all, the second film offered a peaceful coexistence of three people who did not share a common language, yet still managed to reach a mutual understanding. Further topics were related to intercomprehension and mediation as well as to cultural barriers in the use of advertisements. In this context, mediation means transferring information from one language to another. Furthermore, intercomprehension is related to multilingual reading: reading texts written in languages that the learners might not have learned but which are genetically or typologically related to the languages in their plurilingual repertoire, be it their mother tongues or foreign and second languages (Lenz & Berthele 2010).

In compliance with the MAGICC project, students performed simulated multilingual and multicultural negotiations. Persuasive argumentation in multilingual circumstances was practised in the form of persuasive talks aimed at selling an idea, service or product to the appropriate audience. To support their claims, presenters were expected to use languages other than the language of presentation and answer the clients' questions or to provide further information in multiple languages. Finally, the topics of the final session were related to the cultural issues in decision-making and multilingual storytelling. Small groups were appointed to work on a simulation aimed at selecting a new company manager. Candidates' multicultural profiles made the choice difficult. As a matter of fact, every group made a different choice and used different reasons to justify its choice.

In multilingual storytelling, a short story was told in groups consisting of five students. The first student read the story and retold it to the next student in another language, who again retold the story to the next one in a different language and so on. Finally, the last version of the story was compared with the original one. The course was concluded with students' reflections on various perspectives of multilingual and multicultural communication. Before each upcoming session, students were expected to reflect on the issues related to the previous session in their learner logs. The purpose of learner logs was to help students follow their learning process and, through this reflection, enhance their multicultural and multilingual awareness.

3.4. The teacher team

Five language teachers and one researcher interested in the multilingual and multicultural issues participated in the pilot. The teachers' strong languages were English, Finnish, French, Russian, Slovak, Spanish and Swedish. Four to five teachers were present at all of the sessions. Despite continuous use of several languages at one time, written instructions were given in English, because English was evidently the participants' lingua franca. Oral instructions, however, were given in languages other than English. In order to inspire the students to activate their entire linguistic repertoire, teachers also shared their own personal linguistic repertoires, including their partial and elementary competences. In compliance with the requirements for students, they attempted to use their weaker languages in both the contact and online communication. Incidental mismatches in the repertoires were regarded as enriching grounds for applying the mediation and intercomprehension strategies between the students and teachers.

In traditional teaching contexts, lesson preparation as well as classroom control and management is the responsibility of a single teacher. In team teaching, however, a group of teachers carries the responsibility for the whole teaching process: planning, teaching, evaluating learning activities and so on. Effective team teaching requires more than the space and time spent together; it also necessitates a change of mindset and teaching practices. Moreover, flexibility and the need to acknowledge the participation and interference of other colleagues are crucial. In our case, multilingual team teaching conducted by teachers of different languages was perceived as an authentic multicultural task demanding mutual tolerance and respect of otherness. Teacher cooperation was to a great extent based on continuous negotiation, which is a typical characteristic of intercultural interaction. Both students and teachers had to acknowledge their own culture-embedded values and conventions, be willing to understand the communicative difficulties that may arise in a particular intercultural context, and constructively deal with them.

4. Reflections and course evaluation

This section offers some reflections from the students as well as the teachers about the course, an evaluation of the course and some implications for the future.

4.1. Student reflections

During the course, students were expected to reflect on their understanding of multilingualism and multicultural interaction. Reflections were related to the topics discussed during the sessions and how they were related to students' previously acquired competences, new ideas that emerged during the sessions, or perceptions on what was learned and what students considered to be interesting or insightful. The comments and student voices below are extracted from the students' learner logs and feedback.

Students boldly involved themselves in various multilingual situations. In the learner logs, they clearly indicated the motivation and the need to employ their entire language repertoire:

> "I loved the idea of changing the language every time and although it was by no means easy, it was just the sort of mental challenge that I enjoy. The task also made me re-evaluate some of my language skills".

Participation in the course for the reason of improving one's language skills and identifying the already existing competences was one of the learning goals. The activation of weaker languages, even acquiring some partial competence in new languages, seemed to be a prevailing reason for participating in the course. Nevertheless, at the same time the weaker languages were perceived to be difficult:

> "The second task was to summarise an article in one of the weaker languages one knows. I tried to explain this really short text about French midwives being on strike, but it turned out to be really hard. Maybe the fact that the people in my group didn't speak French also affected the situation, but I was still pretty stiff with my explanations. It was a really educational moment: This happens when you don't use your languages".

Multicultural issues made the students reflect on the multicultural competences and their importance in communication:

> "Communication is a complex phenomenon and all communication takes place in a specific context and under the influence of a culture.

> I think that culture creates a frame for almost all we do and especially for communication. Our culture affects communication together with our individual characteristics. One can either emphasise the individual view or the environmental one, but they are both always present. I think our discussion about genes and whether all kinds of communication knowledge can be learned or not, was very interesting".

Multilingualism was not perceived only as the use of one or more languages, but also as a matter of knowing the culture and history as well the social and political situation of a country. It was further seen as acknowledging the other participants, their ethnicity, gender, educational background and other various situational, circumstantial and interpersonal factors which affect the process of communication. Students considered contextualisation to be important, seeing it as, on the one hand, taking historical, social, political, economic and other contexts into account and, on the other, the use of the language (e.g. the type of the language, language proficiency, language policy). Personal experience of various communication situations was also mentioned.

Multilingualism as a result of growing international mobility was mentioned by several course participants. For example, according to one student, multilingualism was equal to speaking a foreign language fluently, "almost as a native speaker". Only after spending some time in a foreign country did the student realise that multilingualism was the sum of various skills and language proficiency, that is, that "speaking a foreign language perfectly" was only a minor part of the whole:

> "Sometimes, when we use certain words in one language, the same words may mean something else in another language. We should understand the whole situation and not the specific words…"

For the non-Finnish course participants, the Finnish-Swedish and Finnish-Russian bilingualism, which is present in Finland as a result of a fairly large population of Finland Swedes and Russian-speaking people, became a source of admiration and sincere interest leading to the re-evaluation of their own concept of multilingualism. The concepts of directness and indirectness in communication, that is, conveying messages by words as well as by other means of communication (e.g. non-verbal communication, body language, and mimicking) were perceived as crucial factors that clearly facilitate interaction.

The awareness of being, or rather, becoming multicultural and multilingual, as well as the intermingling of linguistic identities, was also addressed by the students. Speaking different languages at different levels, in various contexts, was occasionally experienced as "becoming someone else". Living in another country was mentioned as a good opportunity to become multilingual and multicultural. Revealing one's linguistic and cultural background is often related to the issue of self-identification. For example, a person can have a multilingual and multicultural identity, even in case of a monolingual and culturally homogenous background.

One student writing an MA thesis on multilingualism and multiculturalism wondered what language actually is, considering that it might be only one of many tools for communication. For example, using English as a lingua franca in interaction with international friends does not reflect the real English culture, rather, it is only a tool of communication. Nevertheless, the interaction may subconsciously reflect English culture as well, because language and culture "always go hand in hand". Similar issues were raised in relation to the degree of language proficiency. One student even wondered if people could be monolingual and monocultural[3].

The concepts of multilingualism and multicultural communication, that is, communication across different cultures, seem best described as the communication between people who come from different cultural backgrounds and search for a mutually understandable way of interaction through negotiating meanings.

---

3. In a strict sense, the answer seems to be no (see Canagarajah 2011b). Nevertheless, on a subjective level, individuals may consider themselves to be monocultural. See Pitkänen-Huhta and Hujo (2012) for a discussion about an older couple of monolingual Finnish adults.

4.2. Teacher reflections and implications

Due to the multilingual and multicultural nature of this team teaching, the teachers, like the students, also reflected on the process of preparing and implementing the course as well as on the various stages of conducting the course. Teachers' collaborative teaching included a thorough, time-consuming stage of planning and preparation. The opinions and views of the researcher involved in the process were a great contribution to the teamwork as well. On a personal level, the preparation of course activities and teaching itself was highly creative, generating multiple ideas for future course projects. To demonstrate this creative process, some excerpts of the teachers' reflections are presented below:

> "Participating in the course teaching team has been a thrilling experience. Despite an excessive workload, I kept looking forward to the upcoming teaching session. I spent a lot time on the preparation of my teaching and did my best to employ all my knowledge and skills on this course. Nevertheless, there are some areas of teaching that might be improved, for example, the activation of students' offline interaction, communication through social media, blog writing or chats".

> "This course offered me completely new insights into teaching the less commonly taught languages. Instead of a general lack of commitment to learning some less commonly spoken, so-called smaller languages, learners' (and teachers') attention should rather be turned to the employment of their overall language repertoire. For example, speakers of some Slavic languages may acquire the passive knowledge of some other Slavic languages due to the mutual intelligibility of Slavic languages and thus get interested in a particular language. The same may be applied to other language groups, such as the Romance and Germanic languages".

The pedagogy of less commonly taught languages (LCTL) emerged in relation to the mutual intelligibility within language groups, such as the mutual intelligibility of languages in the Slavic or Romance language family:

> "I got the impression that quite a few students were wavering between the more traditional goals, viewing the course as an instrument to improve the skills of the languages they already knew, and the way of identifying their already existing competences as a practical tool of communication".

5. Concluding remarks

The Use Your Languages course was a teaching experiment focused on enhancing students' multilingual and multicultural communication and activating their linguistic repertoire. We feel that this course objective was reached, even though not all students believed that they had enhanced their communication skills in the weaker languages. Nonetheless, they acquired some new insights into multilingual communication and clearly enriched their linguistic repertoire. Unlike in more traditional language instruction, the main focus was not on the correctness of language but on agency, that is, on what the learners could do with their existing language competences. Students also recognised the importance of acknowledging and adapting to various multicultural communication situations.

As for the teachers' perspective, the course was perceived as a challenge due to the excessive workload, especially in the preparation and planning of the team-teaching approach. However, it was also an enriching teaching experience. The teachers became students and proceeded through the same stages of employing their entire linguistic repertoire in teaching situations. Thus the course enhanced the teachers' multilingual and multicultural communication and activated their linguistic repertoire. The stage aimed at preparation of learning activities was perceived as a highly creative process, one that, together with the positive atmosphere within the teacher team, contributed to the successful implementation of the pilot course.

In the future, the course may be implemented in more personal learning environments and include, for example, extended use of social media and multimodal interactive online resources. We believe that personal learning environments may contribute to the increase of learners' multilingual and multicultural awareness. Furthermore, simultaneous use of many languages, referred to as, among many other terms, code meshing (for more, see Canagarajah 2011b; Lewis et al. 2012a, 2012b)[4], where the languages used are "a part of a single integrated system" (Canagarajah 2011a: 403), may result in distinguishing students' competencies as semiotic wholes, what in the end, may reduce the traditional compartmentalisation of languages. This perspective could also demystify multicultural communication as it compares to monocultural communication. With this mindset, the most challenging task for language teachers will be to find the balance between accurate language use (e.g. in writing) and effective language use in terms of communication and interaction.

References

Blommaert, J. 2010. *The sociolinguistics of globalization*. Cambridge: Cambridge University Press. doi:10.1017/CBO9780511845307

Blommaert, J., Leppänen, S. & Spotti, M. 2012. Endangering multilingualism. In J. Blommaert, S. Leppänen, P. Pahta & T. Räisänen (eds.), *Dangerous Multilingualism. Northern Perspectives on Order, Purity and Normality*. Houndmills, Basingstoke: Palgrave Macmillan, 1–21. doi:10.1057/9781137283566.0006

Brown, P. & Levinson, S. 1978. Universals in language use: politeness phenomenon. In E. Goody (ed.), *Questions and Politeness: Strategies in Social Interaction*. Cambridge: Cambridge University Press, 56–311

Brown, P. & Levinson, S. 1987. *Politeness: some universals in language use*. Cambridge: Cambridge University Press.

Canagarajah, A. S. 2011a. Codemeshing in academic writing: identifying teachable strategies of translanguaging. *The Modern Language Journal*, 95 (3), 401–416. doi:10.1111/j.1540-4781.2011.01207.x

---

4. An example of the concepts expressing the same or almost the same meanings used within different frameworks. Other related terms used in the literature are metrolingualism, polylanguaging, polylingual languaging, heteroglossia, heterography, translingual practice, flexible/dynamic/holistic bilingualism, multilanguaging, hybrid language practices, pluriliteracy, transcultural literacy/writing, multiliteracies , continua of biliteracy, fluid lects (Cf. Canagarajah 2011b: 2; Lewis et al. 2012a: 650; 2012b: 655-656).

Canagarajah, A. S. 2011b. Translanguaging in the classroom: emerging issues for research and pedagogy. In L. Wei (ed.), *Applied Linguistics Review 2*. Berlin: De Gruyter Mouton, 1–28. doi:10.1515/9783110239331.1

Figueroa, E. 1994. *Sociolinguistic metatheory*. Oxford: Pergamon.

Garcia, O. 2009. *Bilingual education in the 21st century: a global perspective*. Oxford, UK: Wiley-Blackwell.

Garcia, O. & Sylvan, C. 2011. Pedagogies and practices in multilingual classrooms: singularities in pluralities. *The Modern Language Journal, 95* (3), 385–400. doi:10.1111/j.1540-4781.2011.01208.x

Goffman, E. 1972. *Interaction ritual: essays on face-to-face behavior*. London: Allen Lane / The Penguin Press.

Gudykunst, W. & Ting-Toomey, S. 1988. *Culture and interpersonal communication*. Newbury Park: Sage Publications

Lenz, P. & Berthele, R. 2010. Assessment in plurilingual and intercultural education - Satellite Study N°2. *Guide for the development and implementation of curricula for plurilingual and intercultural education*. Geneva: Council of Europe, Language Policy Division. Retrieved from http://www.coe.int/t/dg4/linguistic/Source/Source2010_ForumGeneva/Assessment2010_Lenz_EN.pdf

Lewis, G., Jones, B. & Baker, C. 2012a. Translanguaging: origins and development from school to street and beyond. *Educational Research and Evaluation, 18* (7), 641–654. doi: 10.1080/13803611.2012.718488

Lewis, G., Jones, B. & Baker, C. 2012b. Translanguaging: developing its conceptualisation and contextualisation. *Educational Research and Evaluation, 18* (7), 655–670. doi:10.1080/13803611.2012.718490

Lo Bianco, J. 2004. Language planning as applied linguistics. In A. Davies & C. Elder (eds.), *The Handbook of Applied Linguistics*. Malden: Blackwell Publishing, 738–762. doi:10.1002/9780470757000.ch30

Mey, J. 2001. *Pragmatics. An Introduction*. Oxford: Blackwell Publishers.

Nakane, I. 2007. *Silence in intercultural communication. Perceptions and performance*. Amsterdam: John Benjamins Publishing Company. doi:10.1075/pbns.166

Natri, T. & Räsänen, A. 2015. Developing a conceptual framework: the case of MAGICC. In J. Jalkanen, E. Jokinen & P. Taalas (eds), *Voices of Pedagogical Development - Expanding, Enhancing and Exploring Higher Education Language Learning*. Dublin: Research-publishing.net, 85–102. doi:10.14705/rpnet.2015.000288

Park, M. S. 2013. Code-switching and translanguaging: potential functions in multilingual classrooms. *Working Papers in TESOL & Applied Linguistics, 13* (2), 50–52.

Pitkänen-Huhta, A. & Hujo, M. 2012. Experiencing multilingualism – the elderly becoming marginalized? In J. Blommaert, S. Leppänen, P. Pahta & T. Räisänen (eds.), *Dangerous Multilingualism. Northern Perspectives on Order, Purity and Normality*. Houndmills, Basingstoke: Palgrave Macmillan, 261–283. doi:10.1057/9781137283566.0020

Räsänen, A., Natri, T. & Foster Vosicki, B. 2013. MAGGICC conceptual framework. Lifelong Learnign Programme. Retrieved from http://www.unil.ch/files/live//sites/magicc/files/shared/Revised_Conceptual_Framework_MAGICC.pdf

Sajavaara, K. & Lehtonen, J. 1997. The Silent Finn revisited. In A. Jaworski (ed.), *Silence. Interdisciplinary Perspectives*. Berlin: Mouton de Gruyter, 263–283.

Spencer-Oatey, H. 2009. Introduction. In H. Spencer-Oatey (ed.), *Culturally Speaking. Culture, Communication and Politeness Theory*. London: Continuum, 1–8.

Swain, M. & Watanabe, Y. 2012. Languaging: collaborative dialogue as a source of second language learning. In C. Chapelle (Ed.), *The encyclopedia of applied linguistics*. Oxford: Blackwell Publishing. doi:10.1002/9781405198431.wbeal0664

Ting-Toomey, S. 1988. A face-negotiation theory. In Y. Kim & W. Gudykunst (eds.), *Theory in Intercultural Communication*. Newbury Park: Sage, 213–235.

Ting-Toomey, S. & Kurogi, A. 1998. Facework competence in intercultural conflict: an updated face-negotiation theory. *International Journal of Intercultural Relations, 22* (2), 187–225. doi:10.1016/S0147-1767(98)00004-2

Ting-Toomey, S. & Oetzel, J. 2003. Cross-cultural face concerns and conflict style. Current status and future directions. In W. Gudykunst (ed.), *Cross-Cultural and Intercultural Communication*. Thousand Oaks: Sage Publications, 127–147.

Watzlawick, P., Beavin Bavelas, J. & Jackson, D. D. 1967. *Pragmatics of human communication. A study of interactional patterns, pathologies, and paradoxes*. New York: Norton.

15. Students' choice of language and initial motivation for studying Japanese at the University of Jyväskylä Language Centre

Pauliina Takala[1]

Abstract

Elective language courses, particularly those starting from the beginner level, constitute their own special group within the communication and language course offerings of universities. The elementary courses of less commonly taught languages (LCTL), such as Japanese, provide students with the opportunity to acquire, among other benefits, a proficiency that distinguishes them from other job applicants. Ordinary language skills, commonly limited to English only, are today regarded as the default and not as any unique international asset. Even partial knowledge of a less commonly taught language and culture broadens one's worldview and increases cultural understanding. The many years of experience in teaching Japanese have evoked in me the desire to analyse my students' backgrounds, studies and employment. The survey described in this article constitutes the basis for a broader study to be conducted in the future. The purpose of the survey was to collect and analyse data on the faculties and major subjects of students who attend elementary Japanese courses, as well as their language repertoires besides Japanese. Their initial motivation, reasons for the choice of Japanese and plans for the future related to Japan and Japanese studies were analysed.

Keywords: Japanese language and culture studies, beginner level language learning, language choice, motivation, employment.

---

1. Language Centre, University of Jyväskylä, Finland; a.pauliina.takala@jyu.fi

How to cite this chapter: Takala, P. (2015). Students' choice of language and initial motivation for studying Japanese at the University of Jyväskylä Language Centre. In J. Jalkanen, E. Jokinen, & P. Taalas (Eds), *Voices of pedagogical development - Expanding, enhancing and exploring higher education language learning* (pp. 337-358). Dublin: Research-publishing.net. doi:10.14705/rpnet.2015.000298

Chapter 15

1. Introduction

Japanese studies at Finnish higher education institutions and at the University of Jyväskylä Language Centre

Elective language courses, particularly those starting from the beginner level, constitute their own special group within the communication and language course offerings of a university. The elementary courses of less commonly taught languages (LCTL), such as Japanese, provide students with the opportunity to acquire a proficiency that distinguishes them, for example, from other job applicants. The knowledge of a less commonly taught language and culture broadens one's worldview and increases cultural understanding.

Japanese language and culture can be studied as a major subject at the University of Helsinki's Department of World Cultures and at the *Fria kristliga folkhögskolan*, a Finland-Swedish folk high school in Vaasa, which operates under the University of Stockholm. The Faculty of Social Sciences at the University of Turku hosts the Master's Degree Programme in Asian Studies, which provides advanced-level Japanese studies. The intermediate studies of Japanese language and culture can be completed as a minor subject at the universities of Eastern Finland and Oulu. In addition, at the language centres or corresponding units of several higher education institutions, such as the University of Jyväskylä Language Centre, students can complete at least elementary courses in Japanese. Smedlund and Uemura (2010) have edited an article collection in which the present-day situation of Japanese teaching and learning in Finland is mapped through expert interviews. Further themes discussed in the collection include the role of Japanese culture and language in a variety of contexts.

Japanese studies have retained their popularity at the University of Jyväskylä Language Centre in recent years despite the natural disasters and economic upheavals Japan has faced. This is partly explained by the general popularity of Japanese culture, but also by the fact that student and researcher exchange between our countries has increased. The Japanese writing system has been experienced as difficult to handle and understand, but modern IT devices and applications have considerably facilitated its reading and writing.

The University of Jyväskylä Language Centre has offered Japanese courses since 1990. Over the past 25 years, the popularity of the centre's Japanese language and culture studies has steadily grown. Students can currently complete a total of 30 ECTS credits in Japanese, consisting of six language-focused courses and one cultural course. Two elementary summer courses have usually been organised with similar contents as the elementary winter courses. In the academic year 2013–2014, a total of 112 students studied Japanese in nine different courses at the Language Centre. Since early 2013, the Language Centre has provided students with the opportunity to compile individual Japanese courses into a minor subject – the basic studies in Japanese language and culture. This has further increased the popularity of the subject.

As Juha Janhunen, Professor of East Asian Studies from the University of Helsinki Asian Studies states, high-quality teaching in students' mother tongue is crucial at the initial stage of learning a foreign language, whereas staying and studying in the target country becomes important at a later stage (Cairns 2010). This view is shared by Annamari Konttinen, University Teacher from the University of Turku Centre for East Asian Studies (Smedlund & Uemura 2010). Continuing one's studies in Japan after the Language Centre courses is a real option: the University of Jyväskylä has six bilateral student exchange agreements with partner universities and several other faculty- and department-level cooperation agreements with universities in Japan. These internationalisation opportunities can be utilised by students as well as staff in order to enhance their language and cultural competence.

2. The research problem and its background

As a university teacher of Japanese language and culture, I encounter heterogeneous student groups. Large elementary courses with as many as 50 participants are condensed into continuation courses attended by fewer participants. My courses comprise both linguistics and elements related to Japanese society, high culture and customs. The elementary course Japanese 1 provides students with the crucial first contact with Japanese studies. At this stage some of the students become passionate about studying more, whereas others realise they prefer to concentrate on other subjects.

The survey for this study was conducted at the beginning of the autumn term 2013 with the Japanese 1 course participants. A link to a questionnaire including 13 questions was emailed to the student group. My aim was to examine course participants' backgrounds, studies and employment by analysing specific student cohorts, which would allow me to develop course content that optimally meets students' needs.

The purpose of the questionnaire was to analyse the learners' backgrounds and to find out why they had chosen to study Japanese. The survey clarified from which faculties the students came to the elementary course, as well as their major subjects. A further aim was to find out whether the motivation for choosing Japanese was connected to the students' plans for the future. The survey also throws light on the participants' language choices and language skills in general.

In the future, the same student cohort will be asked to respond to additional questions. The follow-up studies will provide an overall picture of the role of Japanese studies in, for example, students' employability. The present, first part of the study will provide a basis for later studies: the results and the problems observed in phrasing the questions will enable us to reformulate and improve the questionnaires.

3. Motivation and choice of language

The focus of this study was on clarifying the choice of language and the initial motivation of a specific student cohort, with the aim of finding out why Japanese is studied in Finland.

The choice of language can be regarded as a direct consequence of motivation. Dörnyei (2001) defines *motivation* as follows: motivation means choosing a specific activity and committing oneself to this activity. Motivation, Dörnyei (2001) suggests, can thus explain a person's reasons to act, the duration of the activity and how persistently the person continues the activity.

My aim was to analyse the motivation of students who had recently begun an elementary course in Japanese. However, it is also necessary to consider the various phases of the motivation process. At the beginning of an elementary course, motivation has already developed past the planning and goal-setting phases, but has not yet proceeded to the phases that include implementing and controlling the activity and evaluating the results. Students' motivation varies while studying a foreign language and even during one single course (Dörnyei 2001).

In this article I concentrate particularly on the first phase of motivation, where students have no exact idea of what the studies will require of them. They have expectations regarding their own success and define the value of their expected success. The more probable and important students consider their success to be, the higher their motivation is. At later phases, it is also essential to sustain interest and arrange time and resources for the studies (Dörnyei 2001; Ushioda 2001). The latter factors may explain why motivated students occasionally interrupt their courses. Initial motivation is one of the main themes in this article: even learners who initially seem very motivated may drop out from the course. This phenomenon is also highlighted by Williams and Burden (1997) and by Matsumoto and Obana (2001).

A positive motivational factor for Finns studying Japanese as a foreign language is that both languages are non–Indo-European and even share some structural similarities (Pensikkala 2010a). Moreover, the Japanese phonetic system is rather easily approachable for Finnish learners. Nevertheless, the Japanese language can also create a strong case of culture shock in Finnish learners (Matsumoto & Obana 2001). This can either reduce or increase a learner's motivation, depending on the individual. Difficulties related to the Japanese writing system are clearly a factor that reduces motivation. These positive and negative motivational factors play an important role in determining whether students continue or interrupt their Japanese studies. In addition, students' prior knowledge of Japanese – or of different languages, in general – affects their expectations regarding success in Japanese studies as well as their commitment to these studies. Realistic expectations regarding one's possibilities to complete the studies are factors that enhance motivation (Matsumoto & Obana 2001).

Internal and external motivational factors are significant for the choice of language and for language studies. Williams and Burden (1997) have drafted a tripartite approach to the concept of motivation, first through external factors. Such external factors as the educational system and study arrangements affect students' instrumental orientation. Instrumental orientation means that the utilitarian viewpoints of learning are emphasised, and orientation is a factor that affects motivation. Instrumental orientation contributes to the development of external motivation. On the other hand, such internal factors as the personal relevance of the content to be learned, feelings of competence, attitudes, age and confidence, have an impact on the development of integrative orientation. Integrative orientation refers to the desire of the learner to identify with the culture of the studied language. This results in the development of inner motivation.

The dichotomy between internal and external motivation has been criticised because it was developed for a specific bilingual context and is not viably applicable to several other contexts (Julkunen 1998). In compliance with Williams and Burden's (1997) views, the problematic nature of the dichotomy is taken into consideration in this study, recognising the simultaneous existence of internal and external motivation. An individual's motivational type focuses more on one of the two, and the emphasis may vary within the different subareas of motivation even for the same individual.

Examples of changes in motivation have been presented by Matsumoto and Obana (2001), who examined students of Japanese in Australia. Their research reveals that during these students' studies their interest in conducting business with the Japanese has relatively decreased, whereas their interest in Japanese culture has grown. Moreover, the participants of elementary courses have commonly expressed their interest in business activities, but those who have proceeded to the continuation course have shown less interest. On the other hand, Matsumoto and Obana (2001) state that students who had planned to interrupt their Japanese studies had ultimately decided to continue, guided by their external motivation, in other words, the potential benefits of Japanese to their future careers.

An interest in business activities with the Japanese can, at least to some extent, be regarded as a sign of external motivation. The significance of external and internal motivation for studies can vary from one stage of the study process to the next, and studying is most effective when both are simultaneously present. Matsumoto and Obana (2001) also emphasise that, because of the extensive and diversified connections between Australia and Japan, many Australians begin to study Japanese based on external motivation. However, internal motivational factors develop later side by side with the external ones. In Finland, the situation is different: beginning students typically have an internal motivation alone, or together with external motivation.

These observations highlight the importance of analysing the development of the same student population also after the elementary course. My intention is to pursue this analysis later, while in this study I have limited my focus to students who have only recently begun to study Japanese.

4. Research method and material

A questionnaire was used to map students' background data, language choices with their reasons, and future plans. The questionnaire was first tested in a 2013 summer course, after which some of the questions were modified. In the autumn of 2013, the target group consisted of 53 students who had registered for the Japanese 1 course at the University of Jyväskylä Language Centre. The survey was conducted via a questionnaire on the internet-based platform Webropol, to which I sent a link to the target group. After three reminders about answering the questionnaire, responses were received from 39 students.

The questionnaire included 13 questions, most of them multiple-choice questions. In some of them, students could choose more than one option, and some were open-ended, allowing the respondents to answer in their own words. The questions provided information on the participants' first year of enrolment at the university, faculty, major subject, minor subjects, first year of Japanese studies at the university, and reasons for beginning to study Japanese. In addition, the respondents were asked whether they were pursuing the basic studies in Japanese, what other languages they studied or spoke, whether they had plans for practical training or student exchange in Japan, and what preliminary ideas they had about employment.

I classified and processed the data by faculty and major subject, as well as based on whether the students answered that Japanese was an advantage in their major subject area, whether their initial aim was to complete the basic studies, and whether they wished to be employed precisely in Japan. In February and March 2014, I processed the data on the Webropol platform by creating tables based on different filters. All the students who had registered for the autumn 2013 Japanese course were emailed another questionnaire in March 2014 in order to determine the reasons for potential interruptions. In addition, the 34 students who had begun another elementary course in May 2014 were asked to submit short essay answers about their reasons for attending the course. This data on study motivation complements the original survey. I processed the complementary data during the summer of 2014 by analysing the open-ended essay answers.

5. Results

5.1. Respondents' background data

Table 1 shows the respondents' distribution by faculty or higher education institution according to the main survey of 2013.

Table 1. Number of respondents in the 2013 survey according to faculty/educational institution

Faculty	Number of respondents
Faculty of Humanities	14
Faculty of Information Technology	10
Faculty of Mathematics and Science	8
Faculty of Social Sciences	2
Faculty of Sport and Health Sciences	1
Faculty of Education	1
Jyväskylä University School of Business and Economics	1
JAMK University of Applied Sciences	1
Unknown faculty	1
Total	39

The respondent numbers correlated to some extent with the number of students in the various faculties of the University. In 2012, the Faculty of Humanities, with its 2,495 students, was the largest of the seven faculties. The second-largest was the Faculty of Mathematics and Science with 1,993 students in 2012, and the Faculty of Information Technology the fifth largest with 1,613 students in the same year (Pöyhönen & Oikari 2013). Table 2 below shows the distribution of respondents by major subject and faculty in the main survey of 2013 and the complementary survey of 2014.

5.2. Language repertoire

A slim majority, that is, 21 of the respondents in the 2013 survey, did not study (or had not previously studied) any elective language besides Japanese at the university. French had been studied by 6 respondents and Chinese by 5. A small number of the respondents had completed elective courses of English, Spanish, Latin, Swedish, German, Russian and Finnish sign language.

The question about proficiency in languages taught outside of the university highlighted particularly French skills, in addition to English and Swedish. For the rest, the language backgrounds echoed the results presented in the previous paragraph.

Table 2. Respondents' background data: number of respondents for each major subject and faculty

Faculty and major subject	Number of respondents in 2013	Number of respondents, complementary survey in 2014	Number of respondents, total of 2013 and 2014
Faculty of Humanities			14 and 3
History	4		
English	2		
Ethnology	2		
Finnish sign language	2		
Intercultural communication	1		
Romance philology	1		
Finnish	1		
Russian language and culture	1		
Literature		3	
Faculty of Social Sciences			4 and 2
Management and leadership	1		
Social sciences of sport	1		
Sociology	1		
Political science	1	1	
Psychology		1	
Faculty of Information Technology			10 and 13
Information systems science	5	4	
Mathematical information technology	5	9	
Faculty of Sport and Health Sciences			1
Physiotherapy	1		
Faculty of Education			1
Special education	1		
Faculty of Mathematics and Science			8 and 14
Chemistry	3	5	
Physics	2	7	
Aquatic sciences	1		
Mathematics	1	2	
Cell and molecular biology			
Unknown major subject	1		
Jyväskylä University School of Business and Economics			1
Accounting		1	
Other educational institutions			1 and 1
JAMK University of Applied Sciences, Degree Programme in Tourism	1		
Upper secondary vocational school / tourism industry		1	
Total	**39**	**34**	**73**

The students attending the Japanese elementary course can be said to represent a broad language repertoire. The respondents who majored in history, chemistry and information systems science possessed particularly broad language repertoires. In addition, a few individual respondents had studied or knew several languages. This can be interpreted such that students who know a non-mainstream or otherwise less common language tend to choose a less commonly taught language also later.

To some extent, it seems that multilingualism was concentrated in a smaller group than could be presumed by analysing the overall survey level or faculty level. Nevertheless, the survey demonstrated that for some of the respondents, Japanese was the first less commonly taught language. Japanese elementary courses thus attract both students who have narrow language repertoires and those with broad ones. The respondents majoring in history and information systems science, in addition to knowing several languages, highlighted the usefulness of Japanese skills in their major subject area.

5.3. Reasons for choosing to study Japanese at the university

The most common reasons for choosing Japanese studies at the University of Jyväskylä Language Centre were the respondent's other interests related to Japan. This is also demonstrated in Table 3, which will be analysed in detail later.

Table 3. Reasons for choosing to study Japanese at the University Language Centre

I wanted to learn one more foreign language.	15
I wanted to continue the language studies I had begun earlier.	13
I wanted to learn some less commonly taught language and happened to choose Japanese.	7
I have other interests related to Japan.	29
Japanese is useful in my major subject area.	11
Other, what?	6

5.4. Students' general achievement goal orientation

The distribution of answers was interesting when the students were asked about their plans to complete the entire basic studies in Japanese or only individual courses. Approximately half of the respondents (20) stated having even initially intended to complete the whole module. Among these respondents, the students of history and mathematical information technology constituted the largest groups.

Those who responded that they intended to complete the basic studies were also the ones most interested in practical training and/or student exchange in Japan. Of the 20 students aiming at the basic studies, nearly all (19) said they were interested in student exchange and 14 also in practical training. We can assume that these 14 learners constitute the most motivated group in the course because they have clear goals. I will focus on analysing this motivated group more thoroughly. Is there a connection between these students' elementary course grades and high motivation?

Within the group of 14 respondents assumed to be the most motivated, 7 had an excellent course grade. Because of some of the following factors, the remaining 7 respondents had no final course grades: one of them left the course based on the recognition of prior learning, one did not attend the course after the initial course meeting, one received a failing grade and did not improve it later, and four interrupted the course.

In March 2014, an inquiry was emailed to the students who had been assumed to be the most motivated but had still interrupted the course. Answers were received from 5 of them explaining their reasons for the interruption. The 2 respondents classified as the most motivated explained that fitting the Japanese course into their other studies had been difficult[2]. In accordance with my earlier

---

[2]. An analysis of all the course dropouts highlighted the following reasons: 4 could not match the course into their schedule because the lessons were arranged too frequently and only in the evening; 2 explained that illness had prevented them from following the course; 1 said having experienced pair and group work as stressful; 4 of the 5 course dropouts expressed their willingness to complete the course later, highlighting their interest in studying Japanese further.

observations, arranging time and other resources for studies is a central element at a later stage of the motivational process (Williams & Burden 1997: 121).

There were 4 respondents who answered that they intended to complete the entire basic studies module and wanted to find employment in Japan. One of them told of having chosen Japanese because of the desire to learn one more new language. Of these 4 respondents, 3 had studied Japanese before coming to the elementary course, and 3 of them also said they had other interests in Japan. Japanese skills were experienced as useful in the major subject area by 2 respondents.

The desire to learn one more new language was a relatively strong motivational factor when deciding to attend the Japanese course, as 14 respondents had included it in their answers. Most of these respondents were from the Faculty of Humanities (4) and the Faculty of Information Technology (5).

For a significant part of the respondents, the reason for choosing to study Japanese was linked to their other interests in Japan. This was the case with 11 students from the Faculty of Humanities; 9 from the Faculty of Information Technology; 5 from the Faculty of Mathematics and Science; and 1 each from the faculties of Education, Sport and Health Sciences, and Social Sciences.

Several respondents identified further reasons for choosing to study Japanese in their open-ended answers for the 2013 main survey and the 2014 complementary survey. Reasons other than career-related ones were commonly mentioned in the open-ended answers. The aim to complete the basic studies in Japanese, planned or agreed exchange studies and stays in Japan, a general interest in languages or precisely in the Japanese language and culture, and hobbies related to Japan were mentioned in several answers.

The impact of Japanese popular culture on the choice of language was mentioned by 11 respondents. A few of the respondents indicated it as the only reason, but for most it was a contributory factor. The observations made by Dörnyei and

Chapter 15

Clément (2001) about the emotional attachment present in the acquisition of foreign languages also explain the strong influence of hobbies, dreams for the future, personal interests and goals for choosing to study Japanese. The choice of a foreign language, commitment to studying, and language acquisition are mainly guided by emotions. Positive feelings toward the target language community and the desire to engage in social interaction with the linguistic community of the target language as well as other foreign languages, are the strongest factors determining the choice of language and study motivation (for more on emotional attachment and language learning, see Dörnyei 2001; Dörnyei & Clément 2001; Ushioda 2001).

Sari Pöyhönen, professor at the University of Jyväskylä Centre for Applied Language Studies, states that studying Japanese can be regarded as a stronger demonstration of identity than studying a more commonly taught language: Japanese studies require more initiative. Those in Finland who want to study such less commonly taught languages as Japanese must independently find out where it can be studied (Pensikkala 2010b).

Even though the opportunities for direct social interaction with representatives of the target language are restricted in Finland, indirect contacts are strong. Through various media channels, students can use their Japanese skills extensively even on a daily basis. In this context, the various media encompass games, music, television programmes and films available via the internet, along with other online resources. The active utilisation of language skills and contacts with the target language enhance students' confidence, which is one constituent of motivation. Study motivation is fundamentally social, even though studying a language, as such, is an academic activity (Clément, Dörnyei & Noels 1994; Matsumoto & Obana 2001).

The results of this survey also comply with the findings of Julkunen's (1998) research on the motivation and language choices of students who study foreign languages. A communicative motivation including cognitive features seems to be crucial in the choice of language studies. Language and culture studies are a means of satisfying one's curiosity about a specific linguistic area as well as of learning and exploring an uncommon language. A motivation of this type manifests a deep inner motivation for studies.

In a report by Leppänen et al. (2013), curiosity is mentioned as an important characteristic of future international experts. This report defines curiosity as the understanding of people's different intentions, which contributes to the recognition of what is essential, for example, in studies or work.

As the report explains, feeding one's curiosity enhances problem-solving skills and the ability to perceive the implications of one's own activities. Curiosity and a spontaneous, emotional search for challenges ensure satisfaction with one's career choice even after graduation. A curious individual discovers the ways in which to utilise acquired skills in a variety of environments.

The explicit curiosity observed in the students of this survey should also be supported. *Being curious together* could more clearly be one of the threads in our future Japanese courses. Phenomena that students find meaningful should be increasingly handled in Japanese lessons. It is no longer relevant to define some topics as important and academic, and others as light and leisure-related. The different dimensions of life are increasingly interwoven, and so-called light matters may become extremely meaningful. It thus has to be asked if today's organised studies are still too distant from the learning that occurs in our leisure time and satisfies our curiosity.

Leppänen et al. (2013) also suggest that an international expert used to be defined as a person who possesses both language skills and cultural skills, in addition to being mobile. However, those international experts who have not participated in student exchange or worked abroad should also be recognised. They are consumers of international media, often also produce content, and are involved in global-level daily interaction. These international experts themselves, as well as employers, should be aware of this often tacit know-how.

Furthermore, present-day and future international experts are able to think beyond their own spheres of experience. They also use their free time for learning and developing their skills as well as act in different communities, irrespective of language or location. The strong international competence hidden beyond the structures of society should be brought out (Leppänen et al. 2013). All these qualities can also be identified in the participants of this survey. It would be important to articulate this competence for the students themselves as well, so that they could develop and express it, for instance, in different professional contexts.

Not all the respondents in this survey explicitly stated that they studied Japanese for pragmatic reasons, such as for the world of work. On the other hand, some stated having pragmatic reasons in addition to other motives, or as the only reason, for studying Japanese. A problem in this survey, as well as more generally, is the excessively narrow idea of the benefits of language and cultural skills. If the questions in this survey had taken into consideration a broader vantage point, more participants would have responded that knowing Japanese was useful to them. Japanese studies should more clearly have been defined as parts of international knowledge and skills, which would have made them appear as more beneficial to the respondents.

5.5. Pragmatic reasons for studying Japanese

The data collected in 2013 indicates that 11 respondents regarded Japanese skills as useful for their major subject or field. The subjects or fields mentioned were ethnology (1), history (2), information systems science (2), mathematical information technology (3), the Master's Degree Programme in Intercultural Communication (1), the Degree Programme in Tourism at JAMK University of Applied Sciences (1), and an unknown major subject in the Faculty of Mathematics and Science (1).

It seems that those who have an external motivation and consider Japanese skills important for their major subject are motivated to study Japanese. When comparing the answer "Japanese is useful in my major subject area" to the respondents' course grades, it was noticed that 8 of the 11 respondents who had regarded Japanese as useful had excellent course grades. Those who answered having studied Japanese already before the elementary course also succeeded well, as could be expected: 9 of the 13 respondents had excellent course grades.

The pragmatic arguments for studying Japanese also included the respondents' statements about their interest in exchange studies and practical training in Japan.

5.6. Employment outlook after graduation

The participants' interests in an international career or vague career desires were typical of all the survey answers related to employment. An international career was mentioned by 9 respondents from the Faculty of Humanities, 6 from the Faculty of Mathematics and Science, 2 from the Faculty of Social Sciences, and 2 from the Faculty of Information Technology. Vague career desires were highlighted in the answers of 8 respondents from the Faculty of Humanities, 6 from the Faculty of Information Technology, and 2 from the Faculty of Mathematics and Science.

However, 5 respondents expressed the desire to find employment in Japan. Their distribution was as follows: the Faculty of Information Technology (2), Humanities (1), Sport and Health Sciences (1), and Mathematics and Science (1).

The findings comply with those of Mäkinen (2004), who concluded that students' idea of their future profession typically becomes clearer during the third and fourth academic year, in other words, during the intermediate and advanced studies. The chosen minor subject studies also contribute to this process. The majority of respondents in this survey were first- or second-year students, which is why their unclear ideas about future employment were an anticipated result.

In addition to the answers obtained via the main survey in 2013, the open-ended answers by participants in the spring 2014 elementary course cast more light on their reasons for attending the course as well as on their motivation. In the 2014 course, 34 participants described their motivation, and some examples of their answers are presented in this context. The demand for Japanese in the world of work is mentioned in the following answers:

> "I'm studying physics, and in my future work I will meet a lot of different people. I may even end up undertaking research with Japanese researchers" (Student from the Faculty of Mathematics and Science, 2014).

> "…Of course, it would be awesome if this were the language that opens doors to future employment" (Student from the Faculty of IT, 2014).

> "In the studies of political science, the University of Jyväskylä requires that I complete courses in two foreign languages. I thought I'd try a less commonly taught language […] because it is useful if I happen to apply for a diplomat training programme or an international job" (Student from the Faculty of Social Sciences, 2014).

These answers demonstrate an awareness of the need to be able to work in diverse work environments and examine the world from multiple perspectives. The objective of studies is to develop broad-based expertise even though there would be no exact idea of one's future employment. These findings are also in line with Mäkinen (2004). Listing professional goals and future benefits as a reason for beginning a language course implies the recognition of future professional needs as well as dreams and expectations. The mental image of one's future career is always to some extent emotional (Järvi 1997). The emotional attachment that colours foreign language studies is thus present also here.

The world of work requires diverse language skills. Even though English would be used in official contexts, the language of the collaboration partner is needed in other contexts and in leisure time. The proficiency of Japanese is important in unofficial situations because they are ultimately also parts of official processes. Furthermore, language skills are essentially related to intercultural competence, which is a definite prerequisite for successful operation in East Asia even with the help of interpreters. In working life, strong subject matter competence and, for example, English skills are the main requirements. In addition to them, one should possess sufficient knowledge of the target country's language and culture. This is the formula for success created by Petteri Kostermaa, who has worked, for example, as Finnair's sales director in Southeast Asia and who also has long and extensive work experience in Japan. Kostermaa's view is shared by several other Finnish experts in science, business and the arts. Examples of experts with strong work experience in Japan include Marko Karppinen, CEO of KONE Japan Co. Ltd; Johan Lindén, Lecturer in Physics at Åbo Akademi; and Yrjö Sotamaa, Professor Emeritus at Aalto University (Riikonen 2010; Valsta 2010; Vihko 2010a, 2010b).

I would like a similar view of linguistic and cultural knowledge to spread among my students as well. Extensive knowledge of Japanese language and culture is not a requirement for all, as even a limited amount of Japanese studies can be sufficient and useful in working life when combined with broad competence in one's own special field.

6. Conclusions

There seems to be no single background factor that explains the choice of language or motivation to study Japanese. However, the emotional factors behind the choice and related commitment to studies are clearly highlighted in the results. Instead of external, pragmatic grounds, most respondents identified personal interests and emotional reasons for beginning Japanese courses at the Language Centre. The knowledge of a less commonly taught language and culture may actually become one of the keys for a student's identity and future professional identity.

Follow-up studies on the theme would be necessary, focusing on continuation courses as well as on those participants who interrupt their studies. This would make it possible to obtain more generalisable information on the relationship between background data and the studies, employment and general identity formation related to Japanese skills. Analysing the connections between motivation, course interruption and learning outcomes proved stimulating and fruitful in this survey, which indicates the need for further research.

The generalisability of the findings in this study is limited because the sample only included participants from two courses, and the number of respondents was rather low. The questionnaire consisted of 13 questions, which is why specifying inquiries will be needed later, as well as analyses of new populations, in order to create a more comprehensive picture. Some questions related to motivation were rather general and will be complemented later by adding, for example, the possibility to provide open-ended answers.

My aim as a teacher is to allocate course content so that it will meet students' individual needs in increasingly effective ways. The learners should be made aware of their own international competence by explicitly considering the following aspects in future Japanese courses: understanding Japanese proficiency as a part of broader international competence, integrating more personal and hobby-related interests with academic contexts in concrete learning situations, and nurturing a generally curious attitude.

Acknowledgement

This article has been translated from Finnish by Sirpa Vehviläinen.

References

Cairns, J. 2010. Kieliosaamisen kehittäminen vaatii resursseja. Juha Janhusen haastattelu. In O. Smedlund & Y. Uemura (eds.), *Japanin kieli Suomessa*. Helsinki: Yliopistopaino, 55–56.

Clément, R., Dörnyei, Z. & Noels, K. 1994. Motivation, self-confidence, and group cohesion in the foreign language classroom. *Language Learning, 44* (3), 417–448. doi:10.1111/j.1467-1770.1994.tb01113.x

Dörnyei, Z. 2001. *Teaching and researching motivation*. Harlow: Pearson Education Limited.

Dörnyei, Z. & Clément, R. 2001. Motivational characteristics of learning different target languages: results of a nationwide survey. In Z. Dörnyei & R. Schmidt (eds), *Motivation and Second Language Acquisition*. Honolulu: University of Hawaii Press, 399–432.

Julkunen, K. 1998. *A2-kielen opiskelijoiden motivaatio ja kielivalinta*. Joensuu: Joensuun yliopistopaino.

Järvi, P. 1997. *Ammattimielikuva. Ammattimielikuva osana ammatillisen suuntautumisen prosessia*. Turku: Turun kauppakorkeakoulun julkaisuja.

Leppänen, J., Lähdemäki, J., Mokka, R., Neuvonen, A., Orjasniemi, M. & Ritola, M. 2013. *Piilotettu osaaminen*. Helsinki: Demos Helsinki.

Matsumoto, M. & Obana, Y. 2001. Motivational factors and persistence in learning Japanese as a foreign language. *New Zealand Journal of Asian Studies, 3* (1), 63–82.

Mäkinen, M. 2004. Mikä minusta tulee "isona"? Yliopisto-opiskelijan ammattikuvan kehittyminen. In P. Tynjälä, J. Välimaa & M. Murtonen (eds.), *Korkeakoulutus, oppiminen ja työelämä*. Juva: PS-kustannus, 57–75.

Pensikkala, J. 2010a. Riikka Länsisalmi haluaa kirjoittaa Japanista suomeksi. Riikka Länsisalmen haastattelu. In O. Smedlund & Y. Uemura (eds.), *Japanin kieli Suomessa*. Helsinki: Yliopistopaino, 65–68.

Pensikkala, J. 2010b. Monipuolisen kielikoulutuksen puolestapuhuja. Sari Pöyhösen haastattelu. In O. Smedlund & Y. Uemura (eds.), Japanin kieli Suomessa. Helsinki: Yliopistopaino, 69–72.

Pöyhönen, M. & Oikari, R. (eds.) 2013. *Humanistinen tiedekunta vuosikertomus 2012*. Jyväskylä: Jyväskylän yliopistopaino.

Riikonen, A. 2010. Tutkijana Japanissa. Johan Lindénin haastattelu. In O. Smedlund & Y. Uemura (eds.), *Japanin kieli Suomessa*. Helsinki: Yliopistopaino, 211–214.

Smedlund, O. & Uemura, Y. (eds.) 2010. Turussa toivotaan Aasia-yhteistyötä korkeakoulujen välille uuden sukupolven kasvattamiseksi. Annamari Konttisen, Outi Luovan ja Annukka Kinnarin haastattelu. *Japanin kieli Suomessa*. Helsinki: Yliopistopaino, 207–210.

Ushioda, E. 2001. Language learning at university: exploring the role of motivational thinking. In Z. Dörneyi & R. Schmidt (eds.), *Motivation and Second Language Acquisition*. Honolulu : Second Language Teaching & Curriculum Center, University of Hawaiʻi at Mānoa, 103–106.

Valsta, S. 2010. Jousiammuntaa saa toki työn ohessa harrastaa –jos siihen jää aikaa. Marko Karppisen haastattelu. In O. Smedlund & Y. Uemura (eds.), *Japanin kieli Suomessa*. Helsinki: Yliopistopaino, 127–130.

Vihko, T. 2010a. Japanin-kaupassa kielitaito on valttia. Petteri Kostermaan haastattelu. In O. Smedlund & Y. Uemura (eds.), *Japanin kieli Suomessa*. Helsinki: Yliopistopaino, 135–138.

Vihko, T. 2010b. Ei siihen tarvita kuin yksi ihminen. Yrjö Sotamaan haastattelu. In O. Smedlund & Y. Uemura (eds.), *Japanin kieli Suomessa*. Helsinki: Yliopistopaino, 223–226.

Williams, M. & Burden, R. 1997. *Psychology for language teachers*. Cambridge: Cambridge University Press.

Name Index

A
Aalto, Eija 226, 238
Aalto, Hanna-Kaisa 32, 50
Aarts, Bas 282, 307
Achard, Michel 282, 284, 307
Adamson, Bob 284, 285, 307
Adamson, Hugh Douglas 92, 101
Ahearn, Laura M. 199, 218
Ahokas, Ira 32, 50
Ahvenjärvi, Kaisa 245, 273
Aira, Anna-Leena x
Airey, John 134, 136, 138, 152, 154
Ala-Kortesmaa, S. 41, 50
Alanen, Riikka x, 199, 202, 218, 219
Alatarvas, R. 37, 50
Albrecht, Terence L. 36, 50
Alho, Irja 290, 307
Almonkari, Merja vi, 5, 31, 45, 51
Amsler, Sarah S. 106, 127
Andrade, Heidi 115, 127
Andrews, Stephen 284, 307
Arend, Bridget D. 124, 128
Aro, Mari x, 208, 215, 216, 219, 227, 239
Arrow, Holly 34, 53
Ashford-Rowe, Kevin 106, 127
Atran, Scott 288, 314
Attwell, Graham 172, 179, 193
Auer, Peter 300, 307

B
Bainbridge, William 287, 307
Baker, Colin 321, 334
Bakhtin, Mukhail M. 60, 81
Bandura, Albert 199, 208, 218
Barabási, Albert-László 34
Barab, Sasha 175, 193, 201, 218
Barcelos, Ana Maria Ferreira 286, 287, 290, 306, 307
Barrett, Helen C. 17, 29
Barry, Andrew 34, 50
Basharina, Olga 63, 66, 77, 81, 202, 218
Basterrechea, María 300, 318
Bastone, Rob 306, 307
Baume, David 95, 101
Beavin Bavelas, Janet 322, 335
Becher, Tony 140, 155
Becker, Howard Saul 126, 127
Beetham, Helen 172, 181, 185, 192, 193, 195
Bell, David 284, 285, 307, 308
Bell, Philip 201, 221
Benson, Phil 286, 287, 306, 308
Bereded-Samuel, Elleni 160, 168
Bernstein, Richard 285, 304, 308
Berthele, Raphael 92, 93, 94, 102, 325, 334
Biggs, John 62, 81, 101, 109, 127, 148, 154
Bilash, Olenka 65, 81
Billings, Andrew C. 287, 311
Bittner, Andreas 290, 308
Blin, Françoise 202, 218
Block, David 284, 308
Blommaert, Jan 90, 100, 101, 321, 324, 333
Bloxham, Sue 108, 127
Boers, Frank 283, 308
Bolinger, Dwight 288, 308

Name index

Bollström-Huttunen, Marianne 249, 273
Bolsmann, Chris 106, 127
Boohan, Mairead 44, 52
Borgatti, Stephen P. 34, 36, 50
Borg, Simon 290, 301, 306, 308
Boud, David 106, 108, 109, 118, 125, 127
Bowerman, Sean 289, 290, 308
Boyatzis, Richard E. 112, 128
Boyd, Danah M. 37, 50
Boyd, Peter 108, 127
Boynton, Andrew C. 9, 10
Bradley, Barbara A. 175, 195
Braine, George 145, 147, 154
Braun, Virginia 70, 81
Brecht, Richard D. 58, 81
Broccias, Cristiano 283, 308
Brown, Alan 280, 300, 308
Brown, Cecil 288, 308, 309
Brown, Christine 106, 127
Brown, David 63, 81
Brown, James 286, 309
Brown, Penelope 323, 333
Brumfit, Christopher 285, 309
Bucholtz, Mary 289, 309
Burden, Robert L. 341, 342, 349, 358
Burleson, Brant R. 41, 50
Burns, Anne 306, 308
Burns, Eila 168
Burt, Ronald S. 31, 36, 50
Byram, Michael 63, 81, 92, 101

C
Cain, Carole 208
Cain, Susan 110, 128
Cairns, J. 339, 356
Cameron, Lynne 227, 228, 239
Canagarajah, A. Suresh 227, 239, 300, 309, 330, 333, 334
Canary, Daniel J. 40, 53
Carnevale, Anthony P. 46, 50
Carolan, Fergal vii, 5, 13
Carpenter, Christopher 202, 207, 220
Castells, Manuel 34, 50, 51
Cazden, Courtney 200, 219
Celce-Murcia, Marianne 300, 306, 309
Chalker, Sylvia 282, 295, 309
Chant, Simon 44, 51
Chapleo, Chris 106, 128
Chavez, Monika 300, 309
Cho, Hichang 47, 51
Cho, Kwangsu 122, 128
Clark, Carolyn 43, 54
Clarke, Alan 73, 81
Clark, Ian 106, 128
Clark, Victoria 70, 81
Clément, Richard 350, 356, 357
Clinton, Katherine 194
Clinton, Katie 274
Coffey, Martin 153, 154
Coiro, Julie 246, 273
Collins, James 90, 101
Conole, Grainne 198, 201, 219
Contractor, Noshir 34, 37, 53, 54
Cooke, David 199, 219
Cook, Vivian 283, 309
Cope, Bill 198, 200, 202, 216, 219, 220, 248, 273

Corder, S. Pit 282, 284, 309
Cotterall, Sara 286, 306, 309
Cottrell, Stella 92, 101
Couper-Kuhlen, Elizabeth 300, 309
Coupland, Nikolas 283, 285, 286, 309, 310, 311
Cox, Roy 137, 155
Croft, William 294, 310
Crossling, Glenda 46, 51
Cruse, Susan 33, 54
Cummins, Jim 136, 154
Cupach, William R. 39, 56

D

Dafouz, Emma 134, 152, 154
Dannels, Deanna P. 33, 41, 51
Darling, Ann L. 33, 41, 51
Davies, Alan 286, 310
Davies, Winifred 290, 300, 310
Davis, Mark 115, 129
Deci, Edward L. 74
Deci, Richard M. 83
De Freitas, Sara 62, 77, 83
Del Pilar García Mayo, María 300, 318
Dennis, A. R. 61, 83
Diaz, L. Alonso 78, 81
Dickson, David 42, 43, 52
Dirven, René 283, 310
Dörnyei, Zoltán 64, 74, 81, 82, 203, 206, 219, 341, 349, 350, 356, 357
Downes, Stephen 179, 193
Drescher, Victor 295, 311

Drexler, Wendy 172, 194
Dufva, Hannele x, 60, 64, 65, 78, 82, 199, 208, 215, 216, 219, 227, 239
Dupré, John 288, 310

E

Edelson, Daniel C. 201, 219
Edwards, Anne 8, 9
Edwards, Derek 287, 315
Edwards, John 285, 287, 290, 310
Eerola, S. 165, 168
Ekholm, Kai 245, 246, 273
Elder, Catherine 286, 310
Ellison, Nicole B. 37, 50
Ellis, Rod 65, 82, 284, 300, 306, 310
Eloranta, Johanna vii, 7, 225
Engeström, Yrjö 9, 10, 63, 82
Entonado, F. Blazquez 78, 81
Entwistle, Noel 63, 65, 66, 77, 82
Eteläpelto, Anneli 207, 222
Evans, Carol 109, 110, 112, 114, 115, 118, 122, 124, 128

F

Fairclough, Norman 219
Falchikov, Nancy 106, 109, 125, 127
Fernández Hawrylak, Maria 202, 222
Figueroa, Esther 289, 310, 322, 334
Fink, L. Dee 183, 194
Fischer, Márta 125, 128
Fitch, Kristine L. 47, 51
Flowerdew, John 138, 139, 143, 154, 202, 207, 219

Name index

Fodor, Jerry 288, 310
Fonteyn, Katarzyna 156
Ford, Sam 246, 274
Forster Vosicki, Brigitte 86, 102, 320, 335
Francescato, Donata 78, 83
Franck, Dorothea 300, 310
Frankham, Jo 34, 51
Fried, Mirjam 300, 310
Frymier, Ann Bainbridge 41, 42, 51

G

Gaboury, Jane 33, 51
Gainer, Leila J. 46, 50
Garam, Irma 156
Garcia, Ofelia 321
Gardner, John 108, 128
Garrett, Peter 285, 287, 311
Gay, Geri 47, 51
Gee, James Paul 172, 192, 194, 227, 228, 239
Gee, Jim 219
Geer, Blanche 126, 127
Gemünden, Hans Georg 38, 55
Gerlander, Maija 45, 51
Gibbs, Graham 106, 128, 153, 154
Gibbs, Raymond Jr. 288, 311
Gidley, Jennifer M. 160, 168
Gielen, Patricia M. 31, 36, 52
Giles, Howard 287, 311
Gillett, Andy 18, 29
Givertz, Michelle 43, 55
Glisan, Eileen W. 295, 311
Glucksberg, Sam 288, 314

Goffman, Erving 323, 334
Goldsmith, Daena J. 50
Gould, Roger V. 34, 52
Graustein, Gottfried 282, 283, 313
Gray, F. Elizabeth 41, 52
Greene, John O. 43, 52
Green, Joshua 246, 274
Gudykunst, William 47, 52, 323, 334
Guerrero, Laura K. 47, 54
Guth, Sarah 172, 194
Guyan, Matt 74, 82

H

Haarmann, Harald 290, 311
Hagstrom, Fran 199, 222
Hakkarainen, Kai 249, 250, 273
Häkkinen, Päivi x
Hakulinen, Auli 246
Halgin, Daniel S. 34, 36, 50
Halliday, Michael Alexander Kirkwood 292, 311
Hallila, Mika 249, 251, 273
Hampson, Gary P. 160, 168
Hampton, James A. 288, 311
Hannafin, Michael J. 201, 222
Hardy, Cynthia 39, 52
Hargie, Colin T. C. 39, 52
Hargie, Owen 42, 43, 44, 52
Harjunen, Elina 285, 290, 311
Harlen, Wynne 108, 128
Harré, Rom 212, 219
Harris, Roy 285, 289, 290, 311
Harvey, Lee 107, 129
Harvey, Penny 35, 53

Hasan, Ruqaiya 283, 311
Hattie, John 109, 125, 128
Hauge, Trond Eiliv 201, 220
Hawks, Val 115, 129
Hayward, Louise 108, 128
Hellekjaer, Glenn Ole 137, 154
Henneberg, Stephan C. 38, 56
Herrington, Janice 106, 127
Hiidenmaa, Pirjo 285, 311
Himanen, Pekka 33, 52
Hirsto, Laura 138, 155
Hoenigswald, Henry 285, 311
Hoeve, Aimée 31, 52
Hoffman, David 226, 239
Holland, Dorothy 208, 219
Holme, Randal 288, 311
Hopper, Paul 288, 312
Hora, Matthew T. 152, 155
Horwitz, Elaine 280, 286, 300, 312
Hosiaisluoma, Yrjö 273
Hosler, Kim A. 124, 128
Hounsell, Dai 108, 128
Hounsell, Jenny 108, 128
Houser, Marian L. 41, 42, 51
Hudson, Richard 290, 312
Hughes, Everett Cherrington 126, 127
Huhta, Ari 198, 218, 220, 221
Huisman, Jeroen 107, 129
Hujo, Marja 330, 335
Hunter, Judy 199, 219
Hunter, Kerry 147, 154
Huotari, Maija-Leena 32, 52
Hurme, Pertti 32, 52

Hussey, Trevor 106, 129
Husson Isozaki, Anna 243, 273
Hvistendahl, Rita Elisabeth 243, 274
Hyland, Ken 126, 129, 135, 136, 139, 155
Hymes, Dell 286, 312
Hyvärinen, Marja-Leena 41, 44, 45, 51, 52

I

Isotalus, Pekka 45, 51, 52, 53

J

Jackson, Don D. 322, 335
Jalkanen, Juha , vi, 1, 7, 202, 218, i, 225, 226
Jalkanen, Katja 243, 248, 249, 274
James, Carl 294, 312
James, David 105, 107, 109, 124, 125, 126, 129
Janicki, Karol 288, 312
Järvi, Pentti 354, 357
Jauhojärvi-Koskelo, Camilla vii, 6, 159
Jaworski, Adam 283, 286, 309, 310
Jean, Gladys 280, 281, 303, 312
Jenkins, Henry 172, 180, 194, 246, 267, 269, 274
Jenkinson, Tim 51
Joensuu, Juri 246, 275
Johannesson, Kurt 290, 312
Johnson, Marysia 60, 61, 63, 64, 82
Jokinen, Elina , vi, 1, 7, i, 241, 245, 251, 267, 271, 274

Name index

Jones, Bryn 321, 334
Jørgensen, J. Normann 90, 102
Joseph, Diana 176, 194
Joseph, John E. 282, 284, 288, 312
Joy, Simy 144, 155
Julkunen, Kyösti 342, 350, 357
Juntunen, Merja 175, 194

K

Kachru, Yamuna 282, 306, 312
Kaipomäki, Emma 45, 53
Kalaja, Paula 199, 202, 215, 219, 286, 287, 290, 307
Kalantzis, Mary 198, 200, 202, 216, 219, 220, 248, 273
Kalliokoski, Jyrki xi
Kallionpää, Outi 246, 267, 274
Karkulehto, Sanna 273
Károly, Adrienn vii, 6, 105
Katz, Nancy 34, 35, 53
Kauppinen, Anneli 290, 307
Kearney, Sean 115, 119, 124, 129
Kelly, Louis G. 290, 312
Keränen, Anna 220
Kincaid, D. Lawrence 35, 55
Kirstinä, Leena 245, 273
Kivelä, Raili 246
Klaassen, Renate G. 134, 135, 137, 145, 155, 156
Kling, Joyce Myra 134, 155
Knight, Peter T. 121, 129
Knobel, Michele 172, 194, 200, 220, 246, 263, 273, 274
Knox, Hannah 35, 53

Kock, N. 61, 78, 82
Kokkonen, Lotta vii, 5, 31, 36, 53
Kolb, David A. 144, 155
Kolhinen, Johanna 156
Komulainen, Erkki 138, 155
Koponen, Jonna 41, 44, 45, 53
Korhonen, Riitta 285, 290, 311
Koskimaa, Raine 246, 275
Kostiainen, Emma 33, 42, 53
Kraimer, Maria L. 36, 56
Krashen, Stephen D. 282, 312
Kress, G. 219
Kumaravadivelu, B. 284, 312
Kumpulainen, Kristiina 199, 212, 220
Kunttu, Kristina 160, 167, 169
Kuosa, Tuomo 32, 50
Kurogi, Atsuko 323, 335
Kuure, Leena xi
Kyppö, Anna viii, 5, 8, 13, 57, 59, 63, 67, 69, 74, 82, 319

L

Laajalahti, Anne 41, 42, 43, 44, 53
Laakkonen, Ilona viii, 7, 171, 174, 175, 194
Lachicotte, William 208, 219
Lähdemäki, Jenna 357
Lähteenmäki, Mika 90, 102
Lakey, Sandra 40, 53
Langacker, Ronald 283, 312
Langfeldt, Liv 107, 129
Lang, James D. 33, 54
Lankshear, Colin 172, 194, 200, 220, 246, 263, 273, 274

Lantolf, James P. 199, 220
Larsen-Freeman, Diane 227, 228, 239
Lasky, Sue 207, 214, 220
Lauridsen, Karen M. 134, 154
LaVan, Sarah-Kate 202, 222
Lave, Jean 192, 195, 208, 220
Lawrence, Thomas B. 39, 52
Lazer, David 34, 53
Leech, Geoffrey N. 282, 283, 284, 295, 313
Lee, Jae-Shin 47, 51
Lee, Mark J. W. 83
Lehmann, Christian 294, 313
Lehtomäki, Elina 160, 169
Lehtonen, Jaakko 323, 335
Lehtonen, Mikko 245, 246, 274
Leitner, Gerhard 282, 283, 313
Lenz, Peter 92, 93, 94, 102, 325, 334
LePore, Ernest 288, 310
Leppänen, Juha 351, 352, 357
Leppänen, Sirpa 90, 102, 324, 333
Leskinen, Raija 38, 54
Leu, Donald J. 246, 273
Levinson, Stephen 323, 333
Lewis, E. Glyn 287, 313
Lewis, Gwyn 321, 333, 334
Liamkina, Olga 284, 313
Liden, Robert C. 36, 56
Lightbown, Patsy 284, 306, 317
Light, Greg 137, 155
Lillis, Theresa 286, 289, 290, 313
Lim, Doo Hun 78, 82
Lindblom-Ylänne, Sari 138, 140, 155, 156

Lindstromberg, Seth 283, 308
Lindström, Jan 300, 313
Linell, Per 289, 290, 300, 313
Linturi, Hanna 32, 54
Linza, Christina 156
Lipponen, Lasse 199, 212, 220, 249, 250, 273
Litjens, Judith 108, 128
Litmanen, Topi 138, 155
Littlejohn, Allison 172, 195
Littlejohn, Stephen W. 36, 54
Littlewood, William 282, 299, 306, 313
Lo Bianco, Joseph 290, 314, 324, 334
Lonka, Kirsti 249, 250, 273
Lor, Winnie 286, 287, 306, 308
Lounavaara, Marja-Terttu 244, 274
Ludvigsen, Sten 172, 195
Luke, A. 219
Lund, Andreas 172, 195, 201, 220
Luukka, Minna-Riitta 200, 220

M

MacArthur, Charles 122, 128
Maiworm, Friedhelm 132, 157
Mäki, Elinita 45, 53
Mäkinen, Mirka 353, 354, 357
Malm, Ritva 244, 274
Malone, Denis 17, 30
Mangen, Anne 75, 82
Marginson, Simon 106, 129
Margolis, Eric 288, 314
Martinet, André 292, 314
Master, Peter 306, 314

Name index

Matonya, Magreth 160, 169
Matsumoto, Masanori 341, 342, 343, 350, 357
Mayes, Terry 62, 77, 83
McBride, Dawn Lorraine 138, 155
McCarthy, John 208, 221
McCloskey, Michael E. 288, 314
McCoy, Mairead 44, 52
McCune, Velda 108, 128
McDowell, Liz 106, 126, 129
McEwan, Bree 47, 54
McGill, Lou 172, 195
McLoughlin, Catherine 83
McMasters, John 33, 54
McVey, Francis D. 33, 54
Mebane, Minou Ella 78, 83
Medin, Douglas 288, 314
Mela, Marjo 244, 274
Meltzer, Ann S. 46, 50
Mercer, Sarah 199, 202, 215, 220, 286, 287, 314
Merriam, Sharan B. 43, 54
Mertova, Patricie 229, 230, 240
Mervis, Carolyn 288, 314
Mey, Jacob 322, 334
Mikkonen, Pirjo 244, 274
Miller-Cochran, Susan K. 15, 30
Miller, Lindsay 138, 139, 143, 154, 202, 207, 219
Mitchell, Roger E. 36, 37, 54
Mitchell, Rosamund 295, 314
Mittilä, Tuula 38, 54
Moate, Josephine xi, 146, 152, 155
Mohammadi, Fatemeh 15, 30

Mokka, Roope 357
Møller, Janus Spindler 90, 102
Molloy, Elizabeth 118, 127
Monge, Peter R. 54
Montgomery, Catherine 106, 129
Moolenaar, Nienke M. 31, 54
Moon, Jenny 95, 102, 148, 155
Mori, Yoshiko 280, 286, 314
Morreale, Sherwyn P. 33, 54
Morris, Michael L. 78, 82
Morrison, Debbie 17, 30
Murphey, Tim 202, 207, 220
Murphy, Pauline 44, 52
Myonghee, Kim 243, 274

N

Nakane, Ikuko 323, 334
Nakata, M. 219
Natri, Teija viii, 6, 8, 85, 319, 320, 334, 335
Naudé, Peter 38, 56
Negueruela-Azarola, Eduardo 287, 314
Neuliep, James W. 35, 54
Neumann, Ruth 140, 155
Neuvonen, Aleksi 357
Newman, Mark 34
Nichols, Adam 63, 81
Nichols, Johanna 292, 314
Niedzielski, Nancy 285, 287, 295, 314
Niemi, Jukani 245, 275
Niemi-Pynttäri, Risto 248, 249, 275
Nieuwenhuis, Loek F.M. 31, 52
Nikula, Henrik 282, 283, 284, 314

Name index

Noels, Kimberly A. 350, 356
Norris-Holt, Jacqueline 74, 83
Norris, John M. 306, 314
Norton, Bonny 208, 211, 220
Núnẽz, Begona 134, 152, 154

O

Obana, Yasuko 341, 342, 343, 350, 357
Obstfeld, David 31, 36, 54
Odlin, Terence 282, 283, 285, 300, 306, 315
Oetzel, John 323, 335
Oikari, Raija 345, 357
Ojajärvi, Jussi 273
Oleson, Amanda 152, 155
Ondrejovič, Slavo 58, 83
Orjasniemi, Mari 357
Ortega, Lourdes 306, 314
Osbon, Michael M. 33, 54
Östman, Jan-Ola 300, 310
Ozkoz, Ana 178, 195

P

Palfreyman, David 138, 155
Palviainen, Åsa 199, 219
Parente-Čapková, Viola 244, 275
Park, Mi Sun 321, 335
Parpala, Anna 138, 140, 155, 156
Parry, Sharon 140, 155
Partanen, Maiju 238, 239
Pasquale, Michael 285, 315
Paunonen, Heikki 285, 315
Pearson, Judy C. 33, 54

Pennycook, Alastair 227, 239
Pensikkala, J. 341, 350, 357
Penttilä, Johanna 161, 169
Perrett, Gillian 283, 311
Perry-Smith, Jill E. 31, 36, 55
Pesonen, Tommi 160, 167, 169
Phillips, Brenna 78, 83
Phillips, Nelson 39, 52
Pietarinen, Margarita viii, 8, 319
Pietilä, Paula xi
Pike, Kenneth 286, 315
Pilkinton-Pihko, Diane 135, 156
Pitkänen-Huhta, Anne 330, 335
Potter, Jonathan 287, 315
Pöyhönen, Maija 345, 357
Pöyhönen, Sari 220, 226, 239
Prahbu, N. 282, 284, 315
Preston, Dennis 285, 287, 295, 314, 315
Pudas, Hanna 243, 248, 249, 274
Puhakka, Antero 32, 43, 46, 55
Pullin, Patricia 45, 55
Purhonen, Pipsa 38, 39, 40, 42, 47, 48, 55
Purushotma, Ravi 194, 274
Pyöriä, Pasi 33, 55
Pyysalo, Riikka 249, 273

R

Raimes, Anna 15, 30
Rajala, Terttu xi
Randle, Jacqueline 51
Rantala, Taina 245, 275
Ranta, Tani 246

Name index

Räsänen, Anne viii, 6, 85, 88, 95, 102, 131, 134, 135, 136, 137, 138, 139, 141, 154, 156, 320, 334, 335
Rasmussen, Ingvill 172, 195
Rättyä, Kaisu 280, 315
Rautopuro, Juhani 32, 43, 55
Reinking, David 175, 195
Rempel, John 287, 318
Repo, Yrjö 245, 246, 273
Richardson, John T. E. 160, 169
Rieger, Borbála 281, 315
Rifkin, Benjamin 286, 287, 290, 315
Riikonen, A. 355, 357
Riles, Annelise 34, 55
Ritola, Maria 357
Ritter, Thomas 38, 55
Robert, L. P. 61, 83
Robison, Alice J. 194, 274
Roehr, Karen 301, 315
Rogers, Everett M. 35, 55
Rosch, Eleanor 288, 314, 315, 316
Rouhiainen-Neuenhäuserer, Maijastiina 41, 55
Ruohotie-Lyhty, Maria 201, 207, 208, 221
Russel, Graham 51
Rutherford, William 282, 284, 295, 306, 316
Ryan, Edward L. 83
Ryan, Richard M. 74
Rynkänen, Tatjana 226, 239
Ryshina-Pankova, Marianna 284
Rytkönen, Henna 140, 156

S

Saarinen, Jaana 207, 222
Saarinen, Lauri 246, 275
Saaristo, Pekka ix, 8, 279, 319
Sajavaara, Kari 323, 335
Säljö, Roger 172, 195
Salö, Linus 134, 154
Sambell, Kay 106, 108, 115, 118, 126, 129
Samter, Wendy 41, 50
Sanders, Robert E. 47, 51
Sandoval, William A. 201, 221
Sapir, Edward 316
Savage, Mike 35, 53
Saville-Troike, Muriel 286, 316
Sawyer, R. Keith 198, 221
Schmidt, Richard 306, 316
Schulz, Renate 280, 300, 305, 316
Schwach, V. 134, 154
Segrin, Christ 43, 55
Selting, Margret 300, 309, 316
Selwyn, Neil 181, 195
Sendziuk, Paul 124, 129
Seow, Anthony 15, 30
Seppälä, Riina ix, 7, 197
Shalley, Christina E. 31, 36, 55
Sharpe, R. 172, 181, 185, 192, 193
Sharwood Smith, Michael 300, 316
Shaw, Philip 137, 138, 145, 152, 156
Shope, Beth 23, 30
Shotter, John 287, 316
Siemens, George 172, 179, 195
Siewert, Charles 287, 316
Sigman, Stuart J. 36, 47, 56
Simard, Daphnée 280, 281, 303, 312

Simard, Jean 29, 30
Skehan, Peter 306, 316
Skinnari, Kristiina 202, 221
Skinner, Debra 208, 219
Sleegers, Peter J. C. 31, 54
Slembrouck, Stef 90, 101
Smedlund, O. 338, 339, 357
Smith, Patrick 106, 129
Smit, Ute 152, 156
Smolander, Jenna 244, 275
Söderqvist, Minna 156
Soininen-Stojanov, Henna 285
Solimeno, Andrea 78, 83
Spada, Nina 284, 306, 316, 317
Sparrowe, Raymond T. 36, 56
Spencer-Oatey, Helen 322, 335
Spitzberg, Brian H. 39, 40, 42, 45, 46, 48, 56
Spolsky, Bernard 282, 317
Spotti, Massimiliano 324, 333
Squire, Kurt 175, 193, 201, 218
Staehr, Lars Stenius 134, 155
Staršova, Tamara 247, 275
Stefanone, Michael A. 47, 51
Stegu, Martin 285, 318
Stensaker, Bjorn 107, 129
Stevens, David 63, 81
Stewart, Mary 78, 83
Stobart, Gordon 108, 128
Strong, Brent 115, 129
Sulkunen, Sari xi
Sullivan, Paul 208, 221
Suni, Minna 226, 227, 228, 239
Svensson, J. 290, 317

Swain, Merrill 321, 335
Sykes, Julie M. 178, 195
Sylvan, Claire 321, 334

T
Taalas, Peppi , vi, 1, 174, 175, 194, 198, 218, 220, 221, i, 226
Taipale, Sakari 246, 275
Takala, Pauliina ix, 8, 337
Tang, Catherine 109, 127
Tarnanen, Mirja xi, 198, 218, 220, 221, 226, 239
Taylor, John 282, 284, 306, 317
Taylor, Talbot J. 289, 290, 311
Thompson, Sandra 288, 312
Thorne, Steven L. 178, 195, 199, 220
Thornton, Sabrina C. 38, 56
Thorpe, Mary 66, 77, 83
Timperley, Helen 109, 128
Ting-Toomey, Stella 47, 52, 323, 334, 335
Toft, Trond Egil 75, 83
Tomai, Manuela 78, 83
Tomlin, Russell 283, 295, 317
Tonkyn, Alan 282, 283, 317
Toolan, Michael 289, 317
Toomar, Jaana xi
Topping, Keith J. 109, 122, 129
Torrance, Harry 125, 126, 129
Tourish, Dennis 39, 52
Trappes-Lomax, Hugh 282, 293, 299, 317
Trevillion, Steve 34, 35, 56
Trickett , Edison J. 36, 37, 54

Name index

Tse, Harry 147, 154
Tukia, Kaisa xi
Tulasiewicz, Witold 65, 81
Tulviste, Peeter 199, 222
Tuomi, Margaret Trotta ix, 6, 159, 160, 167, 169
Tuominen, Visa 32, 43, 55
Turner, Joan 290, 317
Turula, Anna 306, 317
Tynjälä, Päivi 198, 221, 249, 275

U
Uemura, Y. 338, 339, 357
Unterberger, Barbara 134, 156
Ushida, Eiko 64, 83
Ushioda, Ema 341, 350, 357

V
Vaarala, Heidi x, 7, 226, 239, 241, 243, 245, 275
Vaattovaara, Johanna 285, 286, 317
Vähäsantanen, Katja 207, 222
Välikoski, T.-R. 41, 50
Välimaa, Jussi 132, 156
Valkonen, Tarja 32, 40, 52, 55, 56
Valsta, S. 355, 357
Valtcheva, Anna 115, 127
Van den Heuvel, Esther 156
Van der Wende, Marijk 106, 129
Van Gulick, Robert 287, 317
Van Harmeleb, M. 178, 195
Van Langenhove, Luk 212, 219
Van Lier, Leo 63, 84, 199, 208, 211, 222, 227, 238, 239

Varis, Piia 90, 102
Vaughan, Norman D. 61, 84
Vehviläinen, Sirpa xi, 238, 273, 356
Veladat, Fahimeh 15, 30
Velay, Jean-Luc 75, 82
Victor, Bart 9, 10
Vihko, T. 355, 358
Violanti, Michelle T. 46, 56
Virkkunen, Jaakko 9, 10
Vygotsky, Lev S. 60, 84

W
Wächter, Bernd 132, 157
Walton, A. Ronald 58, 81
Wang, Feng 201, 222
Ward, Ian 46, 51
Wassell, Beth A. 202, 222
Watanabe, Yuko 321, 335
Watkins, Ryan 73, 84
Watts, Duncan J. 34
Watzlawick, Paul 322, 335
Wayne, Sandy J. 36, 56
Webb, Christine 51
Webster, Leonard 229, 230, 240
Weigel, Margaret 194, 274
Weinert, Regina 300, 318
Wellman, Barry 37, 56
Wells, Gordon 135, 138, 145, 152, 157
Wenden, Anita 286, 287, 318
Wenger, Etienne 192, 195
Wertsch, James V. 199, 222
Wesely, Pamela 286, 318
Westerheijden, Don F. 107, 129

Westerholm, Kirsi x, 6, 131
Westney, Paul 283, 318
Wetherell, Margaret 287, 315
Wheeler, Leone 160, 168
Widdowson, G. 283, 284, 303, 318
Wiggins, Grant 183, 195
Wikforss, Åsa 288, 318
Wiliam, Dylan 106, 108, 109, 130
Wilkins, David A. 282, 283, 285, 289, 290, 300, 318
Wilkinson, Robert 137, 145, 157
Williams, Angie 285, 311, 318
Williams, Geoff 295
Williams, Marion 341, 342, 349, 358
Willis, Jane 60, 84
Wilmot, William W. 35, 56
Wilson, Brent Gayle 84
Wilton, Antje 285, 318
Winters, Margaret 288, 318
Wolff, Jan 156
Wuethrich, Matthew xi

Y
Yip, Virginia 282, 284, 306, 318
Ylönen, Sabine 218

Z
Zanna, Mark 287, 318
Zegers, Vera 145
Ziegler, Arne 300, 318
Zorn, Theodore E. 46, 56

www.ingramcontent.com/pod-product-compliance
Lightning Source LLC
Chambersburg PA
CBHW021829220426
43663CB00005B/180